La Nouvelle Agence
7, rue Corneille
75006 Paris

A COMMON STAGE

A Volume in the Series

CONJUNCTIONS OF RELIGION

AND POWER IN THE MEDIEVAL PAST

Edited by Barbara H. Rosenwein

For a list of titles in the series, visit our website at

www.cornellpress.cornell.edu.

A Common Stage

THEATER AND

PUBLIC LIFE IN

MEDIEVAL ARRAS

CAROL SYMES

CORNELL UNIVERSITY PRESS

Ithaca and London

Publication of this book was made possible, in part, by a grant from
the Campus Research Board of the University of Illinois at Urbana–
Champaign.

First published 2007 by Cornell University Press

Printed in the United States of America

Library of Congress Cataloging-in-Publication Data

Symes, Carol.
    A common stage : theater and public life in medieval Arras /
Carol Symes.
            p. cm. — (Conjunctions of religion and power in the
medieval past)
    Includes bibliographical references and index.
    ISBN 978-0-8014-4581-1 (cloth : alk. paper)
    1. French drama—To 1500—History and criticism.   2. Theater
and society—France—Arras—History—To 1500.   3. Theater—
France—Arras—History—Medieval, 500–1500.   I. Title.
II. Series: Conjunctions of religion & power in the medieval past.

PQ511.S96 2007
792.0944'27—dc22

                                    2007011001

Cornell University Press strives to use environmentally responsible
suppliers and materials to the fullest extent possible in the publishing
of its books. Such materials include vegetable-based, low-VOC inks
and acid-free papers that are recycled, totally chlorine-free, or partly
composed of nonwood fibers. For further information, visit our
website at www.cornellpress.cornell.edu.

Cloth printing   10 9 8 7 6 5 4 3 2 1

For

Eckehard Simon,

my parents,

and the people of Arras

CONTENTS

ACKNOWLEDGMENTS

I have been wrestling with this project since the fall of 1993. At the dawn of 2007, I wish that I could extract a promise of blessing from my co-combatant, as Jacob did. Since I cannot, I would like to thank those who have already blessed me.

First, I acknowledge with gratitude my mentors Thomas Bisson, Michael McCormick, and Eckehard Simon. They alone know how much I owe them. I am also very grateful to Barbara Rosenwein and John Ackerman of Cornell University Press, who have been assiduous in their encouragement, to the anonymous readers whose comments on successive drafts of this manuscript were of great assistance, and to the editorial staff who brought this book into being. I also thank another reader whose advice and support have been invaluable, Diane Koenker.

In pursuing my research, I have become deeply indebted to the denizens of the Salle des manuscrits of the Bibliothèque nationale de France; the librarians of the Bibliothèque municipale d'Arras; Bénédicte Grailles, Jean-Eric Iung, and the staff of the Archives départementales du Pas-de-Calais; and the clergy of Notre-Dame-des-Ardents d'Arras. I benefited from the kindness of Dave and Aralynn McMane of Paris, and was truly blessed in the hospitality of the sisters of the Monastère Sainte-Claire in Arras, who not only allowed me the run of their guesthouse during the long winter of 1996–97 but also gave me my own stall in choir and a part in singing the office.

Material support for this initial period of inquiry was provided by the Georges Lurcy Fellowship Program. Further research was made possible by the University of Illinois at Urbana-Champaign, the Mellon Foundation, the Centre nationale de la recherche scientifique and the Groupe d'étude du théâtre médiéval in Paris, a William and Flora Hewlett International Research Travel Grant, and a visiting fellowship at the Katholieke Universiteit Leuven.

Among the friends and teachers on whom I relied while at Harvard, I offer thanks especially to Matilda Bruckner of Boston College, who was an early and generous reader, and to my cousins Margaret and Bruce Gelin. I am also grateful to Jan Ziolkowski and Charles Donahue, and to many of my fellow scholars, particularly Gregory Pass, who was a great help during the early stages of this project, and Robert Berkhofer, whose labors in the vineyards of Saint-Vaast preceded and facilitated my own. I also thank Robert Epstein and my students in the History Department and History and Literature concentration, as well as the students in Eckehard Simon's course "The Medieval Stage" during the fall of 1993 and the spring of 1996, who were partners in the formulation of this topic.

Special thanks are due my colleagues at Bennington College from 1998 to 2002, teacher-practitioners who made it possible for me to attempt the enactment of theater history and to carry forward many aspects of this project, especially Janis Young, Stephen Siegel, and Gladden Schrock; and to all my extraordinary students there, among them Heidi Sulzdorf, Melis Belgin, Amanda Parla, and Chandler Williams. I am also grateful to participants in seminars and colloquia hosted by Princeton University, the University of Chicago, Columbia University, Loyola University, the Newberry Library, Boston College, New York University, the University of Western Ontario, the University of California at Davis, and Oxford University, as well as to many new colleagues and friends, including Julien Chapuis, Lori Humphrey Newcomb, Tim Newcomb, Tamara Chapman, C. Stephen Jaeger, Anne D. Hedeman, Megan McLaughlin, Richard Burkhardt, Peter Fritzsche, Antoinette Burton, Dana Rabin, Clare Crowston, Tim Duis, Jeff Dolven, David Smyth, Alistair Hobson, Stuart Weber, and Thomas Wilson.

All that is good in this book bears the mark of many past teachers, some of whom made an impression in the public schools of Guilford, Connecticut—notably Joseph Rutland, Linda Baxter, and Donald Kaufman; I can never thank them enough. Perhaps the most indelible marks have been made by the extraordinary medievalists I was lucky enough to encounter as an undergraduate at Yale: John Boswell, Jaroslav Pelikan, Ralph Hexter, James Schulz, Margot Fassler, Robert Stacey, Robin Chapman Stacey, and my former roommate Ellen Joyce. I am also grateful to my Oxford tutors, Henry Mayr-Harting and James Campbell, and to Paul Hyams, now of Cornell, who will want to go on record as having counseled me to write two separate and very different books.

The most fundamental thanks belong to my sisters, Julia and Kimberly, the best of friends; my brother-in-law, Patrick Moreland; my mother, Lynne; and my father, Ernest Symes, who read numerous drafts of this book and offered substantive critique, and who also assisted in the preparation of the manuscript for publication. I don't know how I would have done this, or anything else, without them.

C.S.

Marlboro, Vermont, and Urbana, Illinois

ON TERMINOLOGY AND TRANSLATION

It is hard to avoid anachronism in describing the cultural and geographic landscape covered by this book, even with respect to the seemingly innocuous terms "France" and "French." When I use them, I try to do so in such a way that their specific, technical meanings—as denoting a modern nation-state and its national language—are clear. The reason for this is that the mechanisms by which Arras became absorbed into the Capetian kingdom after 1191 are important to the argument of this book, as is the process whereby the regional dialect of Picardy spoken in Arras was appropriated by this newly constructed "France" and melded with the regional dialects of Champagne, the Île-de-France, and other northern provinces to form something recognizable to later philologists as "French." (The medieval equivalent of this "French," spoken very widely throughout Europe and in many places where the French king had no political presence, was known as *roman*, "romance.") I therefore prefer to distinguish among the different varieties of this northern vernacular: Picard for Picardy, Francien for the Île-de-France, and so on.

Terms like "the North" may also require clarification. Among historians who study the medieval antecedents of France, Belgium, Holland, and Luxembourg, "the North" usually refers to the culturally and economically interdependent territory then comprising northeastern Francia, Flanders, and the Low Countries, as well as some portions of modern-day Germany. It was within this nexus that Arras was situated, and to which it remained tied even after it was wrested from the control of Flanders in 1191 and incorporated into the kingdom centered on Paris. Arras itself formed the nucleus of a region called the Artois, which in 1237 became a fief held by the newly created count of Artois on behalf of his brother Louis IX. Picardy, of which the Artois could be called the heartland, was a linguistically unified region made up of wealthy trading towns and their fertile environs, among them Saint-Omer, Tournai, Douai, Calais, and Cambrai—towns that could, at any one time during the Middle Ages, form individual parts of the French kingdom, Flanders, the imperial county of Hainaut, or the English empire. Later, some of these towns became part of the duchy of Burgundy, and thereafter of the Habsburgs' Spanish Netherlands. This was also the fate of Arras, which formally changed hands in 1384, 1482, 1493, and 1659, and continued to be on the front lines of nearly every major European conflict up to and including World War II.

If this seems complicated, it is. As Robert Fossier has observed, Picardy is perhaps the only region on the Continent that has never, at any time in its history, formed part of a single principality. To my way of thinking, this has something to do with the character of a medieval theater in Arras. Nevertheless, the consequent destruction of this region's archives and its built environment, almost wholly complete by 1915, makes the study of that theater especially challenging.

So does the absence of any medieval terminology consonant with what we would use to describe the pervasive theatricality of the Middle Ages. Those medieval texts that modern scholarship has designated as "plays" are seldom labeled as such in their manuscripts, and when they are, the words for "play" (ludus, jeu, Spiel, etc.) retain their association with gaming and playfulness, eliding the distinction between formal, scripted drama and other varieties of entertainment, usually impromptu and resistant to writing. Moreover, the terms in which medieval people described their experiences of performance are themselves slippery, localized, imprecise, and not cognate with either classical or modern vocabularies, even though some of the same words might be used. In speaking of "a common stage," then, I refer to a wide terrain of performative practices from which these plays have been excavated, some of these practices being self-consciously representational or mimetic, some symbolic and ritualized, some civic. My title thus refers to the original meaning of the Greek word theatron, "a place for seeing," a place where "performed actions," drama, are submitted to public scrutiny and made meaningful through their association with other actions. By this definition, Arras in the thirteenth century can be viewed as "a medieval theater," but so can any other medieval community. Hence, the methodology of this book aims to catch glimpses of what transpired in medieval places for seeing and hearing, whether or not these theatra eventually produced texts that would satisfy the aesthetic and formal requirements for drama on which most modern scholarship insists and continues to rest.

This approach will be recognizable to some theater historians and literary critics as akin to performance studies, which has a similar thrust, but it may prove frustrating to these same scholars because of its resistance to the establishment of an alternate taxonomy, with clear distinctions made between play scripts, dramatized narratives, dialogic song, staged or spontaneous debates, public proclamations, legal proceedings, preaching campaigns, and a variety of other performances which used the same communicative strategies. It is no part of my project to replace one set of anachronisms with another. The more attentive one is to the ambiguities of the historical record, the more impossible it is to treat a complex set of phenomena as relatively transparent and easily brought into conformity with modern, or even postmodern, expectations. An analogy can be made to historians' erstwhile reliance on the concept of "feudalism," the abandonment of which has led to some initial confusion, but which has also inspired a more careful treatment of evidence and yielded some alternative, organic paradigms that more accurately reflect medieval conventions.

Where possible, I have accordingly used indigenous vocabulary to describe the people, offices, and institutions of medieval Arras: maieur ("mayor," leader), grand siège ("great seating," major feast), carité (confraternity, charitable brotherhood), préau ("court," ceremonial enclosure), échevins (elected officials). If speaking specifically of the Carité de Notre Dame des Ardents d'Arras, otherwise known as the confraternity of jongleurs, I make Carité a proper noun. When I have felt it advisable to adhere to the orthography of medieval Picard, the word is placed in italics: *mayeur, grant siege, karite, praiiel, eskievens*. The reader will find these and other terms defined at greater length in the pages that follow. At the same time, the reader will note that some words familiar to modern speakers of French and English carry very different meanings when applied to the Middle Ages, notably *bourgeois*, the residents of a *bourg* ("town"), and *commune*, a *coniuratio* or sworn association resulting in the formation of a *communio*, a collective body with shared political, economic, and social goals. When taken in its medieval context, the latter term easily retains its contemporary meaning; but because of the very strong Marxist flavor adhering to the former, which has given rise to some misrepresentations of medieval urban culture in secondary scholarship, I have chosen to refer to the "inhabitants" or the "townspeople" of Arras rather than to "the bourgeois of Arras" or "the bourgeoisie." When referring to the *cité* and *ville* of Arras, which were separate geopolitical entities throughout the Middle Ages, with different alliances, laws, and bureaucratic structures, I use the equivalent English words, capitalized as proper nouns: City and Town.

With respect to the citation of personal names, I have maintained an internal consistency throughout the book. I have preferred the Picard form of Jehan Bodel's given name (only the alien Francien dialect would have rendered it "Jean") and have likewise favored local versions of other first names, for the same reason. The citation of surnames is trickier. I have regularized the various forms of Jehan's last name (or nickname?) in accordance with his own *Congé* and the memorial record of his death in the Carité's funerary register, which give it as Bodel rather than Bodiaus; I have done the same for other persons whose names are spelled variously in original documents. And because students of French literature will be more familiar with "Adam de la Halle" than with "Adans le Boçu" or "Adam d'Arras," I have generally referred to him by this name.

When evoking the names of plays, I give their modern French titles rather than their Old French *incipits* or *explicits*, unless these are relevant to the discussion: for example, the *Jeu de saint Nicolas* instead of *Cest li ius de.S'.Nicholai* ("This is the Play of Saint Nicholas"), or the *Jeu de Robin et de Marion*, rather than *Chi conmenche li gieus de Robin et de Marion c'Adans fist* ("Here begins the play about Robin and about Marion which Adam made"). When quoting directly from these and other manuscript sources, I have not added modern diacritical markings (accents), nor have I regularized spelling and punctuation. Citations from published editions of Old French texts, where available, are provided for the reader's convenience, but my own examinations of the originals will often be reflected in changes to punctuation or the avoidance of editorial interventions designed to modernize the appearance of a text.

All translations are my own, unless otherwise indicated.

ABBREVIATIONS

AASS	Acta Sanctorum, ed. Joannes Bollandus et al., 68 vols.
AdPC	Archives départementales du Pas-de-Calais
AHOEc	Adam de la Halle: Œuvres complètes, ed. Badel
AHR	American Historical Review
Arsenal	Bibliothèque de l'Arsenal, Paris (manuscript)
BAV	Bibliotheca Apostolica Vaticana, Rome (manuscript)
BCdMhPC	Bulletin de la Commission départémentale des Monuments historiques du Pas-de-Calais
BHP	Bulletin historique et philologique du Comité des travaux historiques et scientifiques
BL	British Library, London (manuscript)
Bm	Bibliothèque municipale (manuscript)
BmA	Bibliothèque municipale d'Arras (manuscript)
BNE	Biblioteca Nacional de España, Madrid (manuscript)
BnF fr.	Bibliothèque nationale de France, Paris, fonds français (manuscript)
BnF lat.	Bibliothèque nationale de France, Paris, fonds latin (manuscript)
BPH	Bulletin philologique et historique (jusqu'à 1715) du Comité des travaux historiques et scientifiques
BSAM	Bulletin de la Société des antiquaires de la Morinie
BUP	Bibliotheca Universitaria di Pavia (manuscript)
Cartulaire	Cartulaire de la commune d'Arras, ed. Guesnon
CCCm	Corpus Christianorum, Continuatio mediævalis
C&D	Chansons et dits, ed. Berger in Littérature et société arrageoises
CdMhPC	Commission départementale des monuments historiques du Pas-de-Calais
Chandelle	La Chandelle d'Arras: Latin and Francien texts of the miraculum, ed. Berger as "Le récit du miracle" in Le nécrologe, 2:137–156
CNRS	Centre nationale de la recherche scientifique
Courtois	Courtois d'Arras, ed. Faral
Coutumier	customary laws of the Carité de Notre Dame des Ardents d'Arras (BnF fr. 8541, fols. 46r–47v)
Épigraphie	Épigraphie ancienne de la ville d'Arras, ed. de Loisne and Rodière
Follye	Factum de domo destructa ad reponendum capsam Beatæ Mariæ in Platea Joannis de Rotunda Villa quæ vocatur Follye, ed. Loriquet
G&A	Le garçon et l'aveugle, in Symes, "The Boy and the Blind Man: A Medieval Play Script and Its Editors"

Guiman	*Cartulaire de l'abbaye de Saint-Vaast rédigé au XIIe siècle par Guimann*, ed. van Drival
JF	*Jeu de la feuillée*, ed. Badel in *Adam de la Halle: Œuvres complètes*
JRM	*Jeu de Robin et de Marion*, ed. Schwam-Baird and Scheuermann
JsN	*Jeu de saint Nicolas*, ed. Henry
MA	*Le Moyen Âge*
MAA	*Mémoires de l'Académie d'Arras*, otherwise *Mémoires de l'Académie des sciences, lettres et arts d'Arras*
MCdMhPC	*Mémoires de la Commission départementale des monuments historiques du Pas-de-Calais*
MGH	*Monumenta Germaniæ Historica*
MSAM	*Mémoires de la Société des antiquaires de la Morinie*
Olim	*Les Olim, ou Registres des arrêts rendus par la cour du roi*, ed. Beugnot
Ordinance	*Ordinance of the rights which those who appear below have from the Carité during the siège. And in what manner things ought to be done*
PL	*Patrologia Latina, cursus completus*, ed. Jacques-Paul Migne, 217 vols.
RN	*Revue du Nord*
ROMRD	*Research Opportunities in Medieval and Renaissance Drama*, formerly *Research Opportunities in Renaissance Drama* (RORD)

Arras and its region

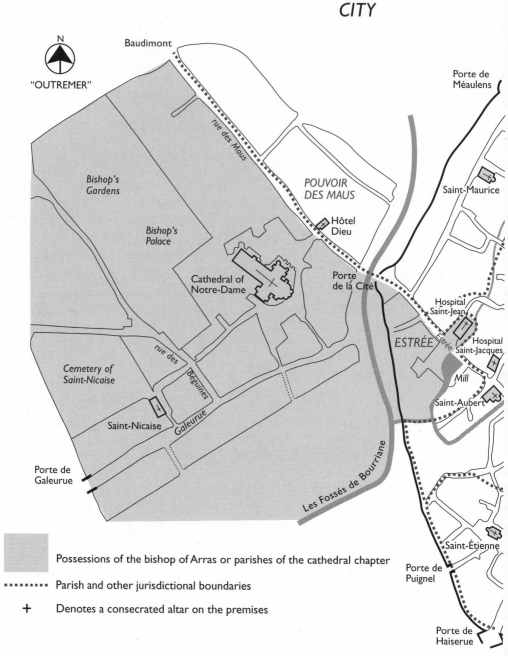

CITY

"OUTREMER"

Baudimont

Porte de
Méaulens

rue des Maus

Bishop's
Gardens

POUVOIR
DES MAUS

Saint-Maurice

Bishop's
Palace

Hôtel
Dieu

Cathedral of
Notre-Dame

Porte
de la Cité

Hospital
Saint-Jean

rue des Béguines

ESTRÉE

Estrée

Hospital
Saint-Jacques

Cemetery of
Saint-Nicaise

Mill

Saint-Aubert

Saint-Nicaise

Galeurue

Les Fossés de Bourriane

Porte de
Galeurue

Saint-Étienne

Porte de
Puignel

Possessions of the bishop of Arras or parishes of the cathedral chapter

Parish and other jurisdictional boundaries

+   Denotes a consecrated altar on the premises

Porte de
Haiserue

Sources: R. Berger, *Littérature et société arrageoises au XIIIe siècle* (1981) and B. Delmaire, *Le diocèse d'Arras de 1093 au milieu de XIVe siècle* (1994), with reference to E. van Drival, *Cartulaire de l'abbaye de Saint-Vaast rédigé au XIIe siècle par Guimann* (1875).

Arras in the thirteenth century

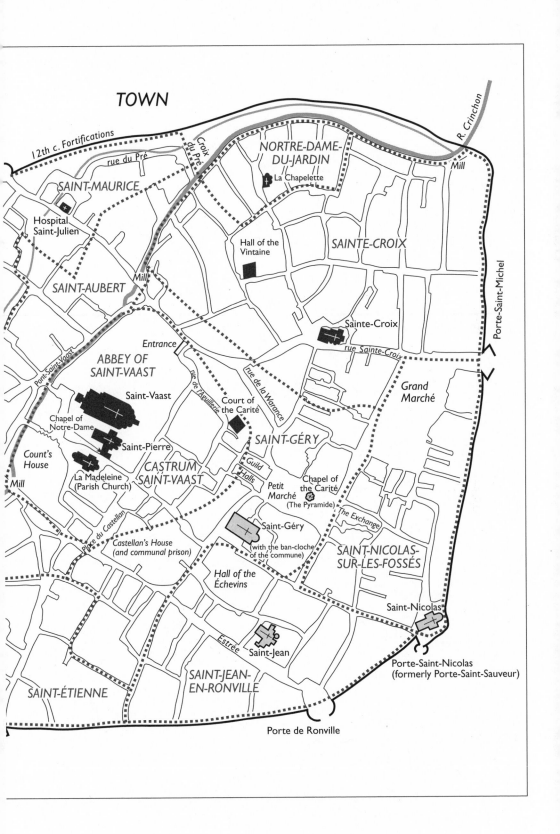

TOWN

12th c. Fortifications

rue du Pré

Croix du Pré

R. Crinchon

SAINT-MAURICE

Hospital Saint-Julien

NORTRE-DAME-DU-JARDIN

La Chapelette

Mill

SAINTE-CROIX

Hall of the Vintaine

SAINT-AUBERT

Mill

Entrance

Pont-Saint-Vaast

ABBEY OF SAINT-VAAST

Saint-Vaast

rue de l'Aguillerie

Court of the Carité

rue de la Warance

rue Sainte-Croix

Sainte-Croix

Porte-Saint-Michel

Grand Marché

Chapel of Notre-Dame

Saint-Pierre

SAINT-GÉRY

Count's House

Mill

La Madeleine (Parish Church)

CASTRUM SAINT-VAAST

Guild Halls

Petit Marché

Chapel of the Carité (The Pyramide)

The Exchange

SAINT-NICOLAS-SUR-LES-FOSSÉS

Saint-Géry (with the ban-cloche of the commune)

Place du Castellan

Castellan's House (and communal prison)

Hall of the Échevins

Saint-Nicolas

SAINT-ÉTIENNE

Estrée

Saint-Jean

SAINT-JEAN-EN-RONVILLE

Porte-Saint-Nicolas (formerly Porte-Saint-Sauveur)

Porte de Ronville

INTRODUCTION LOCATING A
MEDIEVAL THEATER

In the thirteenth century, Arras was at the center of an increasingly urbanized, cosmopolitan, and swiftly changing world. It was a world in which the newly consolidated power of emerging monarchies was balanced by the mercantile power of independent towns situated within international trading networks, where vernacular literacy was beginning to challenge the hegemony of Latin, and when the production of written records was transforming the ways that people in a predominately oral society communicated with one another. Out of this crucible, five remarkable artifacts emerge: the earliest vernacular plays of medieval Europe, the only plays to be produced in a secular milieu prior to the fourteenth century. For the first time since the fathers of a fledgling Christianity had protested against the licentious shows of Rome nearly a thousand years before, surviving scripts indicate that sophisticated, organized entertainments were being devised and performed for spectators who had not gathered for the sole purpose of religious instruction or divine worship.

They are a motley assortment, these plays. The *Jeu de saint Nicolas* (The Play of Saint Nicholas), the work of the minstrel Jehan Bodel, is a historical allegory dramatizing the local impact of the French king's expansion into Flanders in 1191, surviving only because of its inclusion in a deluxe manuscript made several generations later. The anonymous *Courtois d'Arras* (The Courtly Lad of Arras) is an up-to-date retelling of the parable of the Prodigal Son, originally composed before 1228 and available today in four separate manuscript redactions, the remains of four distinctive performance traditions reaching into the fourteenth century and extending into Italy. A satirical sketch called *Le garçon et l'aveugle* (The Boy and the Blind Man), datable to around the year 1265, is copied somewhat incongruously onto the leftover leaves of a long chivalric romance, and was continuously adapted for repeat performance over the course of the next few hundred years. And two plays by the trouvère Adam de la Halle, the *Jeu de la feuillée* (The Play of the Bower) and the *Jeu de Robin et de Marion* (The Play about Robin and Marion), composed respectively around 1276 and 1285, are chiefly preserved in an unusual authorial corpus of Adam's musical and poetic oeuvre, the same Arrageois anthology that preserves the *Jeu de saint Nicolas*.

These five plays predate by over two hundred years the much-studied Corpus Christi cycles of England and the advent of large-scale civic spectacles on the Continent. And they differ significantly, in content and in form, from contemporary liturgical dramas, as well as from the handful of vernacular or macaronic plays on biblical themes which were produced in ecclesiastical contexts. They are also unlike the many cosmopolitan Latin comedies composed in the eleventh and twelfth centuries, which are not attached to particular locales and which circulated widely throughout Europe until they influenced the playwrights of the Renaissance.[1] The plays of Arras, by contrast, are marked by the extreme topicality of their plots, which involve local people and deal with the immediate concerns of local audiences. And they are further set apart from the vast majority of medieval entertainments by the fact of their written remains, since most medieval plays, like most medieval poetry, music, narrative, and ritual, were devised and performed without the support of texts. What is remarkable about Arras, then, is not merely that it was the first medieval town to produce vernacular plays, but that it was the first to produce scripts recognizable to modern eyes *as* plays.

Yet this book avoids limiting the study of medieval theater to a set of conventionally defined plays and challenges the premises by which some texts have been designated as functionally "dramatic" while others have been rejected as "nondramatic" or "unperformable"—either in conformity with anachronistic categories borrowed from the *Poetics* of Aristotle or adapted from the enclosed theaters of modernity. Instead, I argue that the malleable forms in which medieval performances survive, and the permeable conditions in which they were devised and received, call for different ways of looking *for* and *at* the evidence of plays and their larger role in medieval public life. This book takes account of the practical and material processes by which these artifacts and their companion texts were created and exposes the teleology that has elevated only a few to the status of drama. It treats *all* premodern texts as potential participants in a culture of performance—some as the residue of performed actions, some as prompts for performance, some as the focal points of performance—and juxtaposes plays with the variety of other activities alongside which they were produced and transmitted: the display of charters, crying of news, taking of legal testimony, exhibition of relics, celebration of liturgies, organization of ceremonies, preaching of doctrine, telling of tales.

In short, *A Common Stage* equates medieval theater with the space available for public business in medieval communities (the Greek word *theatron* means "a place for seeing") and construes plays as the scripted remains of activities that drew on a shared language of visual display, aural stimuli, and spatial orientation (the Greek word *drama* means "action"). This approach is warranted by the fact that medieval performers were seldom assigned the task of filling a preexisting place with a performance of material deemed

---

1. On the surviving plays in various European vernaculars, see Eckehard Simon, ed., *The Theater of Medieval Europe: New Research in Early Drama* (Cambridge, 1991), especially 119–128 (English), 155–158 (French), 170–171 (Italian), 189–190 (Spanish and Catalan), 208 (German), 227 (Dutch). On contemporary Latin comedies, see Carol Symes, "The Performance and Preservation of Medieval Latin Comedy," *European Medieval Drama* 7 (2003): 29–50.

appropriate to that place (a theater, a concert hall, a courtroom, a church), but usually had to attract attention by carving out a venue and occasion for performance within a space already in use for other purposes. With this in mind, it becomes clear that any understanding of how a given play functioned must begin with an understanding of the much larger culture of performance which gave it meaning.

The special value of Arras in this endeavor lies in the fact that here we can discern the workings of a medieval theater rather more clearly than we can anywhere else in Europe because of this town's precocious tendencies toward representative governance and its precocious habits of recordkeeping. Arras provides us with our earliest opportunity for studying the relationship between dramatic enactment and daily interaction in an age when plays were not confined to purpose-built structures and were only occasionally recorded for posterity in documentary forms. Its history of performed activity therefore compels revision of the traditional narrative of theater's history, in which the thirteenth century has long been relegated to "a kind of limbo," and according to which the study of drama is regarded as a subspecies of literary criticism.[2] At the same time, it reveals how groups and individuals conveyed information, asserted opinion, negotiated conflicts, and exercised agency during a period when theater was open to all, before the construction of playhouses restricted access to paying audiences and required plays to meet the demands of the humanists' classical canon and the censors of the early modern state. In fact, I argue that the common stage which came into being in Arras testifies to an early manifestation of what Jürgen Habermas delineated as "the public sphere," calling into question the notion that purposeful public discourse is reliant on a very specific kind of literacy associated with the Enlightenment, supported by the proliferation of the cheap news sheet and the availability of discrete venues for discussion (the coffeehouse, the salon).[3] By studying a single place and time in which vernacular literacy was beginning to flour-

2. Glynne Wickham, "Introduction: Trends in International Drama Research," in Simon, Theater, 1–18 at 4. This observation is borne out by David Bevington's otherwise invaluable anthology Medieval Drama (Boston, 1975), in which there is a sizable gap of more than two centuries between plays from the Carmina Burana manuscript (ca. 1230) and the Banns of the English N-Town cycle. Although its editor has noted that he had wanted to include a number of other plays, neither Arras nor the thirteenth century appears in that list of desiderata: see David Bevington, "Drama Editing and Its Relation to Recent Trends in Literary Criticism," in Editing Early English Drama: Special Problems and New Directions, ed. Alexandra F. Johnston (New York, 1987), 17–32 at 25–26.

3. Jürgen Habermas, Strukturwandel der Öffentlichkeit: Untersuchungen zu einer Kategorie der bürgerlichen Gesellschaft (Darmstadt, 1962), e.g., 17–22, 172. Hereinafter I cite the English translation by Thomas Burger and Frederick Lawrence, The Structural Transformation of the Public Sphere: An Inquiry into a Category of Bourgeois Society (Cambridge, 1989). Even Habermas's critics take the modernity of the public sphere for granted, as does the complementary argument of Armand Mattelart, L'invention de la communication (Paris, 1994).

ish, and examining how that development affected collective life and shaped the technologies that supported public media for communication, this book demonstrates that we can view the theater of Arras as constituting a medieval public sphere.

In this it is possible that Arras was somewhat unusual. One of the wealthiest and most populous towns in northern Europe during the century that followed its incorporation into the kingdom of France, it combined within its walls a bewildering array of political, social, economic, and cultural institutions. It was a monastic center, diocesan see, comital capital, self-governing commune, and (after 1191) a royal baillage. It was also the cradle of confraternities and trade guilds, including one of the first and most extensively documented lay associations in Europe, the Carité de Notre Dame des Ardents, better known as the confraternity of jongleurs. And the often uneasy coexistence of these and other entities is, as we shall see, inextricably linked to some of the developments that contributed to the variety of medieval theater evinced in Arras. Other towns would rise to prominence in the later Middle Ages, when Arras was already in decline (its central location would make it a strategic site for many of the bloodiest battles from the Hundred Years' War to World War I). But in the long thirteenth century covered by this book, it is arguable that no other urban area—not Paris, not London, not Florence, not Bruges—combined such a dense variety of local institutions with so many advancing national and international interests. The result was a creative maelstrom of conflicting politics, unprecedented economic opportunities, and unfamiliar types of social mobility. And all of these competitive forces staked their rival claims in the open spaces of Arras through the use of public media directed at "all those seeing and hearing these current things," as medieval charters (scripted for performance) call the people who also constituted the audience for plays.

Some of these plays have been known to scholars of French literature since the eighteenth century, but they have never before been treated as the coherent products of a particular historical environment. This neglect is a function of the disciplinary, linguistic, and nationalist divisions that have long impacted the study of the Middle Ages and continue to govern the study of its theater.[4] Current narratives of dramatic development put together by scholars of Middle English literature routinely make little reference to the Continent and to plays in other languages (Latin or vernacular), while those by Francophone scholars valorize the plays in medieval French dialects as prototypically "modern," breaking definitively with the Church and heralding the birth of a secular "French" theater.[5] As

4. Elisabeth Lalou, "Le théâtre et les spectacles en France au moyen âge: État des recherches," in *Théâtre et spectacles hier et aujourd'hui: Moyen Age et renaissance* (Paris, 1991), 19–32 at 10 and 16. See also Alan E. Knight, "France," in Simon, *Theater*, 151–168.

5. E.g., Michel Rousse, "Le Jeu de Saint Nicolas," in *Arras au moyen âge: Histoire et littérature*, ed. Marie-Madeleine Castellani and Jean-Pierre Martin (Arras, 1994), 153–162 at 153; and idem, "Propositions sur

a result, the plays of Arras are either marginalized or omitted altogether in English-language histories, while in France they must adhere to the aesthetic and political standards demanded of this "modern" "French" theater, considered (because of its modernity and Frenchness) to be hostile to religion and the aristocracy by definition, and hence the precursor of Revolutionary fervor or the socialist state.[6] This is the lens through which Arras is viewed in the single published monograph devoted to the plays' urban context, Marie Ungureanu's *La bourgeoisie naissante: Société et littérature bourgeoises d'Arras aux XIIe et XIIIe siècles*, still cited by scholars in America and England even though it has been subject to stringent historical critique on the Continent since the time of its publication in 1955.[7]

In offering an alternative, this book draws upon models provided by recent scholarship on the theater of later medieval centuries, but with some essential modifications mandated by the nature and limitations of older sources. For example, Eckehard Simon's analysis of the records relating to civic theatricals in late medieval Germany shows not only how pervasive were the performance of plays but also how communities small and large were articulated around and through dramatic display;[8] Sarah Beckwith's reading of the dramatic and municipal records of York reveals how the annual performance of the city's Corpus Christi cycle came to be a defining force in local politics and in the creation and fragmentation of social identities;[9] and Gail McMurray Gibson's study of fifteenth-

le théâtre profane avant les farces," *Tréteaux* 1 (1978): 4–18. See also Richard Axton, *European Drama of the Early Middle Ages* (London, 1974), 60, 131, 105, 108. Rainer Warning has detected in all of these narratives a "hermeneutic helplessness" with respect to drama's historical context, especially in France; see Warning, *Funktion und Struktur: Die Ambivalenzen des gesitlichen Spiels* (Munich, 1974), trans. Steven Rendall as *The Ambivalences of Medieval Religious Drama* (Stanford, 2001), 2 and 249–260.

    6. E.g., Jean-Charles Payen, "Théâtre médiéval et culture urbaine," *Revue d'histoire du théâtre* 35 (1983): 233–250; and idem, *Littérature française*, vol. 1, *Le Moyen Age* (Paris, 1984), 156. See also Graham Runnalls, "Towns and Plays: Social Aspects of Drama in Late Medieval France," and "The Theater in Paris in the Late Middle Ages," in *Études sur les mystères: Un recueil de 22 études sur les mystères français, suivi d'un répertoire du théâtre religieux français du Moyen Age et d'une bibliographie* (Paris, 1998), 61–100.

    7. See Henri Roussel, "Notes sur la littérature arrageoise du XIIIe siècle," *Revue des sciences humaines* 87 (1957): 249–286; and Ursula Peters, *Literatur in der Stadt: Studien zu den sozialen Voraussetzungen und kulturellen Organisationsformen städtischer Literatur im 13. und 14. Jahrhundert* (Tübingen, 1983), 61–96. The only other full-length treatment, Susan Johnson Clark's Ph.D dissertation, "The Theater of Medieval Arras" (Yale University, 1973), yields many insights; but it is not an attempt at historical contextualization. The painstaking studies of Roger Berger, while invaluable, do not address the plays directly: *Le nécrologe de la Confrérie des jongleurs et des bourgeois d'Arras (1194–1361)*, 2 vols. (Arras, 1963 and 1970); and *Littérature et société arrageoises au XIIIe siècle: Les chansons et dits artésiens* (Arras, 1981).

    8. Eckehard Simon, *Die Anfänge des weltlichen deutschen Schauspiels, 1370–1530: Untersuchung und Dokumentation* (Tübingen, 2003).

    9. Sarah Beckwith, "Ritual, Theater, and Social Space in the York Corpus Christi Cycle," in *Bodies and*

century East Anglia demonstrates how much we can learn about plays by surveying the wider landscape in which they were conceived and received.[10] Indeed, Gibson's discussion of the ways that theater contributed to a burgeoning "self-consciousness—national, civic, and personal" applies equally well to Arras, as does Theresa Coletti's description of late medieval Norwich as a "thriving textual community of clerical and lay writers and prosperous gentry and noble readers who engendered the region's literary culture."[11] Nevertheless, the historian of an earlier medieval theater cannot rely on the evidence to which these scholars have access, comprising not just play scripts and performance records but extant wills, personal narratives, municipal archives, letters, and chronicles, as well as funerary monuments, domestic sculpture, parish churches, wall paintings, and even the well-preserved topography of certain late medieval towns.[12] Before 1400, everywhere in Europe the picture looks very different: where we have plays, we have no records of their production; where we have records, we have no plays. As a result, we cannot say for certain who enacted the plays of Arras, who commissioned or wrote the manuscripts that preserve them, or when and where they were performed. Given these constraints, research into the parameters of any medieval theater prior to the fifteenth century requires the collection and analysis of sources that usually lie far beyond the present purview of theater studies. Nor is the resulting body of material very extensive in the case of Arras, owing to the almost total destruction of the town's medieval archives during World War I.[13] But the necessity of this new methodological venture has engendered an important

---

Disciplines: Intersections of Literature and History in Fifteenth-Century England, ed. Barbara Hanawalt and David Wallace (Minneapolis, 1996), 63–86; and idem, Signifying God: Social Relation and Symbolic Act in the York Corpus Christi Plays (Chicago, 2001).

10. Gail McMurray Gibson, The Theater of Devotion: East Anglian Drama and Society in the Late Middle Ages (Chicago, 1989).

11. Ibid., 68 and 137–138; Theresa Coletti, Mary Magdalene and the Drama of Saints: Theater, Gender, and Religion in Late Medieval England (Philadelphia, 2004), 9.

12. Alan E. Knight, "Drama and Society in Late Medieval Flanders and Picardy," Chaucer Review 14 (1980): 379–389; Eckehard Simon, "Organizing and Staging Carnival Plays in Late Medieval Lübeck: A New Look at the Archival Record," Journal of English and Germanic Philology 92 (1993): 57–72; Wim Hüsken, "Civic Patronage of Early Fifteenth-Century Religious Drama in the Low Countries," in Civic Ritual and Drama, ed. Wim Hüsken and Alexandra F. Johnston (Amsterdam, 1997), 107–123.

13. Thanks to the heroism of the departmental archivist, the records of the counts of Artois (filed under the letter "A," designating the archives of the local secular authority) survive in their entirety; but of the vast, partly inventoried archives of the region's powerful monasteries ("H"), and the vast, uninventoried archives of the commune and diocese ("F" and "G"), only a few stray documents remain. See M. G. Besnier, "Pas de Calais," in "Chronique des Archives départementales: Années 1926 et 1927," ed. A. Vidier and H. Courteault, BHP (1926–27): 399–403. For an update, see État des inventaires des Archives départementales, communales et hospitalières au 1er janvier 1983, vol. 2 (Paris, 1984), 854–871. The remains

discovery: namely, the inseparability of premodern theater history from the history of communities.

Some Medieval Theaters

It has long been noted that medieval theater was very different from the state-sponsored religious festivals of classical Athens and the civic spectacles of ancient Rome, as well as the proscenium arches and darkened auditoriums of modern theater buildings. Yet these differences have been invariably regarded as deficiencies rather than as evidence of open access and artistic license; they have narrowed, not expanded, the scope of a medieval theater. Despite significant developments in the scholarship of the past half-century, the old story of theater's alleged suppression by the medieval Church is still so frequently invoked that even many medievalists accept the tale of its eradication at the hands of religious zealots, its descent into a hell of liturgical boredom, and its slow release from ritual at the dawn of modernity. As O. B. Hardison remarked in 1965: "The best one can say of the standard histories is that first there was medieval drama and then there was Elizabethan drama. In practice, the introduction and handbooks to English drama do just that, devoting a chapter or two to summaries of Chambers and Young and then proceeding to the sixteenth century with scarcely a backward glance."[14] Forty years later this is still true, except that the chronology has been pushed back a hundred years: it is now the fifteenth century on which the gaze of scholarship rests, the abundance of obvious dramatic material available at that late date—plays and the records of their production or regulation—misleadingly construed as evidence for increased theatricality rather than as a function of more ingrained habits of documentation and the increased authorial, scribal, and official control of public culture.[15]

---

of the diocesan archive have since been inventoried by Bernard Delmaire, whose manuscript handlist was donated to the AdPC in 1977 (hereinafter cited as Delmaire handlist). The holdings of the monastery and cathedral libraries have fared better, but were drastically depleted in the early part of the nineteenth century, when an enterprising librarian cut up all but 45 of the 779 volumes, selling over 40,000 leaves (of an estimated 130,000) to collectors and tourists. See Philip Grierson, "La bibliothèque de St-Vaast d'Arras au XIIe siècle," *Revue bénédictine* 52 (1940): 117–140; Adolphe Guesnon, "La collection de Sir Thomas Phillipps et les archives communales d'Arras," *MCdMhPC* (1909): 1–11.

14. O. B. Hardison, "Darwin, Mutations, and the Origin of Medieval Drama," in *Christian Rite and Christian Drama in the Middle Ages: Essays in the Origin and Early History of Modern Drama* (Baltimore, 1965), 1–34 at 29. Hardison refers to the works that established the agenda and sources of English-language theater studies in the twentieth century: E. K. Chambers, *The Mediaeval Stage*, 2 vols. (Oxford, 1903); and Karl Young, *The Drama of the Medieval Church*, 2 vols. (Oxford, 1933).

15. See M. T. Clanchy, *From Memory to Written Record: England 1066–1307*, 2nd ed. (Oxford, 1993); Sylvia Huot, *From Song to Book: The Poetics of Writing in Old French Lyric and Lyrical Narrative Poetry* (Ithaca,

Although theater scholars have largely rejected the Darwinian model of the evolution of medieval drama from simple to complex forms, the model that informed the labors of E. K. Chambers and Karl Young, more powerful presuppositions about the sources and nature of a medieval theater continue to determine not simply the way it is studied but *what it is supposed to be*. Drama is still spoken of as something that needs an "origin" rather than as something vital to a culture that was "absolutely theatrical," and therefore closely akin to other medieval practices of representation, as Jody Enders and Michal Kobialka have shown.[16] Moreover, the very criteria used to identify certain texts as "plays" have been shown to derive from the capricious tastes of seventeenth-century antiquaries, eighteenth-century bibliophiles, nineteenth-century philologists, and twentieth-century critics—not from medieval generic conventions or indigenous performance conditions. Not one of the four different copies of *Courtois d'Arras*, for example, is labeled a "play" or presented as any more or less stageworthy than the hundreds of bawdy and moral tales with which it shares space in its manuscripts.[17] As Andrew Gurr has remarked, with reference to the plays of Shakespeare, "centuries of habituation to the written word have conditioned us to conceive as fixity what is really flux."[18] Or, as Elie Konigson put it, "The peculiarity of medieval theater is that it was not dependent on any theory of theatrical space specific to the theater."[19]

What, then, *was* a medieval theater dependent on, and is there any way of defining it that comes close to a contemporary understanding? In the *Didascalicon*, an encyclopedia compiled around the year 1125, the Parisian canon Hugh of Saint-Victor divided all human endeavor into two broad categories, the seven "liberal" arts of the mind ("liberal" because free from day-to-day cares) and the seven "mechanical" arts necessary to the survival of mankind. Under the latter rubric he placed "theatrics" (*theatrica*) or "the knowledge of

1987); Paul Zumthor, *La lettre et la voix de la "littérature" médiévale* (Paris, 1987); Margot Fassler, *Gothic Song: Victorine Sequences and Augustinian Reform in Twelfth-Century Paris* (Cambridge, 1993).

16. The phrase is from Paul Strohm, "York's Paper Crown: 'Bare Life' and Shakespeare's First Tragedy," *Journal of Medieval and Early Modern Studies* 36 (2006): 75–101 at 75–76. See Jody Enders, *Rhetoric and the Origins of Medieval Drama* (Ithaca, 1992), *Death by Drama and Other Medieval Urban Legends* (Chicago, 2002), and "Theater Makes History: Ritual Murder by Proxy in the *Mistere de la Sainte Hostie*," *Speculum* 79 (2004): 991–1016; and Michal Kobialka, *This Is My Body: Representational Practices in the Early Middle Ages* (Ann Arbor, 1999).

17. Carol Symes, "The Appearance of Early Vernacular Plays: Forms, Functions, and the Future of Medieval Theater," *Speculum* 77 (2002): 778–831; idem, "Theater," in *Arts and Humanities through the Eras*, vol. 5, *Medieval Europe, 814–1450*, ed. Kristen M. Figg and John Block Friedman (Farmington Hills, Michigan, 2004), 377–417; and idem, "Manuscript Matrix, Modern Canon," in *Oxford 21st-Century Approaches to Literature: Middle English*, ed. Paul Strohm (Oxford, 2007), 7–22.

18. Andrew Gurr, *The Shakespeare Company, 1594–1642* (Cambridge, 2004), 120.

19. Elie Konigson, *L'espace théâtral médiéval* (Paris, 1975), 78.

playing" (*scientia ludorum*), alongside agriculture, hunting, and medicine: basic arts made possible by the still more basic trivium of clothing manufacture, the making of tools and shelters, and trade. Calling attention to the perennial importance of restorative leisure, Hugh chose a term derived from a type of structure that no longer existed, "the place where the people used to gather for the purpose of playing." He chose it "not because a theater was the only place in which such play could happen," he hastened to add, "but because it was a place more often frequented than the rest." And he went on to list some of the other venues in which playing could take place—public buildings, gymnasia, amphitheaters, arenas, halls, temples—and the many types of sport available even in the absence of specific buildings: dramatic performances and recitations featuring actors or puppets or masked figures, ritual processions, wrestling matches, races on foot or horseback or in chariots, boxing, banqueting, music making (vocal and instrumental), dancing, storytelling, and games of chance. Finally, he noted that "in sanctuaries, in solemn seasons, they sang the praises of the gods." While Hugh's use of the past tense underscores the changes that had taken place in the centuries since the ruined theaters on the Left Bank of the Seine had been built by Roman colonists, his catalogue also emphasizes certain significant continuities in the types and places of playing available in Paris, many of which were familiar to his students. He concludes this entry by saying that the ancients "counted all these diversions as legitimate activities" because they allowed for the healthy release of pent-up energies, and he extols the wisdom of his pagan forebears in providing the designated *theatra* which his own society lacked: "Since it is necessary for people to get together in some place for playing, they decided that certain spaces for playing should be set aside, lest people should go off in various groups and get up to all sorts of mischief and misbehavior."[20]

Hugh's definition of theater was widely known and often cited in the thirteenth century. As the Dominican friar Saint Bonaventure (1221–1274) would remark, in an extended commentary on the *Didascalicon*, theater is "sufficient unto itself" (*patet sufficientia*), essen-

---

20. Hugh of Saint-Victor, *Didascalicon*, ed. Charles Henry Buttimer, 2 vols. (Washington, D.C., 1939), 2:27: "Theatrica dicitur scientia ludorum a theatro ubi populus ad ludendum convenire solebat, non quia in theatro tantum ludus fieret, sed quia celebrior locus fuerat ceteris. . . . in fanis tempore solemni deorum laudes canebant. ludos vero idcirco inter legitimas actiones connumerabant . . . quia necesse fuit populum aliquando ad ludendum convenire, voluerunt determinata esse loca ludendi, ne in diversoriis conventicula facientes probrosa aliqua aut facinorosa perpetrarent." On Hugh's antecedents and influence, see W. Tatarkiewicz, "*Theatrica*, the Science of Entertainment from the XIIth to the XVIIth Century," *Journal of the History of Ideas* 26 (1965): 263–272. On the intellectual and theological context in which this definition emerged, see Donalee Dox, *The Idea of the Theater in Latin Christian Thought: Augustine to the Fourteenth Century* (Ann Arbor, 2004), 85–87. Hugh's *theatrica* also frame Charlotte Stern's study *The Medieval Theater in Castile* (Binghamton, 1996), 55–62.

tial, ubiquitous, and universal.[21] Contemporary critics saw it as *too* universal, and naysay-
ers in medieval ivory towers would continue to sputter their worn-out condemnations of
theater professionals, quoting Tertullian (ca. 155–ca. 230), Augustine (354–430), or
Isidore of Seville (ca. 560–636), detractions that merely provide a useful barometer of theatrical activity. As Jonas Barnish has shown, an "outburst of antitheatrical sentiment tends
to coincide with the flourishing of the theater itself" and is invariably marked by the
conflation of actors with any "undesirable" elements in a given society: barbarians and
women in antiquity, indigents and prostitutes in the Middle Ages, Jews and homosexuals
in the twentieth century.[22]

Contemporary clerics who worked in the world approached the problem more practi-
cally. They knew that the only way to discourage unwholesome play was to counter it with
something else. When Lambert le Bègue (d. 1177), a parish priest from Liège, observed
the behavior of his parishioners on Sundays and feast days, he saw that "they would set
aside manual labor only because they were then directing their attention to mimes, dancing girls, and actors, devoting their time to drunkenness and dicing, calling for the seductive caroling of women (either taking part or watching), singing obscene songs and
making lewd gestures even outside of churches, and around the tombs of their ancestors
and kindred." This, he felt, was "not so much playing as raving," but it was also the by-
product of the too successful pursuit of the other mechanical arts practiced in prosperous
Liège, a mercantile town not unlike Arras.[23] Possibly indebted to a reading of Hugh, Lambert recognized that playing was necessary and natural, but that it had to be shaped and
directed to salubrious ends. His response was to invent pious entertainments that would
attract Sunday revelers and encourage more appropriate uses of the church and churchyard. So he taught his parishioners to perform versified vernacular translations of the Acts
of the Apostles and the letters of Paul, directed them in the enactment of episodes from
the life of Christ and the Blessed Virgin, and encouraged dramatic, affective responses to
the celebration of Mass.

21. From the *Reductio artium ad theologiam*; quoted by Tatarkiewicz, "*Theatrica*," 268.

22. Jonas Barish, *The Antitheatrical Prejudice* (Berkeley1981), 66, 38–65, 450–477. See also Dox, *Idea*,
87–92.

23. "Vidi infinitam multitudinem utriusque sexus Dominicam diem non restaurationi negligenta-
rium, sed multiplicationi gravius peccando deputare; sollempnibus etenim diebus a labore manuum
tantum abstinentes, ad mimos, saltatrices, histriones intendebant, ebrietatibus et aleis vacabant, choreis mulierum illecebrosis aut ducendis aut spectandis insistebant, obscenis canticis et gestibus impu-
dicis pro foribus ecclesiarum et super tumulos parentum at affinium suorum . . . non ludebant sed
insaniebant." See Lambert of Liège, "L'*Antigraphum Petri* et les lettres concernant Lambert le Bègue, conservées dans le manuscrit de Glasgow," ed. Arnold Fayen, *Compte rendu des séances de la Commission royale
d'histoire* 68 (1899): 255–356 at 349–350.

What Lambert did was probably not unusual—he mentions a similar dramatization of the Psalms made by "a certain schoolmaster from Flanders"—but it is fortunate for us that he was forced to defend his *theatrica* against ecclesiastical censure or we would not be privy to this valuable record. Like other aspects of day-to-day existence, medieval theater is likely to leave traces only when something goes wrong. We are told, for instance, that the future abbot of St. Albans in England, Geoffrey de Gorron (fl. 1119–1146), would not have taken monastic vows (or found his way into the abbey's venerable history) if the costumes he had borrowed for his students' production of a play about Saint Catherine had not been destroyed the night after the performance when a fire started in his rooms. Thanks to this mishap, we know that the kinds of plays "which we commonly call 'miracles'" were ordinary occurrences; but because they were so commonplace, there was no need for the chronicler to say anything more about them.[24] We do not even know whether this *miraculum* was scripted, or in what language it was performed—Geoffrey's native Norman? his young scholars' native Anglo-Saxon or Anglo-Norman? Latin?—and we have a similarly casual reference to a Resurrection play performed in an English churchyard around 1220, but only because a boy was injured when he fell off the church roof, whither he had climbed to get a better view of the action.[25] The record is eloquent in its silence. We cannot rely entirely on descriptions of performances or the surviving texts of plays for evidence of a medieval theater.

Luckily, we are told where else to look and what to look for. When William FitzStephen wanted to attract pilgrims to the London birthplace of the new Saint Thomas Becket, he did so by enumerating "the plays [ludi] of the city, since it is appropriate that a city be not only useful and important, but also a source of delight and diversion." His lengthy advertisement, appended to an account of the saint's life and martyrdom written in 1174, paints a tantalizing picture of the hospitality awaiting travelers in a place whose *theatrica* included "frequenting churches, honoring the ceremonies of God, the keeping of feast days, the giving of alms, reception of guests, the confirmation of betrothals, making of marriages, celebration of weddings, the preparation of merrymaking, entertainment of merrymakers, and also the observance of funeral rites and the burying of the dead." Unlike ancient Rome, he says, where pagan spectacles were confined to theater buildings, London "has plays of a holier kind, representations of the miracles worked by holy confessors, or representations of the sufferings that glorified the constancy of the martyrs." Moreover, he says, it boasts Carnival plays, tournaments and processions, mock naval battles, hunting

24. *Gesta abbatum monasterii Sancti Albani*, ed. Henry Thomas Riley, 2 vols. (London, 1897), 1:72–73: "quemdam ludum de Sancta Katerina—quem *miracula* vulgariter appellamus."

25. William Tydeman, *The Theater in the Middle Ages: Western European Stage Conditions, c. 800–1576* (Cambridge, 1978), 126.

and hawking, summer games of athletic skill, and winter sports such as bearbaiting and ice skating.[26] If you require a theater, William says, look around you.

But would strangers to William's London evaluate its theater in the same way that he did? Would the use of those spaces, at those times, be equally meaningful to them? A common stage is characterized not only by access but also by consensus, a shared understanding of the purposes of playing. How can we be sure we know a play when we see it, and how can we tell the players without a program? The laconic account of a failed theatrical experiment in 1205 illustrates what Philippe Buc has termed "the dangers of ritual" and shows how easy it is for one culture to misapprehend the theater of another.[27] In his chronicle history of the Baltic region, completed around the year 1225, Henry of Livonia recalled what happened when a group of German-speaking missionaries arrived in Latvia and decided to put on a play. Their plan backfired: "*Concerning the big play put on in Riga.* That same winter, an extremely well-produced play of the prophets was put on in the middle of Riga, in order that the folk might be taught the rudiments of the Christian faith as though through eyewitness. The subject matter of this play was most carefully explained to new converts, as well as to the pagans who came to see it, through an interpreter. At the place where Gideon's soldiers were fighting with the Philistines, however, the pagans began to run away, fearing that they would be killed—and could only be coaxed back with some care."[28] The reference to "a play of the prophets" is casual, since Henry assumes his readers' connoisseurship of liturgical drama. *We* are scarcely the wiser, however, since none of the plays that have come down to us resemble the one he brags about, and none include a battle scene: another reminder that surviving scripts are only remotely

---

26. "Non puto urbem esse in qua sint probabiliores consuetudines, in ecclesiis visitandis, ordinatis Dei honorandis, festis feriandis eleemosynis dandis, in hospitibus suscipiendis, in desponsationibus firmandis, matrimoniis contrahendis, nuptiis celebrandis, conviviis ornandis, convivis hilarandis; etiam, in exequiis curandis et cadaveribus humandis. . . . Amplius et ludos urbis veniamus, quoniam non expedit utilem tantum et seriam urbem esse, nisi dulcis etiam sit et iocunda." The *Descriptio nobilissimae civitatis Londoniae* was eventually included as an appendix to John Stow, A SURVAY OF LONDON. Conteyning the Originall, Antiquity, Increaſe, Moderne eſtate, and deſcription of that City, first published in 1598 and reprinted in 1603, ed. Charles Lethbridge Kingsford, 2 vols. (Oxford, 1908), 2:218–229 at 225–226.

27. Philippe Buc, *The Dangers of Ritual: Between Early Medieval Texts and Social Scientific Theory* (Princeton, 2001). See also Catherine Bell, *Ritual: Perspectives and Dimensions* (Oxford, 1997), especially 1–89 and 160–161.

28. "De ludo magno, qui fuit in Riga. Eadem hyeme factus est ludus prophetarum ordinatissimus in media Riga, ut fidei christiane rudimenta gentilitas fide disceret oculata. Cuius ludi materia tam neophitis quam paganis, qui aderant, per interpretem diligentissime exponebatur. Ubi autem armati Gedeonis cum Phylisteis pugnabant, pagani timentes occidi fugere ceperunt, sed caute sunt evocati." Henry of Livonia, *Chronicon Livoniæ*, ed. L. Arbusow and A. Bauer (Würzburg, 1959), 44; ed. and trans. James A. Brundage as *The Chronicle of Henry of Livonia* (New York, 2003), 53.

representative of what went on in a medieval theater. More important, we are invited to ask whose frame of reference determines the meaning of this performance. The actors' intentions were clear, but only to themselves. They assumed that an explanation of the play's plot and its moral message would be enough, and that their form of mimetic representation would be obvious even to an uncomprehending audience used to real violence perpetrated by some of the same men now playing at war. One of the Latvian spectators would surely have described the scene very differently, in an account that would probably not look like a dramatic record; it would read more like the report of imperialist atrocities.

This is a cautionary tale: it is hard to avoid the missionaries' mistake, and it is discomfiting to be placed in the position of the outsider who does not know what he is seeing. Yet I suggest that this is the position in which modern scholars of medieval phenomena are often placed when they ignore a dramatic event's complex historical setting or fail to recognize a dramatic event because it comes couched in an alien format. These expert witnesses alert us to the challenges and advantages of locating a medieval theater, pointing to a whole spectrum of theatrica that were considered by contemporaries as the larger context in which plays were performed: gambling, churchgoing, socializing, charitable deeds, sport, ceremonial observances, and the fulfillment of public duties. Their testimony indicates, overwhelmingly, that a medieval theater was more capacious, its potential sources more plentiful, and its plays more fundamentally important to our understanding of the entire age than modern theater histories have hitherto disclosed. This is borne out by the plays' manuscripts and the contemporary importance accorded to the enactment of everything from charters to chansons de geste.[29] Logically, therefore, the historical investigation of a medieval theater must take account of many other artifacts while promoting the use of performance as an analytical category.

The Enactment of Evidence and the Scripting of Plays

The dramatic impulse is innate in humans, as Johan Huizinga and Erving Goffman (among others) have observed.[30] In the Middle Ages it was so pronounced that it informed the production of the very evidence on which we rely for our knowledge of the past. Per-

29. Symes, "Appearance" and "Performance." See also David Mills, "Modern Editions of Medieval English Plays," in Simon, Theater, 65–79; Stern, Medieval Theater, 264–278 ("A Call for a New Poetics"); and Darwin Smith, "Les manuscrits 'de théâtre': Introduction codicologique à des manuscrits qui n'existent pas," Gazette du livre médiéval 33 (1998): 1–10.

30. Johan Huizinga, Homo ludens: A Study of the Play Element in Culture, [trans. R. F. C. Hull] (Boston, 1950); Erving Goffman, The Presentation of Self in Everyday Life (Harmondsworth, 1959). The theatricality of medieval life is a central premise of Huizinga, The Waning of the Middle Ages: A Study of the Forms of Life, Thought, and Art in France and the Netherlands in the Fourteenth and Fifteenth Centuries, [trans. F. Hopman] (New York, 1924).

formance was presupposed by the act of writing.[31] John of Salisbury (ca. 1115–1176) described the letters of the alphabet as performance prompts for the speaker. Roger Bacon (ca. 1220–1292) considered editing and punctuation forms of musical notation, "because all these things consist in the raising and lowering of the voice and are therefore like some kind of chant." The great jurist and reformer Pope Innocent III (1161–1216) could concentrate properly only while listening to a text, and so had everything read aloud to him.[32] Audiences everywhere were made aware of the advantages to be gained by participation in literate culture precisely because they were constantly hearing and seeing its effects.[33]

The degree to which all medieval texts are predicated on performance not only has broad implications for the study of plays but also suggests that the historical analysis of any document must consider the public contexts that dictated its inscription and reception, even when that document would seem to have little to do with performance, or is one in which a performative element is so fundamental that it has gone unremarked.[34] The use of performance as a category of analysis thus takes the historian beyond the stage of strip-mining a document for facts. It enlivens the residue of human communications

31. Brigitte Bedos-Rezak, "Civic Liturgies and Urban Records in Northern France, 1100–1400," in *City and Spectacle in Medieval Europe*, ed. Barbara Hanawalt and Kathryn L. Ryerson (Minneapolis, 1994), 34–55; Leo Treitler, "Oral, Written, and Literate Process in the Transmission of Medieval Music," *Speculum* 56 (1981): 471–491; Paul Saenger, *Space between Words: The Origins of Silent Reading* (Stanford, 1997); William A. Graham, *Beyond the Written Word: Oral Aspects of Scripture in the History of Religion* (Cambridge, 1987); Ralph G. Williams, "I Shall Be Spoken: Textual Boundaries, Authors, and Intent,'" in *Palimpsest: Editorial Theory in the Humanities*, ed. George Bornstein and Ralph G. Williams (Ann Arbor, 1993), 45–66; John Dagenais, *The Ethics of Reading in a Manuscript Culture: Glossing the "Libro de buen amor"* (Princeton, 1994).

32. Clanchy, *From Memory*, 253–285.

33. Franz Bäuml, "Varieties and Consequences of Medieval Literacy and Illiteracy," *Speculum* 55 (1980): 237–265; Michael Camille, "Seeing and Reading: Some Visual Implications of Medieval Literacy and Illiteracy," *Art History* 8 (1985): 26–49; Joyce Coleman, *Public Reading and the Reading Public in Late Medieval England and France* (Cambridge, 1996); Evelyn Birge Vitz, *Orality and Performance in Early French Romance* (Cambridge, 1999).

34. Joaquín Martínez Pizarro has demonstrated this for the *Histories* of Gregory of Tours, Brigitte Bedos-Rezak for the making of charters, Jeff Rider for Galbert of Bruges's narrative of Charles the Good's murder, Steven Justice for the creative uses of writing in the English Peasants' Rising of 1381, and Natalie Zemon Davis for the records of requests for royal pardons in early modern France. Joaquín Martínez Pizarro, *A Rhetoric of the Scene* (Toronto, 1989); Brigitte Bedos-Rezak, *Form and Order in Medieval France: Studies in Social and Quantitative Sigillography* (Aldershot, 1993); Jeff Rider, *God's Scribe: The Historiographical Art of Galbert of Bruges* (Washington, D.C., 2001); Steven Justice, *Writing and Rebellion: England in 1381* (Berkeley, 1994); Natalie Zemon Davis, *Fiction in the Archives: Pardon Tales and Their Tellers in Sixteenth-Century France* (Stanford, 1987).

encoded in and manufactured by texts, reminding us that they participated in a communicative process that ancient and medieval rhetoricians called *actio*, enactment.[35] It thereby provides a tool for the reembodiment of the historical record and the reexamination of the causal relationships between texts and events. As R. G. Collingwood once asked: "If, then, the historian has no direct or empirical knowledge of his facts, and no transmitted or testamentary knowledge of them, what kind of knowledge has he: in other words, what must the historian do in order that he may know them?" Answer: "The historian must re-enact the past in his own mind."[36]

This enactment of evidence constitutes an archaeology as fundamental to the historical method as the distinctive archaeologies of Thucydides or Michel Foucault, precisely because it calls attention to the way stories are told (J. L. Austin, Hayden White), as well as to the material conditions through which those tellings are mediated or silenced (Michel de Certeau, Gayatri Chakravorty Spivak). Musing on the limitations of writing as a recording device, an eyewitness to a splendid series of spectacles remarked in 1496, "It is not at all within the capacities of any man living on this earth to know how to describe in writing something that has been accomplished through affect."[37] The sudden-seeming appearance of certain records of performance practice, plays, and other doings "accomplished through affect" is accordingly dependent on the convergence of crucial forces: modern scholars' judgments about the dramatic qualities of certain texts and the medieval development of the vernacular as a language of record, coupled with the influence of contemporary institutions which made some aspects of theatricality worthy of remembrance. A similar observation can be made of the supposedly "late" appearance of liturgical drama in the ninth and tenth centuries, which was driven by the development of musical notation, new trends in the representation of the sacred, and the proselytism of religious reformers.[38] It has also been identified as the process whereby Homeric epics

35. Enders, *Rhetoric*, especially 20–30.

36. R. G. Collingwood, *The Idea of History* (Oxford, 1946), 282. See also Lloyd S. Kramer, "Literature, Criticism, and Historical Imagination: The Literary Challenge of Hayden White and Dominick LaCapra," in *The New Cultural History*, ed. Lynn Hunt (Berkeley, 1989), 97–128.

37. "Il n'est poinct en la possibilité d'homme vivant sur la terre le scavoyr si bien rediger par escript qu'il fut exécuté par effect." Cited by Enders, *Rhetoric*, 16–17.

38. James McKinnon, "The Emergence of Gregorian Chant in the Carolingian Era," and David Hiley, "Plainchant Transfigured: Innovation and Reformation through the Ages," in *Antiquity and the Middle Ages: From Ancient Greece to the 15th Century*, Man and Music 1, ed. James McKinnon (Basingstoke, 1990), 88–119 and 120–142, respectively. Musicologists are still debating whether or not the inscription of the chant repertoire in the lands of the Carolingian Empire during the ninth century would have been facilitated by the preexistence of an earlier written tradition, even a written archetype, or based on a number of local oral traditions. See Andrew Hughes, "Charlemagne's Chant or the Great Vocal Shift,"

and the earliest tragedies of Athens were written down in a century when literacy was new to the people of Hellas.[39]

What future generations might take to be a record of gestation, therefore, is much more likely a record of technological innovation (writing, neums) or of loss (the memorialization of a dying tradition) or a record of control (censorship, canonization). That is why the plays of the later Middle Ages were often grouped together into presentation volumes commissioned by wealthy patrons or fair-copied into official registers maintained by civic authorities. And that is why some of them exist today. The *Miracles de Nostre Dame par personnages*, for example, a group of forty plays making up a sizable portion of the fourteenth century's dramatic record, are preserved in a deluxe manuscript copied between 1382 and 1389—the very years when a series of royal edicts banned the confraternal assemblies for which these plays had been devised and performed for nearly fifty years. The texts that provided the exemplars for this codex, the oldest of which might have dated from 1339, no longer survive, while the plays themselves were dead letters by the time they were copied, since continued royal strictures made their revival impossible.[40] In other words, the eradication of these plays as components of a lively medieval theater is what enables our knowledge of them as fossilized texts. Even more disturbingly, it has schooled us to think that trends new in the late fourteenth century were normative for the entire millennium we call the Middle Ages, when it really invites us to consider the troubled relationship between what little is visible on the manuscript page and how much might once have been visible or audible in performance.

Helpfully, the five plays associated with Arras are situated at various points on a broad spectrum of experimentation and formality, from the loose laissez-faire of improvisational comedy to the relatively strong artistic control sought by the auteur. And they are informed by their own textuality, self-conscious of their location on a frontier between performance and documentation. Indeed, all ten of the scripts currently constituting the "canon" of medieval vernacular drama before 1300 (see the table in the Appendix) display scribal awareness of writing's strangeness as a mode of transmission for practices that

---

Speculum 77 (2002): 1069–1106; Kenneth Levy, *Gregorian Chant and the Carolingians* (Princeton, 1996), 5–13 and 109–140; and Leo Treitler, "Reading and Singing: On the Genesis of Occidental Music-Writing," *Early Music History* 4 (1984): 135–208.

39. Eric A. Havelock, *The Literate Revolution in Greece and Its Cultural Consequences* (Princeton, 1982); John Herington, *Poetry into Drama: Early Tragedy and the Greek Poetic Tradition* (Berkeley, 1985); Rosalind Thomas, *Oral Tradition and Written Record in Classical Athens* (Cambridge, 1989); Gregory Nagy, *Homeric Questions* (Austin, 1996).

40. BnF fr. 819–820. See Graham Runnalls, "The Manuscript of the *Miracles de Nostre Dame par Personnages*," *Romance Philology* 22 (1968): 15–22; and idem, "*The Miracles de Nostre Dame par personages*: Erasures in the MS and the Dates of the Plays and the 'Serventois,'" *Philological Quarterly* 49 (1970): 19–29.

were usually held in the memory or passed down orally.[41] The drama known as *Sponsus* was an aide-mémoire for skilled monastic singers copied into a collection of liturgical tropes and exegetical poetry around the year 1100, along with the first extant vernacular songs in the Occitan language of southern France.[42] The *Auto de los reyes magos* (Act of the Magi Kings) was the product of an intensive program of cultural consolidation and translation centered on Toledo at the beginning of the Castilian Reconquista, the same project that resulted in the redaction of the epic El Cid.[43] The lone designated play in the Francien dialect, the *Miracle de Théophile* of Rutebeuf, copied into two miscellaneous collections of versified stories toward the end of the thirteenth century—and indistinguishable from them—testifies to the relatively late ascendancy of Parisian French as a literary language.[44] The *Ordo representacionis Ade* ("The Way of Representing Adam," also known as the *Jeu d'Adam*) and the *Seinte Resureccion*, by contrast, bear witness to the intensity of linguistic competition in the highly literate lands of the Anglo-Norman realm which, in the twelfth and early thirteenth centuries, included England, much of northern France, the Aquitaine, and the Midi.[45] Finally, the five plays in the Picard of Arras underscore the degree to which the dialects of wealthy border towns in French-speaking Flanders and Champagne had already achieved a certain prestige by the end of the twelfth century, providing the earliest written and spoken standard for a language that was not yet tied to national identity nor focused on the Île-de-France.[46] (In fact, the oldest surviving artifact in Old French,

41. On the problematic construction of this canon, see Symes, "Appearance." On the inscription of the vernacular, see Marc Van Uytfanghe, "Le latin et les langues vernaculaires au Moyen Âge: Un aperçu panoramique," in *The Dawn of the Written Vernacular*, ed. Michèle Goyens and Werner Verbeke (Louvain, 2003), 1–38. On the difficulties of transcribing improvisational praxis, see the essays collected in Timothy J. McGee, ed., *Improvisation in the Arts of the Middle Ages and Renaissance* (Kalamazoo, 2003), especially Domenico Pietropaolo, "Improvisation in the Arts," 1–28.

42. BnF lat. 1139; see Symes, "Appearance," 790–802, and "A Few Odd Visits: Unusual Settings of the *Vistatio sepulchri*," in *Music and Medieval Manuscripts: Paleography and Performance. Essays in Honor of Andrew Hughes*, ed. John Haines and Randall Rosenfeld (Aldershot, 2004), 300–322.

43. BNE C. Toledo Cax-6, 8. See Stern, *Medieval Theater*, 6, 42–49; María Teresa Echenique Elizondo, "Nivellement linguistique et standardisation en espagnol (Castillan) médiéval," in Goyens and Verbeke, *Dawn*, 337–350; Ronald E. Surtz, "Spain: Catalan and Castilian Drama," in Simon, *Theater*, 189–206; and Charles E. Stebbins, "The *Auto de los Reyes Magos*: An Old Spanish Mystery Play of the Twelfth Century," *Allegorica* 2 (1977): 118–143. On the play's manuscript context, see Dagenais, *Ethics*, 43–44.

44. BnF fr. 837 and 1635. See Jakob Wüest, "Le rapport entre langue parlée et langue écrite: Les *scriptae* dans le domaine d'oïl et dans le domaine d'oc," in Goyens and Verbeke, *Dawn*, 215–224 at 221.

45. BnF fr. 902 and BL Add. 45103 (*Seinte Resureccion*) and Tours Bm 927 (*Adam*); see Symes, "Appearance," 802–810. See also Lydia A. Stanovaïa, "La standardisation en ancien français," and Tony Hunt, "Anglo-Norman: Past and Future," in Goyens and Verbeke, *Dawn*, 241–272 at 244–248 and 379–389, respectively.

46. Gabrielle M. Spiegel, *Romancing the Past: The Rise of Vernacular Prose Historiography in Thirteenth-*

after the famous Oaths of Strasbourg, is a liturgical sequence dedicated to Saint Eulalie and written down in the French of Flanders, specifically the dialect of Picardy and/or Wallonia.)[47]

The manuscripts of the plays from Arras also demonstrate a broad range of possible uses and potential audiences. Not only do they call attention to the other drama with which plays kept company, but they defy all attempts to stereotype the people who would have enjoyed them, the elite or popular or secular "mentalities" to which they have been confidently assigned, and so forth; in this way, the study of a medieval theater also signals the need for a reevaluation of theories about medieval cultural commodities and their consumption.[48] The very fact of the preservation of the Jeu de la feuillée in a codex prepared by expert copyists at the probable behest of an aristocratic patron refutes, in itself, all prevailing interpretations of the play as politically subversive. Yet this does not mean that it couldn't have been received as such in performance. By the turn of the fourteenth century, the miscellanies that preserve most of the materials approximating the performers' repertoire were obviously made for well-to-do collectors, but the materials themselves were suitable for taverns or halls or market squares, streets or fairs, feasts or campfires. "The Boy and the Blind Man" makes use of some of the same plot lines and devices that would later be recycled in the comic interludes or farces sandwiched between longer, more serious plays in later centuries.[49] Courtois d'Arras, which could have been intended for performance by a single jongleur with the help of his fool's bauble (the jester's puppet scepter), could also have been expanded and divided into parts, and its circulation among the jongleurs' "greatest hits" certainly indicates that its Arrageois provenance was portable: it brought "Arras," a branded stereotype of urban decadence, to other medieval theaters. Two abbreviated versions of the Jeu de la feuillée are similar products of an effort to capital-

Century France (Berkeley, 1993); Godfried Croenen, "Latin and the Vernaculars in the Charters of the Low Countries: The Case of Brabant," and Liselotte Biedermann-Pasques, "Quelques aspects du développement de l'écriture du français à travers des manuscrits et des incunables (IXe–XVe siècle)," in Goyens and Verbeke, Dawn, 107–125 and 225–240 at 226, respectively. See also Uytfanghe, "Latin," 21; Wüest, "Rapport," 221–222; and Stanovaïa, "Standardisation," 256–268.

47. Valenciennes Bm 150, fols. 140r–141v; see Roger Berger and Annette Brasseur, Les séquences de Sainte Eulalie (Geneva, 2004).

48. Stern, Medieval Theater, 267–275; Zumthor, La lettre, 132 and 245–268; Aron Gurevich, "Popular and Scholarly Medieval Cultural Traditions: Notes in the Margins of Jacques Le Goff's Book," Journal of Medieval History 9 (1983): 71–90; Thomas Bestul, Texts of the Passion: Latin Devotional Literature and Medieval Society (Philadelphia, 1996), 11.

49. See Darwin Smith, Maistre Pierre Pathelin: Le miroir d'orgueil. Avec l'édition et la traduction de la version inédite du Recueil Bigot (XVe siècle) (Saint-Benoît-du-Sault, 2002); and Symes, "Appearance."

ize on the notoriety of its author, while the *Jeu de Robin et de Marion* also circulated in different formats, traveling from the Angevin kingdom of Sicily back to Arras, as well as to Paris and Provence. Underscoring the contingency and fragility of the dramatic record, by contrast, the lone text of the *Jeu de saint Nicolas* suggests that those medieval plays most intimately associated with their communities are probably the least likely to have traveled, or to have survived: had it not been for the fame of Adam's artistry, which prompted the documentation of his major works in a single splendid manuscript (see figures 1–6), this valuable record of a medieval community's response to current events would not exist.

Each of these five plays forms the nucleus of one chapter in this book, beginning with an investigation into the circumstances that produced the *Jeu de saint Nicolas* and the distinctive theater discernible in Arras during a long thirteenth century, a common stage whose antecedents can be traced back to the last decades of the eleventh century and whose effects were still palpable in the early decades of the fourteenth. Chapter 1 therefore reaches back into the history of local institutions formed in response to the restoration of the diocese of Arras in 1093 and the establishment of its commune in 1127, while looking closely at the upheavals of 1191–1214, a crucial period in the history of France and its national language, to which crises Jehan Bodel's play is closely tied. Chapter 2 continues this analysis of the long-term and proximate causes of a medieval theater by playing two contemporary dramas off each other: the fictional story of a local prodigal, the *Courtois d'Arras*, and the distinctive storytelling and documentary strategies that led to the foundation and aggrandizement of the confraternity of jongleurs in Arras. Chapter 3 takes its cue from the attention-grabbing techniques of "The Boy and the Blind Man," whose deft manipulation of the basic components of a medieval theater—sight, sound, space—invites examination of the ways in which people in this community were able to access public media for the exchange of information and the participation in public affairs; it argues for the vibrancy of a medieval public sphere. Chapter 4 carries this discussion forward into a reconsideration of Adam de la Halle's *Jeu de la feuillée*, invariably interpreted as the most "modern" of all medieval plays, in order to demonstrate that it is, on the contrary, one of many contemporary responses to specific religious, social, economic, and political changes in Arras during the latter part of the thirteenth century. Finally, Chapter 5 goes behind the scenes of the *Jeu de Robin et de Marion* and the making of the anthology commemorating Adam de la Halle's reported death in southern Italy and the repeat performance of this play in Arras; it reconstructs the experiences of entertainers in the household of Count Robert II of Artois while arguing that their careers, and that of Robert himself, are equally relevant to the understanding of urban theatricality, and can in fact be shown to undermine the familiar binary of popular and aristocratic cultures.

Throughout the book I insist that the plots and scripts of these five plays, while worthy of special attention for all of the reasons I have cited, cannot and should not be extracted from the particular historical milieu that gave them life. At the same time, I hold them up as examples of the possibilities for meaningful exchange that are to be discovered in any medieval theater, possibilities inherent in any community's history of public interaction—and independent of that community's capacity to produce modern-looking scripts.

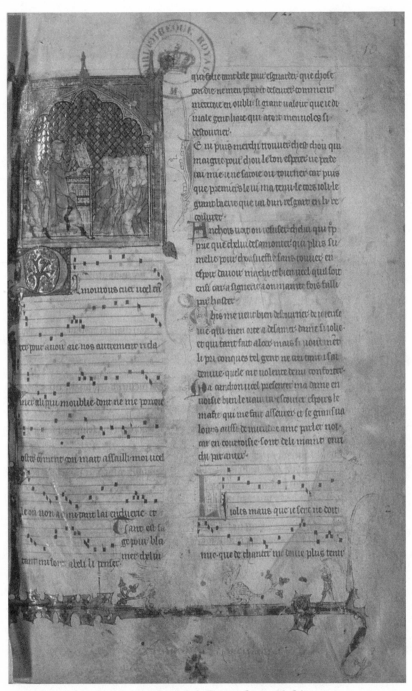

FIGURE I. *Les canchons maistre adan de la halle* (BnF fr. 25566, fol. 10r)

FIGURE 2. *Li ius de pelerin* (BnF fr. 25566, fol. 37r: detail)

FIGURE 3. *Chi conmenche li gieus de robin et de marion cadans fist* (BnF fr. 25566, fol. 39r)

FIGURE 4. *Li dis Adans* or *Li ieus de le fuellie* (BnF fr. 25566, fol. 49r: detail)

FIGURE 5. *Cest li congies Adan* (BnF fr. 25566, fol. 66v: detail)

FIGURE 6. *Cest li ius de.S'.Nicholai* (BnF fr. 25566, fol. 68r: detail)

CHAPTER ONE A HISTORY PLAY

THE JEU DE SAINT NICOLAS AND THE

WORLD OF ARRAS

By the last few decades of the twelfth century, the profile presented by Arras to the outside world was an advertisement of its prosperous diversity: the height and number of its belltowers, the size of its churches, the industry of its windmills' sails, the welcome of its water gates and portals, the strength and beauty of the white stone walls encircling its streets and squares. These were still prominent features of Arras as it looked to travelers even in the eighteenth century, and they belie a cultural historian's attractive characterization of the early modern city as "a theater without walls"—which suggests that theaters, properly speaking, *have* walls, while conveying the mistaken impression that towns do not.[1] In point of fact, a community's walls were one of the factors that promoted the interaction of plays and public life during the Middle Ages, helping to create the theaters in which people could gather "for the purposes of playing," as Hugh of Saint-Victor had put it.[2]

In some significant towns, walls also contributed to "the liberating function" of the medieval marketplace, which had been noted by Galbert of Bruges long before it was articulated by Henri Lefebvre.[3] In 1127, the same year that the commune of Arras was chartered by the count of Flanders, Galbert observed that new forms of civic governance and the unprecedented economic growth of Flemish towns had promoted the emergence of new forms of communication *in forensicis locis*, in all the "public fora" or marketplaces. Because weapons were now forbidden in places set aside "for common use," opinions and ideas could be as readily exchanged as money and goods. It seemed, in fact, that "anyone could defend himself with the power and eloquence of oratory if he were attacked, or if he attacked his enemy . . . for there were even many unlearned men [*illiterati*] in whom Nature herself had implanted the means of eloquence and the endowments of reason, the ways of conjecture and argumentation." In other words, those whose social status might have denied them the right to bear arms outside the walls of towns now had the advantage within those walls and could fight with words against the men who were usually armed

1. Peter Burke, *Popular Culture in Early Modern Europe* (New York, 1978), 178.
2. See Christopher Page, "Court and City in France, 1100–1300," in McKinnon, *Antiquity*, 197–217. See also the collection of essays edited by James D. Tracy, *City Walls: The Urban Enceinte in Global Perspective* (Cambridge, 2000).
3. Henri Lefebvre, *La production de l'espace* (Paris, 1974), 305–306.

FIGURE 7. The Grand' Place d'Arras (Grand Marché): author's photograph taken from the site of the Porte-Saint-Michel, looking southward toward the Petit Marché

with swords. They were also a match for "those trained and instructed in the rhetorical arts."[4]

In the prosperous towns of Flanders, then, people saw themselves as social and political actors, and they represented themselves to one another and to the world at large through their unique forms of governance and their access to a marketplace of ideas. Such spaces were rare and prized; few towns had one, which is why the parishioners of Lam-

4. Galbert of Bruges, *De multro, traditione, et occisione gloriosi Karoli comitis Flandriarum*, ed. Jeff Rider (Turnhout, 1994), 7 (c. 1): "Tandem videns gratiam pacis omnibus jucundam, indixit per terminos regni ut sub quietate et securitate absque armorum usu communiter degerent, quicumque aut in foro aut infra castra manerent et conversarentur, alioquin ipsis plecterentur armis quae ferrent. Sub hac ergo observantia arcus et sagittae et subsequenter omnia arma postposita sunt in forinsecis [sic] locis sicut et in pacificis. Qua pacis gratia legibus et justitiis sese regebant homines, omnia ingeniorum et studiorum argumenta ad placita componentes ut in virtute et eloquentia rhetoricae unusquisque se defensaret cum impetitus fuisset, vel cum hostem impeteret qua colorum varietate oratorie fucatum deciperet. Tunc vero habuit rhetorica sua exercitia et per industriam et per naturam. Erant enim multi illiterati, quibus ipsa natura eloquentiae modos et rationabiles praestiterat conjecturandi et argumentandi vias quibus nullatenus illi qui disciplinati erant et docti artem rhetoricam obviare vet avertere poterant."

FIGURE 8. The Place des Héros (Petit Marché): author's photograph showing the site where the
Pyramide of the Sainte-Chandelle once stood (looking southward)

bert le Bègue held their dances in the cemetery.[5] The people of Arras were more fortunate:
they had two. The fairground called "the forum" in the first attested reference of 1090 lay
just within the eastern gate, the Porte Saint-Michel (Figure 7). This Grand Marché, still
measuring 18,000 square meters (4.35 acres, about the size of six football fields), was
large enough to contain the muster of armies in the time of Jehan Bodel, and was later
the venue for lavish tournaments hosted by Adam de la Halle's future patron, the brash
young count of Artois. But the more important center of activity was the adjacent Petit
Marché, home of local businesses and the official site of all assemblies, bounded by taverns and shops, the cloth industry's guildhalls, and the currency exchange (Figure 8).
Like many of the marketplaces in other northern towns, it would come to be institutionalized as a theater in the fifteenth century, precisely because it had served that function all
along.[6]

According to Hugh's *Didascalicon*, the flourishing of medieval *theatrica* depends on the

5. Jacques Heers, *La ville au Moyen Âge en Occident: Paysages, pouvoirs et conflits* (Paris, 1990), 385–386,
399, and 433.

6. Konigson, *L'espace théâtral*, 113–204.

flourishing of agriculture, textiles, and trade, the other "mechanical arts." This is borne out by the theater which already flourished in Arras before Jehan Bodel composed the first of its plays. By 1191, when it passed from Flanders to France, it was the hub of the fastest-growing, most densely populated, and most affluent region in Europe. Surrounded by some of the Continent's richest farmland, Arras was captain of the North's three major industries—wheat, wool, and woad—that is, the staple grain of the medieval diet and the staple materials (cloth and dye) of which nearly all medieval garments were made; clothing manufacture alone accounted for over 50 percent of all overland traffic. It was also a convenient stopping place on the Oise-Scarpe-Escaut artery, one of the most lucrative commercial routes in Europe, and the clearinghouse for the Burgundian and Rhenish wine trade.[7] And because it was part of Flanders, it benefited from the rule of law to which Galbert ascribed the growth of a public sphere, as well as from a stable currency that traded throughout the known world—a currency minted in Arras, which was the most important European banking capital of the time.[8]

To the extent to which medieval drama has always owed a debt to the Church, it can also be said that Arras owed its theater to the early prosperity fostered by the abbey of Saint-Vaast. One of the largest Benedictine monasteries in Europe, it had been established in the seventh century to house the relics of Saint Vedastus (d. 539), the first bishop of Arras, when the diocese was transferred to Cambrai. This left the ancient Roman urbs, the City of the bishop, vacant, and led to the aggrandizement of the Town that grew up in the shelter of the abbey's fortifications. By the end of the tenth century, the abbey had become the most powerful presence in the region, harnessing a network of far-reaching roads and canals to the marketplaces just outside its walls, which were enclosed in dazzling lime-

---

7. Alain Derville, L'économie française au moyen âge (Paris, 1995), 123, 182–185, and 279–282; Gérard Sivéry, Les capetiens et l'argent au siècle de Saint Louis: Essai sur l'administration et les finances royales au XIIIe siècle (Villeneuve d'Ascq, 1995), 23–25 and map 4; N. J. G. Pounds, An Economic History of Medieval Europe, 2nd ed. (London, 1994), 301–305; and Henri Dubois, "Le commerce et les foires au temps de Philippe Auguste," in La France de Philippe-Auguste: Le temps de mutation, ed. Robert-Henri Bautier (Paris, 1982), 689–709. See also David Nicholas, Medieval Flanders (London, 1992), 103 and 112–117; Elisabeth Carpentier and Michel Le Mené, La France du XIe au XVe siècle: Population, société, économie (Paris, 1996), 172–175, 279–282, and 317. In general, see Robert Lopez, The Commercial Revolution of the Middle Ages, 950–1350 (Cambridge, 1976).

8. Raoul C. van Caenegem, "Coutumes et legislation en Flandre aux XIe et XIIe siècles," in Les libertés urbaines et rurales du XIe au XIVe siècle (Brussels, 1968), 245–279 at 255; Alain Derville, "Le nombre d'habitants des villes de l'Artois et de la Flandre wallonne (1300–1450)," RN 65 (1983): 277–299 at 288–289; Robert Fossier, La terre et les hommes en Picardie jusqu'à la fin du XIIIe siècle, 2 vols. (Amiens, 1968), 1:12, and "Arras et ses campagnes au moyen âge," in Castellani and Martin, Arras, 15–25; Georges Jehel and Philippe Racinet, La ville médiévale: De l'Occident chrétien à l'Orient Musulman, Ve–XVe siècle (Paris, 1996), 199 and 219–234; Nicholas, Flanders, 71 and 77–89.

stone after 1103, the contribution of Count Robert II of Flanders.[9] Ultimately, though, the monks' hegemony was threatened by their own successful initiatives on two fronts: first by the reestablishment of the diocese in 1093, when Urban II decided that the booming population of Arras necessitated this, and then around 1111 by its own former serfs, now canny businessmen who bound themselves together in a *coniuratione*, the commune whose governing body was ratified by the count of Flanders, William Clito, in 1127.[10]

Arras therefore came to consist of two separate geopolitical entities: the episcopal City, which was the temporal domain of a bishop under the immediate suzerainty of the French king, and the Town, part of the independent county of Flanders and under the lordship of the abbey of Saint-Vaast, but with its own representative government. By the time Jehan Bodel composed a play representing the further complications brought about by his town's incorporation into the kingdom of France in 1191, Arras had sustained this form of association for several generations, vesting public power in a group of échevins (*scabini*, *eskievins*) who collectively wielded the same symbolic powers as secular and ecclesiastical lords, exercising justice within the league of encircling territory known as the banlieue, which was defined as the area within which the commune could cry its banns effectively— the space within the walls—and where public authority was exercised in assemblies and legitimized by the authentication of documents using the town's corporate seal.[11] Elected for only a year, the échevins were drawn from a relatively large pool of men whose good character made them prudhommes (*probi viri*), "proven men."[12] For Jehan to cast one such

9. David Nicholas, *The Growth of the Medieval City* (New York, 1997), 116.

10. H. van Drival, ed., *Cartulaire de l'abbaye de Saint-Vaast rédigé au XIIe siècle par Guimann* (Arras, 1875), 170, hereinafter cited as Guiman; R. Dhoehaerd, "Note sur l'histoire d'un ancien impôt. Le tonlieu d'Arras," *MAA* (1943–44): 177–201, and (1946), 27–42 at 28–39. See also Louis Carolus-Barré, "Philippe Auguste et les villes de commune," in Bautier, *La France*, 677–688 at 678, and "Origine et sens du mot 'Commune': Essai sur la naissance et la nature du mouvement communal," in *Les chartes et le mouvement communal* (Saint-Quentin, 1982), 83–104.

11. Brigitte Bedos-Rezak, "Towns and Seals: Representation and Signification in Medieval France," in *Town Life and Culture in the Middle Ages and Renaissance: Essays in Memory of J. K. Hyde*, ed. B. Pullan and S. Reynolds (Manchester, 1990), 35–47 at 39; "Les types des plus anciens sceaux des Communautés urbaines du nord de la France," in *Les chartes*, 39–50; and "Civic Liturgies," 25–36. On the banlieue and the *bannum*, see Jean-Loup Abbé, "Rayonnement urbain et seigneuries autour d'Arras et de Douai au XIIe siècle," *RN* 65 (1983): 400–410; Léopold Génicot, "Aristocratie et dignités ecclésiastiques en Picardie aux XIIe et XIIIe siècles," *Revue d'histoire ecclésiastique* 67 (1972): 436–442; Fossier, "Arras," 15–18. In general, see Adalbert Erler, Ekkehard Kaufmann et al., eds., *Handwörterbuch zur deutschen Rechtsgeschichte*, vol. I. (Berlin, 1971), 306–311; and Oscar Bloch and Walther von Wartburg, eds., *Dictionnaire étymologique de la langue française*, 5th ed. (Paris, 1968), 55.

12. Adolphe Guesnon, ed., [*Cartulaire de la commune d'Arras: Recueil des documents tiré des archives de la mairie.*] *Inventaire chronologique des chartes de la ville d'Arras*. [*Suivi du livre aux sermens*] (Arras, 1863), 3–6 (no.

Prudhomme as the hero of a play, therefore, was merely to heighten one form of representation, political, by overlaying it with another, dramatic. In the world of the Jeu de saint Nicholas, as in the theater of Arras, he stood for everyone. And when an alien king camped outside those walls, which fostered "the means of eloquence and the endowments of reason, the ways of conjecture and argumentation," it was the Prudhomme who was equipped "to defend himself with the power and eloquence of oratory if he were attacked." The play in which he appears is a history play in three senses. First, it is the distinctive product of specific historical circumstances which directly and indirectly inform its plot, themes, and characters. Second, it is a creative historical narrative of the significant changes brought about by the local implementation of a new imperial regime. Finally, it exemplifies the ways in which a medieval theater lent itself to the expression of public opinion on matters of tremendous historical moment.

The Play of Saint Nicholas

According to the Preacher who provides its prologue, the play is set on the frontier between an unnamed Christian town and the land of "a pagan king" (uns rois paiiens, v. 9).[13] War breaks out when the pagans invade this community "just at that feint / Where they had let their own guard faint" (en itel point / Que il ne se gaitoient point, vv. 13–14). They take two key hostages: the Prudhomme, an elected representative of the town, and an image representing Saint Nicholas, before which the Prudhomme is discovered in prayer. The significance of these two representatives, and the reciprocity of their relationship, is highlighted in the miniature placed directly below the rubric introducing the play in its manuscript: Cest li ius de .s'. Nicholai (Figure 6): it depicts the Prudhomme kneeling in homage before a statue of the seated bishop-saint, his hands clasped in supplication, mirroring the bishop's gesture of gracious benediction. Impressed by the Prudhomme's devotion, the heathen King questions him about the icon's powers and learns that the saint is venerated by the men of the town because he "multiplies and yields a profit" (multiploie et pourfite, v. 39) on anything entrusted to his care. The King is intrigued but calls the Prud-

---

4) and 8–14 (no. 9); hereinafter cited as Cartulaire. See also M. Taillar, "Recherches pour servir à l'histoire de l'abbaye de Saint-Vaast d'Arras jusqu'à la fin du XIIe siècle," MAA (1859): 173–501 at 41–42. While the échevins would later be chosen from a group of about fifty families forming an urban "patriciate," this was not the case at the time of the commune's formation or for at least a century and a half afterward; see Nicholas, Flanders, 132–135, and Growth, 127. See also Susan Reynolds, Kingdoms and Communities in Western Europe, 900–1300 (Oxford, 1997), 209; Jehel and Racinet, La ville, 241.

13. All citations refer to the edition of Albert Henry, Le "Jeu de saint Nicolas" de Jean Bodel, 3rd ed. (Paris, 1981), abbreviated JsN. The Preacher's prologue consists of 114 verses. The play itself contains 1,419 verses. The only available published English translation is that of Richard Axton and John Stevens in Medieval French Plays (Oxford, 1971), 77–134.

homme's bluff: he will set the icon to guard his own treasure, but if Saint Nicholas does not "keep account" (*rendre conte*, v. 49) and turn a speedy profit, the Prudhomme will be executed. Subsequently, three thieves break in and steal the King's ransom, yet the Prudhomme's faith is unshaken. He prays to his patron saint, who orders the thieves to replace the treasure. The King converts after witnessing the miraculous increase of his gold and causes his pagan followers to be baptized also.

This prologue, as Albert Henry has argued, "was designed to frame an already existing text and to recast it in a more conventional mold," and was almost certainly composed by someone other than Jehan Bodel.[14] It represents the *Jeu de saint Nicolas* as a generic saint's play, based on a preexisting legend, and attempts to control the play's reception by providing a simplified synopsis of its plot, assuring us that everything will be performed "according to the script" (*selonc lescrit*, v. 61) while at the same time warning of the script's dubious authority. The Preacher even admits at one point that "What's told here could be better said / Were we to find the saint's life read."[15] When he recounts the imprisonment of the play's hero, he says, "But here the letter of the tale / Says that the charter is his jail," which is to say that in the text on which the play is based, the prison is founded on the authority of written record.[16] In other words, the prologue signals an awareness that both the play and its audience are poised between a culture that accepts performance itself as authoritative and one in which performances must be grounded in writing. The Preacher himself embodies this uneasy posture. After all, he is probably not a preacher; he is an actor speaking as a preacher, attempting to represent something flexible as fixed:

Signeur, che trouvons en le vie		My lords, this is what's in the life
Del saint dont anuit est la veille	105	Of him whose vigil is tonight
Pour che n'aiés pas grant merveille		But don't be too surprised, you might
Se vous veés aucun affaire;		Detect some other business, too.
Car canques vous nous verrés faire		But anything you see us do
Sera essamples sans douter		Will be a genuine effort
Del miracle representer	110	To represent the true report
Ensi con je devisé l'ai.		As I described it to you all.
De miracle saint Nicholai		From Saint Nicholas's miracle

14. Henry in JsN, 42–50. This view is corroborated by Joseph A. Dane in *Res/Verba: A Study in Medieval French Drama* (Leiden, 1985), 61. I have not been convinced by arguments in favor of Jehan's authorship, e.g., Tony Hunt, "The Authenticity of the Prologue of Bodel's *Jeu de saint Nicolas*," *Romania* 97 (1976): 252–267; and Jean Dufournet, "Variations sur un motif: La taverne dans le théâtre arrageois du XIIe siècle," in *Hommage à Jean-Charles Payen. Farai chansoneta novele: Essais sur la liberté créatrice du Moyen Age*, ed. Jean-Louis Becker et al. (Caen, 1984), 161–174 at 162.

15. "Che nous content li voir disant / Qu'en sa vie trouvons lisant." JsN, vv. 8–9.

16. "Mais issi le conte le lettre / Qu'en se chartre le fist remetre." JsN, vv. 79–80.

Est chis jeus fais et estorés.	Was this play made and set down here.
Or nous faites pais, si l'orrés.	Now hold your peace, so you can hear.

The legend is held up as an authoritative account drawn from the hagiographic record, while the performance is called into question because it may well depart from the script. Its reliability is only partly vouchsafed by its having been "set down," or established in writing: the final couplet emphasizes this by rhyming *orrés* with *estorés*.

Jehan Bodel's play opens with a different sort of speech, spoken by a character designated as Auberon the Courier and directed to a character addressed simply as "King." Greeting this King in the name of his god, "Mahom," Auberon reveals that neighboring Christians are mustering an army on "this frontier" (*cest marche*, v. 128), and advises him to make a defensive strike on their territory. Already the Preacher's prologue is shown to be misleading: the play's Christians are actually more threatening to the pagans than vice versa. The King, swearing by Apollo, blames his golden idol Tervagan for the Christians' encroachments and threatens to melt the statue down into specie if the god does not come to his aid. His Seneschal rebukes him, however, warning that "neither count nor king" (*ni conte ni roi*, v. 148) should take such liberties with the gods. The King then begs the idol's pardon and asks for an exemplum or dramatization of the battle's outcome, using the word the Preacher's prologue reserves for the play itself (*essample*). So Tervagan weeps and laughs at the same time, a show that the Seneschal interprets correctly: they will win the battle but lose the war. Undaunted, the King rallies his troops "from the Orient to Catalonia" ("D'Orient dusqu'en Kateloigne," v. 223), switching from octosyllabic couplets to alexandrine hexameters in order to emphasize the epic proportions of his undertaking.

When the Seneschal summons a crier to broadcast the news of a general levy, the reader begins to realize that the play is actually taking place in Arras and not in some foreign land—something that would have been apparent to contemporary spectators all along. For the crier who calls the banns in the name of the King of Africa (*Je faç le ban le roy d'Aufrike*, v. 227) is Connart, later revealed as an employee of the City of Arras, who might well have been played by a real crier of that name making a cameo appearance as himself. So although the authority in whose name he acts is said to be from "Africa," and the spectators are harangued as citizens of Prester John's farfetched lands, the distinction between the exotic world of the King and the workaday world of Arras has been collapsed. When the herald Auberon is dispatched to deliver sealed summonses to the King's most powerful vassals—"Show my letters and my seal openly and everywhere" (*Moustre par tout mes lettres et mon seel apert*, v. 243)—he wades through the crowd as if intent on his exotic errand but stops at a tavern in the marketplace of Arras, where the sale of Burgundy is regulated according to the laws of the Town (*au ban de le vile*, v. 258). There he cools his heels and engages in an altercation over methods of payment for the wine he has consumed, prefiguring the way the town will soon be overrun by obnoxious foreigners, ignorant of its customs and currency. Meanwhile, the emirs of Konieh, Orquenie, Oliferne, and Outre l'Arbre Sec journey from the lands of Outremer, their fanciful names drawn from the *Song of Roland*, their homeland known to the people of Arras as the port city of Acre and its crusader kingdom. They arrive with rich tributes—all except Outre l'Arbre Sec, who explains that in his country the only coins are millstones. This is bad news for a King in need of hard cash, who had threatened to turn his god into gold.

Preparing for war, both pagans and Christians express their valor in heroic alexandrines, the triumphal measure of *chansons de geste*, although the Angel who appears to comfort the doomed townspeople speaks in the humbler octave of everyday couplets, the local vernacular of the fabliaux. This draws attention to possible uses of different linguistic and discursive registers, to be revisited later in the play. The manuscript encapsulates the ensuing battle in a single terse stage direction: "Now the Saracens kill all the Christians" (*Or tuent li Sarrasin tous les Crestiëns*, rubric after v. 450). The only survivor is a Prudhomme captured by the emir of Orquenie, discovered in prayerful veneration of an icon of Saint Nicholas, termed "a horned Mohammed" (*un mahommet cornu*, v. 458) in the pagan's estimation. Waiting to be led hostage before the King, the Prudhomme receives a second visitation from the Angel, who urges him to keep faith in the saint's powers. When he is questioned by the King and his council, the Prudhomme accordingly extols the virtues of Saint Nicholas, saying that "he makes good all the losses" of those who venerate him (*Il fait ravoir toutes ses pertes*, v. 521), protecting travelers and repelling thieves, guarding money, and increasing treasure. He then makes the saint's usurious powers the subject of a wager: he bets his life against the saint's business acumen. Duly impressed, the greedy King consigns his prisoner to the "charter" (*chartre*, v. 546) of Durant the jailer before recalling the crier Connart, whom he sends out on another mission: to announce that his treasure has been left unguarded, save for the horned icon, and that it could easily be stolen.

In the course of carrying out these instructions, Connart revisits the world of Arras, the Town of which the Prudhomme is a representative, and describes himself as a lifelong employee of rival officers, "the échevins of the city" (*eskievins de la chité*, v. 601). As such, he becomes embroiled in an argument with another crier, Raoulet, who has been advertising wine in accordance with the laws established by the "men of the town" (*homes de le vile*, v. 606). Insults and blows are exchanged until the Taverner settles the question: he explains that Connart's rights of publicity extend to all news cried on behalf of the King or the échevins of the city, but that Raoulet is still authorized to make certain announcements on behalf of the town. As we shall see, the play's seemingly confused jurisdictions are a direct reference to the very real ambiguities of jurisdiction in Arras, which were heightened by the conquest of Philip Augustus in 1191.

With the action of the play ever more firmly tied to local concerns, there follows a long scene set in the tavern. Here, three gambling ne'er-do-wells—Pincedés, Clikés, and

Caignés—play at a confusing dice game called Hasard (Chance), eventually deciding to make another "good play" (*bon gieu*, v. 1055) by attempting to steal the treasure they heard about from Connart. They succeed, but Saint Nicholas himself intercedes while they sleep off their celebratory binge, ordering that they restore the treasure and its guardian icon. In the meantime, the King has a dream foretelling his winning of a "new crown" (*couronne nouvele*, v. 1383): not just the crown of religious conversion in the world of the play, but the very real benefits of the converted gold crowns with which the capture of Arras has filled his coffers. Bested by the icon of Saint Nicholas and its superior financial wizardry, the King's idol Tervagan is dashed to pieces, uttering a last cabalistic quatrain of unintelligible verses (vv. 1512–15), a species of vernacular rhymed and metered like the Christians' Picard but otherwise devoid of meaning. Once again language is at stake, and the symbolic power of words is equated with the symbolic power of money; the weakness of the King's own coinage and his poverty prior to the capture of the town are matched by the weakness of his native dialect.

This is underscored when the play's final confrontation revolves around the obstinacy of Outre l'Arbre Sec, the only emir unacquainted with the value of money, who is now reluctant to exchange his old god for new gold. His steadfast loyalty to his own traditional values contrasts sharply with the hypocrisy and opportunism of the King, who had earlier threatened Tervagan's liquidation and who has precipitously seized on the more fertile currency supplied by Saint Nicholas. In the end, Outre l'Arbre Sec is forced to convert to both the religion of Saint Nicholas and the innovative economic practices that have been presented as the central tenet of Christianity in the world of the play. His reluctant capitulation is the signal for the Prudhomme to begin the hymn Te Deum laudamus, often sung at the close of liturgical dramas as well as at the ends of battles. As if reinforcing this pious resolution, the manuscript anthology preserving the play concludes: "Here ends the Play of Saint Nicholas that Jehan Bodel made, Amen."[17]

"Every history of medieval theatrical space is the history of the reduction of the universe to the image of the city," observed Elie Konigson. In the *Jeu de saint Nicolas*, the simultaneity of medieval staging techniques both heightens and collapses the distinction between reality and fiction, offering an allegory of current affairs that maps global events onto the familiar, contested landscape of Arras and its two interlocking spheres, the City and the Town. If set in the large marketplace of Arras, the battle scene would call to mind recent occasions when armies had been quartered there by powerful men bent on crusade. If it were played in the Petit Marché, the merchants' currency exchange at the eastern end of the square would provide a fitting backdrop for the Prudhomme's treasured shrine to Saint Nicholas the banker. If mounted in a church, it would draw on the perennial asso-

---

17. *Chi fine li jeus de Saint Nicholai que Jehans Bodiaus fist, Amen.* BnF fr. 25566, fol. 83r[b] (title as given in the *explicit*).

ciations of liturgical plays, which regularly staged the betrayal and arrest of virtuous men, the violence of kings, shady dealings in crowded inns, angelic announcements, and exotic gifts.[18] To make a modern analogy, it calls to mind Saul Steinberg's *New Yorker* cartoon of 1976 in which the world is telescoped through the lens of downtown Manhattan, with Ninth Avenue as the perpetual foreground beyond which lesser realms recede into the distance. The *Jeu de saint Nicolas* gives us the Arrageois view of the world, looking westward from the marketplace and taverns of the Petit Marché, with the bishop's City, the Île-de-France, and the crusaders' Outremer on the far horizon. In contemporary terms, it expresses the mingled chauvinism and extroversion of a mercantile *mappa mundi* often copied during the thirteenth century into the books of traveling entrepreneurs and entertainers, cataloguing the goods available in the wealthy market towns of the North, of which Arras headed the list, encompassing everything from the butter of Norway to the peppers "and all spicery" of Jerusalem, Egypt, and the Sudan and extending all the way to Tartary, a proud expanse of silk and cloth-of-gold. "And from all these kingdoms and lands come merchants and merchandise to the land of Flanders . . . because there is no land that can compare in merchandise to the land of Flanders."[19] This is the material world that produced the *Jeu de saint Nicolas* and that supported the labors of its author, Jehan Bodel.

The Works and Days of Jehan Bodel

Jehan Bodel may be compared to William Shakespeare, who also flourished in times of rapid change which produced new literary genres, and who was also unusually sensitive to the larger movements and mundane problems of his day. Each was a man about whom we know little that cannot be inferred from his own artistry, and each was employed in a capacity that gave him a special command of the fledgling literary language which was, in large part, coined or re-coined by himself, and which enriched a series of timely but timeless compositions whose superior quality was recognized by near contemporaries and then recognized again by generations of scholars, who made them a mirror of their times. Even the tenuous survival and delayed publication of most of Shakespeare's plays, and their collective elevation to the status of a national monument, echo the reception of Jehan's *Jeu de saint Nicolas*, lauded as "thoroughly secular," the firstborn of the "modern" "French" theater.

18. For an imaginative staging, see Michel Rousse, *La scène et les tréteaux: Le théâtre de la farce au Moyen Âge* (Orléans, 2004), 127–143.

19. E.g., BnF fr. 25545, fols. 18v^a–19r^b: "Et de tous ses roiaumes et terres desus dites. veinnent marcheant et marchandises. en la terre de Flandres. . . . Par coi nule tere nest conparee de marcheandise en contre la terre de Flandres."

Jehan Bodel was probably born around 1160. This was when the canons of the cathedral were embarking on an ambitious plan of rebuilding and expansion; when the young Philip of Flanders, newly wed to the heiress Elizabeth of Vermandois, was beginning to act on behalf of his father the count and to distinguish himself as one of the most powerful princes in Europe; and when stories of the miraculous candle given to jongleurs by the Blessed Virgin were gaining narrative power and prestige. During his boyhood, he probably attended the cathedral school in the city, or the school run by the abbey of Saint-Vaast. As a youth, he may have been present on the first occasion when the commune of Arras publicly affixed its seal, around 1175, and he might already have become a member of the jongleurs' Carité, whose foundation legend was redacted in Latin around the same time. He would have witnessed the readings and displays of comital charters in the Petit Marché of Arras, the building of the hospital dedicated to Saint-Jean in 1177, and the addition of a new portal to the gleaming white walls of the Town: for now, like Thebes of old, Arras was seven-gated. Perhaps he frequently passed through that gate and took the road to Compiègne, to Reims, Cambrai, or Saint-Quentin, a second-hand fiddle on his shoulder, a few good coins of Arras in his purse, and assurance of safe travel guaranteed by Count Philip, now among the patrons of Chrétien de Troyes. In 1180 he heard about the death of the pious king of the Franks, Louis VII, and the accession of his young son Philip II, called "Dieudonné" at the time of his "God-given" birth, later to style himself "Augustus" and "king of France." Maybe he took the opportunity to travel into France, to sing at celebrations in towns en route to Paris or Beauvais. In 1183, when the parish church of Saint-Nicolas was built and its nearby gate renamed in the saint's honor, Jehan could have learned much about that saint's miracles through the performance of liturgies and legends, hearing how appropriate his patronage was to the people of a commercial center like Arras. In 1184, when the abbot of the Cîteaux became the bishop of Arras, Jehan may have been among the jongleurs who renegotiated the terms of corporate privilege with this new, foreign pontiff or his strangely surnamed archdeacon, Raoul de Chapeau Cornu. With other loyal men of Flanders, he may have rejoiced at the second marriage of his lord the count, a widower since 1182, and speculated on the possibility that the royal bride from Portugal might yet produce an heir. The following year he may have seen the horses of Count Philip's men-at-arms stamping on the packed earth of the Grand Marché, later returning defeated at the hands of the count's namesake and former ward, Philip of France, and his former brother-in-law, Baldwin of Hainaut.

Around this time, or perhaps earlier, Jehan became a clerk to the échevins of Arras, turned seriously to the composition of songs he could preserve in writing, and tuned his ear to the way that domestic quarrels could be overlaid with the rhetoric of crusade. In that capacity, perhaps, he witnessed the departure of Count Philip, bound for Acre, in 1190; received the news of his tragic death on the first of June the following year; and waited with the échevins to receive a new, usurping lord when a king rode post from Outremer to the Town of Arras by summer's end.

A decade passed, marked by change. Then another, very dark.

Jehan Bodel died between Candlemas and Pentecost in the year 1210. We know this because the name "Bodel" was inscribed after the heading for the Virgin's Feast of the Purification (February 2) in the funerary register kept by the confraternity of jongleurs.[20] Normally, membership in the confraternity was a guarantee of proper burial as well as perpetual prayer and memorial rites, but there is some question as to whether Jehan would have received the former benefit. He appears to have contracted leprosy some years before, a calamity that would have entailed his effective exile from the community, its social structures, and this charitable institution. Whether or not it would have entailed his incarceration in one of the leprosaria outside Arras is less certain. In the *Congé*, or "Leave-Taking," a long farewell poem in which he describes his illness and announces his departure, Jehan mentions one of two such establishments, the aptly named house of Saint-Nicolas at nearby Méaulens.[21] But it is just as likely that he lived out the remainder of his life alone; as we shall see, the will of his close contemporary, Bishop Raoul, attests that many lepers in and around Arras maintained a certain independence.

In death Jehan Bodel became a legend. In life he was a self-promoting pioneer of new poetic forms, regarded by his contemporaries and local successors as setting the standard that would make Arras as famous for its cultural capital as for its capital revenue in the century following his death. The *Congé* had two admiring imitators there, Baude Fastoul (d. 1272) and Adam de la Halle (d. ca. 1288), and their subsequent efforts would enshrine it as a literary form sui generis. Perhaps in emulation of Virgil, another nostalgic city dweller, Jehan also composed a group of *pastourelles*; pastoral poetry, too, would take on renewed life in the hands of Adam de la Halle.[22] In addition, nine of Jehan's fabliaux have survived, and he is usually considered to be the coiner of the term.[23] Following in the tradition of the *Chanson de Roland*, and inspired by the recent conquests of the French king, Jehan also began to compose an epic, the *Chanson des Saisnes*, ostensibly celebrating Charlemagne's victory over a Saxon warlord but obviously dedicated to Philip Augustus.[24]

Jehan was an innovator even with respect to the very idiom in which he composed,

20. BnF fr. 8541, fol. 6v[b]. See Berger, *Le nécrologe*, 1:110 and 2:34–36.

21. Jehan Bodel, *Congé*, in *Les congés d'Arras*, ed. Pierre Ruelle (Paris, 1965), vv. 167 and 488. On the leprosaria in Arras, see Albert Bourgeois, *Lépreux et maladreries du Pas-de-Calais (Xe–XVIIIe siècles): Psychologie collective et institutions charitables* (Arras, 1972), 90–109.

22. "Les *Pastourelles* de Jehan Bodel," ed. Annette Brasseur, in Castellani and Martin, *Arras*, 257–302.

23. John W. Baldwin, *The Language of Sex: Five Voices from Northern France around 1200* (Chicago, 1994), 38.

24. Jehan Bodel, *La Chanson des Saisnes*, ed. Annette Brasseur, 2 vols. (Geneva, 1989), 1:x–xii and 2:v.

144.

largely inventing a poetics that made the Picard dialect of Arras a vernacular that could be understood and emulated outside the immediate region.[25] He even altered his surname to match the rhyme schemes of his verse. The most convenient form was "Bodiaus," and this is how his name appears in the anthology preserving the *Jeu de saint Nicolas*, as well as in the prologue to the *Chanson des Saisnes* and in one of his fabliaux. Indeed, it is possible that he chose the euphonious term *fabliau* on purpose, flourishing the rhyme like a panache: "The jest of Jehan *Bodiaus*, / A rhymster making *flabiaus*."[26] In the *Congé*, however, he matched his altered fortunes with an altered form of his name, bidding farewell to his friends as Jehan Bodel; and this was the name recorded by the Carité at the time of his death.[27]

Jehan's facility for manipulating language was only one of many talents. In his youth, as his own compositions suggest, he had been an itinerant performer, a singer of tales and ballads, a teller of bawdry. Although in later life he made some attempts to distance himself from common minstrels—and from the pieces he himself had helped to popularize—the lofty strain of the *Chanson des Saisnes* reveals a tongue-in-cheek intimacy with their rough-and-ready craft, somewhat incongruously expressed in the impressive consonance of the *laisse*:

Seigneurs, this song should not be mixed with fabliaux,	*Seignor, ceste chançons ne muet pas de flabliaus,*
But is concerned with love, knighthood, and valiant blows.	*Mais de chevaleries, d'amours et de cembiaus.*
Those bastard jongleurs who tramp 'round from show to show,	*Cil bastart jougleour, qui vont par ces viliaus,*
Their instruments old, tuneless, all mended on the go,	*A ces longes vïeles a depeciés fourriaus,*
They'd sing of Guiteclin with asinine bellows.	*Chantent de Guitechin si com par asseniaus;*
Those hacks who can't do more should stick to furbelows: 30	*Mais cil qui plus en set, en est tous fins muiaus,*
For they can't either sing or fathom what I know:	*Car il ne sevent mie les riches vers nouviaus*
The verses new and rich, the songs of Bodiaus.	*Ne la chançon rimee que fist Jehans Bodiaus.*

25. JsN, 51–56; T. B. W. Reid, "On the Text of the *Jeu de Saint Nicolas*," in *Studies in Medieval French Presented to Alfred Ewert in Honour of His Seventieth Birthday*, ed. E. A. Francis (Oxford, 1961), 96–129. See also the discussion later in this chapter.

26. "Tant que lo sot Johans Bodiaus / Uns rimoieres de flabiaus." *Li sohaiz desvez*, vv. 208–209, in *Les fabliaux de Jean Bodel*, ed. Pierre Nardin (Dakar, 1959), 45–50; *Chanson des Saisnes*, 2:713–714, vv. 31–32: "Car il ne savent mie les riches vers nouviaus / Ne la chançon rimee que fist Jehans Bodiaus." BnF fr. 25566, fol. 83r: "Che fine le jeus de saint Nicolai que Jehans Bodiaus fist, Amen."

27. "Wibert de Biaumont et Ansel / Salue par Jehan Bodell." *Congé*, vv. 160–161.

Jehan did not leave the enjoyment of lasting fame to chance. Remarkably, he took care that at least some of his compositions were preserved, since fabliaux, epic, *Congé*, and play were all entrusted to parchment. This is where the seemingly unrelated duties of Jehan's "day job" are exposed as directly relevant to the promotion of his reputation as a playwright: the *Congé* tells us that he worked as a clerk to the échevins of the Town, so he himself could have ensured the survival and circulation of his work in written form, using the same techniques that allowed him to keep track of what was heard and seen by the prudhommes elected to public office in Arras, men memorialized in the character of the Jeu's heroic Prudhomme. Wedded with his performers' know-how, Jehan's clerical capacities enabled him to produce texts that are regarded today as providing the basis for several medieval literary genres, as well as for the very language of France.

The intellectual climate of mid-twelfth-century Arras fostered the conditions that allowed Jehan to acquire these skills. It has been estimated that the monastery school at Saint-Vaast and the cathedral school of Notre-Dame were each capable of educating two hundred students, many more than would be required or inclined to join the ranks of either choir or to spend their remaining days in the abbey's scriptorium or bishop's chancery. Although this cumulative figure is surely too high for the years when Jehan would have received his schooling, it seems that there were usually at least sixty *clericuli*, or choirboys, in training at the cathedral, and not all of them would have taken major orders upon reaching adolescence.[28] This means that successive generations of literate children would grow to literate adulthood, becoming engaged in business or the learned trades that supported business, or in the minstrelsy for which Arras was already famous. Even those who stayed in the Church often participated in these activities. Some famous Artesian trouvères have been identified as members of the cathedral chapter, while forty-eight monks from the abbey were affiliates of the confraternity of jongleurs.[29] Those who prayed and performed therefore drew practitioners from the same pool of educated or half-educated schoolmen, and it is reasonable to suppose that many medieval clerics possessed talents that ran beyond the preparation of documents and their oral delivery. They would have acquired a working knowledge of honorifics and etiquette, the *cursus* and rhyme, the law and storytelling, mathematics and rhythm. Some could have worked as criers or heralds, jobs that required similar preparation and whose dramatic capacities are showcased in the *Jeu de saint Nicolas*. The historian Albert Rigaudière, in a lyrical encomium to the public notary who played so significant a role in many southern French cities, provides us with a glimpse of Jehan Bodel's standing in his own community when he describes this key figure as an

28. Bernard Delmaire, *Le diocèse d'Arras de 1093 au milieu de XIVe siècle. Recherches sur la vie religieuse dans le nord de la France au Moyen Age*, 2 vols. (Arras, 1994), 1:346–347.

29. Berger, *Le nécrologe*, 2:34; Adolphe Guesnon, "Recherches biographiques sur les trouvères artésiens," BHP (1894): 420–435.

"actor and chronicler of its history," guardian of "the memory of the town, in which he recognized, even in the smallest details, horizons far and wide."[30] One thinks of how the *Jeu de saint Nicolas* circumnavigates the globe, encompassing the world within the walls of Arras.

Although we know little about the clerks who worked for the échevinage of Arras in the late twelfth and thirteenth centuries, there is no good reason to question the testimony of the *Congé*, which speaks at length of its author's "fief," or salaried position with the commune.[31] In the decades around 1200, Jehan and his colleagues were called *sargeants*, and were expected to perform a range of duties as scribes, secretaries, heralds. They would have been bilingual, at the very least, and in border towns and commercial centers like Arras most would have spoken Flemish as well as Picard and Latin, and some would probably have had a knack for English, German, Occitan, or Italian. As the thirteenth century wore on, they received more lofty training—and titles to match. While the first known holder of the office of "clerc de la ville" in Arras (attested in a charter of 1222) is called simply "Thibaut," his successors generally bore the honorific *magister* or *maistre*, implying that they had received a university education. Master Henri li Boçu was one such, and his son Adam le Boçu—Adam de la Halle—was "master," too.[32] In the normal course of things such men may have taken higher orders but found instead that a worldly life suited them better. This was just as well, since the Fourth Lateran Council made the existence of lay notaries necessary when it decreed in 1215 that no cleric could pronounce or help to carry out a sentence of death, "nor shall any cleric write or dictate letters directed toward a punishment to be satisfied by blood, so that in the courts of princes this care should be committed not to clerics but to laymen."[33]

Not only did Jehan's education help to ensure the survival of the *Jeu de saint Nicolas*, but his acquaintance with legal procedure, accountancy, and the paraphernalia of written records also informs many aspects of the play, which makes constant reference to charters, seals, accounts, and other instruments. Jehan's documentary expertise also figures in the *Congé*, which takes on a quasi-legal character in the final stanzas. Having said good-bye to Arras and all its people (*Arras et toute a conmune*, v. 459), the unhappy poet implores his audience:

---

30. Albert Rigaudière, *Gouverner la ville au Moyen Age* (Paris, 1993), 265 (evoking Edmond Faral's portrait of the jongleur; see chapter 2).

31. Here I side with Baldwin, *Language*, 3, *contra* Ruelle, *Les Congés*, 34 and 149.

32. Berger, *Littérature*, 74. In Old French usage, the article "li" can denote a masculine nominative singular, while "le" denotes the genitive case; hence, Henri is "the hunchback" but Adam is "[son] of the hunchback." Confusion results when this distinction is ignored, as Adam himself pointed out (see chapter 5).

33. Giuseppe Alberigo et al., eds., *Conciliorum œcumenicorum decreta*, 3rd ed. (Bologna, 1973), 244 (Lateran IV, c. 18): "Nec quisquam clericus literas scribat aut dictet pro vindicta sanguinis destinandas, unde in curiis principum hæc solicitudo non clericis sed laicis committatur."

Pitiés, qui en moi es esprise—		Have pity, you who see my worth—
Ne sai k'autre mes i eslise—	470	I know not who else to send forth—
Porte au maieur d'Arras ce brief,		Bring Arras's maieur this sad brief
Fai tant c'on devant lui le lise:		And have it read out, face-to-face.
Se Dieu plaist et sa gentelise,		For, please God's goodness and his grace,
Ja en lui ne perdrai mon fief.		I'll keep the favor of my fief.
Et as eschievins de rechief	475	The échevins, for my relief,
Le fai lire de chief en chief		Should each one have it read in turn
Tant que pités lor en soit prise		That they might pity me, not spurn
Car, se j'ai anui et meschief,		Me in my sorrow and my grief:
Par raison lor doit estre grief:		It's only right they should do this,
Avenus m'est en lor servise.	480	They've had the faith of my service.

The Congé describes itself as an official letter (bref) to be delivered to the maieur and échevins of Arras and read aloud to them. Under normal circumstances, Jehan himself would have performed this task. Now he asks that his employers levy a taille, like the tax raised by the king to finance his wars, so that it can be used instead "to further this battle" (a parfournir ceste bataille, vv. 484–485) and contribute to his upkeep. Several generations later, the Arras-trained artist responsible for illustrating the Congé understood this reference to the poem as a formal petition interceding on its author's behalf. He depicted Jehan standing before a crowd of onlookers, his leper's rattle hanging by his side, the tragic mask of the leper's hood at his feet, and the scroll containing the Congé unfurled, bridging the distance between the poet and the people of Arras (Figure 9). Jehan's right hand brandishes the writing while his left hand gestures imploringly, as he performs the last public act of his career.

Arras and Its Others

Modern readings of the Jeu de saint Nicolas run along two lines. One the one hand are those derived from the conviction that Jehan must have adapted an older legend about Saint Nicholas, summarized in the (spurious) prologue, and that the play was therefore intended for performance on the eve of the saint's feast (celebrated on December 6 or, occasionally, May 9).[34] On the other are the interpretations that celebrate the play's imagi-

---

34. E.g., Patrick R. Vincent, The "Jeu de Saint Nicolas" of Jean Bodel of Arras: A Literary Analysis (Baltimore, 1954); Charles Foulon, "La représentation et les sources du 'Jeu de saint-Nicolas,'" in Mélanges d'histoire du théâtre du Moyen-Age et de la Renaissance offerts à Gustave Cohen (Paris, 1950), 55–66 at 60–65; Clyde W. Brockett, "Persona in Cantilena: St. Nicholas in Music and Medieval Drama," and Lynette R. Muir, "The Saint Play in Medieval France," in The Saint Play in Medieval Europe, ed. Clifford Davidson (Kalamazoo, 1986), 11–29 and 123–130, respectively; Peter F. Dembrowski, "Literary Problems of Hagiography in Old French," Mediævalia et Humanistica 7 (1976): 117–130; and Arnold Arens, Untersuchungen zu Jean Bodels Mirakel "Le Jeu de Saint Nicolas" (Stuttgart, 1986).

FIGURE 9. Jehan Bodel's leave-taking: miniature illustrating his *Congé* (Bibliothèque de l'Arsenal 3142, fol. 227r: detail)

native fictionality and nascent modernism, on the assumption that Jehan was creating a fantasy world of unlikely comic juxtapositions which actually defy hagiographic models.[35] No analysis has seriously considered the immediate historical circumstances that

35. E.g., Charles Foulon, *L'oeuvre de Jehan Bodel* (Paris, 1958), 57; Tony Hunt, "A Note on the Ideology of Jean Bodel's *Jeu de saint Nicolas*," *Studi Francesi* 20 (1976): 67–72; Michel Zink, "Le *Jeu de saint Nicolas* de Jean Bodel, drame spirituel," *Romania* 99 (1978): 31–46; Henri Rey-Flaud, *Pour une dramaturgie du moyen âge* (Paris, 1980), 7, 12, and 43–48; D. A. Trotter, *Medieval French Literature and the Crusades (1100–1300)* (Geneva, 1987), 229–244; Jean-Claude Aubailly, "Réflections sur le *Jeu de saint Nicolas*: Pour une drama-

framed the play's composition and production, and that may have provided much of the raw material for its plot and characters. Although the date 1191 has occasionally offered a *terminus a quo*, the alterity of the play's King has always seemed to preclude any meaningful identification with Philip Augustus.[36] Even the most perceptive readings have proceeded from the premise that Arras had long been "French" in 1191, and thereby elide the different political affiliations of City and Town.[37] Others obscure the fact that "prudhomme" is a term with specific legal and political connotations, treating it instead as a synonym for "old man" or "good man."[38]

In actuality, Jehan Bodel used the vocabulary of alterity available to him—the portrait of Islam familiar from the *Chanson de Roland*—to describe an Other closer to home. In this he was not so much anticipating the "Orientalism" of Edward Said as adopting strategies similar to those later used by political pundits under the ancien régime, when a roman à clef written around 1750 waggishly disguised Louis XV ("Louis Kinze"), king of the "Frankois," as the exotic African king Zeokinizul of Kofirans.[39] Nor was he copying any known legend; rather, he was participating in a contemporary trend which used the miracles attributed to Saint Nicholas as vehicles for cutting-edge treatments of hot topics, such as the liturgical dramas collected in the so-called Fleury Playbook which explore, among other issues, the changing attitude toward homosexuality in a monastic context.[40]

---

tologie," MA 95 (1989): 419–437; Rousse, "Le Jeu de Saint Nicolas," 153–162. The corpus of literary criticism devoted to the plays of Jehan and Adam is extensive, and I engage it more fully in "A Medieval Stage: Theater and the Culture of Performance in Thirteenth-Century Arras" (Ph.D diss., Harvard University, 1999).

36. E.g., María Pilar Suárez, "L'autre dans le Jeu de saint Nicolas de Jehan Bodel," in Castellani and Martin, Arras, 163–173; Jean Dufournet, "Du double unité: Les sarrasins dans le Jeu de saint Nicolas," in Studies in Honor of Hans-Erich Keller: Medieval and Occitan Literature and Romance Linguistics, ed. Rupert T. Pickens (Kalamazoo, 1993), 261–274.

37. David Raybin, "The Court and the Tavern: Bourgeois Discourse in Li jeus de saint Nicolai," Viator 19 (1988): 176–198; Claire Sponsler, "Festive Profit and Ideological Production: Le jeu de saint Nicolas," in Festive Drama: Papers from the Sixth Triennial Colloquium of the Society for the Study of Medieval Theater, Lancaster, 13–19 July 1989, ed. Meg Twycross (Cambridge, 1996), 66–79. It takes a Dutch scholar to note that Arras was politically and culturally Flemish, and to treat this play as the earliest dramatic artifact of the Low Countries; see Hüsken, "Civic Patronage."

38. E.g., Andrew Cowell, At Play in the Tavern: Signs, Coins, and Bodies in the Middle Ages (Ann Arbor, 1999), 56; Dane, Res/Verba, 48. This is the case in modern French commentaries as well as in English translations.

39. Robert Darnton, "An Early Information Society: News and Media in Eighteenth-Century Paris," AHR 105 (2000): 1–35 at 14–16. See Edward Said, Orientalism (New York, 1978), 60; and Michael Camille, The Gothic Idol: Ideology and Image-Making in Medieval Art (Cambridge, 1989), 135.

40. V. A. Kolve, "Ganymede/Son of Getron: Medieval Monasticism and the Drama of Same-Sex Desire," Speculum 73 (1998): 1014–67. See also Charles W. Jones, The Saint Nicholas Liturgy and Its Literary Re-

If there was resistance to such innovation, it was countered by the saint himself, who was depicted as a champion of novelty and an active promoter of his own cult. An example of this can be found in a thirteenth-century manuscript from Arras. When a certain haughty prior would not allow a new and beautiful office composed in honor of Nicholas to be chanted by his monks, he was beaten like a wayward schoolboy until he succeeded in learning it. A miniature accompanying the story shows the humiliated monk crouching submissively at the feet of the mitered saint, studiously conning his lesson from a little book (Figure 10).[41] In The Golden Legend, Jacobus de Voragine would later attempt to excuse this prior's conservative response by explaining that the office was unworthy of the saint, being a series of "new, worldly songs composed by clerks, a kind of jongleurie."[42] Jehan Bodel's play certainly belongs in this mixed category. As a jongleur, he would have been intimately acquainted with different modes of dramatic storytelling, including those of liturgical dramas in which villainous kings like Herod, Marmorinus, and Darius profess the religion of "Mahom," Apollo, and Tervagan. And as a clerk, he would have performed a variety of administrative and diplomatic tasks, like the herald Auberon who opens the Jeu de saint Nicolas, acting as an intermediary in the negotiations between an avaricious king and a usurious bishop. His play spoke directly to current events: the symbolic representation of power, the debasement of coinage, and the appropriation of culture.

Any effort to understand the history of Arras must begin with the fact of its peculiar political geography; the same can be said of its theater, particularly of this play.[43] Arras was not the only place to have a mercantile bourg and an ecclesiastical cité, between which there was always a natural rivalry, but it is frequently held up as the example par excellence of the medieval "binary town," riven by internal competitions and disputes.[44] The pope's restoration of the diocese in 1093 had given the bishop of Arras only a tenuous footing in what was otherwise a vast monastic domain, in which even the count of Flanders paid an annual ground rent to the abbey; the bishop's fiefdom, which he held from the king of the Franks,

---

lationships (9th–12th c.) (Berkeley, 1963), especially 4–5 and 43–44. There is no need to posit a direct relationship between this codex (Orléans Bm 201) and the JsN; see Patrick R. Vincent, "Jean Bodel and the Fleury Play-Book," Symposium 20 (1966): 367–378.

41. BmA 307, fol. 116vᵃ.

42. Jacobus de Voragine, Legenda aurea, ca. 181: "nova sæcularium cantica clericorum, immo jocularis quædam." Cited by Jones, Liturgy, 48.

43. Adolphe Guesnon, "Les origines d'Arras et de ses institutions," MAA (1895): 183–258.

44. John W. Baldwin, The Government of Philip Augustus: Foundations of French Royal Power in the Middle Ages (Berkeley, 1986), 348; Nicholas, Flanders, 103; Pounds, Economic History, 239–241 and fig. 6.4; Heers, La ville, 146–202; Carpentier and Le Mené, La France, 43. In general, see Alain Derville, Villes de Flandre et d'Artois (900–1500) (Villeneuve d'Ascq, 2002). On the extremes generated by such divisions in fourteenth-century Rodez, see Ann Wroe, A Fool and His Money: Life in a Partitioned Medieval Town (London, 1995).

FIGURE 10. A haughty prior is beaten like a schooboy until he learns a new office in honor of Saint Nicholas: from an Arrageois manuscript featuring the lives and miracles of the saints in vernacular prose (BmA 307, fol. 116v: author's photograph)

did not even extend to the other side of the Roman road that ran past his makeshift cathedral, a district known as the *pouvoir des Maus* and held by the abbey. And he had only one stake in the valuable real estate of the Town, just over the river and along the well-traveled thoroughfare that gave its name to the tiny demesne of the Estrée. There, within a few hundred square meters, he controlled a mill, a market, and all of the traffic through the western gate. He thereby gained a right to a share of the *tonlieu*, or market-tax, levied by the abbey, as well as jurisdiction for himself and the échevins of his City within the walls of the Town.[45] But by 1191 the urban *enceinte* built during the lifetime of the first Bishop Lambert, under whom these accommodations had been hammered out, had become an increasingly

45. A. C. F. Koch, "Continuité ou rupture? De la justice domaniale et abbatiale à la justice urbaine et comtale à Arras," RN 40 (1958): 289–96; Delmaire, *Le diocèse*, 1:76–80; Guesnon, "Les origines," 215–231.

powerful instrument for protecting the Town from the rival City and its foreign political alliances. This was clarified in a new charter issued by Count Philip of Flanders, perhaps during Jehan's tenure as a functionary of the commune, "in order that the contentions which are apt to arise should be laid to rest." Its terms were harsh: "Henceforth, no man who is from the community of the Town of Arras, who keeps the customs of the count in that same Town, can cross over for the purpose of remaining outside the walls in the bishop's district, without the consent of the count; nor should any man of the bishop remain within those walls, without the consent of the bishop."[46] The visitor from the City was thus a perpetual outsider, more distinctive and farther alienated than the *hom de forain* or *homo foraneus* mentioned in the laws of 1163: the foreigner from abroad need only take up residence in the Town for a year and a day, after which a public proclamation would declare him a legal resident.[47] No such ceremony could naturalize the foreigner from the City.

But just as in the *Jeu de saint Nicolas*, there was traffic between these two worlds. In particular, the bearers of news were allowed to pass from one Town to its Other. Specifically, the herald of the count and the commune's criers were authorized to proclaim "the banns which are made in the Town of Arras by order of the count and his échevins" within the bounds of his City as well.[48] In 1194 Philip Augustus would revisit the issue of criers and their purviews, now that his lordship in Arras had lent a new unity to some of the former divisions. Thenceforth, his banns could be cried everywhere. Still, he stipulated that certain banns of the Town should remain in the special control of the échevins of the commune, namely, "The banns of wine and the banns of salable items costing less than 60 sous and the banns concerning *tremel*," a local term denoting games of chance.[49]

---

46. "Ad sopiendas contentiones que emergere solent. . . . Preterea nullus hominum qui sit de communitate ville Atrebatensis, qui consuetudines comiti debeat in eadem villa, poterit transire ad manendum extra muros in districto episcopi, absque assensu comitis, nec aliquis hominum episcopi infra muros, absque assensu episcopi." BnF lat. 9930, fols. 21v–22v; ed. Adolphe Guesnon as "Charte de l'Estrée" in "Les origines," 256–258. See also Benoît-Michel Tock, *Les chartes des évêques d'Arras (1093–1203)* (Paris, 1991), no. 174.

47. *Cartulaire*, 8–14 (no. 9). The French text is given in M. Taillar, ed., *Recueil d'actes des XIIe–XIIIe siècles en langue romane wallone du Nord de la France* (Douai, 1849), 36–43 (no. 11). See also Roger Berger, "Les bourgeois dans la littérature romane (Zone ouest)," in *Bourgeois et littérature bourgeoise dans les anciens Pays-Bas au XIIIe siècle*, ed. Georges Despy and Pierre Ruelle (Brussels, 1978), 429–436; in the same volume, see Alain Derville, "Le bourgeois artésien au XIIIe siècle," 389–406.

48. "Charte de l'Estrée," 256–257 (see n. 33): "bannum quoque, qui fiet in villa Atrebatensi per comitem et scabinos suos."

49. *Cartulaire*, 13; Taillar, *Recueil*, 38: "Banni vini et banni venalium a sexaginta solidis et infra et banni de tremerello remanebunt hominibus civitatis. // Le ban del vin et le ban des veneus et le ban de tremel remanront a hommes de le chite." Frédéric Godefroy glosses *tremeleor* as a "player of *tremerel*" and, by

With this in mind, it becomes clear that Connart the crier's two appearances in the *Jeu de saint Nicolas* mark the passage of time. Before the battle, Connart has access only to the immediate subjects of the King and no right to the airwaves in the town of "this borderland." The herald Auberon, too, can operate "beyond the banlieue" only to summon the King's liegemen (v. 247); when he stops in at the tavern, he does so to get a drink, not to tell his news. The second time that Connart is sent out on the King's behalf, however, his exchange with Raoulet signals that the Town is under new management. Describing himself as a crier by birth, and for sixty years the servant of the échevins of the City (vv. 599–603), Connart avers that he now has the authority to challenge Raoulet, who describes himself as the official crier of wine, working for the men of the Town (vv. 605–606). They wrangle because they have both been used to the old days when Connart's activities were confined to the City, where the King had some power. Now things have changed: the King has won his "new crown," and Connart's job has taken on a new dimension. As the Taverner explains, he can have his banns cried anywhere. And yet, according to the charter of Philip Augustus issued in 1194, as well as to the well-informed Taverner, the men of the Town retain certain privileges:

Connart, tu crieras le ban,	630	Connart, you therefore cry the banns
S'iers au roi et as eskievins		Of both the king and échevins
Et Raouls criera les vins.		And Raoul will cry the wines.

It is interesting to speculate on the effects of this scene if the play were performed in the marketplace, where taverns and criers were prevalent. It would not be the only occasion when the cacophony of news and the confusion of authorities occasioned a quarrel there (see chapter 3).

The Bishop's Hornèd Hat

In 1093 Urban II's reasons for removing Arras from the control of Cambrai had been covertly political: he had cited the urban population boom, but his ulterior motive was to diminish the number of ecclesiastical territories in the hands of the German emperor (Cambrai was in neighboring Hainaut) and to strengthen those of the French king. This is why the diocese was not simply restored but established as a separate political enclave within the archdiocese of Reims. Eventually this provided a much-needed boost to Capetian authority: in 1127, when the murder of Count Charles the Good left Flanders without

---

association, a trickster; he cites this as the only instance of the word's appearance, but it also occurs in *Courtois d'Arras* (see chapter 2); see *Dictionnaire de l'ancienne langue française et de tous ses dialectes du XIe au XVr siècles*, 10 vols. (Geneva, 1982), 8:39.

an heir, Arras became the base of operations for Louis VI, who engineered elections from there.[50] Generations later, this peculiar alliance played even more significantly into the hands of Philip Augustus, when the reigning pontiff, Pierre (1184–1203), showed himself to be a staunch supporter of the king's claims in the region.[51] He was even named as the patron of a chronicle devoted to Frankish royal history, the *Historia succincta de regibus Francorum* by André of Marchiennes, a French-speaking monk living on the border of the Holy Roman Empire, whose view of the king as a leader of "our people" was not universally shared.[52]

This curious relationship between king and bishop is mirrored in the *Jeu de saint Nicolas*, which depicts the King as attacking the town from a secure position on its borders, and as making use of the City's criers to disseminate his message. But it is more strikingly evinced in the saint's willingness to perform financial miracles on the King's behalf, increasing his treasure by taking it into his care and, over time, turning a profit. Indeed, this is such an obvious feature of the play that it is surprising how seldom it has been noted: in the long history of its reception, only one critic has compared Jehan's Saint Nicholas to "a banker of Arras, capitalist, and usurer."[53] Perhaps this reluctance stems from the fact that usury was technically illegal, though very widely practiced. In Arras it was even practiced by the bishop—or, in 1191, by the bishop's deputy, who bore a remarkable resemblance to the bishop-saint of Myra in a number of ways. Like Saint Nicholas, whose relics had been translated to the Italian coast of the Adriatic only a century before the events dramatized in Jehan's play, both the reigning and incumbent bishops of Arras were foreigners who had come from the South. Pierre was a Burgundian; Raoul, his successor-designate, hailed from the Dauphiné and the diocese of Vienne. And both stand out as peculiar

---

50. Galbert, *De multro*, cc. 47, 106, and 110. See F. L. Ganshof, "Le roi de France en Flandre en 1127 et 1128," *Revue historique de droit français et étranger* 27 (1949): 204–228; Ferry de Locre, *Chronicon Belgicum ab Anno CCLVIII ad Annum vsque M.D.C. continuo perductum*, 3 vols. (Arras, 1614–1616), 231–238; Delmaire, *Le diocèse*, 1:39 and 2:425; Guesnon, "Les origines," 212.

51. H. Delaborde et al., eds., *Recueil des actes de Philippe Auguste roi de France*, 4 vols. (Paris, 1916), 1:346–348 (no. 774); Léopold Delisle, ed., *Catalogue des actes de Philippe Auguste* (Paris, 1856), no. 793. See Benoît-Michel Tock, "Les élections épiscopales à Arras de Lambert à Pierre Ier (1093–1203)," *Revue belge* (1987): 709–721; Bernard Guillemain, "Philippe Auguste et l'épiscopat," in Bautier, *La France*, 365–384; Baldwin, *Government*, 65–66 and 182–183; Guesnon, "Les origines," 209.

52. BmA 453. See Auguste Molinier, *Les sources de l'histoire de France dès origines aux guerres d'Italie*, vol. 3 (Paris, 1903), 88; and Karl Ferdinand Werner, "Andreas von Marchiennes und die Geschichtsschreibung von Anchin und Marchiennes in der zweiten Hälfte des 12. Jahrhunderts," *Deutsches Archiv für Erforschung des Mittelalters* 9 (1952): 402–463.

53. Alfred Adler, "Le *Jeu de saint Nicolas*: Édifiant, mais dans quel sens?" *Romania* 81 (1960): 112–120. In Cowell's analysis (*At Play*, 84–87 and 92–98), the King and the thieves are the characters accused of usury.

among the men who had filled the office prior to Pierre's election in 1184, and who would continue to fill it after the death of Raoul in 1221; until the end of the thirteenth century, all the other bishops of Arras, save these two alone, were natives of the North.[54] Raoul, moreover, was an archdeacon of the new school, "the bishop's eye," as Innocent III had it, trained in the tenets of Romano-canonic procedure, a veteran of the diocesan courts with extensive parochial experience, who was probably more visible in Arras than the bishop himself.[55]

We do not, therefore, have to upset the dating of the play in order to connect this future bishop with the "horny-hatted" Saint Nicholas, whose nickname Raoul also shared. Known to modern historians as Raoul de Neuville, he was called "de Capello Cornuto" in his own day, "Hornèd Hat." "Chapeau Cornu" was an ancient toponymic in the Bas-Dauphiné near Vignieu and the surname of its lord Siffroi, Raoul's own father. In Arras, however, it took on new meaning when its owner prepared himself for episcopal dignity, since the bishop's miter was "horned," its double peaks inviting comparison with the horns of demons, idols, and cuckolds, or even the peaked cap worn by jongleurs. Accordingly, the icon of Saint Nicholas is *un mahommet cornu* to the infidel conquerors (vv. 458, 585) and *cest cornu menestrel* to the gamesters in the tavern (v. 999). Indeed, the "hornèd" version of Raoul's surname was used more often among the Arrageois than it had been in his homeland, probably because its owner's episcopal dignity gave it local relish. In obituaries of the cathedral, where yearly prayers were offered for the souls of Raoul's parents and nephews, the scribes underlined the joke: "the lady of the Hornèd Hat, from the diocese of Vienne, mother of lord Raoul, bishop," or "Raoul of the Hornèd Hat, nephew of that same bishop, deacon and canon of this church."[56]

The similarities do not end there. When Pope Innocent wrote to complain about the re-

---

54. Of the seventeen bishops elected or appointed between 1093 and 1293, four came from Flanders and one from the Brabant, at least two and possibly as many as five from the Île-de-France, one from Chartres, two from Picardy, and two from the Artois. See Delmaire, *Le diocèse*, 1:165–168, and "Le testament d'un évêque d'Arras originaire du diocèse de Vienne en Dauphiné (1220)," ed. Bernard Delmaire in *Papauté, monachisme, et théories politiques: Études d'histoire médiévale offertes à Marcel Pacaut*, vol. 2, *Les églises locales*, ed. P. Guichard et al. (Lyon, 1994), 453–460.

55. Jacques Pycke, *Le chapitre cathédral de Notre-Dame de Tournai de la fin du XIe à la fin du XIIIe siècle: Son organisation, sa vie, ses membres* (Brussels, 1986), 145–153.

56. Brussels, Bibliothèque royale, 21532–35, fol. 16r: "Domina de Capello Cornuto, Viennensis diocesis, mater domini Radulphi episcopi"; BmA 290, fol. 78r; and BmA 424, fol 25r: "Radulphus de Capello Cornuto, nepos episcopi ipsius, dyaconus et canonicus hujus ecclesie." See also Delmaire, "Le testament," 455–457. The name was still borne by episcopal functionaries at the end of the century. In 1291 the provost of the bishop of Arras is identified as Guillaume "called Cornu," and one Jakemes de Cornu is identified as a clerk of the count and his advocate in the episcopal official's court in 1299: AdPC ser. 3 G 3 "Hostel Dieu LIIII [Cité XV]" (Delmaire handlist, no. 46), and ser. A 152.27.

ported increase in usurious traffic at Arras in 1208, the bishop's own activities were tac-itly implicated in this censure.[57] The nature and extent of his dealings are also revealed in a document of a kind almost as rare in the North as the script of a play: the bishop's will. Taken down in November 1220, four months before his death on March 26, 1221, it bears witness to Raoul's investment portfolio and, intriguingly, to a special devotion to Saint Nicholas. Alone of all the churches in Arras, the parish of Saint-Nicolas was singled out for a special legacy. The rest, including "our church of Arras," the cathedral, were excused only from paying back *some* of the money they owed to the bishop at his death; the sum Raoul still expected to collect (augmenting the treasures he posthumously stored on earth) amounted to 670 livres.[58] But like Saint Nicholas, he could be generous to those he found deserving. Gautier, the clerk who wrote his will, received 10 livres as a legacy, the amount also paid to Nicholas, the bishop's head chef, and to his two chaplains. Even Raoul's laundress, whose name he did not know, received 40 sous, a sizable sum and the same amount paid to most of his household officers. The remainder of his goods and chattels, divided into four parts, was invested in both temporal and spiritual ways. One part was bequeathed to the poorhouses of La Brayelle and La Fosse. Another went to the executors themselves, the archdeacons Pons and Simon (Raoul's successor and nephew, respectively); the dean of the cathedral, Barthélemy; and Robert of Douai, master of the cathedral school. A third part was put out to use, and the interest earned on its investment went to finance a memorial Mass and the distribution of alms in the bishop's memory.

The final portion was halved and a sum bequeathed to "all the houses of lepers that are in our bishopric, in which there are many lepers living communally together, and to all those lepers that are round about Arras, to the distance of a league, however much they should keep to themselves."[59] Too late, alas, to help Jehan Bodel, whose demise had been recorded a decade earlier and whose illness began around the time of Raoul's pontificate. One wonders, though, whether the *Congé* produced its desired effect on the bishop as well as the échevins. Members of his household might have been among the confrères of the Carité who bade farewell to Jehan and later prayed for his soul, while the patronage of the bishop himself is invoked in the preamble to the Carité's constitution (see chapter 2).

57. Georges Bigwood, "Les financiers d'Arras: Contribution à l'étude du capitalisme moderne," *Revue belge de philologie et d'histoire* 3 (1924): 465–508 at 466 and 769–819 at 772–784. See also John Baldwin, *Masters, Princes, and Merchants: The Social Views of Peter the Chanter and His Circle*, 2 vols. (Princeton, 1970), 1:298.

58. The original does not survive; a copy, made in 1769, forms part of the Colléction Moreau in the Bibliothèque nationale (vol. 128, fol. 60r–v); see Delmaire, "Le testament," 453–457, and *Le diocèse*, 1:166. On the growth of urban testamentary practices in Picardy, see Fossier, *La terre*, 2:583.

59. "Omnibus domibus leprosorum que sunt in nostro episcopatu in quibus sunt plures leprosi communiter viventes et omnibus illis qui sunt circa Attrebatum per unam leugam, quamvis singulariter maneant." Delmaire, "Le testament," 458–459.

Viewed in this light, it looks very much like a bequest made in memory of the town's most famous leper by the mortal namesake of his hornèd saint.

The King's Crusade

Since its "discovery" in the eighteenth century, the *Jeu de saint-Nicolas* has been viewed as a crusading tract. In 1783 the first cataloguer of its manuscript compared it to Corneille's neo-medieval classic *Le Cid*.[60] In 1843 Jean-Baptiste Onésime LeRoy saw it as an inspiration to compatriots who had taken up the white man's burden in Algiers, asking "what Frenchman worthy of that name" could fail to rejoice should a conversion like that of Jehan's pagan king be worked upon a troublesome African chieftain.[61] And in 1957 Henri Roussel declared that the idea of crusade "haunted" Jehan Bodel and the people of Arras, as the specter of communism haunted cold war France.[62] These views, each colored by the historical circumstances of its time, do not match the historical evidence, which indicates that crusading was not a popular activity in Jehan Bodel's Picardy in any sense of the word. Some thirty-one aristocrats from the region participated in the Third Crusade, probably riding in the train of Philip of Flanders, but only one prominent resident of Arras is known to have taken the cross at that time.[63] The Fourth Crusade attracted only two participants of note: Amaury, the provost of Arras, and Vaast Hukedieu, who receives a special mention in Jehan Bodel's *Congé*.[64]

When the people of Arras did feel crusading fervor, it was in their purses. Vast sums of money were raised by the great lords and magnates who besieged Acre in 1190, and both Philip of Flanders and Philip of France levied new taxes to support their armies. So if the Arrageois were "haunted," it was by the constant presence of the count's bailiff. And they were haunted all over again when Philip of France led his army to Arras from Outremer, to the tune of 3,000 livres of the new money coined in their own mint. According to a historian of medieval Flanders, the annexation of Arras by the king of France was a flagrant act of confiscation, driven by greed.[65] In the *Jeu saint Nicolas*, coincidentally, the mecha-

60. Guillaume de Bure, *Catalogue des livres de la bibliothèque de feu M. le duc de la Vallière*, 2 vols. (Paris, 1783), 2:232.

61. Jean-Baptiste Onésime Leroy, *Époques de l'histoire de France en rapport avec le théâtre français, dès la formation de la langue jusqu'à la Renaissance* (Paris, 1843), 85–89 and 94–101. See also his *Études sur les Mystères, monumens historiques et littéraires, la plupart inconnus, et sur divers manuscrits de Gerson* (Paris, 1837), iii–iv.

62. Roussel, "Notes," 275.

63. Fossier, *La terre*, 2:610; H. Van Werveke, "La contribution de la Flandre et du Hainaut à la troisième Croisade," *MA* 78 (1972): 55–90.

64. Jean Longnon, *Les compagnons de Villehardouin: Recherches sur les croisés de la quatrième Croisade* (Paris, 1978), 192; Guesnon, "Les origines," 228–229.

65. James M. Murray, *Notarial Instruments in Flanders between 1280–1452* (Brussels, 1995), 17.

nisms of the takeover are personified in the open avarice of the King and the corruption of his sycophantic Seneschal, a "new man" like the new king's bailiff of Arras, Nevelon the Marshall, condemned for his rapacity by chroniclers from Béthune to Wales.[66] They can also be seen in the co-opted local jailer Durant, whose prison is the king's "charter," and the ineffectual idol Tervagan, symbolic of the outdated "religion" of political economy in the Île-de-France, where land-poor lords were still, like Outre l'Arbre Sec, tied by a trade in millstones.

The architect of the sophisticated fiscal machinery that fell to the king of France in 1191 was Count Philip of Flanders, who had governed his domain for nearly a quarter-century, so well that his economic policies, coupled with the excellent administration of his towns, had long set an example for the relatively impoverished kings on his borders. Flanders was the first lay court in Europe to have a permanent chancery, and the first to have reliable sources of income that were not derived from violence or extortion. Empowered by these, the count eventually began to express territorial ambitions that prefigured those of his protégé, the new king of the Franks.[67] Indeed, it seems likely that the younger Philip's expansionist policies were modeled on those of his former mentor.[68] In 1180, the year Philip II ascended his father's throne, Philip of Flanders had already arranged for his protégé to marry his own wife's niece, Isabella of Hainaut, whose chief attraction was the Flemish dowry provided by the count, who may have regarded the young king as a potential heir. This constituted the most valuable portion of French-speaking Flanders, roughly equivalent to what would later become (in 1237) the county of Artois: the towns of Arras, Bapaume, Saint-Omer, and Aire, with Béthune and the valuable castellany of Hesdin. Under the terms of the agreement, however, the region would pass into the king's hands only after the count's death—and on the condition that Philip and Isabella produced a male heir. It was a bold plan on Count Philip's part because it gave him a permanent hold over the king and the potential power to dictate policy in the North indefinitely.

But Philip of France proved a wily adversary, determined to pursue his own imperial policies. In 1182 he debarred the elder man's claim to Amiens and the Vermandois, which

66. That is, the Anonymous of Béthune and Gerald of Wales: Baldwin, *Government*, 125 and 135; the phrase "the king's new men" is Baldwin's. Nevelon was in office by 1201 or 1202, and may have been in place sooner; he held the post until 1224. See Alain Derville, *Saint-Omer: Des origines au début du XIVe siècle* (Lille, 1995), 126; Sivéry, *Les capetiens*, 119–120 and 125.

67. Raoul C. van Caenegem, "Law and Power in Twelfth-Century Flanders," in *Cultures of Power: Lordship, Status, and Process in Twelfth-Century Europe*, ed. Thomas N. Bisson (Philadelphia, 1995), 149–171; Thomas N. Bisson, "Les comptes des domaines au temps de Philippe Auguste: Essai comparatif," in Bautier, *La France*, 521–539 at 532; Baldwin, *Government*, 7–8 and 59–64.

68. Spiegel, *Romancing*, 34; Nicholas, *Flanders*, 73–74; Baldwin, *Government*, 16–26. In general, see Léon Louis Borrelli de Serres, *La réunion des provinces septentrionnales à la couronne par Philippe Auguste* (Paris, 1899).

Philip of Flanders had inherited on the death of his wife, Elizabeth of Hainaut. The count refused to surrender these lands, however, and further exacerbated the situation by marrying again in 1184 and giving every indication that he and his new bride intended to produce an heir, thus potentially nullifying King Philip's eventual inheritance of the Artois. In fact, the count assigned his new wife portions of what had been Queen Isabella's dowry, with the result that her royal husband threatened to divorce her. In the ensuing war, Baldwin of Hainaut sided with his son-in-law, the king, against his former brother-in-law, the count, who was forced to concede defeat at the battle of Boves in 1185. Then the birth of the future Louis VIII in 1187 seemed to confirm the king in the eventual possession of the Artois, although no one could be certain that the arrival of an heir to the county of Flanders might not shatter all his plans.

Notwithstanding the volatile climate at home, both Philip of Flanders and Philip of France took the cross in 1187, and both spent the next three years levying taxes to finance their expeditions.[69] Finally, in 1190, on the eve of his departure for the Holy Land, the count issued a new charter to the town of Arras, reasserting his lordship over the region to which it belonged.[70] But on the first day of June the following year, six weeks after his arrival at the siege of Acre, Philip of Flanders died. The city fell to the Christians a month later, yet Philip Augustus was not there to share in the victory. He was bent on his own crusade: the pursuit of his "God-given" rights in the Artois. In the same year that Acre became a Christian town, Arras converted to France.[71]

What John Baldwin calls "the traditional Capetian policy toward towns" had been one of passive and intermittent profit until the acquisition of the Artois. Under Philip Augustus, however, towns became special instruments of royal power.[72] Their importance is underlined in an outpouring of documents issued by the royal chancery established in Paris after the notorious loss of the royal archive during a campaign at Fréteval in 1194. Arras received its charter that year, and in the comprehensive Register of 1205 it is listed twice, under episcopal cities and among the thirty-nine communes owing military service to the king. In the latter list it is distinguished by the number of troops to be levied: one thousand strong, in comparison to five hundred from Beauvais, the next-largest number. Still more significantly, Arras and Beauvais alone are noted as having the option to substitute a cash payment of 3 pounds per head.[73] Arras was, of course, eminently capable of pay-

69. Jean Richard, "Philippe-Auguste, la croisade, et le royaume," in Bautier, La France, 411–424; Baldwin, Government, 23.

70. Cartulaire, 3 (no. 3); idem, "Les origines," 234.

71. Baldwin, Government, 79; van Werveke, "Contribution," 61 and 73; Nicholas, Flanders, 74.

72. Baldwin, Government, 59; Carolus-Barré, "Philippe Auguste," 677–688.

73. Michel Nortier, "Les Actes de Philippe Auguste: Notes critiques sur les sources diplomatiques du règne," in Bautier, La France, 429–451; Bisson, "Les comptes," 530; Sivéry, Les capétiens, 20–29 and 43–47; Baldwin, Government, 158.

ing the money, and this was one of the few ways that Philip could exact such a large amount at one time, since the communes formerly belonging to Flanders were exempt from the arbitrary exactions of the royal *taille*. (This was the sort of privilege Philip would never allow the communes of his own patrimony, the most powerful of which—at Laon, Étampes, Beauvais—would be dissolved, while Paris, Orléans, and Bourges were always denied the freedoms enjoyed by the former Flemish towns of the Artois.)[74] New sources of wealth, they also served as centers from which Philip could promote his administrative agenda, because the many duties of the king's bailiff were facilitated by the well-oiled bureaucracy already in place there. As Robert-Henri Bautier remarks, "The great novelty of his reign was exactly this constant recourse to writing," a trick that France had learned in Flanders.[75]

The history of French royal expansion therefore dates from 1191, when Philip Augustus arrived in Arras, and the town's continued importance to the survival of France is shown in the royal policies of monarchs for centuries to come. And it was undoubtedly the acquisition of Artois and its wealth that prompted Philip Augustus to establish a permanent treasury in Paris for the first time, in that very year—the definitive moment in the history of French royal finance. How satisfying for the king, after a hard day's work at the Exchequer in its "Temple" on the Right Bank, to retire to his private chapel in the round tower of the Louvre, hard by the market of Les Halles. Here he could offer his devotions to the saints venerated on counting days, giving thanks at an altar dedicated—appropriately—to Saint Nicholas.[76]

Riens qui en se garde soit mise		Nothing that's to his guard vouchsafed
N'iert ja perdue ne maumise,		Will be diminished or misplaced
Tant ne sera abandonnee		Or lost, or ever left behind.
Non, se chis palais ert plain d'or		Were all this palace full of gold
Et il geust seur le tresor:	530	He'd keep and treasure it, all told—
Tel grasse li a Dieus donnee.		God's grace to him is of that kind.

As the Prudhomme of Arras had assured the pagan King, the bishop-saint was a very reliable banker.

---

74. Carolus-Barré, "Philippe-Auguste," 679; Baldwin, *Government*, 62.

75. Robert-Henri Bautier, "Le règne de Philippe Auguste dans l'histoire de France," in *La France*, 11–27 at 17.

76. Bisson, "Les comptes," 521–523 and 529. See also John Baldwin, "L'entourage de Philippe Auguste," in Bautier, *La France*, 59–75, and *Government*, 60 and 344.

Passing Current: Uses of Coins and Words

When Abbot Guibert of Nogent (d. 1124) retold the popular story of a rich man from the Artois who "had fattened his purse with ill-gotten gains" and was damned for amassing "mountains of metal coins," he could be sure that his audience would recognize the type.[77] To him, as to most people in Europe, the word "Artesian" literally meant "money": not just the wealth that everyone in Arras was supposed to have but the coin in which that wealth was vested and expressed, the petit denier of Flanders, minted in Arras. So tenacious was the association of artésien, a coin, with monnaie, coin in general, that this equation caused considerable confusion throughout the ensuing century, long after the coin of Artois had been swallowed up by that of France, and long after the petits deniers of Flanders were no longer minted in Arras. It would take more than the availability of the parisis, or the royal authority behind the coin, to alter habits of reckoning in Flanders and the towns it had lost. It took time. For the next half-century at least, the inhabitants of the Artois would continue to draw up charters in which wealth was exchanged, at least theoretically, in the artésien of blessed memory. Only by the close of the thirteenth century did the livre parisis become money of account, after it was tied to the strong currency of Tours.[78]

The monetary atelier at Arras was the most important cog in the sophisticated fiscal machinery designed by Philip of Flanders. Its very efficiency ensured that the Parisian coin of King Philip could replace the Artesian coin of Count Philip in scarcely more time than it would take the argentiers to change the matrices, a substitution that has been described as "very clean, and brutal."[79] The diffusion of Parisian coin from Arras was only one manifestation of Paris rule, but it was the most immediate local symbol of Philip Augustus's presence there. For just as the King of the Jeu de saint Nicolas had spoken of his desire to turn the ineffectual idol of his ancestors into ready cash, so the king of France needed a stable currency like that of Flanders. The local coin of his inherited domain had never been an instrument for international trade. Large and clumsy, the Parisian grand denier was heavily alloyed and unreliable, while the petit denier of Arras had remained small only be-

77. Guibert of Nogent, De vita sua 3.19, trans. Paul J. Archambault as A Monk's Confession: The Memoirs of Guibert of Nogent (University Park, 1996), 206.

78. C. Richebé, Les monnaies féodales d'Artois (Paris, 1963), 99, 124–126, and 148; Peter Spufford, Handbook of Medieval Exchange (London, 1986), 167–172. See also J. Ghyssens, Les petits deniers de Flandre des XIIe et XIIIe siècles (Brussels, 1971). In general, see Raymond Monier, Les instititions financières de comté de Flandre du XIe siècle à 1384 (Paris, 1948); and Bryce Dale Lyon and Adriaan Verhulst, Medieval Finance: A Comparison of Financial Institutions in Northwestern Europe (Providence, 1967).

79. Richebé, Monnaies, 124. The mints of Arras and Saint-Omer had been the biggest in Flanders: ibid., 52, 100; Nicholas, Flanders, 111; Françoise Dumas, "La monnaie dans le royaume au temps de Philippe Auguste," in Bautier, La France, 541–574.

cause it was pure. Philip Augustus's liquidation of the artésien thus altered the size and quality of the coinage current there.[80]

Had the facts not been plain enough, the monks of Saint-Vaast could have interpreted the novelty in a traditional way, by leafing through their worn copy of Isidore's *Etymologies*. They would read: "Money is so called because it warns [*monet*] lest any fraud should enter into its composition or weight. The piece of money is the coin of gold, silver, or bronze which is called *nomisma*, because it bears the imprint of the name [*nomen*] and the likeness of the prince."[81] Toward the end of Jehan's play, when the change in the criers' respective jurisdictions signals the change from one ruler to another, there is a corresponding change in currency—and expressions of the anxiety attending that change. When some new coins are tossed onto the gaming table, even the trickster Pincedés looks at them askance. "That's only play money," he declares, *Che fu au jeu de pairesis* (v. 1147). In other words, the *jeu* has become a game played for coins worth nothing (*parisis*), or perhaps a *jeu* "de pas ici," a game and coin "not from here" and mistrusted in Arras. King Philip's economic sleight-of-hand is interpreted as clearing the way for other types of fraudulent activity, since tampering with the value of one potent symbol, the coin, sets a precedent that may lead to the depreciation of others, such as words, or to arbitrary changes in other rules—of dice games, or of grammar.[82]

The change in coinage in Arras after 1191 is another important element that has been absent from interpretations of the *Jeu de saint Nicolas*, compounding the considerable confusion over the Taverner's reckoning of Auberon's wine tab.[83] As we recall, the herald pays a visit to the tavern before it is integrated into the realm of the King, when the Taverner explains that he sells wine at the price set by the town, *au ban de le vile* (v. 258). If Auberon puts a denier down for his first pint, he can have a second pint for a *maille*, a local coin worth half a denier in Arras.[84] The ensuing quarrel actually stems from the fact that buyer and seller are used to two different currencies, each with its own denominations and rates of exchange. The retail price of wine did not always accord with the value of the coins in

---

80. Dumas, "Monnaie," 542–543; Spufford, *Handbook*, 170.

81. Isidore of Seville, *Etymologies* 16:17 and 18, quoted by R. Howard Bloch, *Etymologies and Genealogies: A Literary Anthropology of the French Middle Ages* (Chicago, 1983), 165. A contemporary catalogue of the library of Saint-Vaast (BmA 323, fol. 71v) includes such a volume; see Grierson, "Bibliothèque de St-Vaast," 133 (no. 173).

82. Cowell, *At Play*, 86.

83. This problem has a long history. A recent treatment is that of Guy Paoli, "Taverne et théâtre au Moyen Age," in *Théâtre et spectacles*, 73–78. On the related problem of the game "Hasard" and the significance of dice games in general, see Jean-Michel Mehl, *Les jeux au royaume de France du XIIIe au début du XVIe siècle* (Paris, 1990), 76–98; and Thomas M. Kavanagh, *Dice, Cards, Wheels: A Different History of French Culture* (Philadelphia, 2005), 30–48.

84. Richebé, *Monnaies*, 148.

a traveler's pocket; and because Auberon is a foreigner and does not possess a maille, he does not want to pay a denier for a pint costing only three quarters of that sum, especially since he might not pass that way again. This was a familiar conundrum. At any given time in Arras, the good petits deniers would have been mixed together with coins brought into town by merchants from all over Europe, including the alloyed deniers of Paris, the faithful *tournois* of Tours, and the *esterlin* of England. All would have been exchanged at different rates, based on the fluctuating strength of the currency and the prestige of its political backer.[85] There was also a multitude of smaller currencies, lordly or communal. Douai, for instance, in an attempt to offset the disparities between its local coinage and that of neighboring Arras, began minting a *merel* or token coin that represented the difference in change between the artésien and the *douaisien*, since it took four deniers of Douai to make a denier of Arras and two to make a maille. The resulting scenario: if someone owed half an Arrageois maille for a pint of wine, he could notionally pay for it with a douaisien, but a taverner might not accept the coin, since it represented the nonexistent quarter-denier in Arras.[86] Auberon's situation was not anywhere near as complicated as those seen by any taverner in Arras, any day of the week.

Not only was coinage the most material symbol of the changes wrought by the new regime, in the play as in life, but it was the most pervasive as well. The ultimate medium of exchange, a coin is both signifier and signified: not just a sign of wealth, or a means of measuring wealth, but the substance of wealth. Or was it? R. Howard Bloch has argued that money became a "floating signifier" during the economic revolution of the twelfth century, detached from its moorings as a result of the proliferation of currencies, the debasement of coinage, and subsequent monetary inflation: witness the metallurgically inferior grand denier of Philip Augustus minted at Arras after 1191. Nicholas of Oresme would later liken such fiscal prestidigitation to blasphemy, since both sins involved falsification of a promise made before God. Seen from his perspective, what Philip Augustus did with the coinage of Arras would have been just another form of usury, cursed by Aristotle as a crime "against nature." Money was a dead thing, naturally unproductive, and in order for it to generate more money, it had to be divorced from its proper role as a symbol for wealth that should rightly be vested in heritable property, lineages, and family fortunes. The notion appealed to those who disapproved of the new social order created by towns, and came to be defined by canon law as any practice whereby a sterile coin could be made to propagate other coins without the requisite labor that earned a fair wage. It

85. Spufford, *Handbook*, 209. For example, the English pound could have been exchanged at anywhere from 64 to 90 sous parisis in the mid-thirteenth century, although it was usually worth 65. But it was valued at 90 sous tournois in northern France and 80 in Paris, and at 49s. 9d. or 49s. 7.5d. in the artésiens which were used as the money of account at Ypres during the same period.

86. Richebé, *Monnaies*, 148. On merels, see Mehl, *Les jeux*, 149–151; see also chapter 2.

was *venditio temporis*, "the sale of time," and included deferred payment, lending at interest, the purchase of goods at an unfairly low price, extortion, fraud, and any kind of gambling.[87]

Jehan Bodel himself dramatized these issues in a fabliau "About Brownie, the Priest's Cow," inviting laughter at country folks' simplistic view of money markets and exchange rates while at the same time lampooning a hypocritical willingness to profit from their ignorance. One holiday, a peasant and his wife hear a sermon about the grace of giving alms, "For God, who hears in times of trouble / Returns it all in time, and double" (*Por Dieu, qui reson entendoit; / Que Dieus au double le rendoit*). Impressed, the peasant decides to put this into practice and gives his best cow to God's representative, the priest. The priest makes no objection, takes the cow, and puts it in a pen with his own. Both cows escape, however, when the peasant's cow breaks down the gate and makes for home, followed by her companion. The peasant is very thankful to receive this earnest of God's bounty; it was just the reward that had been promised in the sermon! The moral of the story, says Jehan, is that God blesses the man of simple heart who gives his wealth freely:

Non cil qui le muce et enfuet;		Not he who grasps and hides away
Nus hom mouteploier ne puet		For nothing can increase that way
Sanz grant eür, c'est or del mains.		Without great luck: the lot is thrown
Par grant eür ot li vilains	70	And by that luck the peasants own
Deus vaches, et li prestres nule.		Two cows, and the priest has none.
Tels cuide avancier qui recule.		So he that gave, is he that won.[88]

The connections between banking, gaming, and the miraculous efficacy of prayer are explicit: all have the potential to make something out of nothing.

The message of the *Jeu de saint Nicolas* is more equivocal. The prosperity of Arras was the product of overland trade and the textile industry, and the extent of this trade was heavily dependent on the stable currency of Flanders, which regulated the exchange of other currencies flowing through Arras. The job of the moneychangers was to convert the cash of merchants from all over Europe, accepting letters of credit, brokering loans. All of these practices were technically usurious, but they were also essential to the emerging European economy. More controversially, they were the means by which men of low birth could empower themselves. When Guibert spoke ill of the Artesian merchant, he probably had such nouveaux-riches in mind. Philip Augustus's court poet Guillaume le Breton, author of the

---

87. Bloch, *Etymologies*, 165–168 and 173–174. See also Alexander Murray, *Reason and Society in the Middle Ages* (Oxford, 1978), 203, and "Time and Money," in *The Work of Jacques Le Goff and the Challenges of Medieval History*, ed. Miri Rubin (Woodbridge, Suffolk, 1997), 3–25; Diana Wood, *Medieval Economic Thought* (Cambridge, 2002), 69–109 and 159–180; Cowell, *At Play*, 86–99; Baldwin, *Masters*, 1:270–311.

88. Jehan Bodel, "De Brunain," in *Les fabliaux*, 40–41, vv. 1–9.

Philippiad, used the same vocabulary half-admiringly when he hailed Arras as a commercial "leader and prince" (*caput et princeps*) and paid reluctant homage to "Powerful Arras, metropolis ancient, swollen / With riches, grasping for gain and delighting in interest."[89] Some men grew "swollen" indeed. By the close of the thirteenth century, the Crespin family could extend loans of as much as 11,000 livres to a single creditor, in this instance to the town of Bruges, where the heading *Extradatum Attrebati pro usuris* appeared every year in the account books, tracking the payment of accruing interest.[90] In the time of Jehan Bodel, however, usurious activity in Arras was undertaken almost universally and on a more modest scale, with small-time merchants engaging in business speculation or advancing loans in a local climate that created very favorable conditions—in a diocese where even the bishop was involved. Indeed, the example set by Saint Nicholas in many legends could be adduced in support of such activities, and perhaps it often was in local sermons. But this did not alleviate the many anxieties attending the uses of coinage and its debasement, which blended with anxieties about the way these now indispensable practices might also debase society, undermining traditional values and the status of older elites. In other communities these anxieties came to be associated with Jews and could provide an excuse for their persecution; but in Arras, where Jews were rare, the average moneylending Christian embodied this alterity.[91]

The *Jeu de saint Nicolas* reveals that people in Arras, long used to representative government and the representations of writing and playacting, were keenly interested in the uses and limitations of all symbolic representation. A coin is like a word or a gesture or an image or an officer, standing in for something else. But what happens when the coin or the word does not stand for something concrete and true? Then it is like the false money of a bad king, the oath of a deceitful man, the ineffectual idol of a pagan. Conversely, what happens when a coin is both valuable in itself and also, at the same time, symbolic of something else? What if it refers to more than one thing, becoming ambiguous? Then it is like a word with more than one meaning, an actor who is himself and the character he por-

89. "Atrebatum potens, urbs antiquissima, plena / Divitiis, inhians lucris et fenore gaudens." Henri-François Delaborde, ed., *OEuvres de Rigord et Guillaume le Breton* (Paris, 1882), vv. 97 and 94–95.

90. Carlos Wyffels and J. de Smet, eds., *De Rekeningen van de Stad Brugge (1280–1319)*, 2 vols. (Brussels, 1965 and 1971), e.g., 1:69, l. 14 (account for the year 1283/4). In 1299 the entire debt was owing to the Crespins. See also Alain Derville, "La finance arrageoise: Usure et banque," in Castellani and Martin, *Arras*, 37–52.

91. William Chester Jordan, *The French Monarchy and the Jews: From Philip Augustus to the Last Capetians* (Philadelphia, 1989), 22–30, 34–36, and 74–78. According to Robert Chazan, Saint-Quentin was the only Picard town with a Jewish community. There is no record of any permanent Jewish settlement in Arras nor evidence of individual permanent residents: see Chazan, *Medieval Jewry in Northern France: A Political and Soicial History* (Baltimore and London, 1973), 207–220.

trays, the sign of the cross that betokens the sacrifice of Christ and an instrument of torture. A coin, set aside, could earn interest. Another coin, bet on a throw of dice, could attract the coins of other gamesters—or magically disappear. A coin given to a beggar out
of charity could earn a greater reward, just as the peasant's simple gift of a cow earned him
the reward of another cow. Like a miracle, a sacrament, a dice game, a play, usury takes
something familiar or singular and turns it into something exotic or double. A crier could
be himself and a crier in a play. A king could be a foreigner from France and a foreigner
from Outremer. The Town of Arras could be the town in a play. The marketplace could be
a theater.

These are some of the connections and disjunctions explored by Jehan's *jeu*, a "game"
or "play" displaying the full range of *scientia ludorum* catalogued by Hugh of Saint-Victor:
storytelling, puppetry, epic, acting, carousing, gambling, contests of strength, and religious ritual. It is an in-kind examination of medieval theatricality, an investigation of re-
alities and their representations, combined with a lesson in how to tell the difference
when it really matters. Characters like Connart and Raoulet have both feet planted firmly
on the ground of Arras; it is hardly necessary to distinguish between their real function as
criers and their playful function as criers. The Prudhomme, representative of the citizens
of Arras in his official capacity and his dramatic one, remains clear-headed, focused, in-
corruptible, and true to his oath of office even when interacting with supernatural beings:
preudomme et loiau de le chite, as the customary laws of Arras expressed it. (Here, Jehan sends
a clear message to his échevin employers while offering advice on how to deal with their
new king.) The thieves, however, are already divorcing themselves from reality when they
engage in their immoderate and nonsensical gaming, which is both economically and linguistically destructive: play is intended to nourish society at large; it is not an escape from
public life and its responsibilities. Eventually the tricksters must be brought back to the
reality of their situation, and this is accomplished through the businesslike intervention
of a figure whose playful practices are charitable and nurturing: the bishop-saint.

It is this same miraculous intervention that succeeds in rescuing the Prudhomme and
domesticating foreign invaders who have hitherto inhabited a realm very different from
that of Arras, where both money and language are useless. The King must learn to set idolatry aside; he must curb his greed. He must learn that the violent extortion of money is not
as profitable as the care of those men, represented by the Prudhomme of Arras, who oversee its careful investment with the help of their saintly bishop in the hornèd hat. He must
learn that the worship of an image (Tervagan, ill-gotten gains) is not the same as the veneration of a holy symbol (the icon of Saint Nicholas, good fiscal policies). The enactment
of the climatic scene of the play would have made this last point very graphically. As
Michael Camille pointed out, Jehan uses the word *ymage* to describe the icon of Nicholas,
suggesting the two dimensions of a symbolic coin, as opposed to the three-dimensional

simulacrum of the idol Tervagan.[92] In performance, then, Tervagan would have been a mere puppet whose freakish animation evoked the prevailing view of idols as possessed, while the substitution of a stately actor for the image of Saint Nicholas would make the distinction clear: only the heathen mistakes signs for what they signify. For the Christian of Arras, there is a meaning behind every image, backing behind the bond, authority behind the coin, truth behind the word.

The good coin, the word made good, and the good play thus stand for something else, something higher and better: peaceful negotiation, sober authority, healthy community. The only forced convert in the Jeu de saint Nicolas is Outre l'Arbre Sec, the emir who had come to the King's aid empty-handed, because in his country there was no such thing as money or long-distance trade. According to this conservative lord, representative of the violent knights who remained hostile to the economic and political culture of Arras, money poses a threat to the status quo. As he tells his companions, "No one should count on me" (onques ne m'i contés, v. 1477). He means it literally. When compelled to submit to Saint Nicholas and his new economic initiative, he makes no secret of his reluctance: "By words alone I am your man, / In faith I am Mohammedan."[93] He has no intention of trading cumbersome, outmoded tenets for portable, newfangled signs stamped with the device of Arras. His empty oath is immediately echoed by a quatrain of Tervagan's incomprehensible dialect (vv. 1512–15). We are given to understand that, although the foreign invaders have a system of values, even a system of communication, these systems are empty and inadequate. They, too, must be converted to the use of Arras. The god of the King can only laugh or cry; he has no capacity for nuance, no language like that of Picardy.

Two-Part Invention: Medieval French, Modern France

It is both fitting and ironic that the history of the Jeu de saint Nicolas, which has been identified as marking a point of origin for "modern" "French" theater, is the history of the time when Arras itself began to be "French" and France began to be "modern." It is certainly ironic that Philip Augustus, the coiner of the realm of France, the first to style himself rex Franciæ (king of a territory called "France") and not rex Francorum (king of a people called "the Franks"), was notorious for his dislike of jongleurs and their vernacular.[94] The

92. Camille, Gothic Idol, 127–135 at 129–134. Axton and Stevens, Medieval French Plays, translate both words as "statue."

93. "Par parole devieng vostre hom, / Mais la creanche est en Mahom." JsN, vv. 1510–11.

94. Edmond Faral, Les jongleurs en France au Moyen Age (Paris, 1910; reprint, New York, 1970, and Geneva, 1987), 288–289; Baldwin, Government, 358–359 and 365. On the changing terminology of kingship, see Charles T. Wood, "Regnum Francie: A Problem in Capetian Administrative Usage," Traditio 23 (1967): 117–147.

old lord of Arras, Philip of Flanders, had been just the opposite: renowned for his gift of oratory, his command of Latin and *roman*, and his ability to read and write in both. It was his captive Picard that would continue to lend its superior cachet to the consolidation of a national language throughout the transitional thirteenth century, far more so than the Francien of the Île-de-France. Those dialects that tend to achieve the most prestige and widespread utility are those whose written forms develop early and reflect to the greatest degree the spoken norm.[95] The career of Jehan Bodel has already exemplified the extent to which the Picard vernacular was becoming a literary and legal language by the last quarter of the twelfth century, and it had long been a language of devotion and entertainment.[96]

With respect to language as well as to coinage, then, Paris began its ascendancy only after it began to trade upon the stronger currency of Arras. Yet throughout the thirteenth century, the French of Flanders would continue to set the written and performative gold standard against which the French of France would weigh itself. This is demonstrable not only in the volume of "literature" produced in Arras and neighboring border towns but also in the *chic* attaching to the use of Picardisms and Wallonisms in texts produced for audiences elsewhere (Champagne, Paris).[97] Indeed, Gabrielle Spiegel has argued that, in the hands of the beleaguered Flemish nobility who survived the encroachments of 1191–1214, the deployment of the French vernacular would become the chief weapon in a "contest over the past."[98]

Jehan Bodel, a witness to the events of 1191 and their aftermath, if not their eventual outcome, does not appear to have shared this bitter nostalgia. Still, the *Jeu de saint Nicolas* suggests that he was critical of the French king's conduct, which continued to place Arras in the midst of contested territory for the next two decades. At the same time, he faulted the braggart Flemings for their quarrelsome, destructive ways. As Matilda Bruckner has shown, his pastoral poem *Contre le douz tans novel* addresses the renewal of hostilities in August 1199, when Philip was again at war with the count of Flanders and Arras again caught in the middle. Indeed, without the benefit of hindsight provided by the outcome of the battle of Bouvines in 1214, four years after Jehan's death, it would be impossible for contem-

---

95. By contrast, a marked disjunction between written and spoken standards usually results in the development of a collective insecurity. In 1973, for example, a study of the residents of New York City showed overwhelmingly that New Yorkers recognized a significant discrepancy between the "correct," standard usage of English as a language of written record and their own spoken vernacular, expressing distaste and embarassment with respect to their own idiom. See Stanovaïa, "Standardisation," 267; see also Wüest, "Rapport," 215–224. A seminal study is that of Gertrud Wacker, *Über das Verhältnis von Dialekt und Schriftsprache im Alfranzösischen* (Halle, 1916).

96. Berger and Brasseur, *Les séquences*, 25–44.

97. Stanovaïa, "Standardisation," 267.

98. Spiegel, *Romancing*, 272.

poraries to say how the conflict would resolve itself.[99] This may explain why Jehan clothed his critiques in fancy dress. It also indicates that the *Jeu de saint Nicolas* would continue to communicate a topical message for quite some time, and that the avaricious king could be identified with each successive threat to local security. The later addition of the play's prologue, and the incorporation of both in the manuscript anthology of Adam de la Halle's work nearly a century later, thus registers its place in a permanent community repertoire.

But Jehan also did what his fellow Arrageois have been forced to do time and time again: he turned the other cheek and turned his talents to the composition of what he himself called history, working in the tongue that Dante Alighieri would later call that of the smooth and facile "yes": "Since man is a most unstable and changeable animal, his language cannot be lasting or constant, but must vary according to times and places as do other human things such as manners and custom." Therefore, the *langue d'oïl* was the perfect medium for adaptation and translation, "as it is more easy, pleasant, and widely known."[100]

Whoever has the time should listen and attend:	*Qui d'oÿr et d'entendre a loisir ne talent*
Be quiet, and you'll hear a song of worthy men	*Face pais, si escout bonne chançon vaillant*
To which history books witness and guarantee!	*Dont li livre d'estoire sont tesmoing et garant!*
(No subject for the hacks who practice jongleurie:	*Jamais vilains jougleres de cesti ne se vant,*
They wouldn't know just how to say the verse, or sing.) 5	*Car il n'en saroit dire ne les vers ne le chant.*
There are three kinds of tales to compass everything:	*N'en sont que trois materes a nul home vivant:*
Of Britain, and of France, and then of Rome the great.	*De France et de Bretaigne et de Romme la grant;*
But all of these stories do not bear equal weight.	*Ne de ces trois materes n'i a nule samblant*
The tales of Britain, these are empty but pleasing,	*Le conte de Bretaigne si sont vain et plaisant,*
And those of Rome are wise and sensible teachings. 10	*Et cil de Romme sage et de sens aprendant,*

---

99. Matilda Tomaryn Bruckner, "What Short Tale Does Jehan Bodel's Political Pastourelle Tell?" *Romania* 120 (2002): 118–131.

100. Dante Alighieri, *De vulgari eloquentia*, ed. Warman Welliver (Ravenna, 1981), 1.10; trans. Sally Purcell as *Literature in the Vernacular* (Manchester, 1981), 24–26.

But those of France tell of the things seen every day.	*Cil de France sont voir chascun jour aparant.*
From these materials, we keep the best to say	*Et de ces trois materes tieng la plus voir disant:*
That high above the rest, the crown of France is seen,	*La coronne de France doir estre si avant*
Among all other kings, ours always reigns supreme,	*Que tout autre roi doivent estre a li apendant*
Steadfast in Christian faith, created by God's hand. 15	*De la loi crestïenne, qui en Dieu sont creant.*
The king of France that first God caused by His command	*Le premier roi de France fist Diex par son conmant*
The angels bright to crown, in majesty and song,	*Coronner a ses angles dignement en chantent,*
He then made his sergeant, to keep the Earth from wrong,	*Puis li conmanda estre en terre son serjant,*
To hold His justice sure, to keep His law and word,	*Tenir droite justice et sa loi metre avant,*
To put down all his foes with fire and with sword. 20	*Ses anemis grever a l'acier et au brant.*

A few scholars have advanced the theory that the *Chanson des Saisnes* was written in 1198–99, to commemorate the French king's continued campaigns against Flanders.[101] But if we take into account Bruckner's argument, which suggests that Jehan was critical of the king's policy with respect to Flanders, it makes more sense to see it as a response to Philip's military and legal victories over King John of England, who could be said to share some of the Saxon King Guiteclin's characteristics; this would make it a project of Jehan's declining years, after 1202, when he had contracted leprosy and exiled himself. The result was a paean to the king of France and the glory of the French language, a departure in many ways from the forms in which his earlier work is couched, but an expansion of the themes explored in the *Jeu de saint Nicolas.* It was seen by at least one Picard scribe as the companion piece to his poetic leave-taking, alongside which it was copied.[102]

Four years after Jehan's death, the militia of the commune of Arras would find itself ranged alongside the other communes of France, behind the banner of the fleur-de-lys.

101. Roussel, "Notes," 258.

102. Paris, Bibliothèque de l'Arsenal 3142 (see Figure 9), hereinafter cited as Arsenal; Huot, *From Song to Book,* 44 and 95–99.

Georges Duby once said that they were "regrouped by a tripartite society, reassembled in good order, in the respect for hierarchies, to conduct—guided by the king—the war of an avenging God." After Bouvines, he further declared, "nothing more could place in question the prodigious extension of the royal domain" which sealed "the destiny of all the States of Europe."[103] Perhaps. But the undeniable confusion leading up to the battle on July 27, 1214, would pose a very real threat to the fragile borders of the new France as, throughout the preceding month, the army of Flanders camped outside the walls of Aire. Once again, Arras was overrun by foreigners, this time in the shape of former countrymen from Bruges, Ghent, and Ypres, who were sent as hostages for safekeeping to the towns so recently severed from Flanders. We are told that the hastily trained communal militia of Arras fought badly on that day. And no wonder: in the past two decades Philip had preferred to take their money; only now, in this extremity, did he prefer to take their lives.[104]

Back in Arras, however, the townspeople would again distinguish themselves. In the general rejoicing that followed the victory in which they shared, they remodeled the southeastern gate named for Saint Nicholas in honor of their king, whose glorious battlefield lay along that road. Reaching for splendid effect, they ignored the modest example of the relatively recent Latin inscription preserved on a lozenge of limestone inside the next-door Porte de Ronville, which reminded them that the Town's defensive towers had been built "in the time of Philip, the most noble count of Flanders and Vermandois."[105] Visible now, inside the Porte-Saint-Nicolas, was a more voluble tribute: a forty-line encomium in rhymed octosyllabic couplets, displayed on four tablets that were each five meters wide and two meters high. It was prefaced by a few lines of Latin over the outside door, giving the year as A.D. 1214, the name of the master builder as Pierre Labaie, and the name of the hero as "Lord Philip, illustrious King of the Franks." Within the walls, the vernacular verses name the protagonists of the battle and end by noting that it occurred thirty-four years and two months (less two days) after the king's own coronation, as well as 236 years after the battle of Aisnes, when his great ancestor, Hugh Capet, had vanquished Otto, the German emperor. Mindful of the Latin pediment, which labeled this as the gate "which is the way into the city of Arras" for travelers from Flanders (vicus est in civitate Atrebatensi), the French vernacular verses also proclaim that "The Flemish gave him great distress. / But

103. Georges Duby, Les trois ordres: ou, L'imaginaire du féodalisme (Paris, 1978), reprinted in Féodalité (Paris, 1996), 451–825 at 815, and Le dimanche de Bouvines: 27 juillet 1214 (Paris, 1973), 239.

104. Baldwin, Government, 212–213 and 339; Spiegel, Romancing, 47.

105. "Tempore Philippi, nobilissimi Flan / driae et Viroman / diae comitis fun data fuit haec / Turris a magistro/ Wilboteim anno / Domini M.C.LXXX.VI." Auguste Menche de Loisne and Roger Rodière, eds., Épigraphie ancienne de la ville d'Arras et supplement, 2 vols. (Fontenay-le-Comte, 1925), 2:856–857 (no. 2141), hereinafter cited as Épigraphie. "Master Wilbotemus" is elswhere surnamed "Whitetower" (Witrotorrensis) in honor of this achievement (see chapter 3).

God did honor to the King / As to the men he was leading."[106] With such strokes as these of sword and chisel a new Other is called into being, and a fiction of French identity is constructed over a door closed to any challengers. A fatal fiction, for it may have been through this triumphal arch that King Philip's great-grandson, Count Robert II of Artois, marched to his terrible death at the head of a French army bound for the battlefield of Flemish Courtrai in the summer of 1302.

This is the oldest known monumental inscription in the *langue d'oïl*, what a local epigrapher did not hesitate to call "the memorial of our first national victory." (Paradoxically, it was demolished by local government officials in 1891 as part of a modernizing initiative condemned at the time as having been "undertaken with such brutality, such unbelievable, unheard-of stupidity, that it will cause astonishment to future generations.")[107] It is also a monument to the apotheosis of a language characterized by Jehan Bodel as celebrating the greatness of the everyday, a language of the real and realpolitik, the language that made a loose configuration of adjacent territories look like the "unification" of France, the expression of a manifest destiny. As Colette Beaune has observed, "The mystique that began to surround it eventually led people to affirm—against all reality—that French was spoken throughout the kingdom, that the language coincided with the nation"; and Benedict Anderson has noted that emerging vernaculars and other indigenous modes of communication are obviously implicated in the promotion of nationalist projects.[108] But the power of the emerging vernacular in Arras proves that it doesn't require a printing press to publicize the uses of a language—or to manipulate public opinion. At the same time, we see that the canonization of the *Jeu de saint Nicolas* as "French" is the result of a two-part invention and two far-reaching colonial processes: the co-optation of Picardy and its precocious cultural élan by a fledgling "France," and the modern nation's appropriation of the medieval past.

---

106. "Flamenc li fisent maint desroi,/Mais Dieus le Roi tant onora/Que as gens que o lui mena." *Épigraphie* 2:857–859 (no. 2142).

107. *Épigraphie,* 2:857.

108. Colette Beaune, *The Birth of an Ideology: Myths and Symbols of Nation in Late Medieval France,* trans. Susan Ross Huston and ed. Fredric L. Cheyette (Berkeley, 1991), 267; Benedict Anderson, *Imagined Communities: Reflections on the Origins and Spread of Nationalism,* rev. ed. (London, 1991), 37–45.

CHAPTER TWO **PRODIGALS AND**

JONGLEURS INITIATIVE AND AGENCY

IN A THEATER TOWN

Decisive moments in the development of certain communities are, according to Karen Hermassi, "accompanied by the brief flourishing of remarkable drama." Her chosen examples are Athens in the fifth century B.C.E., Elizabethan London, Berlin in the late 1920s and 1930s, and Hollywood in the 1940s and 1950s.[1] The same can be said of Arras in the century after its annexation by Philip Augustus. But why? As I have argued, the visibility of this theater is partially dependent on the availability of technologies for its recording; yet the achievement of "remarkable drama" cannot be reduced to that. Rather, it calls for an understanding of "the social conditions which provoked and called forth these compositions," as Eric Havelock observed when looking into "the crisis that occurred in the history of human communication" which generated the cultural products of classical Greece.[2]

Such an understanding is not easily achieved with respect to ancient Athens or medieval Arras, although in the latter case it has been treated as a relatively straightforward prospect. One scholar has posited that the birth of "French" theater in Arras was the direct result of its becoming "French," which naturally led to "the development of French literature."[3] A pair of economic historians formulate a cultural calculus of supply and demand: as "rich men[,] . . . the townspeople had the leisure to devote to the cultivation of culture. It is not by chance if the banking center of northern France, Arras, was also the preeminent place for la littérature bourgeoise of the thirteenth century."[4] A similar argument made by a literary critic, that "culture rose rapidly" in Arras under the aegis of France and the patronage of the bourgeoisie, presupposes that the implementation of an authoritarian regime and a steady flow of cash are the main ingredients in the creation of art.[5] According to another theory, the emergence of this medieval theater is an entirely un-

1. Karen Hermassi, *Polity and Theater in Historical Perspective* (Berkeley, 1977), x–xi.

2. Eric A. Havelock, *The Muse Learns to Write: Reflections on Orality and Literacy from Antiquity to the Present* (New Haven, 1986), 1 and 127.

3. Pascale Bourgain, "L'emploi de la langue vulgaire dans la littérature au temps de Philippe-Auguste," in Bautier, *La France*, 765–784 at 771 and 783.

4. Carpentier and Le Mené, *La France*, 271. See also Philippe Wolff, "Les villes de France au temps de Philippe Auguste," in Bautier, *La France*, 645–676 at 666.

5. Joseph A. Dane, "Parody and Satire in the Literature of Thirteenth-Century Arras," *Studies in Philology* 81 (1984): 1–27 and 119–144 at 2.

precedented phenomenon, equally distinct from the gyrations of popular culture and the lofty entertainments of the aristocracy.[6] And unfortunately, these reductive explanations are not placed in perspective by the sophisticated scholarship on Middle English theater, which is confined to explaining "community drama, as it emerged in the fifteenth century"—that is, in England.[7] Even Glynne Wickham's respected study of the "total theater" of the Middle Ages posits that the theater of worship will give way to the theater of towns and finally to the "pay-per-view" theater of the playhouse, rather than embracing the coexistence of theatrical variety.[8] More dogmatically, a recent history of "the French theater of the Middle Ages" declares that the rise of "a comic theater born in the thirteenth century," and in Arras, must have eradicated the tedious religious drama which had preceded it, on the grounds that "the appearance of each new [dramatic] form is accompanied by the decline of the other."[9]

These economic, political, and social models are inapplicable to the reality of medieval performance conditions, as well as to the conditions in which performances became part of the written record. In seeking alternatives, we should probably resist the romanticism of the American medievalist Henry Adams, who famously compared the creative powers of "the Virgin and the dynamo," to the disparagement of the latter ("All the steam in the world could not, like the Virgin, build Chartres"); yet it is hard to get around the fact that the making and preservation of medieval art is almost always a collective process.[10] Jehan Bodel and Adam de la Halle bid fair to being among the half-dozen most authoritative figures of their day, but we would know little or nothing about them had it not been for the initiatives of unknown actors, scribes, and audiences. The unusual efflorescence of a medieval theater in Arras is therefore contingent on forms of association far more basic, and thus far more significant, than has usually been supposed. As Susan Reynolds has observed, "Relatively large populations concentrated in relatively small and well-defended areas were peculiarly well-fitted both to maintain old customs and to develop new ones."[11] Community drama in Arras was the natural product of community life in Arras,

6. Payen, "Théâtre," 242–243; Leonard Goldstein, "On the Origin of Medieval Drama," *Zeitschrift für Anglistik und Amerikanistik* 19 (1981): 101–115.

7. Alexandra F. Johnston, "What If No Texts Survived? External Evidence for Early English Drama," in *Contexts for Early English Drama*, ed. Marianne G. Briscoe and John C. Coldewey (Bloomington, 1989), 1–19 at 6; see also Clifford Davidson, "Material Culture, Writing, and Early Drama," in *Material Culture and Medieval Drama* (Kalamazoo, 1999), 1–15.

8. Glynne Wickham, *The Medieval Theater* (London, 1974), 1 and 4.

9. Charles Mazouer, *Le théâtre français du Moyen Âge* (Paris, 1998), 11.

10. Henry Adams, *The Education of Henry Adams* (Boston, 1918; reprint, 2000), 388.

11. Reynolds, *Kingdoms*, 164. See also David Nicholas, "The City as Theater," in *Urban Europe, 1100–1700* (New York, 2003), 167–172; Jehel and Racinet, *La ville médiévale*, 448 ("the city is the mother of the-

reflecting "the ambiguity and fluidity" of a society in which everyone was aware that public roles were bolstered by dramatic representation: authority derived from the adoption of certain manners, purchase of certain commodities, and election to certain offices.[12]

The opportunities and hazards of this society are showcased in the story of *Courtois d'Arras*, and in the contemporary history of the Arrageois jongleurs who would have enacted the plight of Courtois in performance, while at the same time proving themselves capable of developing a corporate identity that successfully challenged the status quo in reality. By the middle of the thirteenth century, thanks to its charismatic mastery of persuasive storytelling, the Carité de Notre Dame des Ardents had established a "lordship" of jongleurs, winning papal approval for the cult of its miraculous relic, founding a prominent chapel in the Petit Marché, and developing an elaborate series of rituals which enabled it to represent everyone in Arras. Its achievements call for a major reevaluation of the roles played by professional entertainers in the construction of medieval communities and explode widespread assumptions about the mutual exclusivity of urban, aristocratic, and popular cultures.

The Courtly Lad of Arras

Four manuscript anthologies preserve four different redactions of *Courtois d'Arras*, an entertainment consisting of some 650 to 700 rhymed verses and described as "The Lay about the Courtly Lad of Arras" (*Li lais de Courtois dArraz*) or, in two cases, the tale "About the Courtly Lad of Arras" (*De Courtois dArraz*) or simply as "Here begins the Courtly Lad of Artois" (*Ci conince de Cortois dArtois*).[13] The only vernacular play of the Middle Ages to have

---

ater"); and Sylvia Thrupp, "The Creativity of Cities: A Review Article," *Comparative Studies in Society and History* 4 (1961–62): 54–64.

12. Fossier, *La terre*, 2:546–582, and "Arras," 20–21. See also Lester K. Little, "Evangelical Poverty, the New Money Economy, and Violence," in *Poverty in the Middle Ages*, ed. David Flood (Werl, Germany, 1975), 11–26 at 13–15.

13. BnF fr. 1553, fols. 498r–501v (649 verses), copied during the second half of the thirteenth century, probably in Arras (the "A" text); BnF fr. 837, fols. 63–66 (708 verses), copied toward the end of the thirteenth century ("B" text); BnF fr. 19152, fols. 82v–85r (678 verses), copied in the latter part of the thirteenth century (the "C" text); and BUP Aldini, fols. 58–62 (655 verses), copied in the fourteenth century ("D" text). For a proposed stemma, see David Robinson, "La tradition manuscrite de 'Courtois d'Arras,'" *Bulletin des jeunes romanistes* 6 (1962): 37–41. See also Knud Togeby, "*Courtois d'Arras*," vol. 11 of *Travaux de linguistique et de la littérature* (Strasbourg, 1973), 603–614; Camille Kennedy Vandeberg, "Authorship Theory: The Case of Courtois d'Arras" (Ph.D diss., University of Illinois at Urbana-Champaign, 1984), 9. In this discussion I refer to the edition prepared by Faral, hereinafter cited as *Courtois*. It is based on the "A" text but takes critical note of variants in the other manuscripts. The edition by Giuseppe Macrì

survived in so many versions, its popularity must surely have owed something to its pliable treatment of a familiar parable whose renewed relevance guaranteed widespread circulation even before *Courtois* was written down for the first time.[14] Bearing witness to this versatility, extant texts preserve several performance traditions, with at least two versions deriving from transcripts made by scribes recalling or listening to live performances. This helps to explain why most of the information required for the enactment of *Courtois* is encoded in the dialogue itself; only occasionally are exchanges between characters supplemented with narrative verse in the scripts that were eventually copied, none of which makes any attempt to apportion lines to speakers or even to name the dramatis personae. Performers were expected to extract such information from context, adapting the play to changing needs and circumstances.

Predictably, though, what is flexible in the manuscripts becomes fixed in modern editions. These convey the false impression that *Courtois* is actually laid out like a modern play, scripted for a certain number of characters, and allegedly different from the hundreds of fabliaux and verse tales of analogous length and style alongside which it appears in its four anthologies. Nor is this fiction the result of passive editorial policy. In the edition of *Courtois* published in 1995, stage directions added to the modern French translation are retroactively rendered into Old French and inserted into the "original" text, encouraging readers to suppose that they are indigenous to the manuscripts. The editor does not mention these interventions in his introduction or in the apparatus accompanying the play. Instead, he claims "to reproduce very faithfully" the manuscript selected as his base text, while at the same time asserting, paradoxically, that "our primordial principles have been exactitude and modernity."[15]

It is precisely such covert and overt falsifications of medieval plays' "modern" appearance that have fed the narrow conceptualization of a medieval theater by imposing artificial restrictions on its sources. *Courtois* is certainly an exceptionally attractive play, but it is not exceptional as a play. It is one of a great many pieces performed during the thirteenth century in Arras and elsewhere, couched in a variety of forms but sharing many of the same functions, audiences, and enactors. This is why all of its scribes have juxtaposed it with

---

is based on the "C" text: Li *"Lais de courtois," commedia francese del secolo XIII* (Lecce, 1977). I cannot recommend the edition and modern French translation of Jean Dufournet, *Courtois d'Arras: L'enfant prodigue* (Paris, 1995), based on the "B" text, for reasons given in this chapter. There is an English translation by Axton and Stevens in *Medieval French Plays*, 141–163; and another (quirky and pleasing) by Genty de Creky, *Courtois of Arras: The Best Seller of the 13th Century, for the First Time in English* (Chicago, 1959).

14. See Gerald B. Guest, "The Prodigal's Journey: Ideologies of Self and City in the Gothic Cathedral," *Speculum* 81 (2006): 35–75; and Nicole Bériou, *L'avènement des maitres de la Parole: La prédication à Paris au XIIIe siècles* (Paris), 477–489.

15. Dufournet, *Courtois d'Arras*, 32. Dufournet's treatment of *Le garçon et l'aveugle* is similarly problematic.

an assortment of related entertainments, and why one of them called it a "lay"—a ballad, a short story in verse. Like all such pieces, it could be adapted for one or more performers. Its interest for us is both general and specific. Generally, it is highly representative of some of the common conventions of a medieval theater. Specifically, it exemplifies the sort of play composed and performed by jongleurs in Arras, as well as the sort of play that could be exported from Arras and performed for French-speaking audiences all over Europe, audiences whose conceptions of Arras—twinned with the sinful city of a biblical parable— would have been conditioned by its representation of life in that metropolis.[16]

In the opening lines of *Courtois d'Arras*, a hardworking father is urging his son to wake up and begin the day's work. The son protests that he's already exhausted by his labors and complains that his younger brother hardly has to do anything at all. "You've taken me to be your serf" (*moi prendes com le vostre sierf*, v. 14), he says. "My brother, though, has a good deal" (*mais mes frere en a bon marciet*, v. 17):

Bien a son tans et son meriel		He has the time, he has the price,
qui boit et jue au tremeriel	26	To drink and play the day at dice—
chou ke nous gaagnons andui!		With everything we earn, we two!

His grievance goes beyond sibling rivalry. It hints at a larger conflict between an old way of life, in which the paterfamilias is within his rights to treat a son as an unfree laborer and can expect him to remain on the land, and a newly available lifestyle of immediate gratification that makes these customs unpalatable and unenforceable. The elder son represents a value system that is potentially endangered by the town and its effects on the behavior of young men like his brother. Perhaps he expects the entire patrimony to come to him intact. He is certainly conservative in his adherence to tradition, swearing "By the faith I owe to you, *mon père*" (*Foi ke doi vouis qui mon pere estes*, v. 23), and not disparaging the heaviness of the work so much as the injustice of his father's double standard and the waste of hard-earned profits. Describing his younger brother's profligate pastimes, the elder even uses a term with specific meaning to contemporary audiences in Arras, *tremerel*, the word for games of chance that were subject to regulation by the échevins of the Town, according to Philip Augustus's charter of 1194.

The father's lame response reveals that he actually shares these concerns but is puzzled by the way the world is changing and powerless to reverse the effects of those changes on his younger son. The errant lad in question now enters the conversation (whether or not he has witnessed the preceding exchange is one of the choices left open to perform-

16. The parable is never mentioned explicitly, but the parallels are obvious. See Pierre Groult, "La drame biblique dans 'Courtois d'Arras,'" in *Mélanges Cohen*, 47–53; W. Kreutzer, "Zum Verständnis des *Courtois d'Arras*," *Vox romanica* 33 (1974): 214–233; and Pascale Dumont, "La perception de l'espace et du temps dans *Courtois d'Arras* et dans la *Moralité de l'enfant prodigue par personnages*," in Castellani and Martin, *Arras*, 175–195.

ers) and announces his intention of leaving the homestead. He also demands his share of the property, and in sound coin:

sec argent nes priseroit nus.		Hard cash is all they take these days.
Donés moi en deniers menus	47	So pay me in those small deniers
mains ke ma partie ne vaille		A part of what is owed to me.

In two versions of the script he uses the up-to-date fiscal terminology of the day, insolently telling his father to treat him as if he were a bailiff come to collect a debt (*Baillez moi*).[17] In all versions, he stipulates that he'll take only the petits deniers of Arras so prized by Jehan Bodel's fictional King and his real-life alter ego, the king of France. The very fact that the younger son expects to have a share of the property shows that he may have different ideas about its division than his elder brother. This difference may be an indicator of the difference in their ages, or of the fact that (in one version of the lay) they are the sons of different mothers and therefore stand to inherit different portions. In any case, a thirteenth-century audience would have recognized this scene as a dramatization of two related contemporary debates: over the disposition of property through partible inheritance versus primogeniture, and over the advantages and ethics of investing liquid capital in speculation or trade versus real estate—the latter being a direct consequence of the new money economy.

Yet it soon becomes clear that the family of *Courtois* are not members of the landed nobility, bent on consolidating wealth by bestowing it on the eldest son while relegating dispossessed cadets to ecclesiastical or military careers. They are small farmers, not the sort of people who have much to do with money, and not the sort to keep much in the house. The father protests that his wealth is vested in land, not in silver. At last, however, he is persuaded to part with all sixty sous in the family purse, delivering a lecture on urban chicanery—"The times are bad and out of joint" (*s'est li siecles del et repoins*, v. 73)—to which the son retorts, "At 'Hasard,' Dad, and at 'More Points' / I know just what it takes to win" (*Pere, a hasart et a plus poins / sai jou trestoute la queriele*, vv. 74–75). Setting himself up for disaster (Hasard was the tricky dice game played by the thieves of the *Jeu de saint Nicolas*), he boasts that those meager sixty sous will be more profitable, in his hands, than all the hundred marks of silver in the treasury of Girart Lenoir, known to audiences in Arras as a wealthy member of the commune's échevinage. (He was also a member of the jongleurs' Carité, and the separate funerary registers kept by the confraternity and the cathedral of Notre-Dame show that he died in April 1228, establishing a *terminus ante quem* for the composition of this play.)[18] Clearly, the alluring possibilities of instant financial success ex-

17. "B" and "D" texts; *Courtois*, 24.

18. Adolphe Guesnon, "Publications nouvelles sur les trouvères artésiens," MA 21 (1908): 57–86 at 61; Berger, *Le nécrologe*, 1:122.

plored in the *Jeu de saint Nicolas* are still very much in vogue, and the young man's analogy between his own prospects of luck at the gaming table and the potential gains of shrewd investment suggests that these activities are considered by some to be similar. Indeed, there are many ways in which *Courtois d'Arras* looks like a direct response to the *Jeu de saint Nicolas*, to the extent that the character Courtois exemplifies the sort of person who might have been prone, on witnessing a performance of Jehan's play, to boil its sophisticated message down to a simple equation. After all, the gambling thieves were saved too, weren't they? And if a bishop-saint can make money magically appear, doesn't that sanctify the talents of all those who turn a profit?

At this point in the action, one version of the play includes an additional scene.[19] Just as the father is bidding his son farewell, their parting is delayed by the lamentations of the youth's sister, who chides her father for driving him from the house. She alleges that his departure is a triumph for her older brother, who has been trying to get rid of his younger rival while at the same time attempting to turn her father against her mother and herself. This glimpse of domestic dysfunction complicates the picture of filial piety drawn by the elder son and represents a response to another issue that was pressing at the time, and may have been of special interest to certain audiences in the later thirteenth century, when this particular manuscript was copied, probably in or around Paris: the political and economic struggles precipitated by remarriage in an era when female mortality was high during childbearing years, and when a second (younger) wife and her children might well feel threatened by the older children of a previous marriage. Of course, conflict could also be engendered by the remarriage of a young widow with children of her own. Indeed, the jealousy between new spouses and their stepchildren had already been enshrined as normative in one of the most important cultural monuments of the day, the *Chanson de Roland*, in the enmity of Roland and his stepfather, Ganelon. With respect to this crisis, too, the father of *Courtois* shows himself unable to cope. He merely protests, weakly, that his younger son will never be kept down on the farm until he has seen Arras.

So, in all versions of the play, the young man takes to the high road, his purse full of coins and his head full of plans—thoughts to which a few lines of narrative make us privy before the lad voices his desire for a meal and some conviviality. Enter a boy signaling that the scene has shifted to Arras: he is advertising good wine from Soissons, good fare, good company, and plenty of good credit. In the ensuing scene, *Courtois* presents a scenario conforming in almost every respect to reality. Later statutes regulating trade in urban hostelries stipulate that innkeepers and their servants were forbidden (and thus apt) to go out into the streets and grab the bridles of passers-by, or to trick travelers into lodging in the wrong place if they were lost and looking for a different address, or to steal away a client

19. Recorded in the "B" text, BnF fr. 837, and incorporated into the edition of Dufournet. See Faral's edition for a list of variants (*Courtois*, 24–25).

who had already alighted at another doorway, or to run rackets that drove up the tally on the customer's tab, and so on. Prostitution, moreover, was so commonly accepted as to be subject to regulation, and many inns doubled as brothels.[20] Furthermore, the location and distribution of hostelries in major towns shows that many were clustered near main gates, so as to better provide for (and lure) passers-by.

Hence, it would have come as no surprise to contemporary audiences that a greenhorn would be collared by a huckster immediately on arrival at the gates of Arras, or that part of the hard sell would involve special mention of two obliging young women, Manchevaire and Porette:

qui caiens mangüent et boivent		They eat and drink here on account,
et s'acroient qanqu'eles doivent	112	And everything they do will count:
n'en paient vaillent un festu		No need to pay a cent up front.

With striking naïveté, the lad gives thanks for the good fortune that has brought him to a place where so many goods are to be had for what seems so little:

Por faire a l'oste escrit et taille.		—Just give the host a written chit?!
Mout est fols ki assés n'acroit.	123	They're fools who won't give lots of those.
Or Dieus i viegne et Dieus i soit!		From God it comes, to God it goes!
Caiens fait plus biel k'an mostier.		This place is fairer than a church.

He quickly establishes himself among the clients of what is called, in one version of the play, an *ostel d'amoretes*, a "lovers' hostel" or "no-tell motel," where he begins to run up a large tab.[21] Soon, he falls into conversation with the two hussies, whom he mistakes for elegant ladies. Manchevaire's elaborate "green" or "furry" (*vaire*) sleeves (*manche*) suggest a brand of cheap finery to be had in commercial centers like Arras, where the elision of social distinctions was facilitated by the availability of luxury goods and affordable knockoffs. A resident of the town would not have been so easily fooled; but to a boy from the country, the hostel's provisions and habitués present the sumptuous appearance of the courts described in chivalric romance, where beautiful, well-dressed women are always on hand to serve the wandering knight, and frequently vie for his attention.

This is how the lad comes to call himself "courtly." In the course of his flirtation, he reveals himself to be from the Artois—but then declares, with poetic haste, that his name is really "Courtois," so as not to be mistaken for a rube.[22] This portion of the dialogue is

20. N. Coulet, "Les hôtelleries en France et en Italie au Bas Moyen Age," and J.-L. Auduc, "Bapaume: Un carrefour routier aux XIIIe et XIVe siècles," in *L'homme et la route en Europe occidentale au Moyen Age et aux temps modernes* (Auch, 1982), 181–205 and 241–254, respectively.

21. "B" text, l. 137; *Courtois*, 26.

22. Later in the play the lad will also introduce himself as "Courtois" to the prudhomme who gives

worth quoting at length, to convey a sense of how quickly and naturalistically the banter is rendered, and to show how much freedom of interpretation is given to the performer(s).

Entreus que cil fait li vin traire,		So while the lad drinks up his share
Entre Porrete et Mancevaire,		Enter Porrete and Manchevaire
Que se seoient les a les,		Who, sitting by him, side by side,
Li dient: Demoisiaus, beves!	150	Say: Drink, good sir! Yes, open wide!
Que Dieu beneie tes ieus!		God bless you and your handsome eyes!
Le remenans en vaura mieus,		What's left will taste like quite a prize
Se cil biel dent et cele bouche		When such good teeth and such a mouth
A no hanap adese et touche.		Have kissed the wine that we pour out.
Ja sambles cous de nostre gent.	155	You seem to know our ways so well.
Beves a cest hanap d'argent.		Drink now from silver: you're a swell.
Encor est chis los tous entiers.		This cask has just been tapped for you.
Ma demoisiele, volontiers,		Thanks, mistress: don't mind if I do,
Car feme ne hai jou onques.		For wine and women are good fare.
Ha! frere, car vous sees donques.	160	Now, darling, you just sit right there.
Dont estes vous. Je sui d'Artois.		Where are you from? I'm from Artois.
Conment aves vous non? Courtois.		And what's your name, then, love? Courtois.
Courtois voire, ma douce amie.		Courtois by name and nature, dear.
Ciertes vilains ne sambles mie;	165	You're not a peasant, that is clear!
Ains croi bien en mon cuer et pens		My heart and head say the same thing:
Q'an vous ait cortoisie et sens.		You're not just clever, good-looking—
Car pleust or a saint Remi		I wish to God (Saint Rémy, too)
Que j'eusse ausi bel ami!		I had a boyfriend just like you!
Par un convent, ne rois ne quens	170	I'll bet there's neither king nor count
N'orent onques tant de lor boens		Has anything like the amount
Com vous aries sans oevre fair.		Of money that you've stashed in there.
Di jou voir, dame Mancevaire?		What's your opinion, Manchevaire?
Oil certes, dame Porrete;		Oh, I agree with you, Porrete!
Bien li saries sorre se dete,	175	Here's a man who pays his debts
Et reubes et ronchis livrer,		And keep his clothes and horse from pawn
Mais k'il se gardast de juer.		Unless he gambles until dawn—
Chi n'afiert nus lons serventois.		But don't let me lay down the law!
Porrete, entre vous et Cortois		You know, Porette, you and Courtois
Avenries mout bien per a per.	180	Now that I look, look quite a pair.
Or, Manchevaire, del gaber!		Ho, now you're talking, Manchevaire!

---

him employment, but in only one manuscript—the "A" text from Arras—is he called "Courtois" by his father (v. 626). Elsewhere, he seems to invent the name himself, in the tavern.

Encore soie jo or tous seus,		Now that you mention it, we do;
Ne puis jou pas entre vous deus?		So can I sit between you two?
Mais je tieng pore fole ki cuide		I think a man could not do worse
Que je parole a borse vuide;	185	Than boast about an empty purse.
Ains a chaiens auchune chose.		I have a few pigs in this poke.
Cortois, chou n'est mie falose:		Courtois, you know it was no joke.
Je connois li tant ce ses mours		I've seen the way she looks at you
Qu'ele vous ainme par amours.		She really is in love; it's true.

Eventually tricked into giving and gaming away all his money—a lengthy process that accounts for over half of the tale's scripted lines and foreshadows the drawn-out humiliation of protagonists in the morality plays of the fifteenth century—the soi-disant Courtois is thrown into the street.

There he laments his fate in a soliloquy composed of five alexandrine quatrains, a loftier register than the octosyllabic verse in which the rest of the lay is couched, and the signal that religious conversion is beginning. Ultimately, he is saved from destitution by a virtuous man of the town, called a "prudhomme" in one version,[23] who inquires into the state of his affairs, reminds him that he still has everything that really matters—life, youth, health—and offers him modest employment as a swineherd. This is Fortune's coup de grâce, since keeping swine had been one of the tasks the lad had shunned at home. Humbly taking up this new and lowlier status, he thus undergoes another transformation, from "courtly" pretender to social outcast. His new employer even gives him a *machue*, a roughly fashioned club usually associated with wild men or lunatics, "So you'll look fit for your new job" (*si sanleras mieus del mestier*, v. 481).

Relieving his varied feelings in a speech whose length—over a hundred lines—marks the passage of time, Courtois renounces his errant ways and returns to the countryside. Of course, he throws himself at his father's feet and receives an enthusiastic welcome. Also true to form, his elder brother is displeased with this turn of events, even professing to mistake his brother for one of the beggars habitually sheltered through his father's misdirected generosity. But in the end, the father has his say, quoting the words of his biblical counterpart in the parable of the Prodigal Son:

Por amor Dieu, biaus fieus, ne dire!		For God's love, my fair son, don't chide!
Cil est en la fin bien prové:	643	The outcome is what matters most:
ne li doit estre reprové.		My son is found, who once was lost.
Dont n'est cho molt grant aventure?		Is not this, then, a happy day?
Damedieus, cho dist en l'Escripture		In Scripture, our Lord God did say,

23. "B" text; *Courtois*, 29. Dufournet adopts this term as a character designation in his version.

fair d'un pecheor gregnor joie,		There's more joy for the sinning lamb
quant il se connnoist et ravoie,		Who strays and finds the path for home
que des autres nonate nuef.		Than for the ninety-nine there safe.
bien en devons tuer no buef	650	So let's go kill our only calf
de joie k'il est revenus.		For joy that he's come back to us,
Chantons Te Deum laudamus.		And sing Te Deum laudamus.

This final, direct reference to the parable of the Lost Sheep (Luke 15:3–7), which prefaces that of the Prodigal Son in Luke's Gospel (Luke 15:11–32), dispels any lingering doubt as to the play's pious sources. A skeptical viewer, however, might well conclude that the biblical message is a mere pretext for the elaborate display of comic vice in the central tavern scene, or for the airing of contemporary controversies over portable wealth, social mobility, and other ills.

There are obvious differences between the *Jeu de saint Nicolas* and *Courtois d'Arras*. Not least of these is length. Jehan's play is twice as long as the longest text of *Courtois*, not counting the prologue, and would require nearly two hours' playing time and a large cast, with a dozen or so speaking parts, as well as a playing space large enough to accommodate a virtual universe. Any production of *Courtois d'Arras* would make far fewer dramaturgical demands, but it would probably make more obvious demands for money. This is not a play composed for a particular audience at a historical crossroads but a play designed by professionals for repeat performance. Its economic and political underpinnings, while topical, require no specialized knowledge and no acquaintance with local affairs. The allusion to an Arrageois miser could be left out or replaced by an allusion appropriate to each performance venue; Picardisms, such as the use of the term *tremerel*, could be dropped, though their meaning is clear enough in context. The play is easily translated, in every sense. It is brief, and could be performed in under an hour; it could also be cut down to less than that, if time were short. It requires only one skillful performer for an effective, bravura presentation; a full enactment could be done with as few as three or four actors. It requires no changes of scene: *Courtois* need only walk across or around the playing area to signal the lapse of time and his arrival in a new place. If it were played in the vicinity of a real tavern—the central setting for the majority of the play—it would not even require any special furnishings or props. Unlike the *Jeu de saint Nicolas*, it is adaptable. The sheer number of available copies, and the differences among them, offer further proof of this: one did not even need a script; hence the contrast between the sole, specialized manuscript of Jehan's play and the four manuscript anthologies preserving *Courtois*, copied alongside samples of the jongleur's stock-in-trade and the crowd-pleasing *exempla* of mendicant preachers, all of which would have been indistinguishable from it in performance. The variability of *Courtois* even extends to its message. Its tacit relationship with a biblical parable need not have been emphasized, but its religious and moral import could have been heightened were it performed in or under the auspices of a church or framed by appropriate evangelical remarks delivered to a holiday crowd in the marketplace.

In short, *Courtois* is not situated in Arras, like *Jeu de saint Nicolas*; rather, it evokes an Arras synonymous with "a newly prominent and newly dominant set of values," to quote Charles Muscatine's description of the fabliaux, symbolizing the potential for self-invention brought about by new economic structures and the relative freedom of new political agents.[24] Yet it also reinforces and extends some of the same lessons. Perhaps most significantly, both plays concern themselves with the ethics of representation in a medieval theater that was an extension of urban reality. We have already seen how this plays out in the *Jeu de saint Nicolas. Courtois* confronts us with more concrete lessons in the personal pitfalls of playacting, the boundaries imposed on self-determination, and the deceits of daily interaction. The Prodigal's first breaths of free town air, his first acquaintance with the intoxicating experience of changing his name, clothing, and manners, are trumped by the more potent deceits practiced by other empowered individuals who know better how the game is played. In town, a few marks made on a slip of parchment may stand for a huge debt, and habits of dress conceal more than they reveal. Mobility and its consequent anonymity may give a man an initial boost by allowing him to adopt any identity he chooses, but this new identity will require constant discursive and material reinforcement, or the Wheel of Fortune will turn and precipitate his downfall. It is but a short descent from the player's *folie* to the madman's *folie*, from the social minefield of the town to the social wilderness of the disenfranchised urban poor who have no means to pay for the trappings of power and no place in the traditional hierarchy of the countryside. The limited power of artifice is therefore captured in the ineffectual performance of a hapless everyman whose story exemplifies the experiences and anxieties common to urban audiences everywhere. But in Arras itself, the performance of a confraternity of jongleurs illustrates a more unusual phenomenon: the extent to which this power could be harnessed by those whose only assets were a measure of geographic mobility, political independence, and social savoir-faire.

The Jongleurs' Miracle

The average jongleur was accustomed to making the best of a poor tale, a poor crowd, or a poor day's takings. He was also accustomed to vilifications, the victim of stereotypes that included Courtois's temporary role of madman and social outcast. It was a commonplace of medieval theology that jongleurs could not hope to be saved; nor was the entertainer's profession deemed one of the *métiers* necessary to society, even though contemporary theorists approved many other illicit trades. The views of the venomous

---

24. Charles Muscatine, *The Old French Fabliaux* (New Haven, 1986), 152.

Thomas of Chobham (ca. 1160–1233/6) are usually taken as paradigmatic: while differentiating among three species of actors, some of whom could sing nobly of princes and saints, in his heart and his manual for confessors he damned them all equally, those transformers and transfigurers of their bodies, those tellers of jokes and purveyors of lies, those players in fantasy and falsehood who seem what they are not. As John Baldwin has observed, anxiety over the "corporeality of the entertainment profession" was emphasized in most official condemnations of the jongleur's art, the canonists drawing parallels between the unseemliness of their distortions and the tricks of prostitutes, the only difference being that the prostitute's profession was said to be necessary to the sexual health of men and thus to society at large.[25]

These old allegations, which can be traced back to Stoic condemnations of Roman mimes, were only slightly tempered by an opposing set of theological metaphors, initiated by Saint Paul and embraced by Saint Francis, which enjoined Christians to be fools for Christ.[26] Much more frequently, the feigned folly of the jongleur and the unchecked folly of the maniac were conflated. Historiated initials of Psalm 52[53], *Dixit insipiens in corde suo*—"The fool has said in his heart, there is no God"—often feature a composite portrait of the professional fool, a jongleur, and the pathological fool, a madman, in conversation with Satan (Figure 11). The negative iconography of folly was rich: fools could be bald, like imbeciles or heretics shorn for penance (as in this image), or as hairy as wild men in the forest. In the thirteenth century they were often shown wearing distinctive headgear, the baubled cap (*burel* or *bura*) of the jongleur calling to mind the "fool's cap" of the idiot, the pointed hat of the Jew, or the bishop's miter, which was compared to a coxcomb in the *Jeu de saint Nicolas*. These crazy fools brandished clubs or, in place of them, the *marotte* or puppet scepter of the jester. They carried tabors (drums) or, in place of them, rounds of cheese, an unwholesome food associated with peasants and lunatics.[27] Their

25. See John Baldwin, "The Image of the Jongleur in Northern France around 1200," *Speculum* 72 (1997): 635–663, and *Masters*, 1:58 and 198–204. See also Faral, *Les jongleurs*, 67–70; and Michel Rousse, "Le théâtre et les jongleurs," in *Naissances du théâtre français (XIIe–XIIIe siècles)*, ed. Jean Dufournet in *Revue des langues romanes* 95 (1991): 1–14 at 3–4.

26. 1 Corinthians 1:25: "Quia quod stultum est Dei, sapientius est hominibus: et quod infirmum est Dei, fortius est hominibus." See Claude Blum, "La folie et la mort dans l'imaginaire collectif du moyen age et au début de la Renaissance (XIIe–XVe siècles): Positions du problème," in *Death in the Middle Ages*, ed. Herman Braet and Werner Verbeke (Leuven, 1985), 258–285 at 264; and Sylvia Huot, *Madness in Medieval French Literature: Identities Found and Lost* (Oxford, 2003), 17–19. See also Jean-Claude Schmitt, *La raison des gestes dans l'Occident médiévale* (Paris, 1990), 266–273.

27. William Willeford, *The Fool and His Sceptre: A Study in Clowns and Jesters and Their Audience* ([Evanston], 1969); Philippe Ménard, "Les emblèmes de la folie dans la littérature et dans l'art (XIIe–XIIIe siècles)," in *Hommage à Jean-Charles Payen. Farai chansoneta novele: Essais sur la liberté créatrice du Moyen Age*, ed. Jean-Louis Becker et al. (Caen, 1989), 253–265, and "Les fous dans la société médiévale: Le témoignage

ixic insipiens in
corde suo: non est
deus.
Corrupti sunt
et abhominabi
les facti sunt in
iniquitatibus:
non est qui fac
iat bonum.
Deus de celo prospexit super filios homi
num: ut videat si est intelligens aut re
quirens deum.
Omnes declinauerunt simul inutiles
facti sunt: non est qui faciat bonum non
est usqz ad unum.
Nonne scient omnes qui operantur ini
quitatem: qui deuorant plebem meam
ut cibum panis.
Dominum non inuocauerunt illic
trepidauerunt timore: ubi non fuit

FIGURE 11. "The fool has said in his heart, there is no God": historiated initial from a thirteenth-
century Psalter (BnF lat. 1328, fol. 69r)

FIGURE 12. The miracle of the Sainte-Chandelle: historiated initial "E" from a thirteenth-century collection of saints' lives and Bible stories in Francien prose (BnF fr. 17229, fol. 352v: detail)

appetites and accoutrements were not merely outward signs of degeneracy, occasionally feigned for spectators; they were perpetually concealed within, like cancer. *Li fols qui est pleins de folie / Dist en son cuer que Diex nest mie,* began a contemporary Picard translation of the Psalm: "The fool, who is full of folly, / Says in his heart: God cannot be."

de la littérature au XIIe et au XIIIe siècle," *Romania* 98 (1977): 433–459. See also Maurice Lever, *Le sceptre et la marotte: Histoire des fous de cour* (Paris, 1983), especially 9 and 42; Monique Santucci, "Le fou dans les lettres françaises médiévales," *Les lettres romanes* 35 (1982): 195–211; Jean-Marie Fritz, *Le discours du fou au moyen âge, XIIe–XIIIe siècles: Étude comparée des discours littéraire, médical, juridique et théologique de la folie* (Paris, 1992), 56–59 and 321–339. See also the excellent illustrations reproduced by Muriel Laharie, *La folie au moyen âge, XIe–XIIIe siècles* (Paris, 1991).

When the jongleurs of Arras formed a brotherhood and insisted that "it was not founded for lechery, or for folly," this is the image against which they opposed themselves. Although odious comparisons between real and artful folly would continue to plague them individually, and are also showcased in the *Jeu de la feulliée*, the respectability—indeed, the spiritual superiority—of their confraternity in Arras shows how little this propaganda mattered in reality. As usual, the frequency and vehemence of ecclesiastical censure is an excellent indicator of lively praxis—a rule of thumb conveniently ignored by those painting a sinister portrait of the medieval Church and its oppressive effects on a medieval theater. When asked "What is a jongleur?" it is more likely that those who made up the professional entertainer's audience (that is, nearly everyone) would have cited some of the characteristics later articulated by Edmond Faral, when he posed that question in 1910:

> A jongleur is a being of multiple personalities: a musician, poet, actor, mountebank; a sort of steward for the pleasures associated with the courts of kings and princes; a vagabond who wanders the roads and puts up shows in the villages; a hurdy-gurdy man who, at a resting place, sings of glorious deeds for the pilgrims; a charlatan who amuses the crowd at the crossroads; an author and actor of plays played on feast days outside the church; a lord of the dance who makes the young people caper and skip; a taborer, a blower of trumpet and horn who keeps time in processions; a teller of tales, a bard who enlivens the feast, the wedding, the watches of the night; a circus rider who vaults onto the backs of horses; an acrobat who dances on his hands, who juggles with knives, who jumps through hoops, who eats fire, who bends himself back in two; a buffoon who struts and mimics; a clown who plays the fool and speaks blarney; a jongleur is all that, and more besides.[28]

Of course, no one could be master of so many skills or practice them all at once. Faral's point is that the professional entertainer's livelihood depended on his willingness to be all things to all people. Not unlike many struggling entertainers today, a medieval jongleur would hold a variety of temporary jobs, working as a servant in the houses of the wealthy when he was not entertaining there, acting as a herald or messenger, or even as a clerk or military attaché; working in the towns where he also performed on street corners and in the market square, as a crier, notary, or huckster; or traveling from place to place, begging for food and doing odd jobs when he could not earn enough money passing the hat. It was a hard life, and it could earn a bad reputation: anyone who was constantly on the move, constantly changing employment, perpetually versatile, lordless and therefore (in a technical sense) lawless, could be an object of mistrust as well as a source of novelty and delight.

28. Faral, *Les jongleurs*, 1.

This is one reason why so much of the anecdotal evidence relating to the status of performers in the Middle Ages is perjorative. The other reason has to do with the other side
of the coin: the itinerant's mobility and rootlessness translated, very often, into personal
mobility and classlessness. Jugglers—jongleurs—crossed all boundaries, territorial and
political, cultural and social. The analogous careers followed by another group of outsiders, the bureaucrats known as *ministeriales*, show that even the humblest could outstrip
men of rank if they were clever enough. Minstrels, like ministers, often began as unfree
hangers-on in the entourages of the powerful, only to become powerful in their own right
through the use of their wits.[29] Hidden behind the theologians' anxieties about acting or
the lawyers' legislation against deviants is the fact that jongleurs had a knack for evading
the censors.

Craftily, the confraternity of jongleurs in Arras was founded on the jongleurs' art of storytelling, via the artful tale of a miracle, which held the negative stereotype of their profession up to scrutiny before turning it on its head. It stressed the importance of its
founders' stigmatization, the better to advertise their ability to act as intermediaries
among different groups of people; acknowledged the variety of their talents, translating
them into a capacity to communicate effectively; celebrated the indeterminacy of their status, making them representative of everyone; admitted their proximity to the "natural"
state of the fool, which rendered them piously receptive to the call of the divine; even disclosed their unsavory criminal pasts, the better to emphasize their rebirths as lawgivers
and lords. In fact, the cunning of their miracle narrative is part of the miracle, as wondrous
in its workings as the effects of the stories told by the minstrels who had brought the miracle about. The tale was probably composed in the third quarter of the twelfth century; an
official redaction in Latin prose was eventually transcribed in a charter drawn up in May
1241 and destined for the papal curia, which was monitoring the claims of local cults
closely during this period.[30] Corroborating it is a slightly expanded vernacular version of

29. Benjamin Arnold, "Instruments of Power: The Profile and Profession of *Ministeriales* within German Aristocratic Society, 1050–1225," in Bisson, *Cultures*, 36–55 at 40. See also Martin Aurell, *La vielle
et l'épée: Troubadours et politique en Provence au XIIIe siècle* (Paris, 1989); Page, "Court and City," 197–202 and
208.

30. The original does not survive, but it was authenticated by a *vidimus* of 1482 (also lost), transcribed
by Philip Thieulaine in 1625. (The inventory of François-Xavier Desmazières suggests that both of these
charters were still extant in 1770.) The early date of 1133 assigned to the Latin text by antiquarians is
based on the claims of later forgeries: e.g., Louis Cavrois, *Cartulaire de Notre-Dame-des-Ardents à Arras* (Arras, 1876), 91; Paul Chevallot, ed., *Notre-Dame des ardents d'Arras: Faits et documents* (Abbéville, 1918), 330–
331. Berger dates it between 1175 and 1200; Berger, *Le nécrologe*, 2:25, 41–46, and 137–140. Some have
conjectured that the legend was cobbled together using elements drawn from the *Miracles de Notre Dame*
of Gautier de Coincy, notably his retelling of the Virgin's cure of the *mal des ardents* and the legend *Dou
cierge qui descendi au jougleour*, told of a minstrel at Rocamadour; see Gautier de Coincy, *Les miracles de Nos-*

the same story, reflecting the traditions of the confraternity as they had developed by the first decade of the thirteenth century. It survives in a Francien translation included in a compilation of New Testament stories and popular saints' lives copied in the second half of the thirteenth century.[31]

"These miracles have been in Latin a long time. Now they have been translated into romance so that laypeople can understand them better."[32] This direct address to a popular audience, and the inclusion of the legend in a non-Picard anthology, constitute the first of many indicators that the jongleurs' story, like that of Courtois, was known well beyond Arras.[33] Its place in the Parisian codex also demonstrates that it had liturgical and didactic functions, since all of the texts alongside which it is copied were scripted for performance. Hence the legend of Saint Catherine, just above it, ends with the reader's resounding "Amen," while the story "About the Candle of Arras" begins with an invocation, "In the name of the Father and the Son and the Holy Spirit, say each and every one, Amen" (De la chandele darraz. En non del Pere et du Fill et del S. esperit, dites tuit et toutes amen). The historiated initial accompanying it plays on the traditional imagery of folly but gives it an original twist (Figure 12). Rather than a single mad fool consorting with a hairy devil, we see the Carité's jongleur-heroes—one with a tabor, one with a pipe—hailing the Virgin with her candle, on equal footing with the holy.

In the days of Bishop Lambert (1093–1115), the story begins, the inhabitants of Arras became afflicted with "that horrible disease that is called 'the fire of Hell.'" This feu d'enfer is now known to be ergotism, also called Saint Anthony's fire, a potentially fatal form of poisoning brought about by the consumption of cereal grains, particularly rye, contaminated by the ergot fungus (Claviceps purpura). It takes two forms: gangrenous ergotism, which leads to the inflammation, distension, and potential loss of limbs; and

---

tre Dame, ed. V. Frederic Koenig, 4 vols. (Geneva, 1955–1970), 4:175–189 and 295–320. But the testimony of the Carité's own publications predate the stories of Gautier by decades, as I demonstrate in this chapter. See also Paul Verhuyck, "Et le quart est à Arras: Le roman de La Belle Hélène de Constantinople et la légende de Saint-Cierged'Arras," in Castellani and Martin, Arras, 111–136 at 120.

31. Chevallot (Notre-Dame des ardents, 330–331) believed that the translation would have been made in or immediately after 1241, when the Latin original was transcribed. It was certainly not made until after 1237, since it mentions the county of Artois, established in that year.

32. "Cest miracles a este en latin lonc tens. or la on en roumanz tranlate por ce que les laies genz lentendront mieuz." The vernacular narrative De la Chandelle d'Arras has been edited by Berger, in tandem with the Latin text, as "Le récit du miracle," in Le nécrologe, 2:137–156; hereinafter cited as Chandelle. Berger makes minor corrections to the edition of Guesnon, La Chandelle d'Arras, texte inédit du XIIIe siècle (Arras, 1899).

33. BnF fr. 17229, fols. 352vb–357va. It was first noted by Paul Meyer in the course of his discussion of a similar manuscript, BnF fr. 6447, published in Notices et extraits des manuscrits de la Bibliothèque nationale et autres bibliothèques 35 (Paris, 1896), 468.

convulsive ergotism, occasionally cited as a possible cause of the sufferings described by the plaintiffs in the Salem witchcraft trials, characterized by burning or freezing sensations, severe itching, headaches, diarrhea, vomiting, spastic muscular contractions, and hallucinations (a chemical derivative of ergot is the basic component of LSD).[34] In the Middle Ages, its seemingly mysterious capacity to strike some communities and not others could easily lead to its interpretation as a sign of divine disfavor, as when the jongleurs' miracle says that it was brought about in Arras by "the growing sins of the people, and through neglect."[35]

The source of this "neglect" is never mentioned, but the implication is clear: the laxity of Saint-Vaast's pastoral care, to which the people of Arras had been entrusted prior to the restoration of the diocese by Bishop Lambert, had allowed them to fall into damnation, so that the fire of ergotism was burning their bodies as "the fire of Hell" would burn their unshriven souls. The suffering people therefore take refuge in the City of Arras, in the freshly consecrated church of the Blessed Virgin. There, day-to-day observance of class distinctions is broken down by their mutual suffering, since the *mal des ardents* afflicts those "living in suburbs and in towns and in castles" with egalitarian ferocity, just as it could strike in any region of the body, including "the secret places of nature."[36] Like all scourges that come from God, "the fire of Hell" is therefore sent to teach a lesson, in this instance by disrupting traditional hierarchies and uniting the people of Arras in an awareness of shared mortality. They are no longer moneylenders and knights, artisans and laborers, prodigals and peasants; they are the *ardents* of Arras, "burning ones" wasting with contagion, burning souls waiting for grace. The miracle that will save them must therefore be one that knits their souls together in true Christian charity, even as it makes their bodies whole.

So much we may understand from the prologue, before the protagonists are introduced. But those who anticipate the story's outcome can see the poetic justice of the Vir-

---

34. Linnda R. Caporael, "Ergotism: The Satan Loosed in Salem?" *Science* 192, no. 4234 (April 1976): 21–26; Mary Kilbourne Matossian, *Poisons of the Past: Molds, Epidemics, and History* (New Haven, 1989), 9–14. Caporael's theory was disputed by Nicholas P. Spanos and Jack Gottlieb, "Ergotism and the Salem Witch Trials," *Science* 194, no. 4272 (December 1976): 1390–94, but their findings were in turn challenged by Matossian (113–122). Interestingly, the plague that Thucydides describes as destroying the fabric of civic life in Athens in 430 B.C.E. (*History* 2.47–55) can also be attributed to ergotism. On its legendary and hagiographic context, see H. Chaumartin, *Le mal des ardents et le feu Saint-Antoine* (Vienne, 1946).

35. *Chandelle*, 141: "succrescentibus peccatis populi et negligentiis . . . morbo illo horribili qui dicitur ignis infernalis // . . . par le pechié du peuple a Arraz . . . de celle horrible mal, dont Diex nos deffende, que on apele feu d'enfer."

36. *Chandelle*, 141: "menanz en bours et en viles et en chastiaux . . . es membres del secré leu de nature."

gin's chosen instruments of grace: Who better to treat the devilish convulsions, the hell-ish dance of pain, the dramatic cries and lamentations suggestive of the madman's folly, than the professional fool, the jongleur? Who better fitted to salve the societal wounds of Arras than a pair of socially estranged outsiders?

Enter the jongleurs, dwelling at that time in different parts of the surrounding region: Ithier in Brabant, Pierre Norman in nearby Saint-Pol. Strangers to Arras, they are sworn enemies to each other: we are told that Pierre Norman killed Ithier's brother sometime previously, so that Ithier has vowed to avenge his brother's murder. These are the mes-sengers chosen by the Virgin for her cause, the unlikely agents for the rescue of burning Arras. Simultaneously, on the very same night, a Wednesday (every detail is important to the story, and to the ritual life of the later Carité), each jongleur dreams independently of a beautiful woman dressed in white, and each receives the same set of instructions: Go to the City of Arras and, "telling the account of the vision you have seen, all in order," advise Bishop Lambert to visit the cathedral of Our Lady on the eve of the Sabbath, when, in the first watch of the day, a woman will descend from the choir "dressed in just what I am wearing now" and carrying a candle whose wax, dissolved in water, will cure the deadly plague.[37] In after years, preparations for the confraternity's annual feast, its grand siège, or "great sitting," will begin on a Wednesday night, commemorating the apparition with which the miracles began. For with the reconciliation of two outcasts will come the heal-ing of Arras, the establishment of a Marian cult, the affirmation of Lambert's episcopal authority, and the institution of a confraternity. What is more, all of these wondrous events are to be brought about through the practice of the entertainer's craft, the accurate re-counting of the unlikely vision vouchsafed to two jongleurs who are instructed to relate it faithfully, "all in order," as good minstrels know how to do.

Ensuring that they will be word perfect in their delivery, the Blessed Virgin appears to each again the following night. On the strength of these two hearings, both jongleurs are ready to act. The next day, Friday, Pierre Norman rises early and makes his way to Arras, some thirty-five kilometers distant from Saint-Pol, traveling on foot. (Hence the mode of ceremonial conveyance later adopted by one of the confraternity's leaders.) Making his way to the cathedral on Saturday morning, he hastens to find the bishop, "saying the whole psalm *Deus misereatur nostri* silently, under his breath, for he was somewhat lettered." Finding Lambert, but "fearing to interrupt his prayers," Pierre falls on his knees until the morning's devotions are complete. Then he tells his story. Lambert is curious at first, but when he hears that the clerical Pierre has taken a stage name, Norman, and that he earns his living by jongleurie (*joculatoria*), he dismisses the tale as an actor's gag.[38] At length,

---

37. *Chandelle*, 142: "visionem quam vides ordine enarrando . . . vestibus vestita quibus et ego . . . // . . . li recorde la vision que tu voiz, et tout en ordre . . . vestue d'autrietiex dras con je sui."

38. *Chandelle*, 144: "totum psalmum dicit sub silentio *Deus misereatur nostri*, erat enim aliquantulum

however, Ithier arrives, having traveled posthaste from Brabant the day before (presumably on horseback, the ceremonial mode of conveyance later to be adopted by another of the confraternity's leaders). Like Pierre, he displays a native piety, standing quietly, "a layman among clerics," while Lambert celebrates Mass. Afterward, he takes the bishop aside to tell his story, the exact story already recounted—unbeknownst to him, and "all in order"—by his rival. Still unbelieving, Lambert asks Ithier for his credentials and is told, "I earn my bread by acting and singing" or (according to the vernacular version) "by singing and jongleurie."[39] The very consonance of the separate accounts thus leads the bishop to suspect that two deceitful mountebanks have leagued together to play a tasteless joke on him.

But just when it appears that the jongleurs have jeopardized the safety of Arras through the practice of their controversial craft, it becomes obvious that their joint criminal past is intended to serve a vital purpose in the Virgin's plan. When Lambert tells Ithier that he has heard an identical tale from the lips of a certain Pierre Norman, Ithier vows immediately to avenge his brother's death. Questioning him further, the bishop learns of the enmity between the two men and realizes that they could not possibly have been cooperating; their story must be true. Moreover, he understands that his role is to facilitate a cure in Arras, beginning with the healing of the breach between the Virgin's chosen representatives. Using his own arts of persuasion, he reconciles them by preaching a homily of *caritas* and brotherly love, comparing their sins to those of Mary Magdalene and offering them the same forgiveness. Finally, "Ithier, in whose mind and whole soul was deadly hate, so that even charity did not spark but burned with fiery flames," is able to receive Pierre's heartfelt apology and put away the "bad love" engendered by their blood feud.[40]

These are the founding acts of charity later institutionalized in the Carité: Lambert's belief in the improbable story of jongleurs brings about their equally improbable reconciliation by soothing their ardent hatred with the healing balm of love, presaging the miraculous cure of the Sainte-Chandelle, whose soothing flame will counter the burning of the ardents in the cathedral of Arras. Their fellowship sealed with a kiss of peace, the members of the new-formed trinity ask prayerfully for the blessing of the Holy Trinity before beginning their vigil in the cathedral choir. A little after cockcrow, right on cue, the Blessed Virgin appears with a lighted candle:

---

literatus . . . timens orationem ejus interrumpere . . . 'O frater,' inquit episcopus, 'jocundis me // . . . tout disant cest siaume *Deus misereatur nostri* coiement, quar il iert petiz letrez."

39. *Chandelle*, 146–147: "solus stetit laicus inter clericos . . . mima et cantu victum acquiro // et estut il seus lais hom entre les clers . . . de chanter et de juglerie."

40. *Chandelle*, 149: "Iterius, in cujus mente et animo totum erat mortificatum odium et charitas, non per scintillas, sed per ignem flammantem ardebat . . . // . . . et ja iert en son cuer morte toute la haine et la male amour."

"You," she said, "who live by jest and acting: come forward. I bestow this singular gift on you, to keep as a perpetual possession for all time. Whenever someone is stricken with that sickness which is called the infernal fire and is infected, the melting wax of this candle should be distilled in water, and the burning lesions sprinkled with water, so that they are quickly extinguished. Whoever believes will be saved, and whoever does not truly believe will be condemned to sudden death."[41]

Impressed by the Virgin's formal grant of the Sainte-Chandelle, and her endowment of the jongleurs with powers of life and death, the bishop bows to their preeminence: "Since this divine gift has been bestowed upon you, I can only hope that you will find me worthy to associate with you! And if you will accept me as your companion (not through my own merits, but by divine grace and your own), I will not cease to support your claim!" This pointed acknowledgment of the bishop's submission to the jongleurs' superiority, which the Latin narrative clearly constitutes as a contractual obligation, is much softened in the vernacular version of the story, perhaps reflecting changes in later conceptions of episcopal authority.[42] In the vernacular, Pierre Norman and Ithier adopt Lambert as one of themselves via an initiation rite, wherein they "willingly and loyally receive my lord the bishop as a confrère and companion, and kiss him in the name of the confraternity."[43]

The miracle culminates in a description of the social effects brought about by the making of this divine contract. On Sunday morning the three confrères busy themselves with the concoction of holy water, which is not only sprinkled on the diseased skin of the suffering ardents but also offered as a soothing drink, "the common beverage of the confraternity." By the end of the morning, twelve dozen men and women have been treated successfully. The thirteenth of the final dozen, however, has fallen victim to the Virgin's

---

41. *Chandelle*, 151: "'Vos,' inquit, 'per mima joculatis, adeste presentes. Hoc unum memoriale in perpetuum reservandum vobis delibero. Quisquis contagio infirmitatis illius que dicitur ignis infernalis fuerit contaminatus, cerei ceram supereffluentem in acqua distillet, et lesura ignis aqua aspergatur, cito extinguetur. Qui crediderit salvus erit; qui vero non crediderit, morte presenti condemnabitur.' // Vos, jugleor,' fet ele, 'qui vivez de chant et de vielle, venez ca. Cest chandoile vos baill a garder a toz jorz mes parmenablement.'"

42. *Chandelle*, 151: "'Quia vobis divinitus datus est, utinam me vobis associare dignemini! Et quod me vobis socium adscitis, non meis meritis, sed divine gratie et vestre hic imputare non desisto.' // 'Por ce que cist cierges vos est donnez de par Dieu et venuz par miracle, la moie volenté feriez vos de moi vo compaignon en ceste chose, nient par merite mes par la grace de Dieu et par la vostre!'" I have adjusted Berger's punctuation of the vernacular text.

43. *Chandelle*, 153: "Li jogleor recurent volontiers et lieement monseignor levesque a confrere et compaignon et le besierent el non de confrarie." The Latin is much less explicit: "Deosculantes ergo se in fraterna vicissitudine joculatores et episcopus."

curse: informed that the libation is water, not wine, he expressed doubts about its potency, and when "he drank with bad belief," he died.[44] This incident would stand as warning to those who scoffed at the sacramental office of the jongleurs or made the mistake of thinking that theirs would be a fellowship of drunken revelry. By the beginning of the thirteenth century, indeed, anyone inclined to question the jongleurs' ceremonial role was deemed *escumenie,* "excommunicate." Moreover, the sober purposes of the confraternity's periodic gatherings were stressed in all of its publications. When it held a "drinking" (*bevée* or, in Latin, *potus*), as it did three times a year, the avowed purpose of these meetings was not drunkenness or "folly" but the remembrance of the dead and the renewal of the confrères' faith through a communal potation of the "common beverage."[45]

With their enactment of this miracle, Pierre Norman and Ithier have undergone a metamorphosis from small-time buskers and petty criminals, to heralds hired by the Blessed Virgin, to quasi-clerics (Pierre "was actually somewhat lettered" and Ithier "stood alone, a layman among clerics"), to miracle workers, to the presidents of a fellowship that would come to represent the community of Arras. The official Latin narrative closes on a scene of civic harmony, with the people of Arras led in festive procession around the cathedral, the founding fathers of the confraternity at the head, the candle held aloft, and the Te Deum laudamus ringing out, as it had at the end of the *Jeu de saint Nicolas* and on the day the errant Courtois came home. But the legend might just as well be describing the processions held every year on the three days of the Carité's great feast, during the week after the octave of Pentecost, beginning on the Thursday after Trinity Sunday. Like the thrice-yearly bevées, the grand siège observed a rule of three by commemorating the founders' trinity and the three days that had elapsed between the jongleurs' Wednesday visions of the Virgin and her appearance on Saturday night. On all of these public occasions, as on any private occasion when a member of the confraternity fell sick, or when the inmates of its hospital were to be dosed for their ills, the heirs of Pierre Norman and Ithier would be summoned to perform the ministry of the Sainte-Chandelle, whose ritual elements were encoded in the story of the miracle just as the instructions for the performance of the Mass are encoded in the Gospels' accounts of the Last Supper. Only the maieurs (mayors) of the Carité's jongleurs would have the keys to the place "where the Chandelle is kept locked up," and only they were authorized to carry the relic and to perform the healing rite: lighting the wick carefully and letting a drop of the candle's precious wax fall into a vessel of water. For the Carité's customary laws dictated that "with some of this water the sick per-

44. *Chandelle,* 152–153: "communem potum fraternitatis // . . . le conmun buvrage de la conflarrie . . . il but par mauvais creance."

45. Customary laws of the Carité de Notre Dame des Ardents d'Arras (in BnF fr. 8541), fol. 46rᵃ, hereinafter cited as Coutumier; see also fol. 46vᵃ.

son should be sprinkled and given the rest to drink, and he should firmly believe in God that by this, the malady will be cured." It was a formula echoing the words of the Blessed Virgin, who had made the jongleurs of Arras her priests forever.[46]

The Virgin and the Dynamics of Power

Whatever the facts behind the jongleurs' miracle, the most important fact is its transcription in a charter which may have been prepared in the episcopal chancery in 1241, and which was sealed by the confraternity's maieurs and ratified by the other ecclesiastical authorities of Arras, chiefly the abbot and convent of Saint-Vaast, along with representatives of the three mendicant orders established there, the Dominicans, the Franciscans, and the Trinitarians. The vernacular version of the story, which does not take the form of a legal instrument, also describes itself in legal terms as constituting "their charter and their rights" (leur chartre et lor droiture), and readings of this confraternal "charter" were key events at the Carité's annual feast.[47] By the middle of the thirteenth century, moreover, a liturgical reenactment of the Virgin's grant came to form part of the celebrations marking the confraternity's observance of Assumption Eve.[48] Solemn inscription and ceremony thereby extended the effects of the miracle, while the competing claims of clerical factions were reconciled through the agency of jongleurs, who claimed the bishop of Arras as their patron and gradually made alliances with the monks of Saint-Vaast and the mendicants.

But why would these established powers acquiesce to such a collaboration? The complex development of political institutions and social structures in twelfth- and thirteenth-century Arras suggests some motives, while its inhabitants' unusual recourse to written record—for the preservation of plays or the promotion of law—suggests some means. As I have already shown, Jehan Bodel's command of language and his engagement in local affairs lent themselves to the composition of the Jeu de saint Nicolas, but it was his clerical

---

46. "Et se nus est entechies de tel mal con apele fu & por andeus les cles i avoier dont li candoile est enfremee. & li maire des iogleors sil i est doit prendre le sainte candoile & porter a[l] [m]alade dedens le cite &. alumer. & son ne true[ve] le maieur des iogleors on quier un deses . . . [line erased] . . . u eschievins. & en un vaissel plain diaue degouter. & de cel eue sor son malage espardre. & del remanant boire. & fermement croire endeu que parcou i ert garis. Et bien sachies ka ceste besoigne doivent li doi maire a coire. sil le sevent & sil nont essoine grant car il ont le clef del saint luminaire." Erasures suggest that there was a later attempt to extend the priestly function of the jongleurs to the échevins of the Carité: Coutumier, fols. 46r^b–46v^a; see below.

47. Chandelle, 155.

48. Ordinance of the rights which those who appear below have from the Carité during the siège. And in what manner things ought to be done, Archives de la Confrérie de Notre-Dame des Ardents d'Arras MS 239, fol. 5v, hereinafter cited as Ordinance; see further discussion later in this chapter. On the celebration of the Feast of the Assumption, see chapter 4.

grasp of documentation that led to its scripting. And while his membership in the Carité de Notre Dame des Ardents during the crucial period of its institution need not imply that he was the mastermind behind its documentary campaign, this does suggest that it was normal for men who called themselves jongleurs to have the talents of diplomats and clerics, and vice versa. These talents were instrumental in advertising the miracle of civic unity vaunted in the legend and in exploiting the rifts within the political structure of Arras. For if a miracle worked by Our Lady could be discovered to have coincided with the pontificate of her first bishop in Arras, a great deal would be gained for the diocese—and for the Virgin, too. Her cult was only just gaining popularity in the late eleventh century, when the City's ramshackle Romanesque church became her cathedral, and her famed championship of social outcasts may well have begun as a tactic of necessity.

Certainly, the Virgin's embattled bishop in Arras had almost as much need of the jongleurs' support as they of his, since he had been trying since 1093 to establish a tenuous authority from scratch, against the concerted opposition of Saint-Vaast. Handpicked for this mission by Urban II, Lambert de Guînes was a cleric of Flemish birth who had served as cantor and archdeacon at the collegial church of Saint-Pierre in Lille. He had, moreover, received his early education at the prestigious cathedral of Beauvais, where the *Danielis ludus* would later be devised and where there is good reason to believe that the gifts of acting and singing displayed by Pierre Norman and Ithier had long been encouraged.[49] The office of cantor was an important one in any community of religious, second only to that of the bishop and his archdeacons, and was often a proving ground for clerical advancement. (Disputes over elections to this office could be serious; in Arras in 1182 a "schism" over the selection of a cantor lasted nearly a year.)[50] Lambert was also politically active, an advocate of the Peace Movement, and the possessor of strong administrative and diplomatic skills.

Yet during his lengthy pontificate (1093–1115), and for nearly a half-century after his death, the monks of Saint-Vaast continued, successfully, to thwart the hard-earned episcopal power passed down to Lambert's less charismatic successors. They supported the claims of a local lord who insisted on an ancestral right to seize episcopal holdings during vacancies between elections, helping himself to revenues and moveable goods from the episcopal demesne and ritually impeding the installation of the new bishop by grabbing the reins of his palfrey upon his entrance to the cathedral close.[51] They also made the

49. Locre, *Chronicon Belgicum*, 226–239; Delmaire, *Le diocèse*, 1:168. I am indebted to David Wulstan for information on the dramatic traditions of Beauvais.

50. BnF lat. 9930, fols. 26v–27r; Tock, *Chartes des évêques*, no. 192, and "Les chartes promulgées par le chapitre cathédral d'Arras au XIIe siècle," *Revue Mabillon* (1991): 49–97 at 51.

51. BnF lat. 9930, fols. 2r^b–v^a. The cathedral canons later secured the support of Alexander III, who forbade these practices.

most of the long episcopal vacancy that stretched between 1147 and 1151, when a disputed election attracted the intervention of Count Thierry of Flanders, King Louis VII and his chief political adviser, Abbot Suger of Saint-Denis, and finally Bernard of Clairvaux and his protégé, Pope Eugenius III. Although the late incumbent, Bishop Alvis (d. 1147), had been a fellow Benedictine, he was unpopular with the monks of Saint-Vaast, so when he died on the road to Palestine (an early recruit in Bernard's crusading efforts), the abbey moved to block the claims of his chosen successor, the archdeacon Hugh of Ostrevant, whose capitular election was mysteriously annulled by Eugenius in 1148. (A contemporary account of miracles purportedly worked by the relics of Saint Vaast reveals that the monks were actually championing Hugh's rival, the archdeacon Luke of Arras, and may have tried to leverage his candidacy through an appeal to Rome.)[52] This bid was foiled when the successful candidate appointed by the papacy turned out to be an outsider, a Premonstratensian canon named Godescalc of Brabant, consecrated at the end of the summer of 1151. But the monks were triumphant again when Godescalc's pontificate was not a success, coinciding as it did with a plague of ergotism and deep divisions within the cathedral chapter; he was driven into retirement in 1163.

Shortly thereafter, the cathedral's star began to rise under the stronger leadership of Bishop André, a former Cistercian abbot who had the full support of Louis VII. And matters further improved during the short reign of Bishop Robert of Aire (1171–1174), who seems to have been appointed entirely on the strength of his business acumen: the former chancellor of Count Philip of Flanders and rumored to be a man of very humble birth— the son of a peasant or blacksmith, it was said—he was unanimously elected by the chapter and quickly confirmed by Pope Alexander III even though he was not in holy orders at the time. So effective was he at cleaning house that, having swept through the diocese of Arras, he was translated to the see of Cambrai two years later.[53] This newly effective promulgation of episcopal authority infuriated the monks of Saint-Vaast and prompted the making of one of the most unusual and extensive administrative records of the twelfth century, the massive survey of the abbey's holdings begun in 1170 by the cellarer, Brother Guiman. Railing against "the arrogance of the canons," and concerned that the still growing population of the commune was encroaching on the abbey's patrimony, he set out to prove "that the entire town of Arras lies within the territory of Saint-Vaast," an enterprise that would take twenty years because, as Guiman boasted wearily, the list of people ow-

52. BmA 734, fols. 106r–113v. This is my own inference, based on the "Miracles de Saint-Vaast," ed. Joseph van der Staeten in Les manuscrits hagiographiques d'Arras et de Boulogne-sur-Mer avec quelques textes inédits, Subsidia Hagiographica 50 (Brussels, 1971), 87–93. This account, composed around 1152, was recopied in the early thirteenth century and now forms part of BmA 734, fols. 106r–113v. On the lengthy vacancy, the causes of which have long puzzled scholars of the diocese, see Delmaire, Le diocèse, 1:160–166 and 181.

53. Tock, "Les élections," 709–721; Delmaire, Le diocèse, 1:162–164.

ing taxes was so long that "if anyone should wish to write it down in full, he would not be able to keep track of them all, nor could the book contain all of their names."[54]

Not surprisingly, it is during this crucial period of episcopal aggrandizement and competitive record keeping that the miracle of Notre Dame des Ardents appears to have been redacted for the first time, during the boyhood of Jehan Bodel. The narrative drew on a growing body of local legend which was already making connections between Marian devotion and miraculous cures of the ergotism which had been endemic in the region since the years just prior to Lambert's installation. Cures for the disease were ascribed to the Blessed Virgin as early as 1089–90, when a chronicler writing in Cambrai noted that "there were many famous miracles" which, "for the most part, happened in churches dedicated to the Holy Mother of God," especially in Brabant and the region around Tournai.[55] This may have been one of the reasons why the new cathedral of Arras was consecrated to Notre Dame in the first place, and the fact that the town was not affected by a plague of the mal in 1108–9 (widely reported by Orderic Vitalis and Ivo of Chartres, among others) may already have been construed as a sign of her miraculous intervention and eagerly seized upon as such. Then, in the 1120s, a series of bad winters and poor harvests led to widespread famine and pestilence in the North until, in 1129, a terrible "plague of divine fire" (plaga ignis divini) was reported in Paris, Soissons, Chartres, Cambrai, and Arras, eventually "alleviated through the miracles attributed to Mary the blessed Mother of God," according to Anselm of Gembloux.[56] When Bernard of Clairvaux passed through Arras in 1146, he may have further emphasized the power of the Virgin's local ministry by connecting stories of past wonders with the dedication of the cathedral as part of his campaign to promote the Marian piety which became, thanks in large part to his zealotry, so ubiquitous in the later Middle Ages.

When the episcopal vacancy of 1147–1151 coincided with another incidence of the mal des ardents in Arras, there were reports not only of miracles but of disputes over miracles as well. A monk of Saint-Vaast grudgingly noted that many cures for the recent plague had

54. Guiman, 241–242 and 272; see also 170, 177: "canonicorum insolentia," "ex precedenti descriptione vicorum atque platearum certissime teneat quod universa civitas Attrebatensis in fundo sancti Vedasti," and "ut si quis ad plenum scribere velit, nec scriptor omnes nosce nec liber nomina continere possit." On the importance of Guiman's undertaking and "the new administrative mentality" of the twelfth century, see Robert F. Berkhofer III, Day of Reckoning: Power and Accountability in Medieval France (Philadelphia, 2004), 81–86 and 119.

55. "In plerisque sanctae Dei genitricis ecclesiis, et maxime Tornaci, piis ejus meritis et gloriosa intercessione facta sunt praeclara miracula." Reported in the chronicle of the abbey of Saint-André in Cateau, 3.13, in PL, vol. 149, 274. Similar plagues are mentioned in the Gesta regum anglorum of William of Malmesbury, among other sources; see Berger, Le nécrologe, 2:39 and 43.

56. Anselm of Gembloux, in PL, vol. 160, 251: "sed mirabilis per sanctam Dei genetricem Mariam extinguitur."

been reported but "that little has been written about these things" (*ut pauca de ea scriban-tur*), implying that all unwritten claims were, by definition, false. He then hastened to stake his own claim, in the proper textual medium: miracles did occur, but they should be ascribed to Saint Vaast, whose relics had been carried in procession around the Town and must therefore have been the agent of those cures. In any case, he remarks peevishly, "the fire of Hell" spoken of in those (unwritten) stories should be understood for what it is, a metaphor; it is not real hellfire, and its alleviation must not be construed as a deliverance from sin.[57] These are veiled but telling references to the miraculous legend of Notre Dame des Ardents, already in circulation and posing a challenge to the spiritual hegemony of Saint-Vaast. Perhaps it was being preached by Bishop Godescalc, a countryman of the legendary Ithier, who would have grown up on his own region's stories of the Virgin's intercession in Brabant. Perhaps it was a song in the repertoire of Gauthier d'Arras (fl. 1165–1170) as well as a tale told by his fellow minstrels, already banding together in semiformal camaraderie.

In any case, the evidence strongly indicates that Saint-Vaast's hostility toward the cult of Notre Dame des Ardents created an alliance that resulted in the cathedral of Notre-Dame's sponsorship of the confraternity and the confraternity's endorsement of the bishop, the very contract expressed in the written redaction of the story—and the contract by which Saint Vaast and his abbey are literally written out of history while at the same time being implicated in the causes of the malady characterized, even more vociferously, as "the fire of Hell." Small wonder that the monks felt the need to take stock of their possessions while also taking steps to revive the cult of Saint Vaast, whose long-dormant relics were now being paraded around the Town on pious errands, displaying an unwonted interest in the spiritual well-being of the abbey's constituents. This new, socially conscious Vaast was not only credited with the cure of the *mal des ardents* but was also alleged to have competed successfully with the Blessed Virgin on other occasions when the two saints engaged in agonistic contests for the souls of the Arrageois in the arena of its streets and marketplaces. The same monastic apologist who had contested the efficacy of the Sainte-Chandelle even claimed that three of the processional routes annually followed by the monks were based on three miraculous journeys undertaken by the relics of Saint Vaast, and that one of these perambulations was the cure for the plague of ergotism. What had *really* happened, he claims, is that the cathedral canons had come in procession to the abbey, accompanied by the entire population of Arras, to beg the intercession of Saint Vaast; only when his more potent relics had joined those of the Blessed Virgin inside her new cathedral was the cure effected. This explanation—replete with insulting sexual imagery—rests on a reinterpretation of the meaning of the shared liturgy performed by both churches on the feast of Saint Mark (April 25), the day for the observance of the Major

57. Van der Straeten, ed., "Miracles de S. Vaast," 87–88.

Litany, when the monks' annual visit to the cathedral church for a concelebration of Mass in the morning was followed by a reciprocal visit from the cathedral to the abbey later in the day.[58] According to the apologist, this solemnity was a commemoration of historical events and as such could be cited as "proof" of the abbey's claim, to the extent that the Litany's introit is said to have been the cry uttered by a herald sent to quiet the clamorous ardents waiting in the cathedral to greet the healing relics of Saint Vaast (*Exaudivit de templo sancto suo vocem meam alleluya. et clamor meus in conspectu eius introiuit in aures eius alleluya alleluya*). Similarly, the monks' Ascensiontide rogations were held up as recalling miracles worked by Saint Vaast at various times of crisis, when his remains were carried around "the outermost extremes of the city, with hymns and songs" (*in ymnis et canticis civitatis extrema perlustrant*), besting the Marian relics of the cathedral.[59]

The very fact that territorial and jurisdictional disputes were articulated in liturgical terms (Guiman followed processional routes when he spiraled through the streets of Arras, making his inventory) underscores the extent to which the skillful manipulation of ritual was at least as important to the waging of a propaganda war as the production of texts, so that an individual or group in control of both media had the tools of power firmly in hand.[60] The denigration of unwritten miracle reports by the monk of Saint-Vaast therefore sounds like a cry of sour grapes, amounting to an admission that the creation of texts was not always so persuasive as performance. As it happens, the jongleurs' lively retellings of their miraculous tale—recited, recalled, reenacted—needed only the gloss of a literary polishing to trump the jaded pageants of the abbey and the monks, who were eventually unable to beat the cult of the Virgin and had to join it instead. By the fourth quarter of the twelfth century, Guiman was reporting Marian miracles connected with the abbey's own parish churches in Arras.[61] By the turn of the thirteenth, the monks had altogether abandoned their futile attempt to deny the powers of the Sainte-Chandelle and had begun to capitalize on it, donating land in the Petit Marché for the confraternal chapel erected in 1200. In 1241 their seal was duly impressed upon the Latin redaction of the jongleurs' miracle, in which no reference to Saint Vaast or his abbey is made. A century later the monks would be claiming that their abbey had been founded by the Virgin herself, deemed to have been working through the humble Vedastus, and they began to swear their oaths of solemn

58. Ibid. The processional route described in the abbey's ordinal of 1308 (BmA 230, fol. 39r^b–39r^a and fol. 73r) matches that given in a thirteenth-century missal from the cathedral, BmA 309, fol. 127; both appear to be of much greater antiquity.

59. Psalm 17:7[18:6]. See Carolus Marbach, ed., *Carmina scripturarum, scilicet Antiphonas et Responsoria ex Sacro Scripturæ fonte in librose liturgicos Sanctæ Ecclesiæ Romanæ* (Strassburg, 1907), 78.

60. For contemporary examples, see Patrick J. Geary, "Living with Conflicts in Stateless France: A Typology of Conflict Management Mechanisms, 1050–1200," in *Living with the Dead in the Middle Ages* (Ithaca, 1994), 125–160. See also Heers, *La ville*, 352; and Buc, *Dangers*.

61. Guiman, 155–158.

profession to her, first and foremost.[62] In the long run, consequently, the alliance forged between cathedral and confraternity would turn out to be too successful for the former's good, since the jongleurs' campaign for power had resulted in the winning over of the monks, giving them new grounds for competition with the bishop.

Accounting for the Carité

The scripted texts of the Carité's founding miracles were intended to verify, ex post facto, the Blessed Virgin's endorsement of the jongleurs' ministry, which had been confirmed in the presence of the bishop of Arras with powerfully binding words and gestures. For the careful architects of these keystone accounts, a written record of the Virgin's verbal deed-of-gift and the bishop's formal promise of support and self-effacement had become a legal necessity. Standards of proof were changing in the second half of the twelfth century, as the anonymous chronicler of Saint-Vaast's miracles had sneeringly reminded would-be competitors. Oral history had to be institutionalized as *legenda*, "things for reading," which entailed maintaining a balance between fidelity and forgery, the usual strategy deployed in most contemporary historiography, legislation, and record keeping. Throughout Europe, the new dependence of power on writing made it necessary for those in power to ensure that there were scripted accounts of their deeds, even if those accounts were often produced and scrutinized after the fact, as part of a performance. By the same token—and this is crucial for our understanding of the jongleurs' power in Arras—recourse to writing made it possible for those with mere *pretensions* to power to make claims to power in similar ways. That is, the articulation of power in writing meant, speculatively, that everyone with access to a scribe could assert a form of power. If one's contemporaries (or the historians of posterity) believed what was written, then the power was no longer potential; it was real. Hence, one could resort to writing in order to authorize a power that had its origins in the distant past, or one could manufacture a credible past for claims to power otherwise unfounded or dubious.

This was not lightly undertaken. One not only made accounts, one was held accountable. Familiar to everyone in this capital of finance and letters, where transactions were carefully notarized, was the description in the Book of Revelation of the accounts to be rendered on the Day of Judgment: "And I saw the dead, great and small, standing before the throne, and books were opened. Also another book was opened, the book of life. And the dead were judged according to their works, as recorded in the books."[63] In the ver-

---

62. BmA 230, fol 141v: "in hoc monasterio quod est constructum in honore sancte dei genitricis Marie et santi Vedasti confessoris atque pontificis."

63. Revelation 20:12; cited by Berkhofer as a passage "known to every man and monk" in the region, *Day of Reckoning,* 162 and 164–165.

nacular, the message was rendered particularly immediate, because the recounting of stories (*contes*) was spoken of in the same terms as the rendering of accounts (*contes*). Hence, Norman and Ithier were warned by the Blessed Virgin that they would have to give an "orderly account" before the bishop would believe them.

The need to keep a careful record of the Carité's foundation is reflected in the Latin narrative redacted around 1175, not only in the "orderly account" of the miracle story but also in the careful recounting of the Virgin's grant of power to Norman and Ithier, Lambert's acquiescence to that grant, and the subsequent "constitution" (*consuetudines*) which tranformed their brotherhood into a confraternity. The vernacular translation also preserves the terms of this incorporation, designated as the "customs and assizes" (*coutumes et assizes*) offered as a template for the bylaws of confraternities elsewhere. In both accounts, Latin and vernacular, the constitution is brief, consisting of a summary of procedures for the admission of new members. Candidates are to be received only once a year, at the Carité's grand siège. Membership is a guarantee of decent burial, since all who enter the Carité's communion will be expected to finance and attend the funerals of their fellows and to remember them in prayer. Membership is to reflect, as far as possible, the divine numerology of the original twelve dozen ardents, with men and women to be admitted in multiples of twelve, with (ideally) a thirteenth to supply the place of the legend's ill-fated ardent and, secondarily perhaps, in memory of the apostles.[64] The initiation fee is set at a little over 6 deniers, a modest sum corresponding to the daily wage of a laborer, which automatically includes the spouse of the new member in the privileges of fellowship.[65] Finally, those received into the confraternity are required to take a solemn oath to keep its customs and its charity, "in the presence of its maieur and échevins."[66]

A decade or so later, during the pontificate of Bishop Pierre (1184–1203) and the upheavals chronicled by Jehan in the *Jeu de saint Nicolas*, the Carité began to amend this constitution, producing the first articles in a series of customary laws written down in Picard and reflecting a new stage in the process of accounting.

> This Carité is held from God and from Our Lady, Holy Mary. And you should know why it was founded: for the ardents, those who were burning with the fire of Hell. It was never established for lechery, or for folly. For God wrought many miracles on the day that it was founded, when seven score and four sufferers were burning with fiery fever in the City of Arras. And after this the confrères entered into the Carité, so that neither they nor any of their children should ever burn with the fire of Hell, nor ever die of a sudden death, so long as they had faith and belief. And since that time, the *confrères* and

64. Coutumier, fols. 46rᵃ and fol. 46rᵇ; see the discussion later in this chapter. This numerology was later adopted by the Carité's imitator, the confraterntiy of Notre-Dame-du-Jardin: BmA 1116, fol. 7r.

65. See Delmaire, *Le diocèse*, 1:156; see also the discussion later in this chapter.

66. *Chandelle*, 154–155: "in presentia majoris et scabinorum."

consoeurs are the beneficiaries of the church of Sainte-Marie, at Masses and at Matins, and in all the prayers that are said there. And this is what they were granted by Bishop Lambert, and afterward by Bishop Robert, and afterward by Bishop Alvis, and afterward by Bishop Godescalc, and afterward by Bishop André, and afterward by Bishop Frumaud, and afterward by Bishop Pierre—and by Bishop Raoul—and by Bishop Pons.[67]

This powerful statement, which reads like a charter, may actually derive from an act ratified by Bishop Pierre (1184–1203), to which the names of Raoul (1203–1221) and Pons were added at the time of the latter's succession in 1221, after the Carité's coutumier was fair-copied in 1217. This was done by a very competent scribe, who skillfully planned the *mise-en-page* of his text in such a way as to highlight the most important statements of the Carité's legitimacy, mirroring the preamble at the head of the first column with a further declaration of the jongleurs' authority at the top of the second (Figure 13). Carefully, too, he left room for descriptive rubrics, although these were never supplied. Instead, within the next three years, eleven more scribes of varying skill would add to the "assizes," while many more hands would make additions, filling the remaining pages and disclosing the high level of literacy among the Carité's members (Figure 14). The result is an astonishing record of internal deliberations and their effect on gradually accrued tradition, interlaced with snap judgments and spur-of-the-moment changes, constituting an eyewitness to the confraternity's negotiations during the period of its most rapid growth in the first quarter of the thirteenth century, which coincided with the rapid growth of Arras.[68] The fact that it was never again recopied is itself suggestive of an attachment to the material evidence of past resolutions, each introduced by a phrase that captures a moment of hard-won consensus—"It was taken down in full accord" (*Ce fu atire en plain plait*) or "The

67. "Ceste Carite tient on de deu et de ma dame sainte marie. Et saves por coi ele fu estoree por les ardans qui ardoient del fu dinfer. Ele ne fu mie establie por lecherie. ne por folie. Ainsi fist dex tels miracles que le ior quele fu estoree ardoieent .vii.XX.&.iiij. ardant en le cite darras. Et puis que en le carite est entres le confrer[e]. ia puis ne il ne ses enfe[n]s qui il ait. nardera del fu dinfer. ne ne morra de mort subite sil foi & creance i a. Et trestot li confrere. & les consereurs sont es biens fais de liglise. me dame sainte marie. Es messes. & matines. & en toutes les ores qui dites i sont. Si quil le requ[i]rent del vesque lambert. & apres del vesque robert. & apres del vesque auvis. & apres del vesque godescal. & apres del vesque andriu. & apres del vesque fruniant. & apres del vesque pieron. & del vesque raoul. et del vesque poncon." Coutumier, fol. 46rᵃ. The roster is accurate save for the omission of Bishop Robert II (of Aire, 1171–1174), probably an oversight.

68. On the recording of customary law in the North at this time, see Paul Ourliac, "Coutume et mémoire: Les coutumes françaises au XIIIe siècle," in *Jeux de mémoire: Aspects de la mnémotechnie médiévale*, ed. Bruno Roy and Paul Zumthor (Montreal, 1985), 111–122, and "Législation, coutume et coutumiers au temps de Philippe Auguste," in Bautier, *La France*, 471–488. See also van Caenegem, "Coutumes," 256–266.

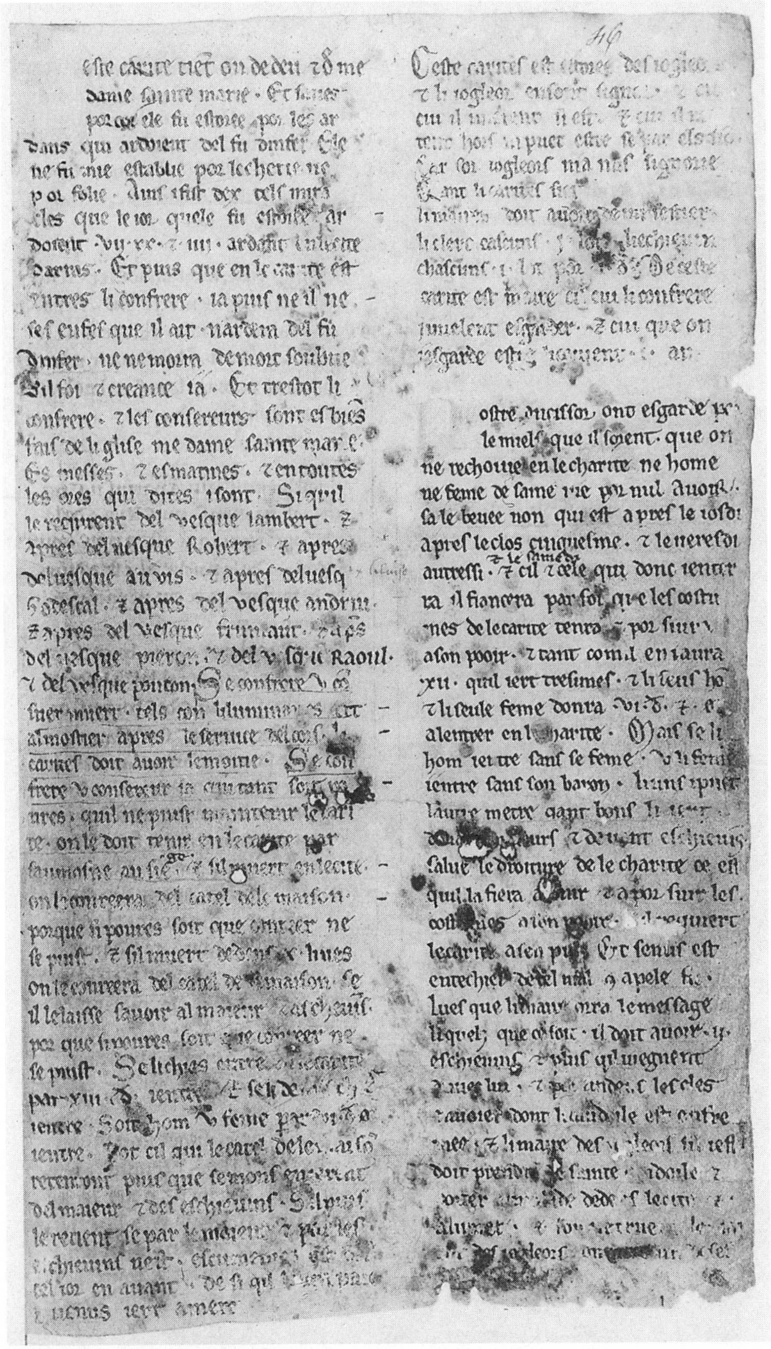

FIGURE 13. Recto of first folio of the coutumier of the Carité de Notre Dame des Ardents, fair-copied in 1217: the professionally trained scribe left spaces for rubrics and initial letters, but these were never supplied (BnF fr. 8541, fol. 46r)

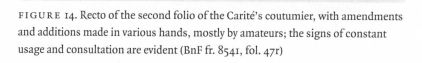

FIGURE 14. Recto of the second folio of the Carité's coutumier, with amendments and additions made in various hands, mostly by amateurs; the signs of constant usage and consultation are evident (BnF fr. 8541, fol. 47r)

Carité's members have established" (Li caritaule ont estore)—and respect for past precedent: "Our ancestors always judged it to be best" (Nostre ancissor ont esgarder por le miels). The wear-and-tear of consultation is also stamped on the dog-eared leaves.[69]

Prior to the Carité's initiation of its remarkable documentary campaign, of which this may be the oldest artifact, the beginnings of an important confraternal movement in Europe can be discerned in only a few scattered sources. In Arras, Guiman's census mentions four charitable institutions sponsored by the abbey, all of which were organized around a single trade and all of which paid yearly tribute in exchange for the monks' pastoral care, which may have extended to the celebration of funerary rites or the offering of memorial prayers.[70] The diocese also appears to have been somewhat active in the formation of such groups, protecting the "carités, as they are called by the people," from being improperly treated by secular and monastic foundations that attempted to charge high fees for burial.[71] Members usually paid dues of a few deniers, most of which went toward the expenses of funerals: "one for the priest that he might pray for the dead, another for candles to stand by at the funeral, and a third to the use of the confraternity."[72]

Similar arrangements would be made by the confraternity of jongleurs for the funerals of its members, but in other respects its initiatives are unprecedented in the annals of laymen's associations anywhere in Europe.[73] It ranks among the first attested of all medieval confraternities and differs significantly from them in the impetus behind its documentation, which was not dependent on outside authorities.[74] Had the original set of custom-

69. The Coutumier is now bound with the Carité's funerary register in the codex BnF fr. 8541, fols. 46–47. The text has been published as the "statuts primitifs" by Cavrois, in Cartulaire, 103–116, and a partial translation was made by Chevallot, Notre-Dame des ardents d'Arras, 23–30. It has also been analyzed and edited incrementally, as the "Règlement général," by Georges Espinas, in Les origines du droit d'association dans les villes de l'Artois et de la Flandre française jusqu'au début du XVIe siècle, 2 vols. (Lille, 1941–1942), 1:80–121 and 2:50–65. The citations here are taken from my own transcription, which is available as an appendix to "A Medieval Stage."

70. Guiman, 191. Chevallot mistook the reference to a payment earmarked for candles ("Porro guilda mercatorum debet viginti quatuor solidos qui dicuntur de candela quos scabini solvent") for a reference to a carité "of the candle," hence a supposed reference to the Carité des Ardents, further misconstruing the payment to be one made on the group's behalf by the échevinage of Arras (Notre-Dame, 23).

71. Tock, Chartes des évêques, no. 73 ("karitates, que vulgo dicuntur confraternitates") and no. 216 bis. See also Delmaire, Le diocèse, 1:175–178.

72. Benoît-Michel Tock, "Les chartes promulgées par le chapitre cathédral d'Arras au XIIe siècle," Revue Mabillon (1991): 49–97 at 94–96 (no. 54): "unum scilicet presbitero ut oret pro defuncto, alterum cereis ut assistant funeri, tercium ad usum confrarie."

73. AdPC ser. 3 G 4/Oblations 3–7 (Delmaire handlist, no. 55).

74. Espinas, Les origines, 1:1; Delmaire, Le diocèse, 1:380–381. An earlier constitution in Latin was drafted for a confraternity in Bergamo in 1159, but by the Vallambrosans; Lester K. Little, Liberty, Char-

ary laws and privileges (dating from the period 1184–1203) survived, they would predate the earliest known legal document written in Picard (dated 1216), as well as the earliest charter in any northern French dialect (written at Douai in 1205).[75] Moreover, the coutumier's remarkable testimony to a process of slow self-invention and triumphant achievement bears little resemblance to the clear-cut statutory laws of the later confraternities based directly on it, notably those drafted by the Dominicans of Arras for the confraternity of Notre-Dame-du-Jardin in 1290.[76]

Also unprecedented is the Carité's decision to keep a register of the dead it buried and remembered in prayer. In the same year that Philip Augustus took steps to ensure the permanence of the royal archive and issued a charter to the commune of Arras, 1194, the Carité de Notre Dame des Ardents ensured that its members should remain "beneficiaries of the church of Sainte-Marie, in masses and in matins, and in all the prayers that are said there." Bound together with the coutumier at a later date, and written by some of the same scribes, the register accounts for a period of 167 years and the names of over 10,500 individuals, listed under the rubrics of the three bevées punctuating the Carité's ceremonial calendar: the four months after Pentecost (a moveable feast occurring the seventh week after Easter, in late May or June), the four months after the feast of Saint Rémy (October 1) up to the Feast of the Presentation of the Blessed Virgin (Candlemas, February 2), and the four months from this feast to that of Pentecost again.[77] It was fair-copied in 1207, but from that year to 1357 (and, sporadically, through 1361), the name of each deceased confrère or consoeur was ceremoniously recorded at the time of burial, allowing for a rough dating of the funeral. We have already consulted it: this is the register recording the death of Jehan Bodel in the wintry spring of 1210.

He! menestrel, douch conpaignon,	Ah, minstrels, my sweet companions,
Ami m'avez esté et bon	You've been my good friends all along,
Conme tres fin loial confrere:	Like loyal brothers, dear to me.
A pourchacier ma garison	To heal the pain of all my grief

---

ity, Fraternity: Lay Religious Confraternities in Bergamo in the Age of the Commune (Bergamo, 1988), 57–69. For a general overview, see Catherine Vincent, Les confréries médiévales dans le royaume de France, XIIIe–XVe siècle (Paris, 1994).

75. Robert Fossier, Chartes de coutume en Picardie (XIe–XIIIe. siècle) (Paris, 1974), no. 84.

76. BmA 1116, fol. 4r.

77. Since its rediscovery in the mid-nineteenth century, there have been disputes over the nomenclature of this artifact. Guesnon, who performed the original analysis, called it a "register," which he defined as "un recueil de rôles mortuaires et comptabilité funèbre" (Le régistre, 7). Berger's use of the term "necrology" is technically a misnomer, according to Nicolas Huyghebaert, Les documents nécrologiques (Turnhout, 1972), 24–25; see also Delmaire, Le diocèse, 1:380. I have therefore returned to the generic term "register."

M'avez fait amour et raison	You've given love and true relief:
Plus que se tout fussiez mi frere.	More kind than true brothers could be.
Diex vous en soit guerredonnere	May God reward you graciously,
Et sa tres douce chiere mere	And his sweet mother too, Marie,
Qui a vous a fait le haut don.	Who gave the greatest gift to you.
Priiés que sa largece pere	Pray that her grace will fall like dew,
En moi, par quoi prit a son pere	Through which I'll pray for the pardon
Et a son fill pour moi pardon.	Of God the Father and her Son.[78]

The dignity with which the Carité honored the deaths of even the humblest of its members—and it often paid for the funerals of unnamed children and nameless indigents as well—adds a human dimension to the gilded picture of obsequies marking the deaths of more exalted personages, about which we have more information. For, as the coutumier states, "no one is so poor that they should not be so accompanied."[79] Regardless of the deceased's status in society, his status in the confraternity warranted a ceremonial guard of twenty of its échevins, who carried the body in procession to the appropriate parish church for the chanting of Mass, and who also took care to ensure the seemly disposition of the body, the deportment of the officers, and the behavior of mourners. The remaining members of the Carité were supposed to arrive in time to witness the removal of the deceased from home, and fines were imposed on those who were late or who did not walk in procession behind the Carité's cross to the church, "because all must be there to sit around the body and do it honor and remain around the body until it is put in the grave and the spades are put down."[80] After the body was interred, custom dictated that an account (*conte*) be drawn up by the maieur of jongleurs and a committee of échevins, none of whom were allowed to leave until the maieur had approved it and sealed the register in which the deceased's name had been entered. The échevins were then responsible for transporting the register to the next ceremonial occasion on which it was needed.[81] If another memorial service was held in honor of the deceased, the register would be carried there, unsealed, and a mark added next to the name to signify that this had been done.[82]

78. Jehan Bodel, *Congé*, vv. 517–528.

79. Coutumier, fol. 46rᵃ: "por que si poures soit que conreer ne le puist."

80. Coutumier, fols. 46vᵃ–46vᵇ: "car tot doivent ester u seir entor le cors por faire le cors honeur. & estre entor lecors tant qil soit en fois & que les peles soient mie sius."

81. Coutumier, fol. 46vᵇ. This appears to be a system designed to ensure that monies entered into account were not done so fraudulently, and to ensure that the accounts were kept in a consistent manner. The later register of the confraternity of Notre-Dame-du-Jardin describes such a system in BmA 1116, fols. 6r–v.

82. I extrapolate from Berger's explanation of these markings (*Le nécrologe*, 1:31–37).

The Lordship of Jongleurs

According to Herbert Grundmann, it is only when a group of laypeople ceases to depend solely on aural instruction that "a new stratum [forms] between laity and clergy," setting up the vernacular as an alternative written authority. He asserted that the group who first "breach[ed] the strict division between Latin-trained clergy and the laity" was female, and can be seen reading (if not producing) vernacular devotional texts around 1300.[83] The confraternity of jongleurs in Arras meets the same criteria over a century earlier, even to the extent of being a gendered group supposedly barred from participation in the more legitimate spheres of masculine influence, and which nevertheless won the support of representatives from within the institutional Church, who in turn helped to cast the jongleurs in their new role as disseminators of social and spiritual values.

But if the happy prospect of harmonious interaction set forth in the history of the Carité's miracle and echoed in the coutumier seems too good to be true, that is because it probably was. Both the vernacular version of the foundation legend and the indigenous legislation drafted by the confraternity in the first few decades of the thirteenth century reveal that the jongleurs' role in the governance of an increasingly powerful Carité was a matter of dispute. This is something that the Latin narrative had either refused to acknowledge or attempted to mask. "And out of reverence for the Blessed Virgin and the miraculous doings of God, that candle given by the hand of the Blessed Virgin Mary was kept by the successors of the jongleurs in the city of Arras, up to the present day," it says, "and through it, the mercy of God is frequently at work among the sick." Ringing down the curtain on the triumphs of Pierre Norman, Ithier, and Lambert, it arranges members of the Carité in a soft-focus tableau vivant: "In memory of the miracle, the jongleurs established a confraternity which was kept up for a while by lowly confrères. But now, in our own time, honorable men and women from the city and other nobles are associated with it, including even clerics and knights, and the prayers and gifts for the sustenance of the poor have increased." That, in Latin, is the end of the story.[84]

83. Herbert Grundmann, *Religiöse Bewegungen im Mittelalter*, 4th ed. (Hildesheim, 1977), trans. Steven Rowan as *Religious Movements in the Middle Ages* (Notre Dame, 1995), 188, 191. Vernacular culture does not form a part of Brian Stock's similar treatment, although he does emphasize the extent to which these new "textual communities" may have gained access to literacy in order to combat a literate authority on its own terms; Stock, *The Implications of Literacy: Written Language and Models of Interpretation in the Eleventh and Twelfth Centuries* (Princeton, 1983), 28 and 90.

84. *Chandelle*,154: "Et ob venerationem beate Virginis et Dei miraculose actionis, reservatus est cereus ille datus per manum beate Marie virginis, per successiones joculatorum, in civitate Atrebatensi, usque in hodiernum diem et per eum in infirmis frequenter operatur Dei miseratio. Ob cujus miraculi memoriam, joculatores constituerunt confratriam, que aliquando per paucos detenta est confratres. Sed nunc, his nostris temporibus, associatis sibi venerabilibus viris et mulieribus civitatis et aliis nobilibus, cleris scilicet et militibus, orationes et beneficia et pauperum sustentationes augmentantur."

But then the vernacular narrator bursts upon the scene, throwing a sudden, harsh light on the picture, in his only significant departure from the official narrative and his only personal intervention in the history's recounting. "And for the remembrance of this miracle, the jongleurs established a confraternity and a charity which was maintained for a long time by a few confrères. But a little while later it became bigger, because the knights entered it, and they set about tearing down and pulling the poor folk from the seat which they had made and kept."[85] For, the narrator goes on to explain, "it seemed shameful and outrageous to the knights of the region that the jongleurs should be masters and lords over them," so they harnessed the power of the confraternity to their own ignoble ends, fomenting an aristocratic resistance to the jongleurs' lordship that went on for eight or nine years during the aging founders' lifetime. Eventually, when Norman and Ithier died, the knights took advantage of this delicate transitional moment to stage a coup. And they were led by "two lords that I know well how to name," the narrator announces: Nicolas, lord of Bailleul and Imercourt, and Jehan de Wancourt, men identifiable as active during the Carité's formative years, between 1184 and 1203.[86] Nicolas, addressing his faction in a fiery speech, explained their rationale: "Lords, this Carité is of great lordship, and we will suffer great shame whenever jongleurs are lords and masters over us in this way. But we don't want them to be part of our group any more, nor come with us to make offerings, nor do anything else that they have been doing, but they should keep their confraternity and charity to themselves, just as we should keep this one among ourselves."[87]

Mortified by their subsidiary position, which would have been dramatically and publicly expressed at the annual grand siège as well as on other occasions, the knights are said to have ousted the jongleurs from their fellowship. Yet they attempted to retain the guardianship of the Sainte-Chandelle, forgetting that the Blessed Virgin had bestowed her gift solely on the jongleurs and their successors: only they have the power to distill its healing potions, while those who violate their lordship are condemned to "the fire of Hell." Thus the Virgin clarifies the terms of her original grant for the edification of the two bad lords of the vernacular legend, who are now stricken with the mal des ardents: "If you ever want to recover your health, amend the wrong of this outrage and return their inheritance

---

85. *Chandelle*, 154: "Et pur la remembrance de cest miracle, establirent li jugleor une conflarrie et une charité qui fu lonc tens meintenue par petit de confreres. Mes en pou d'eure fu molt grant, quar li chevalier i entrerent, qui doivent rentes a conreer la povre gent au siege qui ert fez et diz."

86. *Chandelle*, 154: "tant que hontes et vitez sembla as chevaliers du pais que li jugleor deussent estre mestre et seignor desor euls. . . . dui seignor que ge sai bien nonmer." On the dating of these events, see Berger, *Le nécrologe*, 2:45–46.

87. *Chandelle*, 154: "Seignor, cest charite est de grant seignorie et nos li fesons grant honte quant li jugleor en sont si seignor et mestre deseur nos. Mes ne voulons quil soient en nostre compaignie plus, ne quil viegnent avec nos offrir, ne quil i aient pooste, mes lor conflarrie et lor charite tiegnent par eus et nos tendrons ceste par nos."

to them, which I enfeoffed them in for all time."[88] The episode's denouement mirrors that of the original miracle, only this time the knightly pretenders to the jongleurs' power must make their way ignominiously, on litters, to the church of Notre-Dame, where they find that their accounts of the Virgin's chastisement are identical. "Then there happened to come, as it seems to me, all the jongleurs who were staying then in Arras. And so they gave back to them, there on the spot, their charter and their rights."[89]

This addendum to the Carité's legend brings the founding miracle up to date and addresses the internal tensions arising from the group's early achievements, offering proofs of authenticity (names, dates) vouched for by the narrator's own testamentary intervention. It would be a mistake to dismiss the incident as mere romance. It stands to reason that the jongleurs' control of the Carité's "great lordship" would be perceived as threatening to certain segments of Arrageois society, blandly described in the Latin narrative as "honorable men and women from the city and other nobles." These were the remains of the old landed gentry—one is reminded of the recalcitrant Outre l'Arbre Sec in the *Jeu de saint Nicolas*—tentatively allied with the nouveaux-riches who were jockeying for power in the commune's échevinage and happy to be mistaken for "other nobles," the very echelons of the urban or suburban aristocracy most likely to be infuriated by a league of prodigals that had become a lordship of jongleurs.[90] The objections voiced by the loudmouthed Nicolas are as much social as political, and are promptly echoed by his yes-man, Jehan: "There is very little worth in them!" he had agreed, "and whenever it looks good to you, we should throw them out and take our rightful share, for they are fools and outcasts. Prevent them from coming here anymore, but let them keep their charity by themselves."[91] He betrays the insecurity of a social climber who has no credibility himself, and whose tactic is to challenge the reversal of fortune which the original miracle had effected, urging a return to the primordial hierarchy that had subsisted before the confraternity confused distinctions of social rank, political privilege, and spiritual authority.

The core issue of the controversy dramatized in the vernacular legend is further cor-

88. *Chandelle*, 155: "Se tu sante veus recevoir james, amande leur tost cest outrage et lor heritage leur rent dont ge les fievai a toz jorz."

89. *Chandelle*, 155: "Lors firent venir, ce me semble, touz les jugleors qui en Arraz erent menant; si leur rendirent en es le pas leur chartre et lor droiture."

90. Theodore Evergates, "Nobles and Knights in Twelfth-Century France," in Bisson, *Cultures*, 11–35. See also Léopold Genicot, "Aristocratie et dignités ecclésiastiques en Picardie aux XIIe et XIIIe siècles," *Revue d'histoire ecclésiastique* 67 (1972): 436–442; Pierre Feuchère, "La noblesse du nord de la France," *Annales E.S.C.* 6 (1951): 306–318; Jean Lestocquoy, *Patriciens du Moyen Age: Les dynasties bourgeoises d'Arras du XIe au XVe siècles* (Arras, 1945).

91. *Chandelle*, 154: "Il a en euls molt pou daquest. font li autre. qan quil vos est bon nos lotroions bien de nostre part quar il sont fol et outrageus. Deffandez lor quil ni viegnent plus, mes tiegnent par euls leur charité."

roborated in the Carité's coutumier: "This Carité was founded by jongleurs, and the jongleurs are lords of it. And those whom they put in, are in. And whoever they keep outside cannot be in, unless they say so. Because there is no lordship with us, save that of jongleurs."[92] The apostolic language of this pronouncement was later tempered by an amendment made when the customs were recopied: "And so it is made known that the jongleurs cannot get rid of anyone, nor can anyone else, except by common accord." Furthermore, a number of checks and balances would be put in place over the next few decades in order to ensure that the *carite nostre dame des ardents* could become a *confrerie des jogleors et des bourgois* while maintaining the jongleurs' unassailable position at the top of the Virgin's hierarchy.[93] Hence, the documents produced by the Carité during the first half of the thirteenth century delineate, more and more thoroughly, the separate roles of the two types of people included in its fellowship: jongleurs and non-jongleurs. The jongleurs had the advantage of rank and seniority. They were the lords of the Carité, the heirs of its founders, while the townspeople of Arras were merely the heirs of those first ardents whose social ills had brought down "the fire of Hell" and necessitated the intercession of jongleurs in the first place. Among this priestly caste, a few were "on the inside" (*dedans*), that is, the four permanent jongleur-officers resident in the confraternal hall known as "Our Lady's house" and who were later listed on the Carité's permanent payroll in the ordinances compiled by 1267. These men were supported by the Carité's remaining jongleur members "on the outside" (*dehors*), who were "foreign" (*forains*) or resident at large.[94] To some extent, this terminology mimicked that of the cathedral chapter, whose "foreign" canons lived outside the shelter of the close, as well as that of the commune, which considered those living outside the banlieue of Arras to be *forains*.[95] But it was also symbolic of the legendary travails of the Carité's history. The pairing of the jongleurs' two maieurs mirrored the original partnership of Norman and Ithier, one of whom was from inside the Artois, the other of whom was *forain*; and the maieurs would take turns riding "on horseback" or walking "on foot" on ceremonial occasions in memory of their founders' journeys and in imitation of the sergeants employed by the échevins of Arras.[96] Within the

92. Coutumier, fol. 46r[b]: "Ceste carites est estores des iogleors & li iogleor en sont signor. & cil cui il metent si est. & cui il ratene hors ni puet estre se par els non. Car sor iogleors ni a nus signorie."

93. Coutumier, fol. 46v[a]: "Et si est asvaoir qu li iogleor nen puent nului oster ne austres se ce nest par le commun plait."

94. Espinas (*Les origines*, 1:94) thought that the jongleurs described as *forains* in the documents of the Carité were "foreign to Arras," which has caused much confusion in subsequent scholarship, e.g., Berger, *Le nécrologe*, 2:50; Ruelle, *Les congés*, 178–179; and Jean-Charles Payen, "L'homo viator et le croisé: La mort et le salut dans la tradition du douzain," in Braet and Verbeke, *Death*, 205–221 at 213.

95. Pycke, *Le chapitre*, 115–126; Paul Bertin, *Une commune flamande-artésienne: Aire-sur-la-Lys dès origines au XVIe siècle* (Arras, 1946), 132.

96. The formula *ke a piet ke a cheval* is used to describe these officials in the record of an inquest held

household, each of the four jongleurs served as maieur for a year in what was ostensibly a four-year cycle; outside, the maieur of jongleurs was selected by a committee of eight "prudhommes" chosen from among the jongleurs living in Arras, with the advice of the four jongleurs "on the inside."

Representing the confraternity's civilian members, a similar pairing of maieurs recalled the two upstart lords and the ill-fated revolt put down by the Virgin. Their predecessors' ignominy was reflected in the manner of their election to office: while the jongleurs' leaders were freely chosen by their professional peers, the townspeople's maieurs had to be vetted by the Virgin herself. After an initial round of nominations solicited from each of the ardents' échevins, the three men who had garnered the most votes would sit on a bench apart from the group. Then each would be given a ball of wax "in one of which is written 'Ave Maria' on a slip of parchment. And he of the three who has the writing becomes maieur for the time to come."[97] The different privileges of the jongleurs' chosen officers and those of the townspeople were also demarcated financially: many of the former were paid to serve the Carité, while many of the latter paid for the privilege. The maieur of ardents was responsible for providing hospitality on several occasions throughout the year, as were the échevins appointed after Easter to oversee preparations for the annual feast. In practice, then, those non-jongleurs eligible for the townspeople's mayoral office would have to possess the wealth and leisure to sustain duties that were particularly heavy during the first year of service and that continued into the next, after a new incumbent had been elected. Indeed, men who had served as maieurs formed something of a ceremonial college and were often called upon to fulfill official duties long after their terms had ended.

The jongleurs' lordship and the ardents' indebtedness to the Virgin's chosen agents were also stressed in the most official of public media: the Carité's seals. In the early thirteenth century, the ardents had not even been represented on the matrix used by the Carité. A description of the seal whose use is frequently attested in its earliest records, and which was appended to the transcription of the Latin foundation narrative in 1241, apparently showed only two men, both playing upon *vielles*.[98] Later, when the confraternity had a pair of seals, that of the ardents showed the Blessed Virgin enthroned, holding the Christ Child on her knee; the other bore a jongleur holding his *vielle* in the same posi-

---

in 1289: AdPC ser. A 1009. See Adolphe Guesnon, "Adam de la Halle et le Jeu de la feuillée," MA 28 (1915): 173–233 at 222. For a different interpretation, see Berger, Le nécrologe, 2:50.

97. *Ordinance*, fol. 7v: "Et si prent on .iij. boulles de chire et si a en lun escript ave maria en .i.billet de parquemin Et chius des .iij. qui a lescript demeure maires pour le temps avenir."

98. This is according to a description of the seal appended to a (lost) act of June 1248; Cavrois, Cartulaire, 115–116.

tion.[99] These designs represent claims to apostolic authority, since the figure of the Virgin often appeared on the devices of cathedral chapters whose main altars were dedicated to her.[100] They also refer to the jongleurs' lordship by way of comparison with courtly nobles who cultivated musicianship alongside their more warlike talents and who exhibited this mastery on their seals: in the twelfth century, for instance, Count Bertrand of Forcalquier had himself depicted on the obverse of his seal in an equestrian pose, while on the reverse he played the *vielle*.[101] The seals' complementary inscriptions reinforce both of these powerful messages, one in Latin and one in Picard: + BVLLA CARITATIS. ARDENTIVM. and + BOVLLE DES IOVGLEORS. Even the choice of the term *bulla* or *boule* for "seal" (rather than the usual *sigillum* or *sceau*) is significant, turning the papal bull into a juggler's ball, the *boule* that could stand for "foolery," "a game," or "a trick," a linguistic sleight-of-hand that is a signature feature of the jongleurs' pardoxical lordship.

Documents and Monuments

In the year 1200 the Carité took up a newly prominent position in the public life of Arras, symbolized by its occupation of a plot measuring "forty feet of earth in length and fourteen feet in width, situated in the Petit Marché of Arras on the property of the church [of Saint-Vaast] . . . on the way toward the butchers' stalls." This was the most valuable real estate in the Town, its ground rents jealously husbanded by the abbey of Saint-Vaast.[102] The abbey also sanctioned (and may have financed) the building of the chapel

---

99. AdPC ser. A.482/56. They are appended to a *quittance* dated July of 1328 and are reproduced by Berger, *Le nécrologe*, vol. 2, plate 1. See also Adolphe Guesnon, *Sigillographie de la ville d'Arras et de la Cité* (Arras, 1865), 25–26 and plate 12.

100. Brigitte Bedos-Rezak, "Women, Seals, and Power in Medieval France, 1150–1350," in *Women and Power in the Middle Ages*, ed. M. Erler and M. Kowaleski (Athens, Ga., 1982), 61–82 at 75–76 and fig. 13 (seal of the chapter of Notre-Dame de Chartres); and "Medieval Women in French Sigillographic Sources," in *Women and the Sources of Medieval History*, ed. J. T. Rosenthal (Athens, Ga., 1990), 1–36 at 7 and fig. 7 (seal of the chapter of Notre-Dame de Nantes).

101. Brigitte Bedos-Rezak, "The Social Implications of the Art of Chivalry: The Sigillographic Evidence," in *The Medieval Court in Europe*, ed. E. R. Haymes (Munich, 1986), 1–31 at 22–23 and figs. 13–14.

102. "XL piedz de terre de long et XIIII piedz de lez seans ou petit marquet dArras ou tresfons dicelle eglise tenant a ladicte cappelle, en allant vers le boucherie." AdPC ser. 1 H 1, fol. 245r. On the significance of this donation with respect to larger trends in urban real estate holdings, see Jean-Pierre Leguay, "La propriété et le marché de l'immobilier à la fin du moyen âge dans le royaume de France et dans les grands fiefs périphériques," in *D'une ville à l'autre: Structures matérielles et organisation de l'espace dans les villes européennes (XIIIe–XVIe siècles)*, ed. Jean-Claude Maire Vigueur (Rome, 1989), 135–199. See also Lestocquoy, *Patriciens*, 118–119.

whose diminutive footprint became the base of the "Pyramide," or "Tower," a small oratory topped with an expensive Gothic spire as high as the cathedral's newly raised roof, adorned with a mounting procession of apostles and jongleurs.[103]

It was a strategic move on the monks' part as well as that of the jongleurs. Relocation could not alter the miracle's story, but it did alter the surroundings in which the story was told. Even though the confraternity's many rituals would still invoke the bishop of Arras, and annual processions still visited the cathedral, the location of the Carité's relic and its altar now situated the miracle, physically, in the marketplace and within the patrimony of Saint-Vaast. Whatever was said about the Virgin's candle—and not said, in the story, about the role of Saint Vaast—would now be countered by the location in which it was said and the backdrop against which the candle appeared. The inscription chiseled in uncial capitals over the chapel door is telling. "This pyramid was erected on the ground of Saint-Vaast by consent of the abbot and chapter, without whose assent an altar could not have been built, nor divine services celebrated, nor anything else done that was done."[104]

For its part, the Carité may have begun courting the favor of the abbey years before the chapel was planned and built, its gaze fixed on a central location where minstrels could profitably practice their arts when they were not performing the ritual business of the confraternity. Perhaps it was in an attempt to curry favor with the monks that it scheduled one of its annual bevées on the feast of Saint Rémy (October 1), a date coinciding with the abbey's day of reckoning, when there was always "a monk sitting at the gates of the church, receiving the *census* in his lap."[105] Not only had the historical Rémy been the mentor of Vaast, and therefore a saint with local connections (Manchevaire swears by him in her seduction of Courtois), but he was also the same Bishop Remigius who had baptized Clovis. So the choice may have been calculated, too, to pay a delicate compliment to the king of the Franks so lately arrived in Arras.

Back in their newly remodeled cathedral, the canons of Notre-Dame had to be content with occasional displays of the Sainte-Chandelle and a handsome cenotaph added to the tomb of Bishop Lambert, crediting the miracle to their founding bishop, "by whom the episcopal dignity of Arras was restored, which for a long time had been accorded to

---

103. For a full description, see Pierre Héliot, *Les églises du moyen âge dans le Pas-de-Calais*, 2 vols. (Arras, 1951 and 1953), 1:237 and 2:352–353; on the relative heights of the other roofs and spires, see 1:220, 250, 237, 350, and 2:353. The chapel was razed in 1791, a year before the confraternity was formally dissolved. An architect's drawing made prior to the demolition is reproduced in Berger, *Le nécrologe*, vol. 2, plate 5.

104. "Anno dominice Incarnationis M° CC°.hec pyramis erecta est in fundo Sancti Vedasti per consensum abbatis et capituli sine assensu nec altare hic potuit erigi nec divina celebrari nec aliud fieri." AdPC ser. 1 H 1, fol. 245r. For a facsimile of the copy made by an antiquary, see *Épigraphie*, 734 (no. 1822).

105. "In die festo sancti Remigii ad valvas ecclesie cum monachos sedens et censum recipiens, in gremium monachi." Guiman, 178.

the bishop of Cambrai. To this bishop and to two jongleurs, Ithier and Norman, Blessed Mary appeared in this church, giving them a candle by which those burning with the *mal des ardents* were cured."[106] An addendum to the Carité's customary laws, dated 1338, further testifies that "the maieur and the échevins of the Carité ought to do the service for Bishop Lambert each year on the day of mid-May," alluding to an annual commemoration that may have taken place at the cathedral.[107] And Lambert's successors still had a very prominent role to play during the confraternity's annual feast. On the first day of its grand siège, the bishop would wait outside the parish church of Saint-Géry, one of the curacies belonging to the cathedral chapter and thus a neutral location in the otherwise alien Town, just south of the Petit Marché; this was the parish in which the Pyramide was situated and, not incidentally, the church whose belfry housed the bell used by the commune for its banns.[108] There the bishop would receive the Sainte-Chandelle from the maieur of jongleurs and carry it in solemn procession back to the Petit Marché—the only time of the year when the relic could be handled by anyone other than a designated jongleur, and a reminder of the way that Pierre Norman and Ithier had magnanimously received the bishop into their fellowship.[109] The handsome silver-gilt reliquary fashioned for the Sainte-Chandelle during the second quarter of the thirteenth century (still extant) also commemorates the bishop's involvement in the Carité's miracle, showing Lambert and the two founding jongleurs in prayerful postures beneath a portrait of the Virgin with her candle, the relic that was now known as the Joyel, the "jewel" of Arras.[110] Nevertheless, the

106. "Anno Domini millesimo centesimo decimo quinto XVI Kalend. Junii. obiit beatae memoriae Lambertus. huius Atrebatensis sedis cardinalis episcopus. Per hunc restituta est dignitas hujus episcopatus. quae per multa tempora Cameracensi episcopo fuerat commendata. Huic episcopo et duobus joculatoribus Itherio et Normanno beata Maria in hac ecclesia apparuit. dans eis candelam. per quam sanantur ardentes igne malo." Guesnon showed that this "epitaph," supposed by modern antiquaries to have been inscribed on Lambert's tomb at the time of his death (Cavrois, *Cartulaire*, 37–38), was really a memorial erected a century later; Guesnon, "La Confrérie des jongleurs d'Arras et le tombeau de l'évêque Lambert," *MCdMhPC* (1913): 6.

107. BnF fr. 8541, fol. 49r: "Et si doivent li mayeur et li eschievin de le carite faire le service du vesque Lambert cascun an au jour de mi ay." See also Espinas, *Les origines*, 2:64. The text is only partially transcribed in Cavrois, *Cartulaire*, 174.

108. Delmaire, *Le diocèse*, 2:427. See chapter 3.

109. Coutumier, fols. 46v^b–47r^a.

110. This is the term employed throughout the *Ordinance*. Jean Lestocquoy has dated the reliquary to the period 1220–1250, advancing the hypothesis that it might have been made by Hugo d'Oignies, monk of the priory of Saint-Nicolas and a famous goldsmith; Lestocquoy, "Deux reliquaires du XIIIe siècle: La custode du Sainte-Cierge et le reliquaire de la Sainte-Epine d'Arras," *MCdMhPC* (1908–1935): 397–407. For detailed photographs, see Berger, *Le nécrologe*, plate 6. A copy is currently on display to the left of the main altar of the church of Notre-Dame-des-Ardents in Arras; the original is usually kept in the episcopal treasury.

bishop was constantly upstaged. In the historiated initial accompanying the vernacular version of the foundation legend (Figure 12), we catch only a glimpse of his balding pate, his eyebrows raised in surprise as he peers over the heads of Norman and Ithier to get a better view of the Virgin, before fading gently into the margin.

The Carité also eclipsed the commune during this period, which had as yet no architectural monuments to its corporate identity, neither belfry nor hall, while the jongleurs had both the Pyramide and the building called "Our Lady's house" (*maison nostre dame*) or "the hall of the ardents" (*hala ardentium*), extant by 1224 and situated just to the northwest of the Petit Marché, off the rue de l'Aiguillerie.[111] The Carité's importance was not merely imprinted on the urban landscape; it was articulated in vivid symbolic language every year on the *relatio Sancti Vedasti*, when it literally led the community of Arras. This was the feast dedicated to "an accounting" in honor of Saint Vaast, on July 15, the day when the saint's relics were paraded around the abbey's ancient *castrum* and then placed atop the high altar for three days. It was also the day on which the commune and the abbey's tenants did homage for their holdings.[112]

Although this ceremony was supposed to dramatize the townspeople's dependence on Saint-Vaast, the jongleurs of the confraternity were adept at somersaulting and grandstanding even when they were supposed to be adopting postures of submissive gratitude. On the morning of that day, at the hour of High Mass, one of the jongleurs' two maieurs carried the Sainte-Chandelle from the Pyramide and through the streets of Arras, accompanied by all of the Carité's members dressed in festal array, with the other maieur of jongleurs carrying the key to the chapel door and the two maieurs of ardents carrying the offerings due Saint-Vaast: a thirty-pound wax candle and an effigy of the saint and his mascot (a bear), also made of wax and weighing six pounds. Proceeding with the same pomp exhibited during the solemnities of the confraternity's grand siège—the abbey insisted on this, explicitly—they were followed by the maieur, échevins, and commune of Arras. As the confraternity's own *Ordinance* directed: "One should carry all these things to Saint-Vaast in plain view, accompanied by banners and trumpets and *vielles* and all other kinds of minstrelsy. And when the trumpeters or other minstrels are outside the abbey, they

---

111. The date is based on references in the Coutumier (fol.47r[a]) in the contemporary *hostagia* of the cathedral, BnF lat. 10972, fol. 35r.

112. See also Delmaire, *Le diocèse*, 1:354–367; and Berger, *Le nécrologe*, 2:28. The ceremony is documented by the Carité in its *Ordinance* (before ca. 1267) and in a sixteenth-century copy of the abbey's cartulary containing, among other texts, the census of Guiman; APdC, ser. 1H 1, fols. 245r–247r. It has been edited by Espinas, *Les origines*, 2:76–79, and (with omissions) by Cavrois, *Cartulaire*, 160–165; I have used my own transcription. The two descriptions are very similar, although the Carité's is shorter. The abbey's dates from November 1315, when some new elements had to be incorporated into the traditional ceremony; see BmA 230, fols. 136r[a]–136v[b] and chapter 4.

should all perform *courtoisies*, each according to his art."[113] Outside the gates of the monastery, on the street still known as the rue des Jongleurs, the maieur bearing the Sainte-Chandelle would wait to be conducted into the abbey church, where the confraternity's treasured relic was placed on the high altar, lending its brilliant aura to the musty remains of Saint Vaast. Meanwhile, the maieur with the key would be outside with "all the minstrels remaining there, each one playing according to his mastery and then going, all still playing on their instruments, before the said maieur carrying the key raised up high."[114] When the ceremony was over, the entire procession would re-form and return to the Petit Marché, the maieur of jongleurs with the Sainte-Chandelle again leading the entire community of Arras, to the tune of the other jongleurs. "And on their way back to the hall one should, for God, give alms to the poor minstrels, each according to his desert."[115]

The increasing involvement of the Carité in the civic life of Arras during this period is simultaneously reflected in the number of funerals over which it presided: sixty per year by 1203, eighty-eight between 1204 and 1213, and over one hundred at its apogee, between 1214 and 1223, when the population of Arras was at its height and approaching 35,000 souls.[116] Bearing in mind that no other confraternities appear to have been formed at this time (that of the barbers was not founded until 1247 or 1248), it may have been the case that the Carité was the only such institution open to people of small means, as well as to those impressed by the social and political consequence of its lordship.[117] The jongleurs of "Our Lady's house" were also charged with continual ministry to the sick, and by 1249 they would be responsible for visiting the hospital established in the name of the Carité, the smallest of the six such charitable institutions in Arras but another of its significant acquisitions.[118] As a direct result of their successful campaign for lordship, then, the jon-

---

113. *Ordinance*, fol. 6v: "Item on doit porter toutes ches coses a sain vaast as avis as confanons a trompes a vielles et a toutes autres menestrandies Et quant il ya trompeures ou autres menestreus de dehors on leur doit faire courtoisies selon che que il sont."

114. APdC, ser. 1H 1, fols. 245v: "tous les mensetrels la estans joues chacun des son mestres et de la aller tous iouant de leurs instrumens devant ledis mayeurs portans ladicte clef en hault."

115. *Ordinance*, fol. 6v: "Et au revenir u praiiel on donne pour dieu as poures menestraus selon che que il sont."

116. Berger, *Le nécrologe*, 2:58.

117. See Roger Rodière, "Testament de Gilles, sire de Pas-en-Artois et d'Allines, BSAM 15 (1929–1937): 208; Berger, *Le nécrologe*, 2:52.

118. The hospital was the bequest of Adam de Bapaume, whose death in 1249 is listed in the register under Candlemas. The number of beds appears to have been limited to three in the early fourteenth century, according to an inquest made between 1324 and 1329 by the bailiff of the Countess Mahaut: "Li maisons des Ardans de Nostre Dame, i sont uns home et une feme et n'ont riens. Si i y a III lis pour les malades ardans"; AdPC ser. A 899. See Berger, *Le nécrologe*, 1:42 and 51; Delmaire, *Le diocèse*, 1:277–293.

gleurs' duties were becoming onerous. Indeed, changes made to the coutumier at about this time reflect a perceived need to limit their charitable operations to a fixed radius, in imitation of the town's banlieue, and reveal that the Carité had begun to pay the wages of those who guarded the Sainte-Chandelle and acted as its sergeants and heralds, while retaining two paid clerics to "make the writing" and to read the Psalter and the funeral prayers.[119]

Eventually, however, the ad hoc arrangements noted in the coutumier were clarified by a new centralized system of bookkeeping and administration overseen by the members of the Carité's household, enshrined in another remarkable monument to the jongleurs' lordship. It is impressively titled *This is the Ordinance of the rights which those who appear below have from the Carité during the siège. And in what manner things ought to be done.*[120] Written down between 1249 and 1267 (Figure 15), it is unlike either the coutumier or the register in that it preserves a clear snapshot of the Carité's *familia* and its festive calendar at a particular moment in time, and in many respects imitates—even anticipates—the household accounts that were just beginning to make their appearance in the princely courts of Europe.[121] In addition to adjusting the protocols for the conduct of funerals, the *Ordianance* presents a reckoning of the preparations to be made for the grand siège and regulates the confraternity's other major feasts, which had come to include the midsummer feast of Saint John the Baptist and the feast of the Assumption. The very making of such a record was a way of aligning the Carité's lordship with that of the aristocracy, as were the *Ordinance*'s detailed displays of hospitality, presentation of gifts, and alms-giving, which involved the minting and distribution of token coins (*meriaus* or merels), at its annual feast.[122]

In general, see Michel Mollat, "Hospitalité et assistance au début de XIIIe siècle," in Flood, *Poverty*, 37–51 at 42–43.

119. Coutumier, fol. 47r[b:] "de lescrit faire."

120. *Chest li ordenanche des drois que chil qui chi apres sensient ont a le carite au siege Et ensement she que on doit faire.* It consists of a single gathering of eight leaves, penned in a large, legible bookhand and carefully rubricated. It is nearly square in shape, measuring 30x29 cm. Now catalogued as BmA, Archives de la conférie MS 239, it was formerly part of the archives of the bishopric of Arras. It is briefly described and edited by Cavrois, *Cartulaire*, 117–127, and by Espinas, *Les origines*, 2:67–75. I have relied on my own transcription and my own proposed dating, which is based on paleographic and internal evidence, that is, the document's presupposition of the hospital acquired in 1249, and the fact that the death of one of the two named officeholders is recorded in the Carité's register in 1267.

121. Malcolm Vale, *The Princely Court: Medieval Courts and Culture in North-West Europe, 1270–1380* (Oxford, 2001), 9, 34, and 47.

122. A number of these coins, cast in lead and stamped with an "A," have been found in the Artois, but Richebé was at a loss to explain their significance since he knew of no texts making mention of merels (*Les monnaies*, 149). On the festive uses of merels—as currency for local goods and services, for

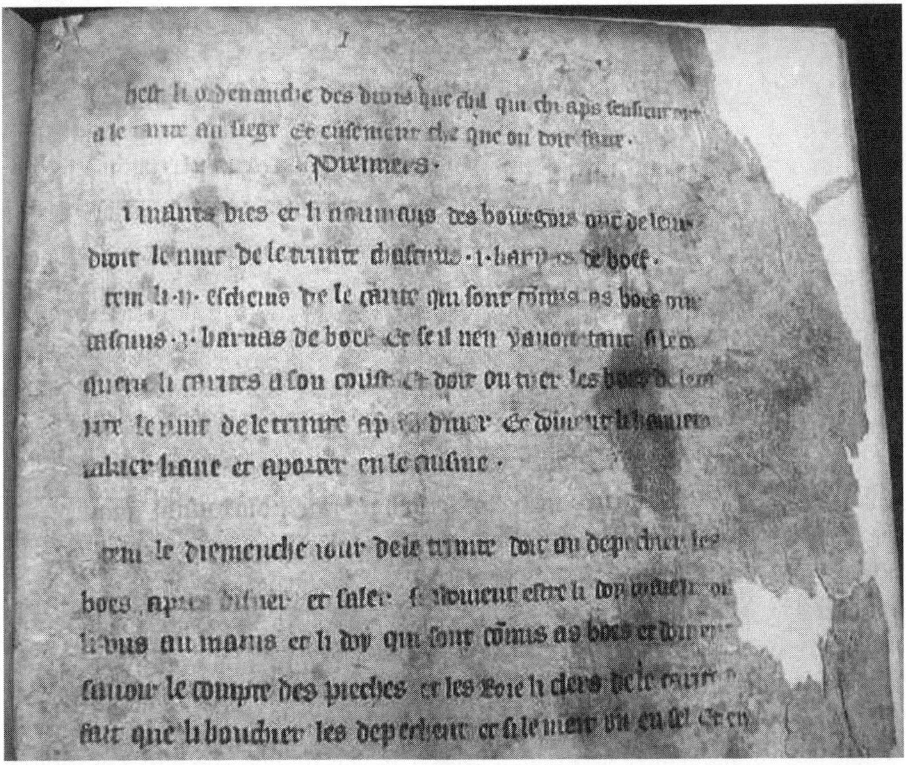

FIGURE 15. Opening page of the Carité's household *Ordinance* (BmA, Archives de la Confrérie MS 239, fol. 1r: author's photograph)

The decision to retain a household on salary, involving an annual expenditure of over 140 livres, further attests to the growth of the Carité's influence and to the increasingly elaborate arrangements necessary to promoting the cult of the Sainte-Chandelle and safeguarding the relic, administering the *potus*, and coordinating a complicated series of large-scale entertainments. For within the space of just two generations, the *maison nostre Dame* of the coutumier had become a *praiiel* or *préau*, a "court" worthy of a *seigneurie*, with retainers paid for services that were now as vital to the interests of the community as to the Carité. First came the jongleur serving as maieur, who earned either 20 livres or 16 livres, 16 sous per annum, depending on whether or not he was "on the watch" or "on guard" (*de l'eswart*), and the three other jongleurs who earned less, 52 sous per annum each, with an additional 52 sous "if they are on the watch, for the inconvenience [*maladie*] of the said watch." The double compensation indicates that being "on the watch" meant

---

gaming in taverns, or as *jetons* handed out by false bishops on the Feast of Fools—see Mehl, *Les jeux*, 149–151. See also chapters 1 and 4.

being on call and ready to administer holy water to the sick or dying at any time of the day or night, while the disparity between the maieur's wages and those of the other jongleurs suggests that the latter's duties were otherwise light enough to allow for employment elsewhere during non-mayoral years. (Since a laborer in Arras at this time earned between 7 and 9 livres per annum, an artisan 16 or 17, and a master craftsman between 23 and 28, the maieur of jongleurs was adequately, but not richly, compensated for the burdens of office.)[123] Along with the maieur, the Carité's other fully compensated employees were the sergeant of the watch, who was the confraternity's master of ceremonies and who earned 16 livres per annum, and the "greater sergeant," who was the steward of the household and earned 17 livres, 8 sous per annum "for his office" and the same amount "for his watch," either because he was constantly on call or because he needed to pay those who were. Also named are four men who earned between 4 and 9 livres apiece, barely a living wage in Arras, and whose duties are not specified, but who may have held the offices of four "lesser sergeants" mentioned elsewhere in the *Ordinance*, whose occasional duties were partly heraldic but may have included sharing "the watch." Finally, the *Ordinance* names two women who worked part-time, probably in the confraternity's hospital, since their fee of 52 sous matches that paid to an unnamed beguine (a lay sister of the religious house recently established in Arras) and to the household jongleurs "on the watch."[124]

Yet there is no mention, in all of this impressive and highly unusual documentation, of any theatrical activity—that is, if one applies a narrow definition of theater to the doings of the Carité. The supposed silence of the record on this head has been seen as surprising: because confraternities were instrumental in the development and production of plays by the end of the fourteenth century, the generations of scholars fascinated by the "origins" of "French" "literature" in Arras have assumed that the confraternity of jongleurs must have been founded for this purpose, and have looked in vain for hard evidence that would link the Carité to the plays by Jehan Bodel and Adam de la Halle.[125] And of

---

123. According to Delmaire, the manual laborer in Arras earned between 6 and 8 deniers per day around the year 1300; he worked, on average, 280 days out of the year. An artisan earned more than twice as much, 18 deniers per day. The annual wages of a master carpenter could amount to 23 livres, and that of a sculptor in wood to 28 livres (*Le diocèse*, 1:156).

124. There were two beguinages in thirteenth-century Arras, one at Baudimont in the City, founded around 1231, and one known as the *couvent le Roy*, allegedly founded by Louis IX in 1260. See ibid., 1:323 and 324.

125. In fact, the first French confraternity founded expressly for the performance of plays was formed at Nantes in 1371, while the "first solid evidence of a confraternity participation in the staffing of a play" comes from the account rolls of the Confrérie de Saint-Jacques aux Pèlerins at Paris in 1324–25; see Robert L. A. Clark, "Charity and Drama: The Response of the Confraternity to the Problem of Urban Poverty in Fourteenth-Century France," in *Le théâtre et la cité dans l'Europe médiévale*, ed. Jean-Claude

course, there is plenty of evidence for theater; it is merely of a different kind, and includes the superior artistry that informs the narrative of the jongleurs' miracle, in which the power of jongleurie is consistently emphasized, and the larger role played by the confraternity in the public life of Arras, through the pageantry of death and the ceremonial ministry of the Sainte-Chandelle. Yet this type of theatricality, and its practice by jongleurs, has frankly puzzled scholars, including the two twentieth-century historians most intimately familiar with the Carité's archive. "What is surprising, after all, is that the care of the dead should have occupied such a preponderant place in the activities of the confraternity!" Roger Berger exclaimed, while Georges Espinas found it very odd that jongleurs should have dedicated themselves to the custodianship of a Marian cult.[126]

Contemporaries would not have regarded this as strange. According to William FitzStephen, "the burial of the dead" had been among the city of London's chief plays. And in a sense, Jehan was staging his own funeral when he made his *Congé*, imitating the protocols of the confraternity as though he were already a corpse being carried through the streets of Arras, or the herald calling the confrères to his own memorial service: "To God I will commend you all / Together, not by calling roll," although he personally greets fourteen men whose names were eventually inscribed in the columns of the register alongside his own.[127] His very choice of the term *congé*, imitated by two later members of the confraternity, Baude Fastoul and Adam de la Halle, echoes the euphemism for unauthorized persons punished with "excommunication" for carrying the Sainte-Chandelle unlawfully: such a one was told that he "could take his leave" (*puet congie*).[128]

Dame, en cui sont tout bien logié,	Lady, in whose care all find reprieve,
A vo candoille pren congié	Of your Chandelle I take my leave,
Que donnastes as jougleours	The gift you gave to the jongleurs.
A li baisier ai renoncié	From kissing it I must refrain
Par un mal qui si m'a blecié	For my ills wound me with that pain
K'aler me couvient kes destours.	As well. I must needs patience learn,
Dusk'a li n'iert mais mes retours,	For fear I never will return,
Mais m'amour li laisse a tous jours,	But love I leave, till my last day.
Et quant iert ou petit marchié	When passing the Petit Marché
De moi iert baisie la tours	I'll blow my kisses to the Tour

———
Aubailly et al. (Stuttgart, 1988), 359–369. For Italy, see Matteo Rabaglio, *Drammaturgia popolare e teatro sacro: Riti e rappresentazioni del Venerdì Santo nel bergamasco* (Bergamo, 1989).

126. Berger, *Le nécrologe*, 1:33; Espinas, *Les origines*, 1:102.

127. "A Dieu vous vueil tous conmander / Ensamble, sans chascun nonmer." Jehan Bodel, *Congé*, vv. 529–530.

128. Coutumier, fols. 46r[b] and 46v[a].

Ou establis est ses sejours,   Where your candle now rests secure
S'avrai cuer mains mesaaisié.   And lay my heart there, it will stay.[129]

For a man who may well have served the confraternity as maieur and performed the healing rites of the Sainte-Chandelle, it must have been devastating to find that Virgin's gift had no powers to allay the scourge of leprosy.

Community Representation

Confraternities were the product of what Jacques Heers has called *la ville éclatée*, "the exploded town," of the Middle Ages, and the disintegration of traditional rural communities. They provided the rootless town dweller with a social and spiritual identity, a sense of professional solidarity, and, sometimes, political power.[130] In Italy, where scholars usually turn for their exemplars, they attracted between 10 and 50 percent of the adult male population by the later Middle Ages, providing opportunities "for regular worship, mutual aid, and social charity."[131] But there is no earlier or more striking example than that of the jongleurs' Carité, whose own archive provides us with something exceptional: evidence that brings us close to power as it was exercised by a group of people whose ordinary lot in life was its passive experience. As individuals, few of the Carité's members were influential; collectively, they participated in a "lordship of jongleurs." This was a phrase that could have provoked laughter, recalling the revelry of carnival, the world-turned-upside-down. Here, it was not an empty jest. It was an articulation of mastery over public media—stories, symbols, and ceremonies—honed to a cutting edge by the newer tools of accountability and diplomacy.

It stands to reason that a confraternity of jongleurs would be well equipped for effective negotiation via the technologies that facilitated communication in medieval theaters and medieval communities: aural, spectacular, linguistic, demonstrative. But like other

129. Jehan Bodel, *Congé*, vv. 505–516. This stanza (no. 43, vv. 505–516) is contained only in the "C" redaction of the *Congé*, preserved in the manuscript Arsenal 3124, made in Arras (Figure 9).

130. Heers, *La ville*, 250. See also Catherine Vincent, "Lieux de piété et lieux de pouvoir à Poitiers entre le XIIIe et le XVe siècle: La confrérie du Corps de ville dite aussi du Cent," in *La religion civique à l'époque médiévale et moderne (chrétienté et islam)*, ed. André Vauchez (Rome, 1995), 429–444; and Alain Derville, "Ghildes, carités, confréries dans le Saint-Omer médiéval," BSAM 19 (1959): 193–211.

131. Nicholas Terpstra, "Confraternities and Local Cults: Civic Religion between Class and Politics in Renaissance Bologna," in Johnston and Hüsken, *Civic Ritual*, 143–174 at 144. André Vauchez focuses almost exclusively on Italian cities in "'Ordo fraternitatis': Confréries et piété des laïcs au moyen âge," and "Patronage des saints et religion civique," in *Les laïcs au Moyen Age: Pratiques et expériences religieuses* (Paris, 1987), 95–104 and 169–186. There is only one brief mention of Arras in all three volumes of G. G. Meersseman's *Ordo fraternitatis: Confraternite e pietà dei laici nel medioevo* (Rome, 1977).

segments of the medieval population represented as negligible or of no account (women, the poor, the disabled), entertainers are often dismissed as having no legitimate role in society, especially by those who prefer to sift through the bad press they attracted. So it is continually asserted that most of them must have been illiterate or indigent, with no desire to make a contribution to the greater good, and no means of participating in civic endeavors: one reads that jongleurs "had no recognized place in any organization, as merchants and artisans did. Their mobility estranged them from the feudal structures of the countryside, as from the artisan organizations and corporations of the town."[132] This is patently false, and not only when applied to the professional entertainers of Arras. An organization providing a near-contemporary parallel is the Sienese Trumpeters' Corps, composed of salaried drummers and instrumentalists who also doubled as criers and heralds. Frank d'Accone describes them as an "indispensable part of the government's household," so much so that theirs were the only offices never endangered by local factionalism. For it was the city's musicians who "represented the commune at all officially sponsored civic, religious, diplomatic, and social events," offering "a concrete and tangible expression of the stability and legitimacy of the government."[133]

Ruminating on the success of the Carité, Edmond Faral wondered whether the fact of having entered into an association could itself alter the status of the jongleur. "For this is what, at first glance, is really new: that the jongleurs of a town could, through a common enterprise, blend in with the rest of the inhabitants, without distinction of profession or of rank."[134] But the Carité went further than that: it inverted the social order and created a new community out of the disjunctions and disharmonies that prevailed in Arras. The craft exhibited by every facet of the Carité's foundation legend, which subtly subverts even the authority of its episcopal patron, is only the first of many indicators that its collective genius could be both creative and interpretive. Later records, even those kept by its ecclesiastical benefactors, confirm that it continued to defy expectation by acting as a public intermediary in Arras to the end of the Middle Ages. In short, it wielded the sort of power best characterized as political, resting as it did on the capacity "to promote policy and cultivate the interests of persons and groups extending beyond lordly solidarity," to quote the definition of Thomas Bisson.[135] Indeed, Espinas considered its formation to be the historic beginning of a more open exhibition of the "ancient impulse" toward associative behavior in northern Europe, seeing it as the earliest manifestation of representative

---

132. Carla Casagrande and Silvana Vecchio, "Clercs et jongleurs dans la société médiévale (XIIe–XIIIe siècles)," *Annales E.S.C.* 34 (1979): 913–928 at 914.

133. Frank A. D'Accone, *The Civic Muse: Music and Musicians in Siena during the Middle Ages* (Chicago, 1997), 625.

134. Faral, *Les jongleurs*, 138.

135. Thomas N. Bisson, "Reply" to "Debate: The 'Feudal Revolution,'" *Past and Present*, 155 (1997): 208–225 at 215.

government, a medieval democracy.[136] Andrew Gurr has advanced a very similar argument with respect to "the Shakespeare Company" in late sixteenth- and seventeenth-century England, calling it "the only effective democracy of its time in totalitarian England."[137]

Perhaps there was "more rhetoric than reality" to the extravagant claims of most medieval confraternities; but then, rhetoric is a powerful force, particularly in the construction of group identity.[138] In this case, its skillful deployment brought real power, real credibility, real estate. It also won widespread publicity and emulation. In Arras itself, the confraternity of barbers was based directly on the Carité, while the confraternity of Notre-Dame-du-Jardin would attempt to usurp the customs, the holidays, and even the symbolic candle of the jongleurs. (The frontispiece of its book of statutes is often mistakenly reproduced in connection with the Carité.)[139] A confraternity in Béthune went so far as to adopt its foundation legend, retooled to give the glory to social-climbing blacksmiths and thereby making nonsense of the jongleurs' sophisticated allegory.[140] And as I have already noted, the Francien translation of the Carité's foundation legend included an outline of its constitution, intimating that other fledgling organizations profited from the example of the jongleurs' lordship. Toward the end of the thirteenth century, surviving municipal accounts from Bruges attest that the city was paying the expenses of actors who traveled to Arras to attend its annual feast, which the *Ordinance* describes as an event involving everyone in Arras, including representatives of all its competing powers and many from the surrounding region.[141] On these occasions the Chandelle would be carried out into the Petit Marché and the ceremony of the *potus* solemnly performed. When the holy water had been entirely distributed (like the Eucharistic elements, all of its sacramental species had to be consumed), leftover pieces of wax were saved in a special bag. Some of these secondary relics were eventually used to dedicate altars to Notre-Dame-des-Ardents in churches throughout Picardy, Flanders, Hainaut, and the Low Countries. As early as 1280 one fragment of wax was cherished in a silver-gilt reliquary called *la torche*, owned by the Confrérie des Damoiseux de Nostre Dame, a group of young men in Tournai. It is still on display in the cathedral treasury.[142] By 1285 there was another fragment in the treasury at

136. Espinas, *Les origines*, 1:8.

137. Gurr, *Shakespeare Company*, xiii and 85.

138. Terpstra, "Confraternities," 144–145.

139. BmA 1116, dated 1290.

140. Espinas, *Les origines*, vol. 2, nos. 13–15.

141. Wyffels and de Smet, *De Rekeningen*, 1: 342 and 454. See also chapter 4.

142. Rosanna Brusegan, "Culte de la Vierge et origine des puys et confréries en France au Moyen Age," in Dufournet, *Naissances*, 31–58 at 38; Jean Dumoulin and Jacques Pycke, *La grande procession de Tournai (1090–1992): Une réalité religieuse, urbaine, diocésaine, sociale, économique et artistique* (Tournai, 1992), 35; Auguste Terninck, *Notre-Dame du Joyel, ou histoire légendaire et numismatique de la Chandelle d'Arras et des*

the monastery of Groenige, at Courtrai; it, too, is still there.[143] In Saint-Omer a market-place chapel was built to house a reliquary containing "some wax which was given miraculously to actors" (*de cera que fuit data miraculose hystrionibus*), and other relics are attested at Pecqeyncourt, near the abbey of Anchin, and at Bruges, Douai, Aire, and elsewhere.[144]

The day that was the occasion for these dramatic expressions of civic harmony and regional pilgrimage was later to become Corpus Christi, which came to serve a similar function in many European communities by the middle of the fourteenth century.[145] It would become, moreover, an important occasion for the performance of plays.[146] The only scholars who have hitherto noted the coincidence have intimated that the Carité held its general assembly on this day *because* it was Corpus Christi, even though the institution of the siège long preceded the eventual promulgation of the feast in 1317. Espinas went so far as to assert that the festivities of the Carité forged the crucial links between Corpus Christi, plays, and confraternities, thus influencing the course of the feast's development into the fourteenth and fifteenth centuries and making Arras the "birthplace of medieval theater" in the most conventional sense.[147] But it is more probable that the *theatrica* later associated with Corpus Christi incorporated a diverse array of local practices.[148] Indeed, the evidence from Arras allows us to see how these practices developed in a particular community, before and after the institutional Church began to crystallize and homogenize them.

---

cierges qui en ont été tirés par les villes et villages de Lille, Desvres, Ruisseauville, Blandecques, Courtray, etc. (Arras, 1853).

143. N. Huyghebaert, "Oorsprong van de 'Heylighe Keersse' van Atrecht de Kortrijk bewaard," in *Verslagen en mededelingen van de Leiegouw* 8 (1966): 279–286.

144. Justine de Pas, "Inventaire des reliques, utensiles et livres de la chapelle de N-D des Miracles à Saint-Omer en 1346," BSAM 9 (1892–1896): 188 (no. 18).

145. In selecting the Thursday after Trinity for the beginning of its annual celebrations, the confraternity had chosen the earliest date on which a festival of any magnitude could be scheduled at that time of the year, since the three days prior to it were sacred to the Pentecostal feast of the preceding Sunday, which was tied to the observance of Easter. See [Antoine-Alexandre] Gosse, ed., "Anciens synodes d'Arras," in *Histoire de l'abbaye et de l'ancienne congrégation des chanoines réguliers d'Arrouaise avec notes critiques, historiques, et diplomatiques* (1786; reprint, Arras, 1972), 574–613 at 575; and Andrew Hughes, *Medieval Manuscripts for Mass and Office: A Guide to Their Organization and Terminology* (Toronto, 1982), 11 and 357.

146. For the beginnings of the feast at Liège (where it is connected with the care of lepers by beguines), its institution by Urban IV (formerly Jacques Pantaleon, archdeacon of Liège), and its promulgation at the Council of Vienne, see Miri Rubin, *Corpus Christi: The Eucharist in Late Medieval Culture* (Cambridge, 1991), 196–199 and 248–267; and Kobialka, *This Is My Body*, 203–205. For the relevant documentation, see *De vita B. Iuliana virgine, priorissa Montis Cornellii apud Leodium, promotrice festi corporis Christi*, in AASS, April 1:437–475 at 459–466.

147. Espinas, *Les origines*, 1:109; see also Verhuyk, "Et le quart," 120.

148. Kobialka, *This Is My Body*, 197–216.

In Arras, the Carité's' Trinity triduum continued to serve the same function as Corpus Christi for more than two centuries after that feast was first mooted, not far away in Liège in 1264, and actually forestalled its regular observance until well after it had become the chief celebration of collective identity in other towns. It does not appear in any local service books until well into the latter part of the fourteenth century and was not celebrated until 1477. And by then the diocese and commune of Arras had to make careful arrangements to ensure that what was being commemorated *was* the feast of Corpus Christi and *not* the feast of the Carité, whose grand siège had been moved to the beginning of the following week. In an agreement ratified by the échevins of Arras, it was explicitly stated that "the members of the confraternity, and everyone else besides, ought to go and make their devotions on this feast of the Sacrament in their own parish churches, and should also accompany the Corpus Christi which is carried this day in procession."[149] The Sainte-Chandelle, however, was also to be carried to the cathedral in procession at the same time, which strongly suggests that the Eucharistic celebration had to be tied to the jongleurs' relic before it was locally legitimated. This is reminiscent of the way the candle had been used to lend credibility to the relics of Saint Vaast at the abbey's own ceremony of homage, and underscores the importance attached to its inclusion in the cathedral's display of relics outside the "great portal" of Notre-Dame, where it was still being exhibited alongside lesser Marian relics, "to the profit and use of the fabric of the church," up to the time of the French Revolution.[150] Moreover, indulgences were still being granted to the faithful who came to venerate it: Figure 16 shows that it was to be displayed in the Petit Marché on June 8, 1749 (the Sunday after Corpus Christi), when it was the subject of a special sermon. A few years earlier, in 1745, it had inspired a lengthy narrative poem which retold the story of Norman and Ithier, with many embellishments of plot, for a contemporary audience.[151] And the relic continues to be renowned for its curative powers. Today, fragments of the original candle are cherished in the episcopal treasury, the ambulatory of the church of Notre-Dame-des-Ardents is ringed with votives, and the thirteenth-century reliquary is set in bas-relief over the door (Figure 17).

In the thirteenth century, Arras became a symbol of all that was worldly, progressive, stylish, excessive, and opportunistic. It held forth the promise of unlimited possibility. Given enough money, audacity, and ambition, anyone could acquire anything, become

---

149. "Les dits caritables et autres plusieurs puissent dorénavant aller et faire leur devotions ledit jour du Sacrement en leurs eglises paroissialles, même accompagner le *Corpus Domini* qui se porte iceluy jour aux pourchessions." Cavrois, *Cartulaire*, 185.

150. AdPC ser. 3 G 2/Fabricque XII (Delmaire handlist no. 30); Cavrois, *Cartulaire*, 184–186.

151. L'Abbé J.-B. du Laurens, *Histoire de la Sainte Chandelle d'Arras*, reprinted by Henry Kristemaeckers (Brussels, [1881]).

FIGURE 16. Announcement of a plenary indulgence granted to pilgrims venerating the Sainte-Chandelle, to be displayed in the Petit Marché of Arras on June 8, 1749—the Sunday after Corpus Christi, which was the last day of the Carité's traditional three-day feast (BmA, Archives de la Confrérie: author's photograph)

anything—or at least make the attempt. The title character of *Courtois d'Arras* exemplifies the adherents to this creed. He is a self-made man, since he not only invents his "courtly" character but also coins his own euphonious name as part of his deception. Cast out of the false paradise in which he had invested his money, identity, and future, he endures a period of alienation before reconciling himself to a stable, if unglamorous, rural existence. His is a story about the limitations of individual enterprise and the disruption of traditional values and obligations. But Courtois is not the only actor who represents Arras. While individual jongleurs were performing the hazards of social mobility in play, a confraternity of jongleurs was rising to a position of actual prominence on the strength of its members' collective self-invention and the cultivation of a religious community that

FIGURE 17. The tympanum over the west portal of the church of Notre-Dame-des-Ardents, dedicated in 1876 and built to house the reliquary of the Sainte-Chandelle, still extant today and depicted here in bas-relief (author's photograph)

could support it. Unlike Courtois, these prodigals reversed the fortunes of their usual lot by inverting the persona of the jongleur. And they sustained that new identity through new forms of political association, making a place for themselves in public life alongside the more established institutions of Arras. Their theatrical initiative gave them real agency and promoted an alternative vision of society and its possibilities.

CHAPTER THREE ACCESS TO THE MEDIA
PUBLICITY, PARTICIPATION, AND THE
PUBLIC SPHERE

In his influential study of the urban "open realm" (*Öffentlichkeit*), a phrase that has been translated into English as "the public sphere," Jürgen Habermas declared that no such thing can "be shown to have existed in the feudal society of the High Middle Ages." His central premise, that a new arena of rational discourse was fostered by the conditions prevalent in some seventeenth- and eighteenth-century towns, depends to a marked degree on a false contrast between the political culture of the Enlightenment and "the forms of domination typical of the High Middle Ages," when the publicity of power "was not constituted as a social realm, that is a public sphere." Whatever validity this argument might have had in 1962, it is now demonstrable that this "feudal society" is a straw man of modern invention. In fact, all of the economic and cultural conditions to which Habermas ascribed the emergence of the public sphere were present in many medieval communities as the result of the very same processes usually claimed as unique to modernity: "the emergence of early finance and trade capitalism," "the rise of long-distance trade," the consolidation of a "network of horizontal economic dependencies" that disrupted traditional hierarchies, and the ways that "the great trade cities became at the same time centers for the traffic in news," opening up a "new sector of communications."[1] All that might be said to be lacking in the public sphere described by Galbert of Bruges in 1127 (see chapter 1) is "commercially distributed news," and that could just as well be a good thing, given the ease with which commercial news outlets can be co-opted and censored.[2] In any case, medievalists have long disputed the hegemony of the printing press as the prerequisite for the circulation of dissenting opinion and the promotion of social change.[3]

---

1. Habermas, *Structural Transformation*, 7, 14–17. See, e.g., David Nicholas, *Urban Europe, 1100–1700* (New York, 2003); Nicholas does not mention Habermas explicitly, but he does take on the similar arguments of Emmanuel Wallerstein and Fernand Braudel.

2. Edward S. Herman and Noam Chomsky, *Manufacturing Consent: The Political Economy of the Mass Media* (New York, 1988). See also the critiques of the Habermasian (Western) model in Miriam Hoexter, Shmuel N. Eisenstadt, and Mehemia Levtzion, eds., *The Public Sphere in Muslim Societies* (Albany, 2002), especially the foreword by Dale F. Eickelman, 1–8.

3. The possibility of alternative modes of effective communication is addressed by David Zaret—with reference to the work of the medievalist Geoffrey Koziol—in *The Origins of Democratic Culture: Printing, Petitions, and the Public Sphere in Early Modern England* (Princeton, 2000), especially 11 and 100–118. Yet

A growing number of historians in Germany and America are beginning to challenge the Habermasian model and to explore the public sphere of the Middle Ages. Geoffrey Koziol and Mary Mansfield have amply demonstrated that ritualized behavior was essential to the construction of any medieval "social realm."[4] Johannes Helmrath has shown how preaching and pamphleteering enabled participants in a late medieval ecumenical council to create a temporary but transnational public sphere, accessible to people at large.[5] Focusing on the eleventh through thirteenth centuries, Gerd Althoff has explored how everyday rituals of friendship and feasting accomplished social and political goals, arguing explicitly that sworn associations—like the commune and confraternities of Arras—mediated between individuals and established institutions in ways analogous to those characterizing the modern public sphere.[6] He has even contended that institutions as seemingly authoritarian and monolithic as kingship were actually collective endeavors, produced by public activities, inseparable from and dependent on the demonstration of kingly attributes legitimized by public opinion.[7] Barbara Rosenwein and Daniel Smail

---

Zaret ultimately follows Elizabeth Eisenstein's famous argument, which rests on a devaluation of oral and manuscript cultures and which has been ably refuted by Clanchy and Coleman, among others. See the essays in Marco Mostert, ed., *New Approaches to Medieval Communication* (Turnhout, 1999), especially Clanchy's introduction; and Coleman, *Public Reading*, 93–97.

4. Geoffrey Koziol, *Begging Pardon and Favor: Ritual and Political Order in Early Medieval France* (Ithaca, 1992); Mary C. Mansfield, *The Humiliation of Sinners: Public Penance in Thirteenth-Century France* (Ithaca, 1995).

5. Johannes Helmrath, "Kommunikation auf den spätmittelalterlichen Konzilien," in *Die Bedeutung der Kommunikation für Wirtschaft und Gesellschaft*, ed. Hans Pohl (Stuttgart, 1989), 116–172. See also Daniel Hobbins, "The Schoolman as Public Intellectual: Jean Gerson and the Late Medieval Tract," *AHR* 108 (2003): 1308–37; and Clementine Oliver, "A Political Pamphleteer in Late Medieval England: Thomas Fovent, Geoffrey Chaucer, Thomas Usk, and the Merciless Parliament of 1388," in *New Medieval Literatures*, vol. 6, ed. David Lawton, Rita Copeland, and Wendy Scase (Oxford, 2003), 167–198.

6. Gerd Althoff, *Verwandte, Freunde und Getreue: Zum politischen Stellenwert der Gruppenbindungen im früheren Mittelalter* (Darmstadt, 1990), especially 119–133 and 182–211; and idem, "Empörung, Tränen, Zerknirschung. 'Emotionen' in der öffentlichen Kommunikation des Mittelalters," *Frühmittelalterliche Studien* 30 (1996): 60–79. See also Gordon Kipling, *Enter the King: Theater, Liturgy, and Ritual in the Medieval Civic Triumph* (Oxford, 1998); Alfred Haverkampf, *Gemeinden, Gemeinschaften und Kommunikationsformen im hohen und späten Mittelalter*, ed. Friedhelm Burgard, Lukas Clemens, and Michael Matheus (Trier, 2002), 207–236; and Gerrit Jasper Schenk, *Zeremonial und Politik: Herrschereinzüge im spättmittelalterlichen Reich* (Cologne, 2003), especially 59–74.

7. Gerd Althoff, "Demonstration und Inszenierung: Spielregeln der Kommunkiation in mittelalterlicher Öffentlichkeit," *Frühmittelalterliche Studien* 27 (1993): 27–50. See also Bernd Thum, "Öffentlichkeit und Kommunikation im Mittelalter: Zure Herstellung von Öffentlichkeit im Bezugsfeld elementarer Kommunikationsformen im 13. Jahrhundert," in *Höfische repräsentation: Das Zeremoniell und die Zeichen*, ed. Hedda Ragotzky and Horst Wenzel (Tübingen, 1990), 65–87.

have shown how the public display of emotion functioned as a key component of meaningful communication and deliberation.[8] Adam Kosto has demonstrated that our lack of
familiarity with certain forms of political representation has masked the structure and
function of viable medieval institutions.[9] And Shannon McSheffrey has problematized
the fundamental categories of "public" and "private" by showing how modern legal
notions have affected the way we read for evidence of intimacy or publicity in medieval
texts.[10]

Coincidentally, Habermas himself subsequently revised his views on the shaping of a
public sphere, and under the influence of an idea that, ironically, derives from one of the
plays produced in Arras. In 1992 he wondered whether "a different picture emerges if *from
the very beginning* one admits the coexistence of competing public spheres and takes into
account the processes of communication." He attributes this paradigm shift to a reading
of Mikhail Bakhtin's influential study *Rabelais and His World*, which was inspired, in its
turn, by a reading of Adam de la Halle's *Jeu de la feuillée* (see chapter 4). His resulting "theory of communicative action" thus "intends to bring into the open the rational potential
intrinsic in everyday communicative practices."[11] That is, Habermas proposes something
like the study of a common stage, while remaining reluctant to explore the many *ineffable*
ways in which meaning can be conveyed; as he says, "I shall ignore nonverbalized actions
and bodily expressions."[12] But Robert Darnton, a cultural historian of the ancien régime,
has shown that news "circulated through several media and by different modes," many of
them oral, even in eighteenth-century Paris, and historians of the twentieth century have
argued that broadcasts of nonverbal communication are as worthy of serious attention as

8. Barbara H. Rosenwein, "Worrying about Emotions in History," AHR 107 (2002): 821–845, and
Anger's Past: The Social Uses of Emotion in the Middle Ages (Ithaca, 1998); Daniel Lord Smail, *The Consumption
of Justice: Emotions, Publicity, and Legal Culture in Marseille, 1264–1423* (Ithaca, 2003).

9. Adam J. Kosto, "Hostages and the Habit of Representation in Thirteenth-Century Occitania," in
The Experience of Power in Medieval Europe, 950–1350, ed. Robert F. Berkhoffer III, Alan Cooper, and Adam
J. Kosto (Aldershot, 2005), 183–192.

10. Shannon McSheffrey, "Place, Space, and Situation: Public and Private in the Making of Marriage
in Late-Medieval London," *Speculum* 79 (2004): 960–990.

11. Jürgen Habermas, "Further Reflections on the Public Sphere," trans. Thomas Burger in *Habermas and the Public Sphere*, ed. Craig Calhoun (Cambridge, 1992), 421–461 at 425, 442, and 444–446;
Mikhail Bakhtin, *Rabelais and His World*, trans. Hélène Iswolsky (Cambridge, 1968). A collection of essays evaluating Habermas's turn toward Bakhtin misses the medievalism of the latter's work: Nick
Crossley and John Michael Robert, eds., *After Habermas: New Perspectives on the Public Sphere* (Oxford, 2004).

12. Jürgen Habermas, "What Is Universal Pragmatics?" in *Communication and the Evolution of Society*,
trans. Thomas McCarthy (Boston, 1979), 1–68 at 1; idem, *On the Pragmatics of Social Interaction: Preliminary Studies in the Theory of Communicative Action*, trans. Barbara Fultner (Cambridge, 2001), 67–84.

blatant propaganda.[13] Accounting for the operation of these techniques is all the more imperative when we consider the "gestural communities" that make up medieval societies (the phrase is that of Jean-Claude Schmitt).[14] In this chapter, I will demonstrate that the history of a medieval theater in thirteenth-century Arras extends these challenges to the conceptualization of the public sphere, by showing how frequently and cannily people without the power to assert themselves through more conventional means (violence, wealth) gained other types of power through the use of public media.

The Boy and the Blind Man

On a busy day in the marketplace, a blind beggar makes his way tentatively through the crowd, jostled and ignored by passers-by. His singsong invocation of the Virgin is half-hearted and ineffectual. He attracts no attention and gets no handouts. Changing his tune, he mutters to himself—or does he speak to you directly?—saying that he'll never get anywhere unless he finds a boy to lead him to a better part of town. As if on cue, a boy appears: a ne'er-do-well who's been leaning against the wall of that tavern over there, his gaze shifty. In fact, you've been keeping an eye on him since you saw him earlier in the day, wending his way past the stalls where the country folk had paused to finger unfamiliar finery, their purses dangling. Suddenly he's alert, stung into action at the sight of the blind man and the sound of his plaintive remarks. He closes in, and you hear the following exchange. In fact, it's hard to ignore it, since they're both speaking so loudly that everyone within earshot has stopped to listen:

Sire vous nales mie bien		Sir, look out: you've lost your way
Vous querres ia en cest celier		You'll fall into that cellar there.
A meredieu veullie me aidier		Mary! Can you help me? Where?
Ki esce qui si bien mavoie		Who's that, who sees so well for me?
Preudons se Jhesus me doint ioie	20	Prudhomme, so Jesus give me glee,
Cou est vns poures triquemers		It's just a luckless passer-by.
Pour dieu ie croi quil soit mult bers		My God, I bet that he's the guy.
Viengne avant a lui veull parler		Come here, I want to talk to you.
Ves me chi.		I'm here.
Te veus tu louer	25	You'll sell me what you do?

13. Darnton, "Early Information Society," 4. See, e.g., Alain Corbin, *Les cloches de la terre: Paysage sonore et culture sensible dans les campagnes au XIXe siécle* (Paris, 1994); and Richard L. Hernandez, "Sacred Sound and Sacred Substance: Church Bells and the Auditory Culture of Russian Villages during the Bolshevik *Velikii Perelom*," AHR 109 (2004): 1475–1504.

14. Schmitt, *La raison,* 19. See also Aron J. Gurevich, *Categories of Medieval Culture,* trans. G. L. Campbell (London, 1985).

Sire a quoi seroi che faire		What, Mister? I don't understand.
Pour mi pour mener sans mesfaire		Just lead me safely by the hand
A vale la cite de Tournay		All 'round the the city of Tournai.
Tu prieras ie canterai		I'll sing for them and you can pray,
Sarons asses argent et pain.	30	And we'll earn coins and bread for two.[15]

You begin to get the feeling that they may not be meeting for the first time. For one thing, they're speaking together in verse; that arouses your curiosity. Impromptu displays of poetic skill are not at all unusual, in your experience, but you are used to the improvised couplets of jongleurs or the occasional flights of fancy attained by preachers who have fallen in love with their pious themes, or their own voices. Of course, you've also heard the local wits (well-born young men and leisured clerics in the company of minstrels) engage in the verbal sparrings the literati call *jeux-partis*, those plays of rhymed one-upmanship meant to seem spontaneous. To be honest, though, you've always thought that some of the lesser competitors tend to cheat, scripting a few generic retorts beforehand and passing them off as something newly coined. These two down-and-outers, now: they look like the real thing.[16]

Yet they also seem to be following some prearranged routine. Notice the way they've advertised this meeting, talking at the tops of their voices, and the way they're mugging and making up to the circle of people who've gathered round, the boy pulling faces that the poor blind man can't see, or shoving him around and pretending to chide the rudeness of someone else. And that "poor" "blind" beggar: what makes you so sure that he is really blind? A con man more likely, and the boy's another. Yes, look again: they're not singing to the Virgin anymore. Now they're giving us the one about that new French king of Sicily, the uncle of young Robert of Artois—the one that's sung to that old drinking song. Cheeky! What if the count comes by? And listen to the mouth on that young lad! Swearing "by Saint Sophia's hole" and "by God's ass"! What makes him think that that will move the crowd? But everybody's laughing. Wait, what did he say? "So by the faith I owe Saint Vaast."[17] You get it now: they're acting. Those are pratfalls, gags—the begging and the blindness are in fun. You thought the reference to Tournai was strange, since we're

---

15. *Le garçon et l'aveugle*, in BnF fr. 24366, 242b–245b. All citations refer to the facsimile and transcription in Symes, "The Boy and the Blind Man," 105–143 at 128–143, hereinafter cited as G&A. (The edition of Mario Roques, reissued in 1989 by Jean Dufournet, should be used with caution, for reasons discussed in this chapter and in chapter 2.) The only English translation is that of Axton and Stevens, *Medieval French Plays*, 196–206.

16. Spontaneous, conversational composition of French verse is attested even in the nineteenth century. See Graham Robb's review of *L'atelier de Baudelaire: "Les fleurs du mal,"* ed. Claude Pichois and Jacques Dupont, in the *Times Literary Supplement*, April 21, 2006, 5.

17. G&A, 243b, l. 16: "Par la foi ie doi saint Vast."

all in Arras. A good joke, really, since the folks in that old burg would probably fall for anything, just like this stupid "beggar" who's shown that clever urchin where he lives and
given him his purse, sending him off to fetch his moll and bring home dinner. As if the
kid will follow through! You'll never see that purse again, buddy; that boy learned everything he knows from good Saint Vaast! There's one born every minute, mark my words.
See, the lad has taken off. It's over now, unless he takes a bow. Either way, they'll pass the
hat. Funny how it doesn't matter whether they're acting or begging or turning a trick,
since the end result's the same for those who watch. Well, whatever their game is, they put
on a good show and you've got to give them something. With things the way they are these
days, there's no telling who's for real and who is not.

The dialogue for "The Boy and the Blind Man" took on its present shape sometime after 1265. It can be dated on the basis of its inclusion of a song recruiting troops for the
campaign of Charles of Anjou, who began to plan his conquest of the kingdom of Sicily
in that year.[18] Although the version of the play sketched on parchment seems to be set in
Tournai—that Flemish city and its environs are mentioned in the text that comes down to
us—the Boy identifies himself as the product of a place famous for its trickery, Arras. As
Courtois discovered the hard way, many Europeans took it for granted that fast-talking
charlatans and cheapjacks came from there. And prior to their scripting, the gags making
up this play could have originated anywhere, while the manuscript preserving them—an-
notated and bowdlerized by five generations of "editors" or performers over the course of
the next two hundred years—was probably copied on an actor's initiative in the region on
either side of the border between the Artois and the imperial county of Hainaut, where
Tournai was then situated. Hence, it is perfectly possible that the name of the town was
routinely altered, depending on the planned performance venue; I have demonstrated as
much for *Courtois*, and this was the ostensible purpose of the later Middle English "N-
Town" script, which leaves the "Name" (*Nomen*) of the targeted town blank, to be supplied
by performers.[19] Alternatively, a reference to Tournai in a play performed for audiences
elsewhere could have conveyed the impression that its inhabitants were especially vulnerable to the superior stratagems acquired in Arras.

As my imagined performance suggests, "The Boy and the Blind Man" emerges organ-
ically from its setting, presupposed by the plot of the play and the plotting of its players to
be a crowded marketplace. In those surroundings it would not have mattered much
whether the audience perceived the performers to be actors, beggars, or con men, or ac-

18. G&A, 243ᵃ, ll. 40–243ᵇ, l. 7. See Jean Dunbabin, *Charles I of Anjou: Power, Kingship, and State-Making in Thirteenth-Century Europe* (New York, 1998), 208. See also chapter 5.

19. Although "Tournai" sets up a rhyme to be completed in the following line, "Tu prieras, je can-
terai," a new couplet could easily be invented if the next day's destination were Saint-Omer or Aire (Cambrai, Douai, and Courtrai would pose no difficulties).

tors pretending to be con men pretending to be beggars, or beggars putting on a good show (the better to win alms), or con men whose begging and acting skills had been honed out of sheer necessity. The bottom line was the same: money; and the getting of money would have depended on successful competition for attention. The intimate relationship between this play and the public activities out of which it was fashioned is therefore exemplary of the way that a medieval theater worked, since the techniques of attracting attention would have been known and cultivated by all whose livelihoods depended on it—jongleurs, kings, criers, preachers, poets, and politicians—as well as by those who required only occasional recourse to public media in order to communicate a particular message or to participate in public affairs. My discussion of the achievements of the Carité, which used its superior understanding of image making to construct a lordship of jongleurs, has already raised some of the important questions: What were the strategies used to gain access to "air time" in Arras? What restrictions could be placed on different modes of communication, by whom, and with respect to what spaces and times? What was generally known about the manipulation of public opinion? In what ways, then, did other groups and individuals in Arras use these same tools, with what degree of success, and to what ends?

Making Space, Shaping Opinion

In 1237 young King Louis IX gave Arras and its surrounding territory to one of his many younger brothers, Robert. This was the richest prize among the lands won by the princes' grandfather, Philip Augustus, and included the wealthy towns of Lens and Bapaume, the castellany of Hesdin, and the port of Calais. It was bestowed on Robert as part of an appanage willed by the late Louis VIII when his sons were little boys, designed to consolidate fraternal support and ease the tensions that might arise among otherwise landless siblings.[20] Yet the bequest created further tensions on the ground in Arras. In the two generations that had followed its annexation by the king of France, few official changes had hitherto been made to the configuration of power at a local level, which remained confusing enough. The monastery of Saint-Vaast and the commune of Arras continued to divide and squabble over rights in the Town, while the monks held on to the strip of territory on the northeastern side of the City's main thoroughfare. Meanwhile, the bishop of Arras continued to exercise high and low justice in the City and in the tiny demesne of the Estrée within the walls of the Town, as well as within the precincts of six out of the nine parish churches, which formed a chain of spiritual and temporal power anchored in the west by the church of Saint-Maurice, extending southward to Saint-Aubert and Saint-Éti-

---

20. Charles T. Wood, *The French Appanages and the Capetian Monarchy, 1224–1328* (Cambridge, 1966). See also Monique Flament, *L'Artois à la fin du XIIIe siècle* (Poitiers, 1981), 24–31; Delmaire, *Le diocèse*, 1:37.

enne, east to Saint-Jean and Saint-Nicholas, and reaching to the church of Saint-Géry, at the edge of the abbey's precincts, the parish whose belfry housed the *ban-cloche* of the commune. These churches, with their cemeteries and tiny *places*, could be used as toeholds of power by the cathedral, and their parish boundaries would be made palpable reminders of diocesan authority on rogation days, when a series of ephemeral lines would be drawn in the sand by the secular clergy loyal to the bishop.[21] Yet there were divisions of power between the bishop and his cathedral clergy, too. The chapter had its own domain, which included temporal jurisdiction within the cathedral close, where the bishop needed permission to gain entrance; and when tensions ran high, new episcopal incumbents were sworn into office at a house on the rue de la Cité, beyond the canons' reach.[22] The cathedral chapter also owned and administered the Hôtel-Dieu founded in the 1220s, located opposite the main gate to the cathedral's north transept and on the abbey's side of the rue des Maus, a site deliberately chosen because it lay beyond the bishop's jurisdiction, while the bishop himself owned a house in "the domain of my lord the abbot of Saint-Vaast," thereby creating an odd alliance.[23]

Across these treacherous urban frontiers, the royal presence of the king of France had been felt chiefly through the person of the king's bailiff, who issued writs and proclamations in the king's name and whose interventions into the tangle of domestic affairs were otherwise limited. With the advent of the royal county of Artois, however, another layer of authority was superimposed on the political palimpsest of Arras. There was now a new count with his household quartered in the shadow of Saint-Vaast, and they were uneasy neighbors: the abbey lay within the county, but the count when he resided in Arras was the abbey's tenant. Together they were supposed to divide the *tonlieu* levied in the marketplaces owned by the monks, an arrangement that soon proved to be untenable when the count's agents tried to wrest control of its collection in 1239. In the end, both parties agreed, separately, to sell their rights in this tax to the commune of Arras in exchange for shares in a perpetual rent. So while the monks retained possession of the ground beneath the merchants' stalls—and the Pyramide of the Sainte-Chandelle—the échevins of the commune now had jurisdiction there.[24] But both the commune and the abbey had to yield to the king's bailiff in matters of royal prerogative and to the count's bailiff in comital affairs, a provision which assumed that these officers and their charges could be easily differentiated. They could not. Both were styled *baillivus Attrebatensis*, the adjective meaning

---

21. On the fixity of medieval parish boundaries, see Delmaire, *Le diocèse*, 1:79–86 and 2:425–431.

22. Delmaire, "Le testament," 459; Berger, *Littérature*, 55–60. The oaths of Guillaume (in 1282) and Gérard (in 1296) are recorded on an otherwise empty page near the beginning of BnF lat. 9930, fol. IV.

23. AdPC ser. 3 G 3/Hostel Dieu liii and liiii [Cité xiiii and xv] (Delmaire handlist, nos. 45–46).

24. Auguste Menche de Loisne, "Catalogue des actes de Robert I, comte d'Artois (1237–1250)," *BHP* (1919): 133–206 at 145–146 (nos. 18–20). For a summary of the transaction, see Delmaire, *Le diocèse*, 1:267–268. See also Derville, *Saint-Omer*, 126.

either "of Artois" (the count's man) or "of Arras" (the king's man). Nor is the confusion all on the side of the historian; contemporary confusions, and the abuses they fostered, led to long periods in which no royal bailiff was posted in Arras, so that the bailiff of Amiens or his subordinate, the provost of Beauquesne, was empowered to intervene there.[25] To make matters murkier still, both bailiffs "of Arras/Artois" had lieutenants (sous-baillis) obliquely designated Attrebatensis, too, and each maintained a string of sergeants to keep the peace. Moreover, some of these men-at-arms may have worked for both bailiffs at once, or for the commune, or even for the castellan of Arras, whose hereditary office had been rendered all but obsolete by Philip of Flanders, save for his vestigial role as keeper of the prison. And the castellan himself was doubly bound, by oath to the commune and by ties of fealty to the new count of Artois.[26]

The makings of a common stage and the shaping of a public sphere in thirteenth-century Arras are very much implicated in this constellation of confusing powers. For neither the dramatic articulation of power nor the powerful articulation of drama could depend on firm physical boundaries, but relied instead on performance to delineate those spaces whose uses and significance "depended on a number of peculiar local conditions, such as ill-defined public authority," as Mansfield observed.[27] Making space for acting or for the exercise of agency meant, equally, carving out that space and imbuing it with meaning—even when that space was preexisting, seemingly permanent, architecturally distinctive. In Michael Camille's words, space is "fugitive rather than fixed," the meaning of any corner or cul-de-sac determined by "contingencies of use" and negotiations among the users. Roads can "ruthlessly demarcate and divide" while at the same time conveying messages and facilitating the flow of traffic.[28] Walls that appear solid will be exposed as

25. Auguste Menche de Loisne, "Chronologie des baillis d'Artois du XIIIe siècle," BHP (1899): 65–78. On the prévôté of Beauquesne, see Guesnon, "Adam," 215 (pièce justificative I). See also Berger, Littérature, 63–66 and 427–428; and Flament, L'Artois, 39–41, and 44–49.

26. On the dual allegiance of the castellan, see Cartulaire, 42 (no. 43) and 509–519 at 511–512 (no. 5 in the Livre aux sermens). See also Maxime de Germiny, Les lieutenants de Robert II, comte d'Artois, gardes et maîtres de toutes ces terres (1270–1299) (Arras, 1898), 6; and Pierre Feuchère, Les châtelains d'Arras: De l'épée à la plume (Arras, 1948), 55–57.

27. Mansfield, Humiliation, 13 and 151. See also Rebecca A. Baltzer, "The Geography of the Liturgy at Notre-Dame of Paris," in Plainsong in the Age of Polyphony, ed. Thomas Forrest Kelly (Cambridge, 1992), 45–64; Noël Coulet, "Processions, espace urbain, communauté civique," in Liturgie et musique (XIe–XIVe s.) (Toulouse, 1982), 381–397; and Joëlle Rollo-Koster, "The Politics of Body Parts: Contested Topographies in Late-Medieval Avignon," Speculum 78 (2003): 66–98.

28. Michael Camille, "Signs on Medieval Street Corners," in Die Strasse: Zur Funktion und Perzeption öffentlichen Raums im späten Mittelalter, ed. Gerhard Jaritz (Vienna, 2001), 91–117 at 91; idem, "Signs of the City: Place, Power, and Public Fantasy in Medieval Paris," in Medieval Practices of Space, ed. Barbara Hanawalt and Michael Kobialka (Minneapolis, 2000), 1–36.

mere constructs when the spaces within them cannot be protected by those who erect them. Open spaces reveal themselves to be enclosures when violated by a traveler who finds himself, unwittingly, a trespasser.

As the inhabitants of Arras walked through its streets and traded in its squares, they were continually aware that frontiers were being crossed and recrossed, most boundaries invisible to the untrained eye but of palpable importance to those who guarded them. Townspeople in the days of Adam de la Halle were still following in the footsteps of monks who were tracing the pastoral boundaries of the abbey's Carolingian foundations and its tenth-century banlieue, as the itineraries of penitential rogations conjured up the ghosts of walls and orchards long since lost in a warren of tenements. Thus the monks laid down ceremonial claims to land and rights over which they no longer exercised material control, claims more lasting than those made by Guiman's census, which had itself borrowed sacral authority by following the same routes. The annual procession on Ascension Day, which symbolically fortified the abbey's most venerable patrimony, the Merovingian *castrum* in which it had originally grown up, was an act of such importance that the fourteenth-century liturgists forbade its cancellation.[29]

Sometimes, then, boundaries were immaterial, articulated or contested only through ritual. At other times, however, boundaries that appeared nonexistent to some were obvious to others. When the bishop of Arras alleged that the young Count Robert II (1250–1302) had ignored "the manifest boundary marker between the sides"—that is, between the Estrée and the Town—he was referring to byways whose significance was mysterious to a newcomer.[30] But even the most obvious of boundaries were subject to reinterpretation and debate and had to be redrawn from time to time, a procedure that was always better effected through an act of publicity than a building campaign. The boundary between Town and City, for instance, was unmistakable, marked by a high wall, a postern gate, a deep ditch, a river, and a canal; but the boundaries between the rights and privileges of those dwelling on either side were porous. In 1258 the king's court held a public inquest to determine whether the échevins of the Town had the right to cross the Crinchon and enter the City in order to view the body of a murdered woman and to sit in judgment on the case. It was the testimony of past precedents gathered from the residents of Town and City which proved that they did not, rather than the existence of the physical barriers demarcating the two jurisdictions.[31] Similarly, an appeal to the public allowed Count Robert

29. BmA 230, fols. 41v^a–54r^b; see also fols. 30v and 34r. The ordinal of 1308 has been edited by Louis Brou, *The Monastic Ordinal of St.-Vedast's Abbey*, Arras Bibl. Mun. MSS 230/907, 2 vols. (London, 1957), 66–67 and 95–96. See also Delmaire, *Le diocèse*, 2:440–441; Mansfield, *Humiliation*, 150 and 162.

30. *Les Olim, ou Registres des arrêts rendus par la cour du roi sous les règnes de Saint Louis, de Philippe le Hardi, de Philippe le Bel, de Louis le Hutin et de Philippe le Long*, ed. Arthur Auguste Beugnot, 3 vols. (Paris, 1839–1844), 1:318–320 and 2:391–394: "usque ad metam inter partes ostensam." Hereinafter cited as *Olim*.

31. *Olim*, 1:46.

II to prove that he and his men had the right to open and close the barbican gate of the Port de la Cité for the defense of the Town, even though this was part of the bishop's domain.[32]

These examples alert us to the importance of public opinion in the making of public space and its meanings, which would shape the meaning of plays and in turn be shaped by them. Consensus was a force to which all claimants to power in Arras had to bow, and which all attempted to cultivate and harness. In 1115, when the completion of the Town's defensive wall divided the parishioners of Saint-Sauveur from the church that was now *extra muros*, a new gate was opened for their convenience after Bishop Lambert ordered that their grievance be "diligently inquired into and aired" (*diligenter inquisita et ventilata*).[33] In 1295, when the abbey of Saint-Vaast managed to persuade the king's bailiff from Amiens to free a woman from the prison of Arras on the grounds that she had been arrested on the abbey's land, the king's high-handed intervention caused a public outcry, because the castellan's prison was kept "according to the law of the town of Arras" and was therefore deemed out of bounds.[34] When the monks attempted to play the other side of the field a decade later, they now invoked public opinion in an effort to circumvent royal justice; "a certain forger of coins" had been arrested in their marketplace domain, and they called for an inquest in the hope of finding that the crime had involved only the circulation of counterfeit money, a lesser offense that could be tried in their own court. But as a scribe in the Parlement of Paris laconically reported, "the case was not proved," the general agreement of the townspeople having been that the offense was forgery.[35]

Legitimacy, then, was dependent on publicity: more specifically, on a general acceptance of the version of reality advertised through public media, conceded by the people whose testimony and subsequent behavior determined and reinforced that reality. Identity, too, was determined and expressed through publication, and not only the identity of the king's "new men" or the jongleurs of Arras or those who aspired to be mistaken for their betters, like poor naïf Courtois. In the exercise of individual and collective agency, as in the exercise of power, appearances mattered, reputation mattered. Power was a fact, but it had to be established again and again; it had to be publicized. Maintaining a high profile depended on putting on a good show, and the higher one's pretensions, the greater and longer running the show had to be, and the larger its audience. The Boy and the Blind Man have modest aims, but they introduce us to the basic tools of expression which lent themselves, universally, to the production of a medieval theater and its allied public

---

32. *Olim*, 1:318–320.

33. BnF lat. 9930, fol. 16r; Tock, *Chartes des évêques*, no. 21. See also Delmaire, *Le diocèse*, 2:89 and 430–431.

34. *Olim*, 2:389–394.

35. *Olim*, 2:246–247 (no. 21): "rubrica non probatur."

sphere. These tools included, but were by no means limited to, the flamboyant seizure of space and time, whether through ceremonious or obnoxious means, often involving the redirection of the gaze through the occupation of the built environment and the capture of aural attention through intrusion on the sonic environment; the adoption of postures, garments, or habits of speech recognizable to the targeted audience; the reiteration and recording of claims to authority (pretended or official) through the production of symbols, monuments, and writings manufactured in public and either permanently or frequently exhibited; and the attempted regulation of noise and behavior in protected spheres of influence advertised as such—or the undermining of these published controls through their deconstruction.

On the Air

Approaching Arras from a distance, the thirteenth-century traveler would have been struck by a vista of belfries and the sounds of bells. There were thirteen belfries in the Town alone, one for each of the nine parish churches and the three churches within the monastery complex of Saint-Vaast, and one for the tower of the Pyramide in the Petit Marché. In the City there were an additional six bell towers: one for the parish of Saint-Nicaise and—shaming Saint-Vaast with its single, blunt tower—five for the cathedral church of Notre-Dame, which had two belfries flanking the west end, two at the north portal, and another atop the transept. The cathedral's elevation was also showy, for at thirty meters it was three times higher than any other building in the region, and would have seemed higher still due to its situation atop a rise, overlooking the Crinchon. By the time the canons' various building projects were completed, around 1270, their church presented an impressive, if highly asymmetrical, silhouette.[36] Saint-Vaast's abbatial church, by contrast, exhibited an old-fashioned, barnlike appearance, impressing more by its bulk and the industrious appearance of construction under way throughout much of the period.[37] It, too, was situated on rising ground, overlooking the river and the proud towers of its rival. But even as the two main churches vied with each other for precedence, they were hedged in by the court of the count, the grand houses of the wealthy, and the hovels of the poor, and challenged by the tower of the jongleurs' marketplace chapel, which was as high as the cathedral's roof.[38]

While the spire of the *hôtel de ville* would later become the symbol of Arras, as in other

36. Héliot, *Les églises*, 1:237 and 2:347–352.

37. Ibid., 1:220, 250, 347, and 350. The abbatial church burned for the third time in 1136, but an ambitious project of reconstruction was not fixed upon until 1259. The new church was finally consecrated in 1295, although much of the work was still unfinished at that time.

38. Ibid., 2:353.

northern towns, there was no such edifice during the thirteenth century. The communal bell was housed in the belfry of the parish church of Saint-Géry, on the ancient street of the moneychangers, convenient to the assemblies held in the Petit Marché. Its authoritative ring could be heard at a radius of thirty kilometers, and thus established the limits of the banlieue.[39] A surviving record from Saint-Vaast's village of Haspres shows how important that carrying power was to those who lived within earshot, since soundings of opinion were taken through *placita generalia*, meetings that were "called together by the sound of the bell and organized by judgment of the échevins."[40] On such occasions, matters of general interest and public policy were—as Bishop Lambert had put it—"aired."

"One sound rose ceaselessly above the noises of busy life and lifted all things unto a sphere of order and serenity: the sound of bells."[41] Huizinga was right, although he did not expose the social and political mechanisms that operated, behind the scenes, to produce that order when there could just as well have been cacophony. Henri Lefebvre also stressed the importance of medieval bells, but (following Jacques LeGoff) thought their belfries must have "dominated space" only because they later housed the clocks that regulated time.[42] On the contrary: bells and their towers were instruments of prosperity, publicity, and order long before the advent of mechanical timekeeping. In the North especially, the bell and belfry were constitutive of communal identity, to the extent that misbehavior on the part of the townspeople of Boulogne would lead to the king's destruction of their belfry and ban-cloche in the 1270s, actions synonymous with the revocation of their charter.[43] The ringing of bells was the most effective long-range communication medium of the day: it gave one the means to call an assembly, to summon aid, to proclaim. So the possession of a bell was a privilege, while the unlawful possession and sounding

39. Abbé, "Rayonnement," 409–410.

40. AdPC ser. 1 H 2807/2. Fossier, *Chartes*, 166–171 (no. 24): "et sonnitu campane convocantur et judicio scabinorum exercentur."

41. Huizinga, *Waning*, 10.

42. Lefebvre, *La production*, 306; Jacques LeGoff, "Au Moyen Age: Temps de l'Église et temps de marchand," *Annales: E.S.C.* 15 (1960): 417–433; reprinted in *Pour un autre Moyen Age: Temps, travail et culture en Occident: 18 essais* (Paris, 1977), 46–65. For a critique of Le Goff's paradigm, see Murray, "Time and Money," 4. On the importance of bells and bell-ringing in the Middle Ages, see Renato Bordone, "Campane, trombe e carrocci nelle città regno d'Italia durante il medioevo," in *Information, Kommunikation und Selbstardellung im mittelalterlichen Gemeinden*, ed. Alfred Haverkamp and Elisabeth Müller-Luckner (Munich, 1998), 85–101. In the same volume, see Michael Viktor Schwarz, "Toskanische Türme: Repräsentation und Konkurrenz," 103–124; Gerold Bönnen, "Zwischen Kirche und Stadtgemeinde: Funktionen und Kontrolle von Glocken in Kathedralstädten zwischen Maas und Rhein," 161–199; and Gerhard Fouquet, "Zeit, Arbeit unde Muße im Wandel spätmittelalterlicher Kommunkationsformen," 237–275.

43. AdPC ser. A 32.34–35 and A 37.4.

of bells were condemned as serious abuses, which is why disorderly bell-ringing was a prominent part of revelry at times of carnival.[44]

Because the height of the tower affected a bell's carrying power as well as its visibility, this was also subject to regulation. Attempting to muffle unwanted competition from the mendicants, the diocese of Arras took steps to ensure that few of their foundations had more than a modest wooden structure enclosing a single bell.[45] The charter of 1233 that gave the Dominicans the right to a church and cemetery in Arras restricted them to a bell tower with a bell small enough that "one man should be able to pull it with one hand." This was reiterated in 1311 at the end of a long dispute argued in the papal curia, a sign of the issue's perceived importance.[46] In 1235 the Trinitarians were allowed two bells, but only because their church was situated well beyond the walls of the Town and therefore out of immediate earshot.[47] In 1262 the Penitential Friars (also known as the Friars of the Sack) were ordered to content themselves with one medium-sized bell supplemented by "their smaller bells and signal bells," like those rung at Mass.[48] By contrast, the leper hospital at Beaurains was denied the right to any public voice at all: "There they will have neither bells, nor any other signs by which anyone could be called to come to divine services."[49] This was fitting: lepers could carry clappers to warn folk away but could keep no bells to draw them near.

According to Jean de Garlande's imaginative etymology, "bells [campanæ] are so called by the peasants who live in the field [campus], who do not know how to reckon the hours except by the bells."[50] But the men and women of Arras were able to discern more than the hour of the day from the ringing of a bell. They could also have identified its provenance and the status of its owner, the nature and importance of a given feast, and further details as well, including what neighborhood they were in. Bells shaped space as well as time. They also communicated specific information in a language that all the Arrageois could understand. On Christmas morning, for instance, the monks of Saint-Vaast would ring their largest bell, "not too late, and not too early," as a signal that it was time for the

---

44. Margot Fassler, "The Feast of Fools and *Danielis ludus*: Popular Tradition in a Medieval Cathedral Play," in Kelly, *Plainsong*, 65–99 at 78.

45. Héliot, *Les églises*, 1:111 and 236–237.

46. AdPC ser. 3 G 4/"Jacobins," ii: "campanam quam unus homo una manu pulsare valeat."

47. AdPC ser. 3 G 4/"Trinité," xiii (Delmaire handlist, no. 61).

48. AdPC ser. 3 G 3/"non coté [Frères au sac]" (Delmaire handlist, no. 43): "cum cymbalis et tintinabulis suis."

49. BnF lat. 9930, fol. 25v (charter of July 1186): "verumtamen ibi, neque campanas, neque signa aliqua habebunt, quibus possint aliquos ad divina officia convocare." See also Tock, "Chartes du chapitre," 53–54.

50. "Campane dicuntur a rusticis qui habitant in campo, qui nesciant judicare horas nisi per campanas." Cited by Le Goff, "Au Moyen Age," 57.

special Mass for children and the sick.[51] If a parishioner fell ill, the parish priest would return to his church and ring its bell, summoning his congregation—effectively defined as those within sound of the bell—to go in procession with him to the invalid's house after Mass, following the Blessed Sacrament.[52] The ringing of a bell could also signify that alms were to be distributed, in commemoration of those who had made such arrangements in their wills. Bishop Raoul "Hornèd Hat" was one, having invested a certain sum to be broadcast annually among the poor after his death.[53] In fact, the status of the deceased could be gauged by the number of bells he or she was allocated, thus providing a helpful barometer that could be "read" by the more discriminating poor. On the eve and day of January 7, for example, all the bells of the cathedral would ring out to commemorate the death of Margaret of Nevers, wife of King Charles I of Sicily, and would continue during the Mass of that day, up to the reading of the Gospel.[54]

Holy days could be heard as well as observed, since nothing but the clamor of bells was heard in the streets from which traffic had been cleared. The synodal statutes of 1280 reiterated the custom observed in the diocese: on feast days all worldly labor should cease, and on the most important holidays the use of carts, carriages, and horses was also forbidden.[55] In this way, the very soundscape of holidays reminded the town dweller, inured to worldly racket, of their special character. A more ominous silence would fall during times of ecclesiastical interdict. The congregations of Saint-Vaast and Notre-Dame would signal its imposition with one pulse of a mid-voiced bell, at the sound of which both choirs would lower their voices and finish the divine office in a whisper. The parish churches throughout Arras would follow suit, and the stillness would be broken only by the enunciated names of wrongdoers.[56] The gravity of the public's collective punishment was symbolized by the closing of what had been spaces for public worship: the doors of the abbey church of Saint-Vaast and the two churches within the abbey walls were ceremoniously shut, and only on very special days could they be thrown open for a time and the bells rung out.[57]

As Alain Corbin has shown, in his important study of acoustic landscapes in nineteenth-century rural France, the reading of the sonic environment is fundamental to un-

---

51. BmA 230, fol. 139rb: "ne trop tart. ne trop tempre."

52. Joseph Avril, "La pastorale des malades et des mourants aux XIIe et XIIIe siècles," in Braet and Verbeke, Death, 88–106 at 98–99.

53. Delmaire, "Le testament," 459.

54. BmA 424, fol. 6v.

55. Gosse, "Anciens synodes," 576–578.

56. BnF lat. 9930, f. 1rb; see Tock, Chartes des évêques, 240–241 (no. 215).

57. Similar provisions were adopted at the Fourth Lateran Council. See Alberigo, Conciliorum, 262 (Lateran IV, c. 58).

derstanding public life in traditional societies; and Bruce R. Smith's analysis of sound-scapes in early modern England deals perceptively with how meaningful noise was both controlled and manipulated, and how very differently the acoustic spaces of the new playhouses were perceived, compared to the open spaces in London where William FitzStephen's *theatrica* had taken place.[58] In a medieval theater, most plays, poems, and songs began with a call for attention (*Oyes*), as did the scripted invocations of proclamations and legal documents, addressed "to all those seeing and hearing." Loud summons, raised voices, and grandiose displays were not merely prerequisites for drama; they were necessary for the delineation of boundaries, the advertisement of authority, and the legitimacy of transactions. When members of the Carité went in procession to Saint-Vaast for the annual renewal of their chapel's lease, the mayor of jongleurs would enter the abbey's cloister, lifting high the key to the door of the Pyramide "so that each one of the people standing around there can see this key."[59] When he renewed the confraternity's oath before the high altar on which the relics of Saint Vaast were displayed, he did so "speaking in a loud voice, so that anyone can hear it."[60]

Publicity was also the key to the judicial process. The very words for punishable offenses and their judgment link the twin requirements of notoriety and justice: *forisfacta*, deeds done openly, and *jurisdictio*, the right of pronouncing law. Justice could be served only when crimes were manifest, and proof of criminal activity consisted of what was generally known; hence the evidentiary importance of *clamor*, a universal outcry, or the visual witness of tumult, breakage, or wounds.[61] In certain cases, to be sure, notoriety could help to exonerate the accused, as when the king's court judged that some of the bishop's men should not be punished for carrying daggers into the Town because they did so "publicly and openly" (*publice et aperte*) and "within the knowledge and sight" (*ad scitum et visum*) of those who had the power to detain them. (In other words, they were merely doing what they had always done.)[62] The only exceptions to the rule of public acknowledgment were crimes warranting excommunication, which the bishop could discern in anyone "impeding our ecclesiastical jurisdiction secretly or openly [*clam vel palam*], directly or indirectly

58. Corbin, *Les cloches*, 13 and 267–268; Bruce R. Smith, *The Acoustic World of Early Modern England: Attending to the O-Factor* (Chicago, 1999), especially 30–95 and 206–284. See also Reinhard Strohm, *Music in Late Medieval Bruges* (Oxford, 1985); Jesse D. Hurlbut "The Sound of Civic Spectacle: Noise in Burgundian Ceremonial Entries," in Davidson, *Material Culture*, 127–140; and R. Murray Schafer, *The Soundscape: Our Sonic Environment and the Tuning of the World* (Rochester, Vt., 1994), 53–63.

59. AdPC ser. 1 H 1, fols. 254r–v: "adfin qui chacun la estant puis icelle clef veus."

60. AdPC ser. 1 H 1, fols. 245v–246r: "en disans a hault voix adsui qui on le puist entendre."

61. E.g., *Cartulaire*, 1–2. See Miriam Müller, "Social Control and the Hue and Cry in Two Fourteenth-Century Villages," *Journal of Medieval History* 31 (2005): 29–53.

62. *Olim*, 1:165 (no. 14 in the octave of All Saints, 1262) and 2:118 (no. 31 in the octave of All Saints, 1278).

in whatever way."[63] Publicity was also the consequence of crimes "notorious in public report," *notorios per famam*, since those convicted had their names read out every Sunday and
feast day until the sentence was lifted. In 1280 deacons, priests, and chaplains were instructed to pronounce this sentence "with candles lit and bells ringing in front of the
church." After 1296 this was to happen between Masses, when the priest made the announcement "in a loud voice."[64]

Having a loud voice was itself an instrument of power, which is why the crying of news
was a major issue in the *Jeu de saint Nicolas*, and in contemporary customary law. The crier
called a community into being. Anyone within hearing had notice of assemblies and other
public business, while those who paid no heed to the banns or who lived beyond the reach
of the crier's voice were political exiles.[65] By the same token, anyone seeking to enlarge
his influence would need to enlarge the compass of his crier's operations. We recall that
Count Philip of Flanders and the bishop of Arras had taken pains to lessen the number of
their disputes by more carefully regulating their criers' respective territories in 1171, but
these arrangements were thrown into confusion by the events of 1191 and parodied by Jehan Bodel in his play. Connart and Raoulet would have known, as most people in Arras
knew, that criers who represented different authorities were expected to remain within
their own jurisdictions, or to cooperate when it came to the publication of news that
crossed boundaries. A charter of agreement made between the monks of Saint-Vaast and
the count of Saint-Pol in 1201 or 1202, a document roughly contemporary with the *Jeu de
saint Nicholas*, stipulated that "the banns and customs of necessity to the town should be
made by the criers of the abbot and count together, according to the following breakdown:
two parts to the church, one to the count."[66] The crier embodied authority and gave it
voice; hence Jehan Bodel's appreciation of the job's twin representations of dramatic and
political power. He was the public man. In the "Book of Oaths" (*Livre aux sermens*) compiled
in the fourteenth century by the commune of Arras, the official crier not only was charged
with the responsibility of ensuring that breaking news was brought to the attention of the
public but also was empowered to do so without consulting any other authority: "And if

63. Gosse, "Anciens synodes," 604–505: "omnes et singulos impedientes nostram juisdictionem
ecclesiasticam clam vel palam directe vel indirecte seu aliquo quomodo."

64. Ibid., 596–597 (article 29): "candelis accensis, campanis pulsatis, in facie ecclesie," and 604–
605: "alta voce." See the essays in Thelma Fenster and Daniel Lord Smail, eds., *Fama: The Politics of Talk
and Reputation in Medieval Europe* (Ithaca, 2003), especially F. R. P. Akehurst, "Good Name, Reputation,
and Notoriety in French Customary Law," 75–94.

65. Thomas N. Bisson, *Assemblies and Representation in Languedoc in the Thirteenth Century* (Princeton,
1964), 300–302; Fossier, *La terre*, 2:208.

66. "Banni et institutiones ville necessarie per nuntium abbatis et comitis communiter fient, de quo-
rum infracturis dues partes eccelesie, tercia comitis erit." Fossier, *Chartes*, 249–253 at 252 (no. 34).

you know anything to the detriment of the échevins or the Town, you will announce it and make it known as quickly as you can."[67]

Media Control and Accountability

Recognition of the inherent theatricality and potential abuses of the crier's public role is not confined to the manuscript of Jehan's play, or to the occasion(s) of its performance. Around the time that *Le garçon et l'aveugle* was conceived, a mocking song composed in Arras used the standard vocabulary of crying to make a nonsensical proclamation. Starting off with a loud "Listen up!" the poet announces that all types of gaming have just been licensed by the king of France; henceforward, only the game of "telling the truth" will be considered an offense:

Li rois fait a cascun savoir	The king makes known to everyone
Ke nus ne jut a dire voir	That games of truth are hereby done.
Voirs est, et bien l'ai entendu,	It's true, that's really what you heard:
Ke le voir dire a deffendu:	That speaking true is now censured;
Ki voir dira il ert honis	Henceforth, who utters truth is false
Et hors de le vile banis.	And banished is, outside town walls.[68]

The questions left open by this Arrageois version of the Liar's Paradox had already been raised in the minds of those witnessing the *Jeu de saint Nicolas*, who heard both the artful cries of Connart and Raoulet and the real cries of the criers who may, in fact, have played those very roles: How do I know whether the proclamations I hear are authoritative? Who is controlling the means of production—of noise, of news? How can I make an informed decision when I hear conflicting accounts of reality? Nor are these playful questions posed by plays; on a daily basis, the people of Arras were challenged to interpret and inflect an array of verbal, visual, and sonic signals, and their response to any scenario (fictive or actual) would be conditioned by a sophisticated knowledge of the public vocabularies on which it drew.[69]

About a century after the upheavals that prompted the composition of Jehan's play, a dispute involving a conflict between criers representative of different authorities was enacted in the same space where Jehan's play was probably performed. That space is identi-

67. *Cartulaire,* 509–519 at 519 (no. 29): "Et se vous savéz aucune cose contraire aux eschevins et à la dite ville, vous le noncherés et ferés savoir au plus tost que vous porrez."

68. "Au cuer trop de duel et d'ire ai," vv. 29–34, datable to 1262–1264, ed. Roger Berger among the *Chansons et dits artésiens* in *Littérature,* 250–258 (no. 24). This collection is hereinafter cited as *C&D,* and is further discussed in chapter 4.

69. "Public noises" (*bruits publics*) of news and gossip circulated via similar channels in eighteenth-century Paris and required the cultivation of similar skills. Darnton, "Early Information Society," 2–7.

fied by a curious phrase, *ad phalam Attrebatensem*, "out in the open of Arras" or "at the Arrageois display place": curious because it appears five times in a single document yet cannot be found in any other sources, and also because it clearly designates a space or set of conditions so well known that it required no further elaboration.[70] The only additional clue as to its meaning is its association with proclamations made *a le breteske*, a Picard phrase occurring twice in the same document and referring to a raised structure, usually made of wood and roofed with thatch, which served as a rostrum for the publication of news and announcements. There were at least two of these in fourteenth-century Arras, one in each of the major marketplaces, and they had probably been there since the twelfth century.[71] Yet the Latin phrase *ad phalam Attrebatensem* cannot be translated or located so specifically. On the one hand, *phalam* appears to be the accusative case of the feminine noun *phalla* or *falla*, variously defined as a tower, a high perch, or a place for the display of merchandise. In practice, the word often referred to a temporary wooden structure, sometimes roofed or thatched; by the later Middle Ages it meant a hall, usually the town hall.[72] But there was no such edifice in thirteenth-century Arras, so *ad phalam* might refer to the place where open-air stalls were located—the marketplace—or to the location of the *breteske*.[73] On the other hand, the common Latin adverb *palam*, "plainly," "manifestly," "in

70. AdPC ser. 3 G 2/"Foires et marchés du cloître et de la cité," cvi): "ad phalam Attrebatensem . . . ad phalam Attrebatensis . . . ad phalam predictam," etc.

71. *Bretesche* is defined as "place publique d'une ville où se font ordinairement les criées et les proclamations" by Godefroy, who quotes from the late medieval *Coustumes générales du comté d'Artois*; *Dictionnaire*, 1:728–729. According to Viollet-le-Duc, the term applies equally to siege towers made of wood and multistory urban towers or abutments added to urban tenements, particularly town halls; he notes that traces of a medieval *bretèche* were still visible on the exterior of the *hôtel de ville* in Arras in the midnineteenth century; *Dictionnaire raisonné de l'architecture française du XIe au XVIe siècle* (Paris, 1858–1868), 2:244–249. According to Battard, the *bretesque* was usually "a small balcony in wood or masonry" jutting out from a belfry; M. Battard, *Beffrois, halles, hôtels de ville dans le Nord de la France et la Belgique* (Arras, 1948), 24. In Arras, by 1382 the phrase "de la bretesque" appears to have indicated a house on one side of the Petit Marché, owned by the échevins and sold by them in 1501, when the *hôtel de ville* was constructed; this became the place for all official announcements and for the exposure of criminals. In the thirteenth century, however, the échevins met in a house on the *place* of Saint-Géry, and all assemblies were held in the Petit Marché, where there seems to have been a pair of rostra, one at each end of the marketplace, noted by van Drival as "des endroits officiels pour l'accomplissement d'actes judiciaires" (Guiman, 453). See Charles le Gentil, *Le viel Arras, ses faubourgs, sa banlieue, ses environs: Souvenirs archéologiques & historiques* (Arras, 1877), 23, 412–418, 444.

72. A. Ernout and A. Meillet, *Dictionnaire étymologique de la langue latine*, 4th ed., 2 vols. (Paris, 1960), 1:213b; Charles du Fresne du Cange, *Glossarium mediae et infimae latinitatis*, ed. Léopold Favre et al., rev. ed., 10 vols. (Graz, 1954), 6:301b; J. F. Niermeyer and C. von de Kieft, *Mediae latinitatis lexicon minus*, rev. ed., 2 vols. (Leiden, 2002), 1:532b and 2:983b.

73. This inference is my own; the Parisian usage of *falae* to mean market stalls, or, by association,

the presence of all," was occasionally strengthened to *ad palam*, and always denoted what was said or done "out in the open," things brought to light, attested, or exposed.[74] It was often placed in opposition to anything furtive, hidden, or exclusive, as in the formula *clam vel palam*, "secretly or openly."[75] Hence, *phalam* may have been a local conflation of *ad palam* and *ad phalam*, evoking more generalized circumstances of notoriety, presumably in the places most frequently associated with public display, the marketplaces. The text of an inquest held in 1289 corroborates this when it describes certain public affairs as taking place *en plaine hale*, defined in the text of the document as meaning "in front of échevins, the council, and the common assembly of the town" (*devant eskievins, le consel de le vile et du kemun de le vile*).[76]

The document featuring these two designations, *ad phalam Attrebatensem* and *a le breteske*, is a brief narrative cartulary compiled in the cathedral's chancery. It recounts a sequence of events that began in the late summer of 1293, when the canons were forced to defend a claim that that they had a right to hold a market in the cloistered forecourt of the cathedral on days when the diocesan synod met in the City, as well as on the eve and day of two important Marian feasts, the Assumption (August 14 and 15) and the Nativity of the Blessed Virgin (September 7 and 8). These were high days in Arras, when pilgrims visiting the cathedral and its Marian relics might be expected to spend a lot of money for food, lodging, and merrymaking.[77] But such a market, whether or not it had been held "time out of mind," as the canons alleged, would have been viewed as detrimental to trade in the marketplaces of the Town, and could have been set up to rival the popularity of the Carité's Sainte-Chandelle, which was displayed in the Petit Marché on these days. So much can be inferred from the document, which reports that the échevins of the Town had instructed their crier to make an announcement *ad phalam Attrebatensem* forbidding the people of the commune to buy or sell anything in the City. Annoyed, the canons appealed directly to King Philip IV, demanding a public retraction of the ban from the very stage *ad phalam At-*

---

the place where stalls were set up, is attested in a charter dated 1375. (The most important open-air marketplace in medieval Paris, which is still called Les Halles, drew its name from the merchants' booths set up there.) See du Cange, *Glossarium*, 3: 98b.

74. For the augmented forms of *palam* (*ad palam*, *in palam*), see Ernout and Meillet, *Dictionnaire*, 2:475b. *Palam* also lent itself to the formation of the neologism *propalatum*, "made known to all," and the verbs *propalo*, "to make manifest," and *depalo*, "to disclose."

75. E.g., Gosse, "Anciens synodes," 574–613 at 604–605.

76. AdPC ser. A 1009; Gusenon, "Adam," 221–233 at 221.

77. AdPC ser. 3 G / "Fabrique," 106–114, and 3 G Carton 2 / "Foires et marchés du cloître et de la cité," cvi (Delmaire handlist, nos. 35–38). Delmaire, *Le diocèse*, 1:368, mentions a market in the cathedral cloister on these days but does not allude to the dispute. Marian feasts were becoming increasingly important throughout the North, and the feast of the Virgin's Nativity became the "official feast" of Tournai in 1284; see Dumoulin and Pycke, *La grande procession*, 21. See also chapters 2 and 4.

trebatensem on which it had been made. The king honored their request, sending out an order to the échevins of Arras dated October 2, the day after the feast of Saint Rémy—an important day for the abbey and its tenants, as I have noted, and the occasion of one of the Carité's thrice-yearly bevées. Apparently the order was ignored, since it was issued again about a month later, before the feast of Saint Martin (November 13). This time the échevins were even provided with a scripted form of words, given in Picard as part of a document otherwise couched in Latin, which shows how seriously the matter of publicity was taken and how much attention was paid to the medium of the message.[78]

The échevins complied with the second order, yet they seem to have given certain interested parties advance warning of the planned proclamation. For when the crier appeared *ad phalam Attrebatensem* to deliver his lines, the count's men also appeared on the scene, ready to contradict the announcement "as soon as it had been made." As the cathedral's chronicler reports, a bailiff named "Colard Lamores" or "Colard Lamous" had the following counterproclamation cried by one of the count's sergeants, a herald called Brenet. The Latin cartulary carefully quotes it, in Picard: "Listen up you lords, and all of you gathered here! We tell you and advise you that this repeal of the ban and prohibition by the échevins is totally against the will and pleasure and consent of my lord the count of Artois. And so we forbid you in his name, all you men and women who consider yourselves his good townspeople, to go selling or buying anything there, under the aforesaid prohibition."[79] The mastermind behind this Bodellian spectacle can be identified as Master Nicolas (Colart) Levoul, the holder (by 1296) of the communal office of clerk: a good indication that this "discordant announcement *a le breteske*" was the result of careful stage management and mediation between the commune and the count, and possibly even the abbey of Saint-Vaast, since all three parties had a vested interest in the revenues of the marketplace and were united in their animosity toward the City.[80] Certainly the outcome was favorable to these allied powers, since (as the canons' cartulary reports) no one from the Town went to the market in the City after that.

King Philip, once again petitioned to intervene on the canons' behalf, responded by sending the bailiff of Amiens to persuade his cousin Robert to revoke the ban "just as pub-

---

78. AdPC ser. 3 G 2/"Foires et marchés du cloître et de la cité," cvi. The texts of these cries are not included in Auguste Menche de Loisne's survey of Picard usage in early charters, "L'ancien dialecte artésien d'après les chartes en langue vulgaire du d'Arras (1248–1301)," *MAA*, 2nd ser., 29 (1898): 1–94.

79. AdPC ser. 3 G 2/"Foires et marchés du cloître et de la cité," cvi: "Oyes signeur et entendes vous tout qui chi estes assanle. Nous vous disons est faisons asavoir que tel ban et tel deffense ke eskievin ont chi rapelle che nest de le volente ne du gre ne de lassentement monsi. le conte dartois ancois le deffendons de par lui quil nesoit si hardis bourgois et bourgoise qui voist vendre ne akater ne ne port devrees pour vendre ne pour akater sous le deffense devant dicte."

80. Berger, *Littérature*, 74.

licly as it had been made" (*ita publice sicut factum fuit*).[81] The count stood his ground. The canons were probably holding a market much more frequently than they had claimed, since their own narrative reveals that merchants and customers who wanted to trade in their cloister were "often" detained in the Town "with force and violence" (*per vim et violentiam*). Indeed, Count Robert seems to have been bracing for a showdown *ad phalam Attrebatensem* as early as August—since the Assumption Day market, perhaps—for it was then that he sought an attorney to represent him at the court of the king, Odo of Saint-Germain.[82] Odo was certainly present at court on February 6, 1294, when the case was heard, but then so was the count himself, the duke of Burgundy, the count of Poitou, the castellan of Nesles, and many other notables: a distinguished company bearing witness to the importance attached to control of the media.

In the end, the case was settled out of court, although this hardly means that it was settled privately. As the cathedral's cartulary tells it, the bailiff of Amiens took a new mandate to the king's palace, where the count's men had gathered, and showed it to them. Then Reynaud Coignet, the count's agent, "read it out loud from word to word" (*de verbo ad verbum legit*) and told the bailiff that he and the count's own man Simon Monnekin, then sheriff of Hesdin, would see to its performance. Back in Arras, they arranged for a public retraction to be made *ad phalam Attrebatensem* on the first day of March, when the assembled audience included the dean of the cathedral, the master of the cathedral school, the future bishop Pierre de Sorra, the canons, and "a multitude of people, who came to hear the revocation of the ban and prohibition aforesaid in the form and manner following." This time an effort was made to choose a crier whose appearance would symbolize concord, someone acceptable to the cathedral but not prejudicial to the count or commune. This was a herald called Colart Beauchant, styled "Sir" (*dominus*) in the canons' record of the dispute and known to the jongleurs' Carité as "Sergeant Colart."[83] His surname (Beauchant) suggests that he was renowned for his beautiful singing voice, the honorific indicates that he was a man of some standing, and his close connection with the confraternity (he may even have been a member of its household) implies that he was entrusted with this task because of his membership in an organization that was regarded as representative of the whole community. Once again, the wording of the proclamation is quoted in Picard.[84]

81. AdPC ser. 3 G 2/"Foires et marchés du cloître et de la cité," cvii (sealed original of Philip IV's letter).

82. AdPC ser. A 38.24.

83. "Le Bauchant serjant colars." His death was recorded in the register between Candlemas and Pentecost of 1317; see Berger, *Le nécrologe*, 2:166.

84. It is noteworthy that Robert II appealed the decision of his cousin in a formal complaint made before the Parlement of Paris in 1300 (he lost again), and his heirs would still be protesting against the claustral market in 1345. See *Olim*, 3:44–45 (no. 8); AdPC ser. 3 G 2/"Foires et marchés du cloître et de la cité," cviii.

The contest *ad phalam Attrebatensem* reveals more about the importance attached to publicity than it does about the competition for trade. However desirable the goods exchanged in the canons' cloister, commercial success is here represented as dependent on advertisements and public opinion. In the cathedral's cartulary, the mandates of the king, and in the proceedings of the Parlement of Paris, concern over the form and content of the messages conveyed to the public emerges as central to the negotiations over access to the media. And in all of these sources it is taken for granted that the townspeople are not just passive recipients of news but political, social, and economic agents; hence the attempts to regulate their behavior are matched by attempts to capture their attention and sway their judgment through painstaking stipulation of the manner and language in which messages should be conveyed, and through the canny casting of certain spokesmen charged with the delivery of those messages.

Moreover, there is good evidence that the people of Arras considered it their prerogative to hold those in power accountable for what was said and done in public. This was something the count's agent, Reynaud Coignet, knew only too well—which is probably why he left Arras abruptly and suspiciously in 1299, when his overhasty exit become the subject of a public lawsuit (which was still being pursued in 1307). The case against him? "Before his departure, he should have had it cried, according to custom," every ten days beginning fifty days beforehand, in order that grudges or suits could be brought against him.[85] For it was within the right of all men in that town to hear and see *en quel guyse et quel maniere* (in what guise and in what manner) a public man had played his part among them.[86] Where power is measured by tolling bells and meaning determined by common consent, a life spent in the manipulation of public media required public evaluation.

Observing the Proprieties

In the autumn of 1266 a lieutenant of the count's bailiff pursued a fugitive into the choir of the cathedral in Arras. The man had sought sanctuary there, yet he was cornered near the altar and severely beaten by one of the bailiff's sergeants. At the same time, a chaplain of the church was struck down when he tried to prevent the bailiff and his men from entering the choir, while a lay caretaker of the church was assaulted when he tried to intervene and stop the beating. On his way out of the church, moreover, the lieutenant had added insult to injury when "he stuck his finger in the eye of Pierre, a married cleric, and

---

85. AdPC ser. A 53.28. In a letter read out to the people of Arras on August 31, 1307, Countess Mahaut asked them to affirm "que avant son partir il avoit fait criier par quinzaines et par quarantaines ensi comme la coustume dous paiis donne." When Reynaud did not answer her summons, she sent a letter to her cousin Charles II of Sicily asking for his assistance in pursuing the offender. AdPC ser. A 49.23. See also de Germiny, *Les lieutenants*, 33–34l; and Derville, *Saint-Omer*, 129.

86. This is a standard formula; e.g., AdPC ser. A 31.18 (inquest of April 18, 1292).

this in the aforesaid church, because Pierre told him that he did an evil deed in causing violence in the church of Arras." (Either he made a rude gesture—"gave him the finger"—or actually poked him in the eye.) Later, an inquest in the Parlement of Paris determined that the lieutenant had also sworn at the chaplain, "called him 'whoreson priest,' and threatened to rip his guts out."[87] The court ruled that the offender be admonished by the bailiff and forced to undergo a form of public penance "by procession" (per processiones).

An example of the kind of ritual that would have been performed by the offending officer is found in the more complete record of a disturbance that occurred a few years later on the feast of the Assumption in 1270. Several of young Count Robert II's companions had gone out to two of the cathedral's rural parishes and driven cattle from the fields into the churchyards. Others had brought a falcon into Mass at Notre-Dame and loosed it there. These were pranks serious enough to warrant excommunication, and two of the rogues, who had actually broken into church buildings, were ordered to make penitential pilgrimages. The rest were sentenced to an exhibition of public humiliation scheduled to take place on the Nativity of the Blessed Virgin, a gala day in the City. On September 8 the perpetrators were led in procession through the holiday crowd, behind the dean whose cathedral had been desecrated by their behavior, dressed only "in sleeves and shirts, without caps or any other concealing garment, in bare feet, carrying rods in their hands."[88] After Mass they had to go out to the parishes where they had done their mischief, in order to take part in more localized rituals, so that justice was seen to be done in the proper places and at the proper times. That was the mimetic purpose of penance: "it satisfied the public's need to see the sinner humiliated" and "held up the victims to the contempt and perhaps the laughter of their social inferiors," as Mansfield has shown.[89]

Indeed, the conceptualization of penitential rites amounted to a dramatic art—in the

87. *Olim*, 1:258 (no. 3 among the cases heard during the octave of All Saints): "Item quod idem subballivus posuit digitum ad oculum Petri, clerici uxorati, et hoc in ecclesia predicta, quia dixerat ei quod malefaciebat quia violenciam inferebat in ecclesia Attrebatensi . . . Item quod vocavit dictum Robertum 'sacerdotem ribaldum,' et comminatus fuit ei quod ipsum evisceraret seu esboelaret." On the basis of the chronology provided by Berger (*Littérature*, 428), the sous-bailli was either Jean Longeleske (attested between 1245 and 1270) or perhaps Jean Blassel, who was already in place by 1269; the bailiff of Arras was Dreu de Bray, in office from April 20, 1265, to November 1267.

88. "In brachis et camisiis sine cuiffa omni alio vestimento circumscripto nudis pedibus, virgas gestantis in manibus in medio processionis vel in fine processionis in cedant." AdPC ser. A 18/26 (accord made on August 16, the Sunday after the feast of the Assumption, 1270), and A 26 bis (vidimus in French by the provost of Paris copied during Lent of 1271). The case was heard by the archdeacon of Bayeux and Guillaume de Chevry, acting for the king. A representative from the chapter met with the judges, who also took depositions from the bailiff and sous-bailli of Arras (Gui le Bas and Robert de Saint-Venant) and others acting on the count's behalf.

89. Mansfield, *Humiliation*, 266 and 269–277.

planning if not always in the performance. Imaginative decisions as to the choice of venue and audience, timing, costumes, and choreography were made in order to address the damage done by the failure to observe proprieties. The young knights of Robert's *maisnie* had been making a show of their seigneurial status through a series of calculated transgressive acts: raiding livestock, trespassing on church property, and sending a bird of prey into the rafters of Notre-Dame while the sacrifice of Christ's body and blood was on the altar. Only a *coup de théâtre* that temporarily stripped them of their prerogatives (fashionable garments, headgear, boots, swords, horses, and hawks) could satisfy outraged opinion and make amends for material and symbolic damages. The transgressions of the bailiff's lieutenant were seemingly less calculated but as symbolically charged: he was the count's man sent on the commune's and castellan's business, whose mistreatment of a suppliant in the canons' cathedral within the bishop's domain was eventually brought to trial in the king's court. His victims were a layman in the employ of the cathedral, a married cleric in minor orders, and a chaplain, as well as Notre Dame herself, whose high altar had been the scene of bloodshed (and would, presumably, require reconsecration), not to mention a man whose person was technically inviolate, since he had thrown himself on the Virgin's mercy. Whatever ritual punishment was eventually devised, it would have been designed to redress, dramatically, these improper actions.

These two incidents, both of which occurred in the heyday of "The Boy and the Blind Man," further illustrate the forces at work in the making and unmaking of space, demonstrating that even the most carefully guarded and unambiguous boundaries in Arras were collapsible. The cathedral's high altar could not be adequately protected by the building's fabric, the spiritual force field exerted by its consecration, or even the celebration of Mass. In theory, it was sacrosanct; in practice, it could be rendered no more safe or seemly than the rowdiest tavern in Arras. The self-conscious knaveries of the count's companions and the blasphemy of the bailiff's lieutenant therefore present two different paradigms of the (disruptive) agency conferred by the (unauthorized) use of forceful vocabularies in public spaces where certain types of activities were expected and others were not. Trumping the power exerted by the built environment or the consensus of the community was the behavior of individuals. Words and actions had the capacity to undo centuries of careful construction, and could be corrected only by other words and actions calibrated to reverse their effects. At the same time, actions and utterances benignly performed at other places and times were rendered newly meaningful as well as dangerous: a falcon flown in the forest is banal, and so is a brawl in a wine shop. Consecrated, enclosed spaces are thus deconstructed and reconfigured by uses to which they are put, while certain types of human behavior, corralled in such spaces, become newly, strangely effective.[90]

Harnessed and directed, such behavior becomes productive of social, political, and

90. Goffman, *Presentation*, 108 ("Regions and Region Behavior").

cultural change—and of a medieval theater. Liminal spaces, such as churches and church-yards, are therefore good places to look for evidence of the ways in which actions could effect such changes or create such theaters. In most medieval towns, the cemetery was the only viable place for public assembly and was therefore the site of dances, fairs, and markets. While such pursuits came to be condemned during the twelfth century, practical necessity made the enforcement of prohibitions difficult, as did a centuries-long tradition of public use and habitation.[91] The earliest set of local canons to have survived from the diocese of Arras, issued in 1280, directed that "cemeteries should be decently enclosed, and not made unclean by the presence of farm animals, whether asses, hogs, pigs, or any other beasts."[92] The second set, issued ten years later, expressed exasperation: "We order and will that cemeteries now lacking boundary lines be provided with boundaries."[93]

For in point of fact, it was hard enough to keep parish churches, which *were* decently and clearly bounded, from being polluted—whether by "feminine effusions," blood shed in violence, or other acts and accidents. "Priests should frequently warn their parishioners not to fight or make disturbances in church, or to allow such things to happen, nor should worldly matters be pursued, nor should they organize dances. And whenever any really shameful thing is manifestly discovered to have been done in the churches, we order that they should be closed at night with strong bars and that the office be celebrated by day."[94] The priest was also to be on the lookout for those who, "under the pretense and sham of praying," frequented his church intent on other pursuits: dancing, gaming, drinking, carousing.[95] Moreover, he was to buttress the fragile sanctity of the building by modifying his own behavior, enacting the gravity and piety he was supposed to be inducing in his congregation. When performing the gesture of Elevation at Mass, the priest was to display "a humble and downcast mien while the bells are rung" and to teach his congregation to "bow reverently."[96] When processing with the Blessed Sacrament, especially on

91. Michel Aubrun, *La paroisse en France des origines au XVe siècle* (Paris, 1985), 152–155; André Vauchez, "La foi des laïcs vers 1200: Mentalités religieuses féodales," in *Les laïcs*, 125–132; Heers, *La ville*, 386–390. In general, see Michel Fixot and Elisabeth Zadora-Rio, eds., *L'environment des églises et la topographie des campagnes médiévale* (Paris, 1994).

92. Gosse, "Anciens synodes," 588 (article 12): "Cimiteria honeste claudantur, ne bestie, anseres, porci, sues, et alia animalia ibidem immundiciam faciant."

93. Ibid., 596 (article 28): "Item precipimus et volumus ut cimiteria que limitatione indigent, limitentur."

94. Ibid., 588–589 (article 12): "Frequenter moneant presbiteri parochianos suos nel in ecclesia pugnas vel contentiones faciant, vel fieri sustineant , nec cause seculares tractentur in illis, nec fiant choree. . . . . Et qui multa inhonesta in ecclesiis perpetrantur, cum aperte reperiuntur, precimus ut de nocte claudantur sub bonis seris, et de die officio celebrato."

95. Ibid., 598 (article 31): "pretextu et sub simulatione orandi."

96. Ibid., 581 (article 3). "Hostiam autem cum honore deferat in vase honesto et mundo, dicendo

visits to the dying and the sick, he was to surround himself with the aura of the church even in the open air, carrying the monstrance "with great reverence," preceded by a candle and a ringing bell, "so that all seeing and hearing may bend the knee just as if they were before their Creator, and with joined hands they should pray until such time as it has passed."[97]

The Church's increased emphasis on the accessibility and "openness of the sacraments," which necessitated the publicity of even "private" acts of contrition, made the theatricality of the priest's role ever more pronounced. Around 1200 the synodal statutes issuing from Paris taught that clergy hearing confessions ought "to choose for themselves a communal place in the church [communiorem locum in ecclesia], so that they can be seen communally [communiter] by everyone."[98] The synodal statutes of Arras, like those of other regional and ecumenical councils convened during the thirteenth century, are more explicit in the connections drawn between the priest's acting ability and the very efficacy of the sacraments performed by him. When hearing confession, he was to create an illusion of magisterial detachment by sitting "in a sideways position, not in a concealed place, but in a place where he can be seen by everyone," keeping "a humble countenance, eyes lowered to the ground." Like the figure of Christ in a scene of the Last Judgment, he was to mete out penance impartially. Moreover, he was to continue this performance for the duration of his acquaintance with those who confessed to him, since the inviolability of the confessional's seal could be guaranteed only if he refrained from revealing his secret knowledge either "by sign or word, whether generally or particularly, as if to say: 'I know what sort of person you are.'"[99] At the same time, canon law insisted that priests and cler-

---

septem psalmos penitentiales vel alias orationes in vultu humili et demisso, cum pulsatione campanule. Sacerdos vero quilibet frequenter doceat plebem suam ut cum in celebrationem missarum elevatur Hostia salutaris, quilibet se reverenter inclinet, et similiter cum portatur ad infirmum." See also Rubin, *Corpus Christi*, 35–49, 55, and 131–132.

97. Gosse, "Anciens synodes," 589 (article 12): "Semper sacerdotes [sanctum Corpus Domini] ferant cum magna reverentia in pixide adminus eburnea bene clausa propter casum et periculum, et cum lucerna precedente et campana sonante, ut omnes videntes et audientes genua flectant tanquam Creatori suo, et junctis manibus quousque transierit, orent."

98. "Ad audiendum confessiones, communiorem locum in ecclesia sibi elegant sacerdotes, ut comuniter ab omnibus videri possint." Cited by Mansfield, *Humiliation*, 9. See also Odette Pontal and Joseph Avril, *Les statuts synodaux français du XIIIe siècle*, 3 vols. (Paris, 1971, 1983, and 1988), 1:62 (Paris, ca. 1200, c. 27).

99. Gosse, "Anciens synodes," 583–584 (article 7): "Sacerdos audiens confessiones, secrete et sigillatim peccata audiat et sedeat in loco publico non in absconso, ut ab omnibus videri possit, et intra Ecclesiam. . . . In confessionem audienda, habeat sacerdos vultum humilem, oculos at terram demissos, nec . . . audeat in aliquo casu revelare confessionem, signo vel verbo, vel generaliter vel specialiter ut dicendo: Ego scio quales estis."

ics not only adopt appropriate postures at special times but also dress distinctively at all times. Their self-dramatization was to be the badge of their profession, a perpetual performance of identity.

Keeping Up Appearances

The inhabitants of Arras could take special advantage of the ambiguities in status fostered by moveable wealth, since the European cloth trade of which their town was the epicenter provided a very material medium for adjusting the rules governing the expression of power. Conspicuous consumption of clothes marked a man out as an aristocrat, or as a pretender to that rank, and the two often looked distressingly alike. "The greater the social challenge to the old nobility from the rising wealth of the urban bourgeoisie, the more visually necessary it became for the nobility to distinguish itself through the adoption of distinctive mode of dress, deportment, and manners," observes Gabrielle Spiegel, but this was a losing battle until sumptuary laws were introduced.[100] Throughout the thirteenth century, the people of Arras were in an excellent position to confuse distinctions. Their economic and political powers, though occasionally harnessed by secular or ecclesiastical lords, were fueled by independence of movement and freedoms of association over which lords could exercise little control. To control was to stifle: that is why the monks of Saint-Vaast preferred to free its serfs and put them to use rather than to keep them unfree and unprofitable. And that is why Philip Augustus gambled with his winnings and honored the charters of Arras and other former Flemish communes: it was more profitable to risk loosening their reins.

Nevertheless, the problem of keeping up appearances among the professional performers of the Church meant that the clergy were more and more subject to restrictions which the laymen of Arras could flout at will. In 1182 the archbishop of Reims scolded the chapter of Arras for the laxity of its dress code, censuring the unsuitable surcoats and hats the clerics wore "for the sake of ornament and pride even in the streets and public squares."[101] Speaking for the Church at large, the Fourth Lateran Council attempted to make the cleric's outward seeming an appropriate reflection of (or mask for) his inner state, addressing those in the priesthood as well as those "resolved to adopt that character" (*personatibus constituti*) and representing the creation of a theatrical persona as essential to the business of pastoral care, not only when celebrating divine service or keeping countenance during confession, but all the time.[102] In Arras, priests and deacons were

---

100. Spiegel, *Romancing*, 21. See also Fossier, *La terre*, 2:609; Pounds, *Economic History*, 301.

101. BnF lat. 9930, fol. 43v: "etiam per vicos et plateas ad decorem et gloriam."

102. Alberigo, *Conciliorum*, 43 (Lateran IV, c. 16). On the self-conscious dramatization of certain professions in a given society, see Goffman, *Presentation*, 40.

therefore ordered not to walk about improperly attired, either within their own parishes or outside them. When carrying the sacred Host to a sick parishioner, it was even more important that they avoid either ostentatious or slovenly apparel but clothe themselves "reverently and decently" (*reverenter et decenter*) in cope and tunic.[103] Furthermore, none of the pursuits appropriate to laymen were to be practiced by those in major orders. Enlarging upon the canons of Lateran IV, which had already called attention to the problem of clerical hooliganism, the canons of Arras forbade the clergy "to play at dice, to attend shows or take part in dancing, to go into taverns alone or for the purpose of drinking, to enter others' houses, or to wander around the streets and public places." They were also forbidden to contract debts, an impossible injunction in this town of universal usury. In place of these pursuits, companions, and habits, priests "should maintain themselves with virtuous contemplation, the study of books, and worthy activities."[104]

These activities included privileges supposedly distinctive to their vocations. The statutes issued in 1296 insisted that only priests should announce and explain parish business, preach, confer indulgences, gather people together for processions by ringing the bells, or announce coming feast days. The only exceptions to this rule were the heralds of the diocese, whose job it was to make proclamations. Like other men in minor orders, they occupied a troublesome middle ground. Because they lived among laymen but were vested with clerical authority and status, their appearance was a matter of even greater concern to the Church, and they had to be nagged continually to dress and act the part, down to the choirboys and charity scholars at the cathedral school, who were known in Arras as *bons enfants cappés* or *enfants à la capette* for the short hooded cloaks they wore.[105] The diocesan synod of 1280 reminded all clerics, "whether engaged in trade, or married men," that they had to dress appropriately "if they wish to rejoice in the privilege of their clerical state." Thus, "they should not wear colorful or slashed clothing" and were to maintain a proper tonsure. The diocese also ventured to describe an appropriate clerical manner as fully as possible: "When [clerics] come to church, they should sit or stand in the chancel, not mixed up with the laity, but between the altar and the laymen, and by keeping themselves there in all innocence, singing, reading, praying, the difference between them and the laity should be apparent." The preoccupation with propriety and its performance reinforces the impression that the church building was not sufficient protection for the holy

---

103. Gosse, "Anciens synodes," 587–588 (article 11).

104. Ibid., 587–588 (article 11), 596 (article 27), and 603–609 (articles 36–38): "Ludere cum deciis, interesse cum spectaculis aut coreis assistere, intrare tabernas causa potandi et sine comite clerico vel laico, domos alienas intrare aut discurrere per vicos aut plateas . . . ne pro defectu solutionis scandalum oriatur . . . bonis meditationibus, studio librorum, et honestis actibus intendant." See also Alberigo, *Conciliorum*, 242–243 (Lateran IV, cc. 15–16).

105. Adolphe Guesnon, *Un collège inconnu des Bons enfants d'Arras à Paris du XIIIe au XVe siècle* (Paris, 1915), 9–11.

things contained within it, although it could be an appropriate frame within which the behavior of the clergy was showcased, the place "where they should listen devoutly to the priest, setting a good example for the laity." Beyond its walls, by extension, clerics' behavior on ceremonial occasions was supposed to help in the building of a spiritual environment for the parade of relics or the Eucharist, as they walked "between the priest and the cross, putting themselves in a position to sing, according to their knowledge, and to repeat the psalms, virtuously and without undue levity."[106]

Repetition of these injunctions betray the fact that they were seldom followed. And when they were, the resulting exhibitions of some men's clerical piety must have seemed very much at odds with their everyday demeanor, and therefore an even more blatant display of theatricality. For despite the Church's attempts to curtail not only the behavior of the clergy but the conduct of their affairs as well, there is ample evidence that even those in major orders were richly engaged in public life. Many of the cathedral canons and even some monks of Saint-Vaast were members of the Carité, and a significant portion of the former can be numbered among the local trouvères.[107] Moreover, the schools kept by both the monastery and the cathedral had, as I have already argued, a direct and indirect impact on the development of a common stage in Arras. It must have been at these institutions that Jehan Bodel, Adam de la Halle, and other clerically minded jongleurs of Arras learned to read, sing, and write, and the Carité's close association with both foundations could have resulted, at least in part, from the continued friendship of men who had been schoolmates. Many of those who had taken orders in boyhood, as part of their initiation as "little clerics" (clericuli), may even have retained these privileges into adulthood so that they could continue to serve in the cathedral chancery or even in its choir: in 1261 the chapter of Notre-Dame granted additional stipends to certain chaplains and jobbing clerics who regularly performed the divine office, which suggests that some of these were paid professionals, living at large. That this could have been a way for talented performers and ex-choirboys to augment their income is further suggested by another charter, made in 1263, which offered pensions to choristers and clerics performing liturgical duties at certain feasts.[108] Indeed, Adolphe Guesnon has argued that Adam de la Halle's continued asso-

---

106. Gosse, "Anciens synodes," 590 (article 13). "Omnes clerici nostre dyocesis tam negotiatores quam uxorati . . . si privilegio gaudere volunt clericali . . . non ferant vestas partitas, sive virgatas. . . . Cum venerint ad eccelesiam, sedeant vel stent in cancello, non permixti laicis, sed inter altare et laicos, in simplicitate ibidem se habendo, cantando, legendo, orando, et appareat differentia eorum a laicis . . . devote predicationem audiant, bonum exemplum laicis prestando . . . inter sacerdotem et crucem decantando secundum suam scientiam et psallendo honeste et sine derisione se habentes."

107. Adolphe Guesnon, "Nouvelles recherches biographiques sur les trouvères artésiens," MA 15 (1902): 137–173; see also idem, "Recherches biographiques" and "Publications nouvelles." See chapter 4.

108. AdPC ser. 3 G 5/Grand Commun xiii and xvi (Delmaire handlist, nos. 65 and 67). In 1435 the text of an oath administered to the chaplains assigned to perpetual service in the cathedral church

ciation with the cathedral is referenced in the opening lines of the *Jeu de la feuillée*, which call attention to the fact that he has once again put on the distinctive habit of the Arrageois scholars who continued their studies at the Collège des Bons Enfants in Paris.[109]

Other shared pursuits of the laity and clergy can be inferred from a famous list of forbidden business dealings articulated for the first time in Arras and later applied to the rest of medieval Christendom. It is unlikely to have been enforced, yet it staunchly declares that clerics should not be fullers, weavers, dyers, horse dealers, bathhouse workers, butchers, traveling dentists, leather workers, shoemakers, or tanners; nor could they engage in any vile trades "by which scandal might be brought upon the clerical orders," including usury, that mainstay of the economy. Moreover, they were to have no "suspect or unworthy companions," no commerce with players, gamesters, perjurers, pimps, whores, or like personages; nor should they have resort to the places where such people could be found, namely, taverns.[110] But the diocesan statutes of 1350, which insist that "clerics must not show themselves off as goliards or buffoons," merely corroborate the popularity of this career choice for the former scholars of the abbey and cathedral schools.[111] The historian Gérard Sivéry is forthright in classing jongleurs among lawyers, bureaucrats, moneychangers, bankers, and hoteliers in a growing "tertiary sector" of service and entertainment industries which was staffed in part by minor clerics.[112] And evidence of rivalries among the entrepreneurs of these emerging industries reveals that anxiety over the impropriety of certain clerical pursuits was not confined to the Church. It was the échevinage of Arras that initially lobbied the papacy to tighten the strictures: petitioning Innocent IV in 1254, they argued that clergy engaging in trade used the public roads, marketplaces, and amenities like everyone else and should therefore be taxed like everyone else. The First Council of Lyon, convened later that year, accordingly divided those within the *forum* of the Church from denizens of the public *forum*, chastising clerics "who mix themselves up in disgraceful affairs, meaning usury, or the frequenting of public taverns night after night, or who engage in forbidden trades."[113] Its terminology con-

---

stressed the importance of their attendance at divine service, which suggests that it was often difficult for the cathedral to field a full choir without the lure of special incentives; AdPC ser. 3 G Carton 5/ "Grand Commun," xxxiii (Delmaire handlist, no. 71).

109. Guesnon, *Un collège*, 9–11.

110. Gosse, "Anciens synodes," 590 (article 13); see also 591–592 (articles 14–15): "Item inhonesta mercimonia non exerceant; non sint fullores, textores, mangones, unctuarii, carnifices, rinctores, nebularii, calceorum factores vel coriorum preparatores, sive huiusmodi vila officia exercentes, per que scandalum fiat ordini clericali." For a more imaginative treatment of the evidence, see Jacques Le Goff, "Métiers licites et métiers illicites dans l'Occident médiévale," in *Pour un autre*, 91–107.

111. Lille, Bm 193, fol. 19v; cited by Delmaire, *Le diocèse*, 1:263, n. 16.

112. Sivéry, *L'économie*, 23.

113. *Cartulaire*, 31–33 (no. 30): "bigamis, seu viduarum maritis, et aliis qui turpibus negotiantibus

trasts the conceptual space encompassed by Christendom, and locally contained within the walls of its churches, with the *forum*, or marketplace, most closely associated with the transactions of public life.[114] Two years later, reiterating his predecessor's decision in a letter to the échevins of Arras dated March 21, 1256, Alexander IV made clerical status dependent on exemplary conduct, not on the technicalities of ordination.[115]

Public opinion was therefore called to the service of canon law, since any judgment about which clerics were properly behaved and which were not would have to be determined on the ground: the papacy could set the standard but could not apply it. The diocese of Arras was quick to educate the public. In the year between the Council of Lyon and Innocent's letter, certain curates from parishes in the district of Ostrevant had already been arraigned in the court of the bishop's official, on charges that they had been enjoying illicit pleasures in taverns and at feasts, "against the statutes and banns solemnly and publicly proclaimed there."[116] But no diocesan court could possibly handle the number of such cases that would arise on a daily basis. In fact, one can read the canons of the Second Council of Lyon, convened in 1274, as an abandonment of this position, which was all the more problematic because of its dependence on subjective judgments formed in the public sphere. This council attempted to impose a more objective standard by disenfranchising only bigamous clerics—that is, widowed and remarried members of the minor clergy—who were henceforth forbidden to wear the tonsure or any type of clerical costuming, and thereby forced to adopt an appearance that placed them beyond the protections of canon law.[117] By defrocking these men, the Church altered only their appearances, but this was enough to create a legal loophole through which secular authorities could demand their share of taxes.

None of this was lost on the people of Arras. In Adam de la Halle's *Jeu de la feuillée*, whose dating is partly dependent on the promulgation of this canon, the playwright's clerical father, Master Henri, remarks: "Rome wrongs a third part of her clerks / Enslaving them and stripping perks."[118] And he admits to having been married twice himself, as though

---

se immiscent, utpote usariis, et tabernariis publicie et continuis, aut qui amplectuntur inhonesta commercia, duntaxat exceptis."

114. Mansfield, *Humiliation*, 49.

115. *Cartulaire*, 33 (no. 31).

116. Letter from the official of Arras in the cartulary of the abbey of Marchiennes, now BL Add. 16611, fol. 188r (Stein no. 2331): "contra statuta et bannos sollempniter et publice proclamatos ibidem." Cited by Delmaire, *Le diocèse*, 1:268–269, n. 68.

117. Alberigo, *Conciliorum*, 303–331 (Council of Lyon II, especially c. 16).

118. "Romme a bien le tierche partie / Des clers fais sers et amatis." JF, vv. 456–457; see also vv. 204, 206. See Frederick W. Langley, "Community Drama and Community Politics in Thirteenth-Century Arras: Adam de la Halle's *Jeu de la feuillée*," in *Drama and Community: People and Plays in Medieval Europe*, ed. Alan Hindley (Turnhout, 1999), 57–77.

inviting spectators to turn him in to the authorities. (They apparently do not.) Meanwhile, Adam and his clerical buddies display their involvement in a whole catalogue of forbidden trades: consorting with fools, charlatans, and prostitutes; drinking in a tavern; practicing pagan rites; and (the crowning irony) appearing in a play. Indeed, the play begins when Adam grabs our attention by flaunting his scholar's gown:

My lords! Do you know why I've changed my clothes and all?	*Segneur, savés por quoi j'ai mon abit cangiet?*
I'm too long with the wife: I'll heed the clergy's call!	*J'ai esté avoec feme, or revois au clergiet*
And so I here reclaim my state before that Fall—	*Si avertirai chou que j'ai piecha songiet.*
But want, before I go, to take leave of you all.	*Mais je voeil a vous tous avant prendre congiet.*

Adam offers his own interpretation of the directives from Lyon. Instead of renouncing clerical attire, he'll put away his wife. No matter that he's been married only once (so far as we know); this excuse is as good as any. Clothes make the man, or make the man into a clerical persona—a *dramatis persona*. No stretch of the imagination is needed to translate the one into the other.

Playing the Crowd

Musing on the fact that the *Jeu de saint Nicolas* begins with a sermon, Paul Zumthor remarked, "If one persists, by virtue of a debatable critical habit, to speak of the medieval 'theater,' preaching has to be included in the category so designated."[119] The scripting of plays in the vernacular coincided almost exactly with the official encouragement of preaching in the vernacular, and it is not surprising that Picardy marched in the vanguard of a movement that produced biblical translations, exempla, and other texts that facilitated communication with the laity; the *Jeu de saint Nicolas* is a case in point.[120] Indeed, it is noteworthy that the manuscript anthology of Adam de la Halle's work depicts the stances and gestures of the protagonists in the *Jeu de la feuillée* (Figure 4) and the *Jeu du pèlerin* (Figure 2) as identical to those of preachers. According to these representaions, the main difference between preaching a sermon and acting in a play seems to lie in audience response. Adam and the Pilgrim are shown interacting with the crowd, members of which

119. Zumthor, *La lettre*, 266. See also Schmitt, *La raison*, 278–284.

120. See Clive R. Sneddon, "The 'Bible du XIIIe siècle': Its Medieval Public in the Light of Its Manuscript Tradition," and Jean-Robert Smeets, "La Bible de Jehan Malkaraume," in *The Bible and Medieval Culture*, ed. W. Lourdaux and D. Verhelst (Louvain, 1979), 127–140 and 220–235, respectively. See also Wickham, *Theater*, 58–60.

FIGURE 18. Differing authorities sanction preaching to the people in the vernacular, according to historiated initials from a manual compiled at Saint-Vaast in the mid-thirteenth century (compare Figure 19); here, a Dominican friar follows the example of God (BmA 657, fol. 89r: author's photograph)

exchange greetings or dialogue with the actors, as their gestures indicate. By contrast, a contemporary manuscript from the abbey of Saint-Vaast shows the respective congregations of a Dominican preacher and Saint Bernard sitting quietly, with their hands folded or thoughtfully supporting their chins (Figures 18–19).[121] Both preachers are speaking to them in Picard, although the Dominican, unlike the saint, does not speak on his own authority but takes his cues from the figure of God hovering over the heads of his listeners.

121. François Garnier, *Le langage de l'image au Moyen Age*, 2 vols. (Paris, 1982 and [1988]), 1:167–169 and 209–211.

FIGURE 19. "Saint Bernard teaches the people as well he knows how" (BmA 657, fol. 97v: author's photograph)

Saint Bernard does not require the same coaching: "He teaches the people as well he knows how," without the direction of the Figura.[122]

As much recent scholarship has demonstrated, urban life in the thirteenth century would come to be characterized by the omnipresence of religion, represented by a variety of professional religious who came in a bewildering array of colors, sizes, and styles. While the vast majority of French towns had only one mendicant house by 1275, Arras was

122. BmA 657, fol. 89ra and fol. 97rb: "ensaigne le peuple bien kil set."

among the twenty-one urban centers that attracted four or more.[123] The first arrivals were the Franciscans, probably around 1220, who almost immediately allied with the Carité of jongleurs.[124] They were followed by the Dominicans in 1233, the Trinitarians, and later by the brethren of the Order of Penance of Jesus Christ, better known as the Friars of the Sack and "popularly known" in Arras as the "Sachettes," who came in 1263.[125] These new foundations added to the intricate geometry of power overlaying Arras, although their immediate impact may have been softened by the fact that most of their activities were consigned to the southeastern edge of the banlieue, where their use of space was as fiercely regulated as their access to the mass medium of bell-ringing.[126] The charter issued to the Trinitarians in 1242 stipulated that although their new foundation stood "in the common street or public way," the bishop's court reserved the right to limit their access to that road, proclaiming that church doors and gates "open only by our will," a sign of lordship also invoked by the cathedral chapter with respect to its close, and by the monks of Saint-Vaast with respect to the Pyramide.[127]

Nevertheless, the main mission of the new orders was evangelism, and this activity did not require a building or a bell. While the diocese of Arras could control access to churches and cemeteries, it could hardly stop itinerant preachers from doing what every jongleur was free to do in the marketplaces or streets: perform. The Dominicans therefore made a virtue of necessity, relying on their personal resources, their charisma, their loud and carrying voices, their glib tongues. Alexander Murray, in a study of the "how-to" preaching manuals written by Humbert of Romans, shows that the head of the Order of Preachers (from 1254 to 1263) focused on technique, drawing on a lifetime's experience in the forensic trenches. He urged preachers to use plain language and suit their homilies to specific occasions and the composition of the audience, and to make ample use of entertaining

---

123. Richard W. Emery, The Friars in Medieval France: A Catalogue of French Mendicant Convents, 1200–1550 (New York, 1962), 5 and 18; Carpentier and Le Mené, La France, 265–267.

124. The first direct reference to the Fransiscans in Arras comes from the register of the Carité, which records the death of "Frere meneut Gheraus" in 1225; see Berger, Le nécrologe, 1:24 and 2:51.

125. AdPC ser. 3 G 3/"non coté [Frères au sac": "qui vulgariter fratres saccorum vocantur." See Berger, Littérature, 39–40; Delmaire, Le diocèse, 1:238–239 and 243. The Order of Penance originated in Provence and was approved by Innocent IV in 1251. The Sachettes' stay in Arras was relatively short-lived, and their convent was given over to the Carmelites in 1311. See Emery, The Friars, 10–11 and 101; "The Friars of the Sack," Speculum 18 (1943): 323–334; and "A Note on the Friars of the Sack," Speculum 35 (1960): 591–595.

126. The exception, for the whole of the Middle Ages, was the convent of beguines located in the bishop's City. The convent still belonging to the Clarisses, which is within the borders of the modern town, was a later foundation (of the fifteenth century) and originally located outside the walls.

127. AdPC ser. 3 G 4/"Trinité," xvii (Delmaire handlist, no. 62): "in vico conmuni sive via publica . . . pro voluntate nostra aperire" (vidimus, dated 1268, of the official's charter of 1242).

narrrative. In fact, as Lester K. Little has argued, storytelling may have been a more effective theatrical and didactic medium in a cosmopolitan context than the ritual vocabulary of the liturgy.[128] Urban crowds were often made up of transients, and these outsiders would not have had the same visceral reactions to the spaces and times of a town, the sight of local relics, the sounds of certain bells. And these audiences—shifting, dispersing, and re-forming—sometimes provided more fertile ground for the spread of doctrine than the churches, to which the poorest folk rarely came. What is more, as Humbert himself had discovered, an attentive, holiday-making crowd has a tremendous *facultas fidei*, a predisposition toward belief and conversion.[129]

The local success of such methods, even in the face of diocesan strictures, appears to have fueled the animosity of cathedral clergy in Arras. In 1286 an inquest was held to determine whether there were grounds for a complaint made by the Dominicans in the Parlement of Paris that a group of canons had harassed and injured preachers of the order.[130] No witnesses could be found to support the charge, but there is plenty of evidence from further afield to show that the popular strategies of the Dominicans were reanimating some old debates centering on the abuses of theatricality inherent in the role of the Church's public figures. Ælred of Rievaulx (1109–1167) had condemned vernacular preaching that relied too much on histrionic affect.[131] Peter the Chanter (d. 1197) had compared the crowd-pleasing techniques of certain priests to those of jongleurs, since "these men are like those singing of fables and great deeds who, when they see that the song of Landricus doesn't delight their hearers, right away begin to sing about Narcissus—and if that doesn't please either, they sing something else."[132] Denouncing a rival religious for his entertaining methods often involved more than insulting comparisons. In 1224 the first Franciscans to arrive in England were "mistaken" for mummers by a group of monks and ridden out of town on a rail.[133]

But if theatricality was an evangelical danger, or an occupational hazard, it also pro-

---

128. Lester K. Little, *Religious Poverty and the Profit Economy in Medieval Europe* (Ithaca, 1978), 31–34 and 198–199. See also Louis-Jacques Bataillon, *La prédication au XIIIe siècle en France et Italie* (Aldershot, 1993).

129. Alexander Murray, "Religion among the Poor in Thirteenth-Century France: The Testimony of Humbert of Romans," *Traditio* 30 (1974): 285–324 at 301 and 317.

130. *Olim*, 2:258–259 (no. 17 among the cases heard at All Saints). The gravity of the charge is proved by the presence of the order's Master General, Jacobus de Bologna.

131. Tydeman, *Theater*, 189–190.

132. "Hi similes sint cantantibus fabulas et gesta, qui videntes cantilenam de Landrico non placere auditoribus, statim incipiunt de Narcisso cantare; quod si nec placuerit, cantant de alio." Cited by Faral, *Les jongleurs*, 288.

133. Ian Lancashire, *Dramatic Texts and Records of Great Britain: A Chronological Typography to 1558* (Toronto, 1984), 336 (no. 1763).

vided an acknowledged and valuable set of tools: an actor can make a poor tale sound powerful, while a skillful preacher can make a difficult doctrine clear. At bottom, the secular clergy's distrust of the mendicants, like the Church's official disapproval of public entertainers, was linked to the fact that all were vying for the same audiences.[134] The example of the Waldensians' legendary founder comes to mind, since the self-professed usurer Valdes seems to have owed his fervor for popular preaching and biblical translation to his spiritual epiphany in the marketplace of Lyon, when he was moved to tears by the story of Saint Alexis—sung by a minstrel.[135] This cannot have been an unusual occurence, and its outcome does not speak well for the record of the heretic's parish priest. Nor does a Latin sermon from thirteenth-century Picardy:

> When in the voice of the jongleur, sitting in the marketplace, it is recited how those errant knights of old, like Roland and Olivier and the rest, were slain in war, the crowd standing around is moved to pity, and oftentimes to tears. But when in the voice of the Church the glorious wars of Christ—that is to say, how he defeated death by dying, and triumphed over the vainglory of the enemy—are daily commemorated in sacrifice, where are they who are moved to pity?[136]

Intended as an indictment of the laity's inattention at Mass, this homily actually shows how frequent were the comparisons between entertainers and preachers, while the story of Valdes's conversion reveals that they not only used the same performance techniques but also shared the same material. Jongleurs were just as likely to sing of the miracles of saints as they were to tell dirty jokes or tales of great deeds. The juxtaposition of devotional materials and popular entertainments in most of the major vernacular anthologies copied

---

134. Baldwin, "Image," 639. See also Alan Hindley, "Preaching and Plays: The Sermon in the Late Medieval French *Moralités*," *Le moyen français* 42 (1998): 71–85.

135. *Chronicon universale anonymi Laudunensis*, ed. Alexander Cartellieri and Wolf Stechele (Leipzig, 1909), 20 (entry for the year 1173). See also Faral, *Les jongleurs*, 287; and Grundmann, *Religiöse Bewegungen*, 42–44 and 190–192.

136. Anonymous sermon in BnF lat. 14925, fol. 132; excerpted by B. Hauréau in *Notices et extraits de quelques manuscrits latins de la Bibliothèque nationale*, vol. 3 (Paris, 1891), 317: "Cum voce joculatoris, in plateis sedentis, quomodo illi strenui milites antiqui, scilicet Rolandus et Oliverius, etc., in bello occubuererecitatur, populus circumstans pietate movetur et interdum lacrymatur; sed cum voce Ecclesiæ inclyta Christi bella, quomodo scilicet mortem moriendo devicit et de hoste superbo triumphavit quotidie fere commemoratur, qui sunt qui pietate moventur?" In another version of this sermon (BnF lat. 3495, fol. 192), the words "in Parvo Ponte" appear in place of "in plateis," indicating that the Petit-Pont in Paris was the popular haunt of jongleurs there, while in northern towns the marketplace was a better performance venue. (This is corroborated by Peter of Blois in his *De confessione*; see Faral, *Les jongleurs*, 287.) On the dramatic performance of the *Chanson de Roland*, see Schmitt, *La raison*, 262. See also Wenzel, *Hören*, 53.

during the thirteenth and fourteenth centuries—including those containing the plays of
Arras—underscores their symbiotic relationship. So does an unlikely pair of manuscripts
made for merchants in the boomtowns of the North: on the one hand, a greasy, dog-eared
codex of fabliaux is prefaced by a table of exchange rates in major textile centers, beginning with Arras; on the other, a richly illuminated collection of Picard saints' lives and devotional lyrics contains the same information.[137]

Set in the marketplaces of Troyes, Provins, Tournai, and Arras, the metatheatrical tales
that have come down to us in these scripted forms provided exempla that could be given
a pious or a prurient turn depending on the mission of the performer and the circumstances of his performance.[138] *Courtois d'Arras* would almost certainly have been pressed
into service by preachers or jongleurs, and who is to say for what purpose it was originally
composed? The same can even be said of *Le garçon et l'aveugle*, invariably described by modern critics as a thoroughly secular play. Yet the favorite biblical text of the well-known
preacher Michel Menot was Matthew 15:14: "Leave them: for they are blind and leaders of
the blind; for if a blind man offers to lead a blind man, they will fall into the pit together."[139] The play begins, we recall, with the Boy saving the Blind Man from just such
a tumble: "Sir, look out! You've lost your way, / You'll fall into that cellar there." Framed
appropriately, this sketch could amuse an audience while at the same time demonstrating
the existential consequences of the pair's blasphemous codependency; perhaps both Boy
and Blind Man ended up in the pit of Hell Mouth. Some plays were designed specifically
to work in this manner: a manuscript compilation made for Dominican preachers active
in northern France during the late thirteenth century contains a number of sermons followed by short dialogues that employ a similar kind of reverse psychology, teaching good
behavior by staging the inevitable outcome of bad.[140]

The residue of vernacular sermons, like that of plays, usually has to be sifted out of
manuscript sources, since sermons were often extracted from—or incorporated into—
longer devotional texts. Consider the Arrageois edition of *Le naissance Ihesu Crist et se mort*,
otherwise known as *Li romanz de saint Fanuel et de sainte Anne et de Nostre Dame et de Nostre Seg-
nor et de ses apostres*, which forms part of the same codex from Saint-Vaast in which the Dominican preacher and Saint Bernard are depicted, and which was obviously intended to
attract the attention of an audience outside the walls of the monastery:

---

137. BnF fr. 25545 and BnF fr. 412. See Robert Lopez, "The Culture of the Medieval Merchant," *Medieval and Renaissance Studies* 8 (1979): 52–73; Derville, *L'économie*, 174 and 191–203; Carpentier and Le
Mené, *La France*, 190.

138. Little, *Religious*, 200, and "Evangelical," 11–26.

139. Étienne Gilson, "Michel Menot et la technique du sermon médiéval," in *Les idées et les lettres*
(Paris, 1932), 93–154 at 117.

140. BnF fr. 12483, fols. 119va–21rb and 203ra–203va. See Symes, "The Boy," 114–116.

Signor por diu entendes mois	Seigneurs, for God listen to me
Arestes vous ici un poi	Stop here a moment, tend to me:
Par .i. couvent que vous dirai	A promise I can give to you
Nostre signour deproierai	As from Our Lord. I pray you, do—
Pour ceus qui ci aresteront	For those who stop by here today
Et ma parole escouteront	And mark the words that I will say
Qui diex lor face vrai pardon	To those will God his pardon give
Si con il fist celui larron	Just as He did unto that thief
Qui ase destre li pendi	Who at His right hand bravely hung
Au iour que passion sosfri	The day He suffered his Passion.[141]

Sections of this versified catechism could have been performed on street corners over the course of several days, or broken into episodes in order to dovetail with the Church's calendar, the time of day, or other local circumstances.[142] In Arras one might choose to perform the Harrowing of Hell, since the first words out of Christ's mouth are a condemnation of usurers: only after addressing them does the Savior turn to address Satan. But there was something for everyone. Eve's direct appeal to the female portion of the audience is particularly striking:

Peceour qui estes umont	O all you sinners of the world,
Souviegne vous de la dolor	Remember you the doleful way
Qui nous sousfrons et nuit et ior	We suffer here both night and day.
Ne traissies pas vos maris	Don't cross your husbands, as you see
Con li miens fu par moi trais	That mine was so betrayed by me
Ci seres vous mis et ietes	Lest you be taken down and cast
Encestre dolor tourmentes	In this sad torment, at the last.[143]

The Jeu d'Adam is hardly more dramatic.

The spiritual success of the mendicants in Arras, which can be inferred from the number of new foundations, their later sponsorship of confraternities, and the proliferation of vernacular texts with religious themes, was obviously of great interest to the monks of

141. BmA 657, fol. 32va. This long poem is preserved in eleven known manuscripts, but the conventional title refers only to the first 850 of 3,971 verses; the second portion, vv. 851–3667, also appears as the Histoire de Marie et de Jésus. See Arthur Långfors, ed., Les incipit des poèmes français antérieurs au XVIe siècle (1918; reprint, Geneva, 1977), 94–95.

142. On the use of such materials by popular preachers, see Nicole Bériou, La prédication de Ranulphe de la Houblonnière: Sermons aux clercs et aux simples gens à Paris au XIIIe siècle, 2 vols. (Paris, 1987), 1:125–129, 496. See also Siegfried Wenzel, "The Joyous Art of Preaching; or, the Preacher and the Fabliau," Anglia 97 (1979): 304–325.

143. BmA 657, fol. 48va.

Saint-Vaast, who were responsible for making this manuscript. They do not appear to have shared the canons' distaste for the Dominicans, perhaps seeing in the Order of Preachers a helpful ally against diocesan competition and an inspiration for the newest phase of their public relations campaign, which had begun as a challenge to the jongleurs' Carité in the twelfth century. A vernacular version of the life and miracles of Saint Dominic is even included in an illuminated anthology of legends and miracles meant to showcase the power of Saint Vaast, who was now being translated into Picard as part of the ongoing effort to overhaul his image. Indeed, the monks had begun to experiment with vernacular preaching even before the mendicants' arrival, as evinced by a notebook containing the outline of a homily probably intended for the Monday rogation before Ascension Day, which compares Saint Vaast to a rainbow shining in the sky and the buds of flowers in springtime, and which is partially scripted in Picard.[144] But what had been expressed in liturgical metaphors or the hard administrative language of Guiman's census in the twelfth century becomes a forthright mission statement in the thirteenth-century compilations of preaching material prepared under the influence of the Dominicans: "Now this section speaks about Aubin the deacon, who explains how one should talk to the people on the day of the feast of Saint Vaast concerning the miracles that happened after his death."[145] The accompanying miniature depicts a Benedictine preaching to an attentive and diverse urban crowd. Another shows the abbot of Saint-Vaast talking to a group of monks, and the text of his discourse reminds them "that Saint Vaast was sent from God in order to preach His name at Arras" and that his holiness was shown every day "through his teaching and miracles." A new generation of monks was being urged to proselytize, and thereby to repair the damages done to the saint's reputation through "the negligence of writers and the laziness of those who know little."[146] The abbey now had three related goals: the education of its monks for public life, the better integration of their activities with those of the community, and a greater degree of access to the media that shaped public opinion.[147]

144. BmA 1067, fol. 98v. This homily is a peroration on Ecclesiasticus 50:8, hence my inference as to its liturgical occasion. See also Delmaire, Le diocèse, 1:597–598.

145. BmA 307, fols. 182–205 at fol. 149vb: "Chi fine li vie mon signeur Saint Veast et de ses miracles quil fist a se vie. or parole apres daubin le diacre qui ensaigne con doit dire a la gente le ior de la feste S.' Vaast. et des miracles apres se mort." The corpus of Vedastian material is found at fols. 152–171v. This manuscript also contains the cycle of Saint Nicholas legends, previously noted.

146. BmA 307, fol. 162rᵃ: "que Sains Vaas qui fu envoies depar du et pour preechier sen non a Arras . . . par ensaignes et par miracles . . . par le negligence des escrivains et par le perece de ciaus qui poi sevent."

147. Of some twelve hundred manuscripts now housed in the Bibliothèque municipale d'Arras, almost half come from the medieval library of Saint-Vaast, and a large number of these are in Picard. They include several thirteenth-century compendia of saints' lives, exempla, and other didactic materials. See van der Straeten, Les manuscrits, 16; and Grierson, "La bibliothèque de St-Vaast," 120–122.

Public Piety

In the early part of the twelfth century, the theologian Honorius Augustodunensis (1075/80—ca. 1156) compared the celebration of the Mass to the performance of a Greek tragedy, drawing parallels between their similar social functions and cathartic effects.

> It is known that those who performed tragedies in the theaters represented to the people, through their actions, the deeds of warriors. So our tragedian represents the battle of Christ to the people in the theater of the church through his actions, and leads them to the victory of his redemption. Thus when the celebrant says, "Pray," he portrays for us Christ in the midst of his trials, as when he exhorted the apostles to pray. . . . Stretching out his hands, he imitates the extension of Christ on the cross. . . . Through communication of the Peace, he signifies the peace given after the Resurrection of Christ and the publication of joyful news. . . . [S]o peace is announced to the people by the judge, and one is invited to a feast.[148]

In this allegory, based explicitly on pagan precedents that no longer seemed threatening at the distance of many centuries, Honorius cast the congregation as participants in the drama of Christ's Passion and Resurrection, while employing a classical model to capture the attention of contemporary intellectuals.

Adjusting the allegory for an audience in Arras is a devotional meditation titled Li senefiance conment on se doit contenir a le messe, "The Meaning Which One Ought to Enact within Oneself at Mass," included in the same codex as Saint-Vaast's handbook of Dominican homiletics, which was later bound together with a famous book of troubadour and trouvère poetry known as the Chansonnier d'Arras. Possibly inspired by Honorius but composed almost two centuries later, it relies on a different set of analogies to capture the rite's inherent theatricality, which is expressed through frequent use of the verb representer, "to make present," "to dramatize." In it the Mass is brought vividly up to date and made vitally immediate with reference to familiar things, activities, and events, "so that one should be able to enter inside of oneself" (si doit on entrer dedens li) and experience it personally, as one could experience the joyeuse entrée of a great prince. Hence, the reading of the Epistle

---

148. "Sciendum quod hi qui tragoedias in theatris recitabant, actus pugnantium gestibus populo repraesentabant. Sic tragicus noster pugnam Christi populo Christiano in theatro Ecclesiae gestibus suis repraesentat, eique victoriam redemptionis suae inculcat. Itaque cum presbyter Orate dicit, Christum pro nobis in agonia positum exprimit, cum apostolos orare monuit. . . . Per manuum expansionem, designat Christi in cruce extensionem. Per cantum praefationis, exprimit clamorem Christi in cruce pendentis. . . . Per pacem, et communicationem designat pacem datam post Christi resurrectionem et gaudii communicationem. . . . pax et communio populo a sacerdote datur." Gemma animae (1.83) in PL, vol. 172, 570. On the intellectual context of this commentary, see Hardison, Christian Rite, 39–77; and Dox, Idea, 74–85.

signals that "a message is coming which carries news that the Lord will be coming with all speed." The Alleluia before the reading of the Gospel is like "the banner-bearers, the jongleurs, the musicians, the *vielles* who come before the Lord to honor him." The Gospel itself is "the true tidings that cannot lie, which say certainly that the Lord is coming. So one should give all his attention to hearing and understanding what the Evangelist says. Because these are the letters which Our Savior dictated with his own mouth, which teach us how we ought to live if we want to be in the household train [*maisnie*] of this very great Lord." Then comes the Sanctus, which signifies the way one is supposed "to dress the place and the table where God feasts his friends, after which one waits for the coming of God. So one ought to do just the same as when a king is about to enter a city, and everyone goes out to meet him, and each one shows him his greatest grief, so as to be well recovered; so we ought to do when the Lord comes." For, we are assured, the Lord is "so courtly to his friends that he protects them from all peril."[149]

The miniature introducing this unique text shows the happy people of a parish attending Mass: the priest standing before the altar at the moment of consecration, the deacon next to him, and the assembled congregation whose social diversity is highlighted by the inclusion of a wealthy lady in her stylish hat. Everyone seems to be smiling (Figure 20).[150] The message here is that the celebration of the Mass is a celebration of community, even though its sacramental effects are individual: all the metaphors evoke collective activities such as the witnessing of charters, the hearing of proclamations, the ceremonies organized to welcome important visitors, the banquets spread on holidays like the Carité's grand siège. Collective participation in the Mass was becoming a major theme of the

149. "Et apres list on lepistle. si dist autant que uns mesages vient qui aporte nouveles qui dist ke li sires venrra hasteement. . . . ce senefie que ce sont les banieres. li iougleour les muses les vieles qui vienent devant le signour pour lui honnourer. apres list on levangile. si dist autant que cest uns vrais mesages ki ne puet mentir ki dist certainement ke li sires venra. Si doit cascuns metre toute sentencion aloir. et alentendre cou que li evangiles dist. Car ce sont les letres que nostres sires dicta de se propre bouke qui nous enseignent conment nous devons vivre se nous volons estre de la maisnie de si tres grant signieur. . . . a pres cante on le loenge des angles. ki sans fin disent. Sanctus. sanctus. sanctus devant le trinite qui descent pour apareillier le lieu et le taule ou dieus repaist les siens amis. apres aten on la venue de dieu. si doit on ausi faire que qant uns rois doit entrer en une cite. tout lun a la desasient al encontre et li moustre cascuns se plus grant maladie pour mieus recouvrer. ausi devons nous faire que qant li sires est venus . . . Car diex est si courtois a ses amis quil les garde en tous perieus." BmA 657, 126r^a–128v^a. The text has been edited by H. Sonneville, "'Li senefiance conment on se doit contenir a le messe': Édition et traduction d'un traité en ancien français," *Recherches de théologie ancienne et médiévale* 44 (1977): 231–236. I have relied on my own transcription, which corrects some of Sonneville's readings.

150. A similar image accompanies a fourteenth-century treatise on the Mass, demonstrating the appropriate postures and gestures that should accompany it: BnF fr. 13342, fol. 47; reproduced in Schmitt, *La raison*, pl. 35. See also Camille, *Gothic Art*, 105–109 and fig. 107.

FIGURE 20. "The Meaning Which One Ought to Enact within Oneself at Mass": miniature illustrating *Li senefiance conment on se doit contenir a le messe* (BmA 657, fol. 126r: author's photograph)

Church's teachings in the thirteenth century, and we have already seen that the earliest articulation of the jongleurs' spiritual lordship in Arras, in the last quarter of the twelfth century, had reserved the confraternity's place "at Masses and at Matins and at all the prayers said" in the cathedral.[151] There was also a strong Eucharistic flavor to the jongleurs' administration of the holy water derived from the Sainte-Chandelle, and an insistence on group solidarity in the solemnization of even the lowliest members' funerals. Yet fashioning a single corporate body from a diverse population was not easy or uncontroversial. Chief among the complaints of the Carité's legendary rebels had been the "shame" suffered by the nobility and urban plutocrats under the lordship of jongleurs, which required men of high standing to associate in public with their social inferiors, especially at church: "But we don't want them to be part of our fellowship anymore, nor come with us to make

---

151. See John Bossy, "The Mass as a Social Institution," *Past and Present* 100 (1983): 29–61 at 51; Jungmann, *Missarum*, 129; Deragnaucourt, "Dernier voyage," 81.

offerings." Walking in procession cheek-by-jowl with jongleurs was considered beneath their dignity, until the Virgin corrected their misguided pride. And she went on to humble the mightier pride of the abbey of Saint-Vaast, which was eventually forced to accept her, and her minstrels' Sainte-Chandelle. So in "The Meaning Which One Ought to Enact within Oneself at Mass," the jongleurs take their rightful place in the procession, heralding "the true tidings that cannot lie" and embodying the Alleluia, the most melodious and most controversial moment of the Mass in the thirteenth century, since its musical elaboration could be characterized as "a kind of jongleurie," to quote the unhappy prior who had condemned the innovative liturgy of Saint Nicholas.[152] Coincidentally, the Carité's *Ordinance* reveals that the confraternity bestowed an annual gift on "all the priests who are in the Carité of Notre Dame, for the three Masses of the year," indicating that a Requiem was being celebrated for the confraternity's dead at its bevées on the feasts of Saint Rémy, Candlemas, and Pentecost.[153]

The example of public piety set by the confraternity of jongleurs in the course of the twelfth century was matched in the thirteenth by an increased level of lay participation in all things spiritual, fueled by the adoption of affective, entertaining methods of instruction by the mendicants and the monks of Saint-Vaast. Although it has been seen as surprising that the abbey did not produce the scripts of any liturgical plays, the evidence strongly suggests that such scripts were hardly needed, nor would they represent the only variety of dramatic activity geared toward religious instruction, outside of the church or in the context of the liturgy.[154] After all, the vast majority of medieval ecclesiastical foundations did not produce such scripts, and this can hardly be taken as a sign that most of the churches in Christendom were silent and empty when festivities were called for in the calendar. It is much more reasonable to posit that the monks of Saint-Vaast and the canons of the cathedral performed plays as an integral part of their liturgical office than to presume that they did not. In fact, the service books that *do* survive from the thirteenth century tell us so little about the celebration of even the most major feasts that we must infer that oral traditions of performance persisted at both abbey and cathedral, or that the relevant *ordines* and part-sheets circulated in some ephemeral medium, like that of the actor's parchment scroll, destined for almost total annihilation.[155] Prior to the making of their ordinal in 1308, the monks of Saint-Vaast appear to have relied largely on the memories

152. Fassler, *Gothic Song*, 10, 30–31, and 43.

153. *Ordinance*, fol. 5r–v: "pour se chartre lire . . . out li prestres qui sont en le carite nostre dame parmi .iii. messes lan."

154. Vincent, "Jean Bodel," 370. The noted exception is an eleventh-century *Visitatio sepulchri* now in Cambrai's Bibliothèque de la ville (MS 75), a liturgical drama that "scarcely deserves the name" in the opinion of Edith A. Wright, *Dissemination of the Liturgical Drama in France* (Bryn Mawr, 1936), 116. It is printed by Young, *Drama*, 1:245.

155. Symes, "Appearance," 825.

of sacristans and senior brethren. At the cathedral, similarly, a lectionary made around 1183 preserves only a shorthand inventory of vestments "beyond the everyday" (*preter cotidianas*), its purpose more fiscal than ceremonial; on the use of those vestments, and the liturgies they would have adorned, the books are largely silent.[156] This is normal. The more elaborate liturgical instructions drawn up in the fourteenth century do not mark the *terminus a quo* of the practices they delineate but rather indicate a more formal articulation of performance traditions, some of which may have been written down because they were threatened with extinction.

At Saint-Vaast these instructions were partly couched in the vernacular, the frequent references to lay involvement in the monks' ordinal further testifying to their interest in public outreach by the end of the thirteenth century. Not only had they taken steps to make the relics of Saint Vaast more accessible and attractive to the people of Arras, but through their more frequent perambulation and through a new preaching campaign, they were also attempting to include the laity in the abbey's liturgical life. On Passion Sunday, for instance, the mimetic opportunities outlined in "The Meaning Which One Ought to Enact within Oneself at Mass" were heightened by the overt dramatization of the Passion narrative, which invited the participation of the congregation at the key moment of Jesus' condemnation and emphasized the community's presence with him at the moment of his death, when a monk ready at the rope of the abbey's deepest-toned bell rang it loudly to commemorate the loud cry with which Jesus had given up his spirit, so "that all may come to the suffering of Our Lord." Even those not present at the ceremony would hear this and know what was happening.[157] The diocese was also working to ensure that its parishioners could play their parts fully and with full understanding in those parishes that did not have the human resources to support a staged singing of the Passion. "Whenever the Passion of Our Lord is read out publicly in the church . . . anyone present should reverently bow, bending the knee." The reader, too, should genuflect, "that his example might increase the devotion of the others, as well as letting them know when this ought to be done."[158] Parishioners were also encouraged "to learn and to repeat the Lord's Prayer and the Creed and the Hail Mary" and were reminded "to come frequently to church to hear the divine office, at least on Sundays and feast days, and on those days they ought to listen to the announcements regarding festivals and fasts."[159]

156. BmA 1049, fol. 60v.

157. BmA 230, fol. 132ra: "Ke tout vieignent a le souffrance nostre seigneur."

158. Gosse, "Anciens synodes," 600 (article 34): "Quotiescumque legetur in ecclesia publice Passio Domini . . . quilibet reverenter se inclinet flectendo genua, et pro tanto ineffabili beneficio, Domino gratias agat humilans et devotus. Lector autem ipse hoc idem faciat, ut ejus exemplo augeatur devotio aliorum, atque sciant quando hoc erit faciendum."

159. Ibid., 587 (article 11): "Presbiteri parochianos suos moneant diligenter ut ad ecclesias frequenter veniant, divinum officium audituri, adminus in diebus dominicis et festivis, in quibus debent

Through these initiatives, the secular and regular clergy of Arras were building on the importance attached to public opinion and the widespread participation in community affairs which was already a feature of life in Arras. They appear to have taken it for granted that most of the laity understood the Latin liturgy and could be trusted to perform their parts in it while joining in the conduct of important parish business that called for an understanding of canon law. Weekly announcements included the posting of marriage banns, which required the vigilance and acquiescence of the community, since anyone who knew of an impediment and did not put it forward at the proper time could be subject to excommunication, as could anyone who made a frivolous objection. This helped to reinforce the idea that "marriage should be celebrated with honor and reverence in front of the church, not with laughter and joking around," and that secret weddings would be condemned as a matter of course: they had to be publicized.[160] Priests also warned their congregations that any betrothals made before the publication of banns should be expressed in the future tense, an indication that the nice distinction between *de præsenti* and *de futuro* contracts was not lost on the average person.[161] Nor, it seems, were many other Latin formulae. Even Pincedés, one of the thieves of the *Jeu de saint Nicholas*, could make the sign of the cross and say the appropriate words accompanying the gesture.[162]

In fact, there were occasions in the life of nearly every person in Arras when she would have been called upon to speak in Latin, or to speak words in the vernacular that were understood to be the equivalent of Latin phrases. Baptism ought to be celebrated with reverence, commanded the synodal statues, and in these words: *Ego baptizo te in nomine patris et filii et spiritus sancti*—although priests told prospective parents, especially mothers, that children could be baptized "using this form of words in their own language" if necessary.[163] Latin was also used in the solemnization of marriage vows, heightening the otherwise homely transaction of a ceremony which began with the bridegroom's gift of gold or silver coins, passed through the priest in a series of gestures that were meant to ensure the couple's fertility—and that of their money. The bridegroom was to take the coins from the priest's hand "and putting it in the hand of the woman, and taking her hand beneath his, let him say after the priest: 'N. with this silver or gold I thee endow, and with my body

---

feriare et audire renunciationes festorum, jejuniorum . . . Frequenter exortentur populum ut adiscant et sepe dicant Dominicam orationem et Credo in Deum et salutationem Beate Virginis."

160. Ibid., 584–585 (article 8): "Matrimonium cum honore et reverentia celebretur in facie ecclesie, non cum risu vel jocose, ne contempnatur."

161. Ibid., 584–585 (article 8): "Caveant autem sacredotes ut in sponsalibus que solent fieri ante proclamationem edictorum seu Bannorum in ecclesiis faciendem, solum utantur verbis de futuro et non de presenti."

162. JsN, v. 1300.

163. Gosse, "Anciens synodes," 581 (article 4): "Si summa necessitas fuerit, debere sub eadem forma in lingua sua cum trina immersione in aqua baptizare pueros."

I thee honor, and over myself and all the goods that I have or will have I make thee lady.'
Then afterward the priest should teach the bridegroom, holding the ring, to say, following after him: 'N. with this ring I thee espouse and with my body I thee honor. In the name
of the Father, and of the Son, and of the Holy Spirit.'"[164] Every person who participated
in this rite would have known that she or he was playing a public role.

The Public Record

"The Meaning Which One Ought to Enact within Oneself at Mass" construes the reading of the Epistle as the arrival of a messenger "who carries news saying that the Lord will
come with all speed" and describes the Gospel as "the letters which Our Lord dictated with
His own mouth, which teach us how we ought to live if we want to be in the household
train of this very great Lord." So "each one should give all his attention to hearing and understanding what the Evangelist says." This was the way the people of Arras could best
understand the Word of God: as a charter read out by a herald, containing important
"rules and ordinances" and thus requiring them "to retain as much as possible." If heeded
and held in the memory, it would grant the listener a place at the Lord's table.[165] If ignored, it might place him in the painful position of a prisoner consigned to the "charter"
of Durant the jailer in the Jeu de saint Nicolas, bound by the power vested in a warrant.[166] To
compare the words of the Evangelist to words dictated by Christ was to remind listeners
that his Gospel had a palpable and public origin. The words now contained in the writings of Scripture had begun as the utterance of a voice.

"To admit that a text was oral, at any given moment of its existence, is to become conscious of an historical fact," wrote Paul Zumthor, a fact that has very little to do with the
"written trace of that text."[167] He refers chiefly to those texts he calls (in quotation marks)
"literary," but the aural and visual impact of other documents also worked to create a medieval theater. "To all those seeing and hearing these present letters, greetings," ran the
salutation that opened most charters, reminding us of the immediate conditions under

164. BmA 466, fol. 19r: "Tunc accipiens argentum illud aut aurum a sacerdote aut ab alio mittens illud in manu mulieris tangens quoque desuper manum suam dicat sacerdote proloquente: N. de hoc ar-
gento aut auro te doto, et de corpore meo te honorifico, et de me et de omnibus bonis meis quæ habeo
et habebo te dominam constituo. Tunc postmodum sacerdos sponsum anulum tenentem doceat dicere
preloquens N. de hoc anulo te sponso et de corpore meo te honorifico. In nomine patris et filii et spiritus sancti Amen." See Jean-Baptiste Molin and Protais Mutembe, Le rituel du mariage en France du XIIe au
XVe siècle (Paris, 1974), 78–79, 181–185, and 297–298 (Ordo X).

165. "Si en doit on retenir cou con puet. Car chest li rieulle et li ordinaires par coi on puet connoitre
le sainte taule et le sainte refection. aveuc nostre signor." BmA 657, fols. 126ra–126va

166. JsN, vv. 541, 546, 558.

167. Zumthor, La lettre, 37. See also his Essai de poétique médiévale (Paris, 1972).

which they were produced, usually in public, for reading aloud in public, with a wax seal that added color to the accompanying public display.[168] When King Philip Augustus of France confirmed the laws and customs of Arras in 1194—taking care to assure everyone "that the rights and customs of the city of Arras remain utterly unchanged"—even those standing at some distance from the herald would have been able to see the yard-long span of parchment and its large green seal, hung with dangling silken cords.[169] A further confirmation, both audible and visible, was issued in 1211, this time in Picard as well as in Latin, the former distinctly rubricated for clear proclamation and easy reference.[170] Seals could also take part in performances that emphasized hearing as well as seeing. While the seal of the bishop's official in Arras suggests the interior space within which judgments were rendered (a roof over a cross with the legend *CURIE. ATTREBATENSIS.+*), the counterseal features a hand writing the cry that rang out every day when judgments were broadcast: *OIES*, "Hear ye!"[171] The process of going over accounts also had an audible aspect, preserved in the modern use of the term "auditing": in 1296, for instance, the officers of Count Robert II of Artois would be called together in public "to hear and to survey" the fiscal record.[172]

The precocious use of Picard as a literary language, and a language for the performance of plays, was matched by its usefulness as a language of public record from the earliest years of the thirteenth century, as we have already seen with respect to the jongleurs' documentary campaign and the career of Jehan Bodel. Even the abbey and cathedral preferred to settle disputes in the vernacular, via local customary law or in the king's court, rather than placing themselves under the Latin canons of Rome. As of Pentecost in 1269, the abbot and convent of Saint-Vaast promised that they would "not drag the bishop to the papal court or into the ecclesiastical court in the ordinary way" when they had a grievance.[173]

---

168. Brigitte Bedos-Rezak, "Diplomatic Sources and Medieval Documentary Practices," in *The Past and Future of Medieval Studies*, ed. John Van Engen (Notre Dame, 1994), 313–343 at 324; and idem, "Civic Liturgies," 32–34. See also Benoît-Michel Tock, *Une chancellerie épiscopale au XIIe siècle: Le cas d'Arras* (Louvain-la-Neuve, 1991), 100–103, and "Auteur ou impétrant? Réflexions sur les chartes des évêques d'Arras au XIIe siècle," *Bibliothèque de l'École des chartes* 149 (1991): 215–248.

169. *Cartulaire*, 3; Delaborde, *Recueil des actes*, 1:565: "Noverint universi presentes pariter et futuri quod jura et consuetudines civium Atrebatensium perpetuo inconcussa manere decernimus."

170. *Cartulaire*, 8–14 (No. 9); Taillar, *Recueil*, 36–43 (no. 11).

171. AdPC ser. 3 G 3/Hostel Dieu liii [Cité xiiii] and 3 G 5/Grand Commun xi (Delmaire handlist, no. 45). My inspection of the two surviving seals does not accord with the report of Germain Demay that the legend reads DIES; see Demay, *Inventaire des sceaux de l'Artois et de la Picardie* (Paris, 1877), 245 (no. 2316). (The only example cited is a charter numbered A.9.15 *bis*, which no longer survives. In any case, the word "day" makes little sense on its own.)

172. De Germiny, *Les lieutenants*, 30–31: "oïr et examiner."

173. *Olim*, 1: 715. "Non trahent ipsum episcopum coram papa, vel in curia ecclesiastica, ordinaria via, nec per modum denunciacionis vel alias."

In 1271, accordingly, a long-standing contention over rights on the Aubigny road was settled following the procedure for proving title to land as laid out in the coutumier of Artois: the bishop and his men showed the bounds to the bailiff of the abbey, witnesses were examined, and written proofs were displayed.[174]

Based on case law and actual judgments, the coutumier which the parties consulted was itself a blueprint for public performance, retaining what Zumthor called "vocal modulation" and proclaiming that "these books speak of the customs and usages of Artois and of the manner in which they should be practiced."[175] A self-conscious theatricality is also exhibited in its format, which consists of a dialogue between an experienced practitioner of the law and an eager student, framing cases laid out like "scripts, whether for jongleurs or for lawyers," as Michael Clanchy put it.[176] The finest illuminated manuscript further dramatizes the law in vignettes designed "to show" (*moustrer*) how a particular plea or claim should be enacted, harking back to the ancient Roman practice of illustrating legal texts with diagrams and images of appropriate stances and facial expressions which exhibit the close relationship between the rhetorical tricks of the courtroom and those of the theater.[177] The image accompanying the ritual of exfestucation (Figure 21; see chapter 5) directs that the gestures be performed "as this figure demonstrates" (*conme ceste figure le moustre*), while the script for the ceremony of homage shows three men witnessing the kiss exchanged between man and lord, alongside a set of instructions:

> To enter into the faith of his lord, a man joins both hands and places them between the two hands of the lord. ¶ "My lord, I come into your faith and become your man by mouth and by hand. And to you I promise my faith and to maintain my loyalty to you against all persons and to keep your law and to hold fast the secrets of your court." ¶ And the lord responds, "And I receive you according to my law, and according to the uses and customs that fidelity owe, and I kiss you in the name of faith."[178]

174. *Olim*, 1:395 (no. 21 in the octave of All Saints). See also BnF fr. 5249, fols. 15v–16r.

175. BnF fr. 5249, fol. 1r: "Che livres parole des coustumes. et des usages dartoys en la maniere on ensoloit use." Adolph Tardif has edited the coutumier based on the two principal manuscripts: *Coutumier d'Artois: Publié d'après les manuscrits 5248 et 5249 fonds français de la Bibliothèque nationale* (Paris, 1883). I have relied on my own transcription from the better manuscript. (The second, BnF fr. 5248, is inferior in quality and contains no images.)

176. Clanchy, *From Memory*, 277–278. See also Zumthor, *La lettre*, 98. Contemporary reports of cases heard by the court of the Common Bench in London were even laid out like play scripts; see Paul Brand, ed., *The Earliest English Law Reports*, vol. 1 (London, 1996), e.g., 6–7 (dower case from 1270, in BL Stowe 386, fol. 138v); and idem, *Observing and Recording the Medieval Bar at Work: The Origins of Law Reporting in England* (London, 1999).

177. Enders, *Rhetoric*; Schmitt, *La raison*, 25.

178. BnF fr. 5249, fol. 22v: "Entrer en sa foi son signeur iondre ses .ij. mains et mettre entre les .ij.

This particular show was familiar to everyone living in Arras, and had been since the early part of the twelfth century, when the ritual of homage became an important urban ceremony.[179] The *Jeu de saint Nicolas* is full of references to it (e.g., vv. 190–191, 350–351), with the saint himself as the *baron* (vv. 21, 1453, 1464) to whom the heroic Prudhomme offers his allegiance (vv. 482–484), and with the play's public as witnesses to the bargain (vv. 1243, 1256) whose reciprocity was communicated physically. Thus, at the moment when the Prudhomme prays to the saint for succor, he reminds his lord of their bond by assuming the appropriate posture, a gesture of submission later adopted by the King at the moment of his conversion, when he says, "My lord, thus I become your man" (*Sire, chi devieng jou vostre hom*, v. 1459). The échevins of Arras performed a version of this same ceremony, taking their oaths between the hands of the maieur of Arras in the presence of the relics of Saint Vaast, inside the abbey's parish church of La Madeleine.[180] The oaths of other officeholders were similarly tactile and dramatic, sworn with a hand placed either on the Gospels or on "the holy image of the precious body of Jesus Christ which you see here before you now" or "which is here right now and that you see and touch."[181]

Public acts of legal significance and the documents they generated, exhibited, and voiced thus played a very large role in the making of a common stage and its vocabulary. When Auberon ventured out on his errand for the pagan King in the *Jeu de saint Nicolas*, he displayed letters patent—literally, "open" or "accessible" writings—from his lord. When Jehan Bodel took his leave of the Arrageois, he imagined his *Congé* as a letter and a legal brief. When Courtois sold his soul to the devils of Arras, he duly signed it away on a receipt. When the jongleurs' prerogatives were usurped by jealous knights, the Virgin gave them back "their charter and their rights." Contextualizing these fictive documentary flourishings would be the many occasions on which everyone in Arras—men, women, and children—saw and heard the charters of the counts of Flanders and the kings of France, the occasions when they would have responded to inquiries like those of Guiman, or had their oral testimonies taken down in depositions made before the bailiffs of king and count, or watched and listened as official inquests were undertaken by secular and ecclesiastical representatives. All would have participated in ceremonies in which agreements were written and ratified, all would have paid regular homage to the sacred books

---

mains sons signeur ¶ Sire ie vieng en vo foy et devieng vos hom de bouce et de mains. et vouz ai encouvent foi et loiaute aporter contre toutes personnes et garder vo droit et celer les secres de vo court. ¶ Et li sires doit respondre, et ie vous rechoif salf men droit et lautrui as us et as coustumes que li fies doit, et vous en baise non de foy."

179. Galbert of Bruges, *De multro*, c. 49. See Dirk Heirbaut, "Galbert van Brugge: Een Bron voor de vlaamse feodaliteit in de XII de deuw," *Legal History Review* 60 (1992): 49–62.

180. *Cartulaire*, 511 (no. 4). See also Berger, *Littérature*, 60.

181. *Livre aux sermens*, in *Cartulaire*, 510–513 (nos. 2–3, 5, 11): "la sainte figure du précieux corps Jhésu-Crist que ychi veés en présent . . . que cy en présent vous veés et atouchiés."

of Scripture, and many would have honored the carefully guarded book of life in which jongleur-clerics recorded the names of the Carité's dead. Such experiences would have trained them to recognize and evaluate the importance of different sorts of texts, even if they could not read them. Writing does not have to be intelligible in order to have a powerful effect, and the function of a text is just as likely to be determined by its form and placement as by its content. The Code of Hammurabi, inscribed on a black basalt phallos eight feet high and displayed in the marketplace of Babylon in the eighteenth century before the Common Era, would have impressed as much by its size, shape, and situation as by the justice of its laws, which the vast majority could not decipher.

The frequency with which written instruments of every kind were read out, translated, explained, and manufactured *ad phalam Attrebatensem* corroborates what Michael Clanchy, Joyce Coleman, and Steven Justice (among others) have revealed about the ways that the publication of medieval documents fostered a cultural literacy of texts that could become a functional literacy of participation. It may even have promoted technical literacy. Consider the many inscriptions that were on view in the public places of Arras. Who could have failed to notice and be impressed by the monumental memorial to the battle of Bouvines, couched in those forty octosyllabic vernacular verses inscribed on ten tablets, each taller than a man and wider than the outstretched arms of two men? Even without a knowledge of the history behind its placement, or the history it told, one would grasp that something of significance was being placed on record. But anyone who had access to a literate acquaintance could have had these lines read out to him, hearing how the valiant Philip of France had defeated the "false emperor" Otto and the men in league with him, "Who found their deaths without delay / En route from Bouvines to Tournai."[182] Every child in Arras, even the girls barred from the schools at Saint-Vaast and the cathedral, probably knew it by heart and could perform it for a penny. They may even have been able to quote the concluding couplet that acknowledged the portal's chief architect: "And Master Pierre de Labaie / Made of this work the mastery" (*Et Maistre Pierres de Labeie/ Fist de cest oeuvre la maistrie*). Descendants of Pierre would have pointed with pride to his name repeated in Latin on the postern side of the gate, where it was joined with that of "Philip, illustrious king of the Franks and his firstborn son, Lord Louis." Visitors taking a tour of all the famous spots would also have been directed to the nearby church of Saint-Nicolas, and the site of the altar at which Saint Thomas Becket had supposedly celebrated Mass when he passed through Arras in 1165—although, in fact, the church had not been built until 1183. Testifying equally to the regional popularity of the saint's cult and the questionable memory of his visit, a marble plaque read, "Here, Saint Thomas would certainly have celebrated Mass" (*Icy S. Thomas celebra messe certainement*).[183]

---

182. *Épigraphie*, 2:857–859 (no. 2141): "Que mort que pris sans nul delai / Entre Bouvines et Tornay."
183. *Épigraphie*, 1:239.

In the cathedral of Arras, which was a venue for many different types of *theatrica*, public writing was also ubiquitous: in stone, lead, and copper, on walls, tombs, and paving stones. There were epitaphs citing the accomplishments of individual bishops, prominent among them the cenotaph erected to commemorate Lambert's role in the miracle of the Sainte-Chandelle.[184] Prominent, too was the notice that the chapter had purchased the right to the investiture of its bishops from Philip Augustus in 1203 for the princely sum of a thousand livres, its importance communicated even to an illiterate audience via accompanying images representing the exchange between Bishop Raoul and the king.[185] Nearby, the epitaph of Bishop "Hornèd Hat" himself, etched in copper, informed the reader of a Latin quatrain that the man who had formerly been master of the City was now "a citizen of heaven" and alluded again to his purchase of the regalia: "Whose features this sculpture displays, / To kingly ransom led the way."[186] Raoul's successor, Pons, who had followed his lead in life, was also versified in death, his towering defense of the bishop's rights contrasted frankly with his apparently diminutive person.[187] The epitaph on the tomb of Bishop Gerard Pigalotti, an Italian who died in 1304 and who was chiefly remembered as a foreigner—the first bishop of Arras who had come from some land other than that of the *langue d'oïl*—began by pointing this out.[188] And public poetry was not solely the province of bishops, or their Latin elegists. In the thirteenth century some altars in the cathedral's side chapels bore inscriptions in Picard, and by the fourteenth century nearly all dedications and votives were in the vernacular, many in verse. Some were quite lengthy; one ran to forty-six lines.[189]

The abbey church of Saint-Vaast was another public arena in which the monks were determined not to be outdone by the cathedral, the commune, the Carité, or the mendicants in the production of verbal propaganda. Here and in the smaller monastic church of Saint-Pierre and the chapel of Notre-Dame, terse inscriptions on altars and reliquaries dating from the eighth century were nearly all replaced or supplemented by more voluble tributes paid to the ancient abbots whose resting places were being fashionably refurbished throughout the thirteenth century. Saint Hadulph, who had slept undisturbed since 728, now found himself the occupant of a new tomb and the subject of a newfangled Latin qua-

---

184. *Épigraphie*, 1:73 (no. 2). See chapter 4.

185. *Épigraphie*, 1:5 (no. 4).

186. *Épigraphie*, 1:6 (no. 5): "Quem sculptura premit, presul regale redemit. / Non facit, antistes, discretas mors tua tristes; / Nam celi civis meritorum pondere vivis. / Hoc elimavit Dionisius fabricavit. Obiit 1220."

187. *Épigraphie*, 1:6 (no. 6): "Quem modo mors nescit, Pontius ille quiescit, / Qui minimis parens, arcendos fortiter arcens, / Atrebatum rexit : hunc nulla potentia flexit."

188. *Épigraphie*, 2:618–619: "Anno 1304 Gererardus Pigalotto, Italus."

189. *Épigraphie*, 1:7 (nos. 6–7) and 8–11 (no. 10).

train.[190] His new neighbors, Abbot Eudes (1206–1228) and Abbot Martin (1236–1249/50), whose internment probably prompted the gentrification of their immediate surroundings, were likewise lauded in a dozen verse lines apiece.[191] Hadulph also found himself in the dubious company of remains claimed by the monks to be those of the Merovingian King Theuderic III (673–691) and his wife, Duodha, who were "discovered" to have been among the abbey's early benefactors.[192] Adding further élan to the atmosphere were the gilded escutcheons and *couchant* beasts of aristocratic patrons, some of which began to carry vernacular inscriptions, the earliest being the brief notice on the tomb of a man who had died on Saint Vaast's own feast day in 1253.[193] The most attractive to a seventeenth-century collector must also have turned heads from the time it was erected, in 1212. This was a *gisant* worthy of Chrétien de Troyes's *Yvain*: a knight supported by four lions and bearing a lion on his shield, whose Latin legend declared him to be "A well-formed youth, both wise and brave in arms: / This was Renaud, whose form a lion adorns."[194]

Reliant as we are on the notes of modern epigraphers, it is hard say how many such inscriptions there would have been in the thirteenth century, and how representative these few might be of writings that became part of the public record. How frequently, and in what formats and venues, did texts in Latin or Picard fall under the eyes of the Arrageois? How were they interpreted, and what did they contribute to the backdrop of its theater? Were they apt to become invisible to those who saw them daily, or was there something inherently special about the written word which would affect the way current events and historical memory were shaped, by its very appearance? The epic proportions of the verbal monument to the battle of Bouvines suggest that Picard poetry, publicly declaimed and permanently publicized, was considered an effective medium for conveying and recording information. For future generations, the writing on the wall would be the medium whereby the Arrageois, and their visitors, would be apprised of sacred and secular history in their local dimensions, as the history of victorious kings was visibly juxtaposed with ambitious public works initiatives, the careers of gifted craftsmen, and the changing topography of Arras. In fact, these public writings recall the *Jeu de saint Nicolas* in the way they associate features of the urban landscape with heroic deeds done in the parallel universe beyond its walls. In similar fashion, visitors to present-day Florence find bricks and byways adorned with stanzas of Dante's *Commedia*, suggesting that the poet's medieval genius is still imprinted on the modern city.

---

190. *Épigraphie*, 2:447 (no. 1151).

191. *Épigraphie*, 2:449–450 (nos. 1153 and 1153 *bis*).

192. *Épigraphie*, 2:451–452.

193. *Épigraphie*, 2:437–438.

194. *Épigraphie*, 2:447–448: "Formosus iuvenis sapiens an[imosus] ad arma iste Renaldus erat quod signat leo[ne] forma."

This leaves a question: How many people in Arras could read their own vernacular? How many could understand spoken Latin, even if they could not read it? How many other tongues did the dealers in luxury goods, the long-distance traders, and the well-traveled jongleurs understand? The evidence suggests that levels of multilinguality and literacy rates were high in Arras, as elsewhere in the cosmopolitan North. They would have to be, in order for business to thrive.[195] Moreover, the availability of low-cost public schooling suggests that a large number of men were not simply literate but relatively well educated, and many would have been able to pass their knowledge on, formally and informally. As I have already noted, the combined enrollment of the cathedral and monastery schools at any given time can be estimated at 400, while the population of Arras at its height can be estimated at 35,000 or, more conservatively, 25,000.[196] If approximately 80 students per year graduated from those schools, and if only half of these remained in Arras, within a generation of twenty years there would be 800 laymen with clerical knowledge, overlapping with an up-and-coming generation and a previous generation of former scholars, say, another 800. Moreover, each of these literate laymen would provide access to the culture of Latinity for his family and neighbors, at least to the extent of being able to decipher inscriptions and the wording of formulaic documents: let us say, for a circle of ten people. This very modest calculation, surely far too low, suggests that 1,600 laymen in Arras at any one time would have been literate in Latin, while 16,000—about one half of the population—would have been functionally literate, since they had ready access to literate modes of communication. And this takes account only of Latin, whereas the practical demands of business in Arras, which relied increasingly on documentation, would have necessitated a basic level of vernacular literacy among all merchants and master craftsmen, with numeracy required of nearly every man, woman, and child.[197] Even Courtois, none too bright in other respects, was familiar with legal terminology and the paraphernalia of promissory notes and could count his pocket change. The confraternity of jongleurs of Arras, on the other end of the lay spectrum, depended on a shared system of accounting and record keeping that involved many different people in daily administrative prac-

195. On the multilinguality of public life in Flemish towns, see Wim Hüsken, "Politics and Drama: The City of Bruges as Organizer of Dramatic Festivals," in The Stage as Mirror: Civic Theater in Late Medieval Europe, ed. Alan E. Knight (Cambridge, 1997), 165–187. On the acquisition and prevalence of numeracy in this period, see Murray, Reason and Society, 188–210.

196. Fossier, "Arras," 15 and 22; Derville, "Le nombre," 288–289.

197. I have used the lowest of the estimates proposed by Berger in his calculation of the schools' annual graduates (he suggests 80 to 100), but argue for a much higher incidence of public (or shared) literacy. His assessment of the number of "men receiving formal instruction" is given as 25 percent of the adult male population; he does not, however, differentiate between technical and functional literacy or quantify the incidence of vernacular literacy or numeracy (Littérature, 110).

tices. Its archives indicate that a basic level of literacy and a high level of numeracy were actually assumed.

This helps to explain the text of "The Boy and the Blind Man." Copied initially by someone familiar with its performance, it became an appendix to a romantic retelling of the deeds of Alexander the Great and was later adapted by generations of actor-redactors who reapportioned some lines and altered others over the next three centuries, each leaving his mark in an emphatic explicit.[198] If, as one scholar has theorized, this play was a vehicle for jongleurs eager to promote "a worldly and popular theater, without literary ambitions or edifying intent," why was it couched in a literate medium and embedded with an edifying chivalric poem?[199] Clearly, some entertainers were not without the resources for translating their work to or from the page. Furthermore, the use of a new communication strategy—writing—by those already attuned to the powers of speech, sound, gesture, and display could create powerful agents, skilled in retouching what Walter Lippman called "the pictures in our heads."[200] This was how the Carité had carved out a space for itself among more established institutions, and similar techniques could be deployed by anyone eager to win notoriety, including social climbers and minor clerics, itinerant preachers and traveling players. They prompted even the monks of Saint-Vaast to learn new tricks, and to reinvent their austere founder as a popular evangelist and healer. The commune, for its part, used its access to the airwaves of Arras to thwart the mercantile designs of the cathedral, while the cathedral attempted to short-circuit the influence of the count of Artois by making public appeals to the king of France and the Parlement of Paris. The competing representatives of king, count, castellan, and City also, in their turn, made public bids for credibility in retaliation for equally public attempts to undermine their credibility. All became participants in the shaping of a public sphere.

198. See the images reproduced in Symes, "The Boy" and "Appearance."

199. Rousse, "Le théâtre," 4. See also idem, "Le Jeu," 54, and "Propositions," 4–18.

200. The is the title of the famous first chapter of Walter Lippmann's Public Opinion (New York, 1922).

CHAPTER FOUR RELICS AND RITES "THE PLAY OF THE BOWER" AND OTHER PLAYS

More so than any other play from Arras, the *Jeu de la feuillée* exploits the relationship between fiction and fact; the intersecting practices of sacral and secular spaces; the intermingled conventions of courtliness, coarse comedy, community deliberation, and clerical wit; the rich vocabulary of a common stage. Like the *Jeu de saint Nicolas*, it is situated on a frontier of the real and the surreal, the normal and the paranormal; like *Courtois* and *Le garçon et l'aveugle*, it seems to be happening in the immediate present. Yet unlike all of these, it has no obvious antecedents and cannot be compared to any other contemporary artifact. It is novel, it is dazzling. It names names, it locates itself, it begs interpretation. It appears to be a seductive oasis in the otherwise featureless desert of medieval anonymity, promising the rare refreshments of circumstantial detail and authorial transparency.[1] But it is really a mirage— or a mirror, or a Rorschach blot, in which each critic sees his own reflected image.[2] Jean Dufournet, who has described the play as presenting a bleak, existential universe, thus downplays the significance of its invitation to worship at the Blessed Virgin's shrine in order to assert that "evil, fraud, violence, and madness triumph in the end."[3] For Guy Mermier, it is "The Play of Madness," "a representation of hell where Adam and—Arras's inhabitants—are held prisoners."[4]

In brief, the history of this play's reception since the eighteenth century has been that of its removal from historical context. For over 250 years it has been hailed as avant-garde,

1. Joseph Dane called it "a monumental work in search of a monumental poet" ("Parody," 4), and there have been many attempts to construct an artistic biography of the playwright based upon it, e.g., Henri Guy's *Essai sur la vie et les œuvres littéraires du trouvère Adan de la Hale* (Paris, 1898; reprint, Geneva, 1970), and Alfred Adler's *Sens et composition du Jeu de la feuillée* (Ann Arbor, 1956). D. R. Sutherland's trenchant critique of this dubious exercise, "Fact and Fiction in the *Jeu de la feuillée*," *Romance Philology* 13 [1960]: 419–428, has not staunched the flow of retroactive Freudian analysis. For an introduction to the play's critical reception since its publication in 1839, see Otto Gsell's edition, cited in note 8. I deal with this topic more fully in "A Medieval Stage."

2. See, e.g., Daniela Musso, "Adam o dell'ambivalenza: Note sul *Jeu de la feuillée*," *L'Immagine riflessa* 8 (1985): 3–26.

3. Jean Dufournet, *Le Jeu de la feuillée* (Paris, 1989), 14.

4. Guy Mermier, *"The Play of Madness": A Translation of Jeu de la Feuillée by Adam d'Arras* (New York and Bern, 1997), xxi.

which means that each successive generation has discerned in it the prophetic character-istics of a perennial present. In the twentieth century, and into the twenty-first, the *Jeu de la feuillée* has been regarded as proto-modern, antiauthoritarian, and neo-pagan. Those critics unabashedly bored or manifestly puzzled by other medieval plays have expressed delight in its air of louche sophistication or earthy populism, *chacun à son goût*. Equally dismissive of performance conditions, probabilities of audience response, and textual provenance, Marie Ungureanu saw it as a collective expression of proletarian political dis-content and therefore denied that the same poet could have composed the *Jeu de la feuillée* and its companion piece, the *Jeu de Robin et de Marion*, since "the political attitude" of the former was clearly "anti-patrician," while the latter toadied to the aristocracy.[5] Others have characterized it as a lighthearted, meaningless romp, the only specimen of medieval theatricality with no spiritual content or edifying message whatsoever, hence "the achieve-ment of the secular drama."[6]

In 2003, the Comédie-Française added its imprimatur, by hailing Adam de la Halle as "notre premier poète-dramaturge profane," inventor of the "théâtre profane du Moyen Âge," and mounting a "revival" of the *Jeu de la feuillée* under the confusing title *Le Jeu d'Adam*, in a new modern translation by Jacques Darras, directed by Jacques Rebotier. Advertised "as a fantasy in verse" and described as originally "staged for the nocturnal Festival of Spring around 1270" (puzzlingly "premiered on the 3rd of June in 1276"), the play was praised as "already heralding the *soties* of the sixteenth century" and "criticizing with fe-rocity the morals of the Arrageois bourgeoisie." Program notes assert that the playing place must have been "a tavern (a *feuillée*, as they said in the Middle Ages), a place of free speech." Yet this fleeting glimpse of a promising public sphere is immediately veiled by a warning: "In order to fully appreciate this work, it is necessary to give up all desire for co-herence or rationality." Is such vaunted incoherence supposed to be proof of the play's familiar modernity or its medieval alterity? Taken out of context, this remark aptly sum-marizes the critical response of the past two centuries; in context, it betrays the prevailing paternalistic posture of the modern vis-à-vis the medieval, that age when theater was al-legedly "prohibited," only to be miraculously "reborn at first in the churches (eleventh century), then in the towns (thirteenth century), at Arras"—a sad reminder of how influ-ential the potted histories of medieval drama continue to be. It is meant to be reassuring that "according to Jacques LeGoff and Nicolas Truong, 'some of these theatrical plays conjure up the image of a medieval Festival of Avignon.'"[7] Yet surely it should be the other

---

5. Marie Ungureanu, *La bourgeoisie naissante: Société et littérature bourgeoises d'Arras aux XIIe et XIIIe siècles* (Arras, 1955), 201, 204; see also 109–111, 196, and 207–210.

6. Axton, *European Drama*, 168.

7. Marcel Bozonnet, "Résumé," in *Comédie Française: Saison 2003–2004* (Brussels, 2003), 22–23: "La pièce a été créée le 3 juin 1276. . . . Montée pour la Fête nocturne du Printemps vers 1270 à Arras,

way around: the Festival of Avignon might conjure up an idea of medieval theater, but the plays of Arras can hardly have been devised with an eye to their modern reception.

This chapter rejects such teleologies. Instead, it proceeds from the radical premise that the *Jeu de la feuillée* is the product of public life in thirteenth-century Arras.

The Speech (or Play) by Adam

"My lords! Do you know why I've changed my clothes?" (*Segneur, savés pour quoi j'ai mon abit cangiet?*).[8] Calling attention to himself, Adam de la Halle—known at home as Adam le Boçu and abroad as Adam of Arras—informs us that he is off to Paris; he plans to resume his studies there. It's therefore an attempt to say good-bye: "Before I go, I want to take good leave of you" (*Mais je voeil a vous tous avant prendre congiet*, v. 4).[9] The miniature accompanying "The speech by Adam" (*Li dis Adan*, later altered by the scribe to read "The play by Adam," *Li jus Adan*) shows him standing before an audience seated on benches (Figure 4). Their faces are sober, and Adam's face is also grave. He raises his right hand high in a gesture of greeting or benediction; his left hand clutches a fringed cloth (a handkerchief?) held tightly against his scholar's gown. Two members of his audience, a man and a woman in the front row, raise their hands, too, in greeting or farewell. But this ceremonious *congé*, delivered to the solemn strain of twelve-footed alexandrine meter, will soon be rudely interrupted. "Yo, dude, what's up with you?" (*Caitis, qu'i feras tu?* v. 12), shouts Rikiers, completing his friend's rhyme but shattering his plans. With his entrance, the play resumes the octosyllabic banter of everyday speech.

---

l'œuvre se situe à la frontière entre le comique, la fable féerique et la satire sociale, et annonce déjà les soties du XVIe siècle. . . . [La compagnie] se retrouve dans une taverne (une feuillée, comme on disait au Moyen Âge), lieu de libre parole. . . . Il faut, pour savourer pleinement cette œuvre, renoncer à tout désir de cohérence ou de rationalité. . . . Du IVe au XIe siècle, le théâtre . . . est prohibé. Il renaît d'abord dans les églises (XIe siècle), puis dans les villes (XIIIe), à Arras, où se succèdent, selon Jacques Le Goff et Nicolas Truong, 'des jeux théâtraux qui suggèrent l'image d'un Festival d'Avignon médiéval.'"

8. All citations refer to the edition of Pierre-Yves Badel in *Adam de la Halle: OEuvres complètes*, hereinafter abbreviated as AHOEc (Paris, 1995), 286–375; the text of the play is abbreviated JF. The best critical edition overall is that of Otto Gsell, "Das 'Jeu de la feuillée' von Adam de la Halle: Kritscher Text und Einführung, Übersetzung, Anmerkungen und einem vollständigen Glossar" (Ph.D diss., Würzburg, 1970). There is an English translation by Axton and Stevens (*Plays*) and another, more creative, by Guy Mermier, cited in note 4.

9. The original *incipit* (BnF fr. 25566, fol 48b) has been independently noted by only two other scholars in all the long history of the play's reception: Guesnon, "Adam," 209; and Jane B. Dozier, "Mimesis and Li jeus de la fuellie," *Tréteaux* 3 (1981): 80–89 at 88–89. Dozier suggests, intriguingly, that the scribe himself may have been "suddenly confronted by the question of *genre*" in the midst of the copying process. For a helpful introduction to the wording of *incipits*, see Huot, *Song to Book*, 48.

Designated in its *explicit* as *Li jeus de le fuellie* and preserved in its entirety only in the deluxe anthology of Adam's oeuvre, "The Play of the Bower" is some 1,100 lines long and boasts seventeen speaking parts, one of which is negligible (probably a cameo role for someone planted in the audience) and eight of which were clearly designed to be doubled by four actors, so that its production would have required a dozen people, about the same number as the *Jeu de saint Nicolas*. With a few exceptions, many of the dramatis personae embodied or mentioned in performance were real people living in Arras, and some would eventually be listed in the funerary register of the Carité de Notre Dame des Ardents.[10] In two abbreviated versions of the play, by contrast, the circumstances of local production are irrelevant and unknown: Adam makes his speech, debates his decision briefly with friends whose identities are also irrelevant and unknown, and then makes his exit. One of these shorter sketches circulated in southern Italy; the other was part of the same traveling repertoire as a version of *Courtois*. Once again, as with *Courtois* and *Le garçon et l'aveugle*, we find that dramatic material premiered in Arras could find a welcome reception in venues where the outer layer of associations and meanings attached to that specific locale could be shorn away and generalized: the audiences of these postprandial entertainments would have heard and seen nothing of the play's proximity to a bower, its cast of fakers and fairies, its devotion to relics, or its culmination in an act of Marian piety. Yet the celebrity persona of the title character was still essential to the playlets' success, since both identify "Adan le Boçu" of Arras as the star, suggesting that jongleurs all over Europe capitalized on his fame. One wonders whether the mystery surrounding his early death and disappearance spawned a cottage industry of "Adam impersonators," just as it gave rise to contemporary rumors that he (like the American idol Elvis Presley) was still alive and touring.[11] But I am getting ahead of my story.

Adam's overture acknowledges that his renewed career at the university may raise a few eyebrows, especially since it means leaving his wife, Maroie, behind in Arras, presumably so that he may be eligible for residence in the house of the Bons Enfants d'Arras in Paris, established for bachelor graduates of the local grammar schools who were pursuing a degree in arts (and the second-oldest foundation of its kind).[12] The historical Adam almost certainly lived and studied in Paris at one time, given his ability—unique among thirteenth-century trouvères—to compose in the new polyphony. Yet it is unclear from the testimony of the play whether or not he was able to return. His buddies Rikiers, Guillos, and Hane certainly do everything they can to discourage him from going, discussing the pit-

---

10. E.g., Dame Douche (d. 1279), Maistre Henri Bochu (d. 1291), Rikiers Aurris (d. 1302), Guillos li Petis (d. 1302), Raoul le Waidier (d. 1311), and the Veelet mentioned in v. 891 (d. 1290). See Berger, *Le nécrologe*, and *Littérature*, 115; Guesnon, "Adam," 183–187.

11. I owe this insight to conversations with Timothy Duis. See also chapter 5.

12. J. M. Reitzel, "The Medieval Houses of Bons-Enfants," *Viator* 11 (1980): 179–207.

falls of student life and the limited scholarly attainments of clerics from Arras, while at the same time challenging Adam's decision to abandon his wife. In his own defense, therefore, Adam launches into the bravura diatribe that was the climax of the play in its abbreviated forms (at nearly a hundred verses, it constituted half their length), a *blazon* of Maroie's youthful charms as deconstructed by the disillusionments of marriage.

For most audiences in thirteenth- and fourteenth-century Europe, this was "the play by Adam": a quarter-hour's worth of sophomoric wit capped by a stock soliloquy, enough material for a few actors, or a tour-de-force for a jongleur who might then launch into a set of Adam's songs. But in Arras, in the shade of the bower, the play continues. Rikiers offers to take Maroie off Adam's hands; she's very much to his taste, even if Adam has tired of her. Then Master Henri li Boçu arrives, echoing the plaint of fathers everywhere (including that of Courtois), since he fears that Adam's scheme will liquidate the family's savings. He'd be better off in Arras, he's told, where he can continue to care for his sick old sire. Hearing talk of illness, a Physician enters and speedily diagnoses Henri's complaint as a malady common in Arras: it is known as greed, and he can name several people who suffer from it. Henri inquires after a cure and produces a urine sample for analysis. In the midst of their medical consultation, a character designated variously as "Douce Dame" or "Dame Douce" appears, carrying her own specimen. Plying his art, the Physician reveals what has caused her ailment: "Too many things are taken lying down" (*Chis maus vient de gesir souvine,* v. 252). Just in case the joke is obscure, someone called Rainneles pipes up to say that Douce is pregnant—probably calling this out from the audience, since he interjects again a while later, and is told by Adam to shut up and sit down (vv. 584–589). After a perfunctory denial, Douce fingers Rikiers as the father of the child, adding defensively that it was conceived "a little before Lent" (*un peu devant quaresme,* v. 285), and therefore within the bounds of propriety.

The Arrageois spectators' reactions to this first segment of the play would have been colored by its casting. Were Adam, Rikiers, Guillos, Hane, Henri, and Rainneles playing themselves? What was the relationship between "Dame Douce" and the Dame Douce whose death was duly noted in the Carité's register just a few years after the play's probable premiere, in 1279? Did she also make a commanding appearance as herself? Was this a loving or a spiteful parody? Were Margos of the Maison des Pomettes and Aelis of "The Dragon" present when their names were mentioned, or did Rikiers merely nod to those two taverns, one on the rue de la Warance running past the confraternity's "court" into the Petit Marché, the other on the market's southern side?[13] Other questions, such as those addressing the interaction between the play's meticulously prepared manuscript and the circumstances of its composition and performance, are related. Were the actors working from a memorized text, or did they perform a species of improvisational comedy, struc-

13. Berger, *Littérature,* 49.

tured around a series of gags and games, later organized and scripted at some time prior to the text's preservation? Does the involvement of people affiliated with the confraternity of jongleurs suggest that it was intended for performance at one of its bevées or at the grand siège? If so, was it performed in the Carité's court, or can we imagine it set in the Petit Marché, near the Pyramide and convenient to the tavern where the final scene of the play is set? What was the significance of "the bower," and why is it mentioned, explicitly, only once? We will return to these questions in due course. For now, we return to the play.

The entrance of Dame Douce prompts general discussion and a roll call of sharp-tongued local wives (were they, too, present?), interrupted by the arrival of a Monk. He carries with him a reliquary, which, he says, contains the remains of an exotic saint from Ireland, Acaire, famous for curing varieties of folly and stupidity (*sos et sotes*, v. 331). He gives his pitch:

Souvent voi des plus ediotes		I've seen the greatest idiots
A Haspre no moustier vient		In church, at Haspres, in our care,
Qui sont haitié au departir,		Completely cured when they leave there
Car li sains est de grant merite.		Because of his great sanctity.
Et d'une abenguete petite	335	And for a very trifling fee
Vous poés bien faire du saint		You too can have the saint's blessing.

Haspres was a monastery located just north of Arras, so the Monk has not traveled too far; in fact, he may have come no farther than the abbey of Saint-Vaast, which was the mother house of Haspres and the place where an arm bone of Saint Acaire—known to cure madness—was kept in a silver reliquary.[14] He has come to the right place: immediately, a Knave (Walés) presents himself as a candidate for the cure, describing himself as *un sos clamés*, "an acclaimed fool" (v. 344), and carrying one of the symbols of the jongleur's stylized madness, a cheese. As in the story of Courtois and the rhetoric of the jongleurs' Carité, he riffs on the various meanings of folly, which in his case is a professional choice, enhanced rather than alleviated by contact with the relics of Acaire—but poignant nevertheless, as Master Henri intimates when he nostalgically contrasts the Knave's career with that of his dead father:

Walet, foy que dois saint Acaire,		By Saint Achaire, whose faith you owe,
Que vauroies tu avoir mis	351	What would you give to have been made
Et tu fusses mais a toudis		As good a minstrel, so it's said
Si bons menestreus con tes pere?		So often, as your father was?

14. Attested in the (lost) inventory of the treasury of Saint-Vaast, AdPC ser. 1 H 426, 428. See *Inventaire sommaire des archives départementales antérieures à 1790*, ed. Henri Loriquet and Jules Chavanon, vol. 1 (Arras, 1902), 303–306. See also Guesnon, "Adam," 215–216.

To which the Knave replies:

Biau né, aussi bon vielere		Old chum, if I could play the *vielle*
Vauroie ore estre comme il fu	355	So well that I could be like him
Et on m'eüst ore pendu		I'd let them hang me on a whim
Ou on m'eüst caupé le teste!		Or, even more, cut off my head.

If the Knave's madness is that of the lesser artist who would sell his soul for a chance at genius, it is soon compared with the antisocial folly of another son, li *Dervés*, "the Dervish," a crazy lad who comes upon the scene accompanied by his Father. These new arrivals interact with each other in a manner similar to that of the Boy and the Blind Man—the one a prankster, the other his straight man—although the Dervish is freed from the constraints of probability imposed on sane characters, so it is hard to know whether anything he says corresponds to lived reality. When he spouts elliptical abuse and accuses Adam of bigamy, do we take this as a mad delusion? Maybe not, since it prompts a topical discussion of the canons issued at the Second Council of Lyon, convened just two years prior to the play's *terminus a quo* of 1276.

With the eventual departure of the Physician, the Knave, the Dervish, and his Father—exits timed to allow for costume changes before the actors' next entrances—Rikiers reveals that the true purpose of the play differs from that proclaimed by Adam's character in the opening address. The audience has been summoned not to hear the playwright's farewell, as advertised, but to witness "A great wonder of fairy folk" (*Grant merveille de faerie*, v. 563). The Lady Morgue and her companions are due any minute, we are told, and will seat themselves at a special table, now indicated for the first time in the text of the play but visible to the audience throughout the preceding scenes, probably sheltered by a bower. "For this true custom's well observed, / That they come always on this night" (*Car c'est droite coustume estavle / Qu'eles vienent en ceste nuit*, vv. 566–567), the dating of "this night" in the world of the play remaining tantalizingly unspecified. Overseeing last-minute arrangements, Rikiers suggests that the Monk take his relics away from the scene lest their presence interfere with the fairies' magic. The Monk, however, declares that he would prefer to stay; his relics do not, after all, have any efficacy.

When Guillos says that he can hear the approach of the fairy king Hellekin's household train, his remark is followed by the entrance of Crokesos, the fairy herald. Catching sight of Dame Douce, Crokesos asks if Morgue has yet arrived, informing her that he has come to Arras at the request of his lord to deliver an amorous message on Hellekin's behalf. Douce avers that she has not seen the lady in question; on cue, Morgue appears with her companions. Ignoring the mortals, she addresses herself to Crokesos in courtly fashion, speaking in the Francien dialect of the Parisian court rather than the Picard vernacular featured in the rest of the play. She then seats herself promptly at the feast spread by Adam and Rikiers, flanked by the fairies Maglore and Arsile. All is serene until Maglore notices a fault in the table setting, which she takes as a personal affront: there is no knife laid ready at her place. (How insulting! Only peasants would expect a guest to supply her own cutlery!) Morgue, with the politesse becoming a fairy queen, tries to set the tone by ignoring the slight, praising the repast and graciously asking who prepared it. Crokesos tells her that the spread is offered by two clerics, Rikiers and Adam, "The one there, in the scholar's gown" (*S'estoit en une cape chiex*, v. 631). Graciously, Morgue replies that these two suppliants deserve appropriate gifts in exchange for their offerings: airily, she bestows vast riches on Rikiers, and to Adam grants that he will be the greatest lover in the world. Arsile, following her mistress's lead, pronounces that Adam will also be handsome and "a good maker of songs" (*bons faiseres de canchons*, v. 665), while Rikiers will be prosperous in all business affairs. Maglore, however, still piqued by the lapse of etiquette, uses her fairy powers to void these gifts, ordaining that Rikiers will never have anything to line his purse and putting an end to Adam's plans—and the play's original purpose:

De l'autre, qui se va vantan		As for the other one, who boasts
D'aler a l'escole a Paris,	685	Of Paris schools and being trained,
Voeil qui'il soit si atruandis		I will that here he be detained
En la compaignie d'Arras		Among the people of Arras
Et qu'il s'ouvlit entre les bras		And that, while lost in the embrace
Se fame qui est mote et tenre,		Of his good wife, loving and kind,
Et qu'il perge et hache l'aprenre	690	He learns to shun and hate that grind
Et meche se voie en respit.		And put his learned journey off.

Morgue and Arsile protest, but Maglore refuses to revoke her curse.

Now that Adam's plan is shattered and the play's original course irrevocably altered, a new plot is revealed. Morgue asks Crokesos for his master's message, a love letter. She reads it, but declares that her affections are already fixed on one Robert Sommeillon. This personage had been mentioned earlier in the play, in a conversation between the Dervish and his Father:

Ha! Biaus dous fies, seés vous jus!		Please, my sweet son, behave! Sit still!
Si vous metés a genoillons!	405	Or on your knees right now, get down!
Se che non, Robers Soumillons		If not, then Robert Someillons—
Qui est nouviaus prinches du pui		Who is the new prince of the *puy*—
Vous ferra!		Will make you!
Bien kië de lui!		He'll take that from me!
Je sui miex prinches qu'il ne soit		I'm more a prince than he can be.
A sen pui canchon faire doit,		You have to make songs at his puy
Par droit, maistre Wautiers as Paus		By rule, like Sir Gautier Big-Toe[15]

15. This Gautier, or Wautiers, has been identified as Walterus ad Pollices ("with the Toes"), a wealthy

Et uns autres, leur paringaus,	410	Or him they call the best-in-show,
Qui a non Thoumas de Clari.		The one named Thomas de Clari.
L'autr'ier vanter les en oï.		I heard them just the other day:
Maistre Wautiers ja s'entremet		That Master Walter's singing fast
De chanter parmi le cornet		Accompanied a trumpet blast,
Et dist qu'il sera coronnés.		And he said he'd be crowned for that.

Morgue, who has not been privy to the Dervish's description of this puy's flatulent proceedings, gives a different account of Robert and his pastimes. She says that he was her champion in a recent tournament held "By the land of the Round Table" (Par le païs a tavle ronde, v. 723), and that he is also the veteran of a fierce joust at Montdidier. Crokesos recognizes his master's newest rival from her description, since his heraldic training has given him a detailed knowledge of the chivalric devices favored by different combatants; he recalls that Robert wears green slashed with red (vv. 730–731). But he is also able to inform Morgue that his master, Hellekin, has already bested Robert in a show of force at Arras, after the latter indelicately bragged about the fairy queen's attachment to him:

Tres qu'il jousta a l'autre fie		For when he jousted recently
En ceste vile, ou marchié droit,	735	In this town, in that market square,
De vous et de lui se vantoit;		He boasted of your love, right there!
Et tantost qu'il s'en prist a courrre,		The instant he was on his horse,
Me sires se mucha en pourre		My lord struck at him with such force—
Et fist sen cheval le gambet		Made his mount sway and stumble so—
Si que caïr fist le varlet	740	That from his perch the knave did go
Sans assener sen compaignon		With great dispatch; it was no match.

Morgue comes to her senses when she hears that her former favorite is capable of behaving in so discourteous a fashion, thus exposing himself as an unabashed social climber in fancy dress.

The spectators' attention is now diverted to a representation of Fortune's wheel set up in the playing area. At Crokesos's request, Morgue identifies the figures who are shown to be rising and falling upon its spokes. At the top, in the place reserved for reigning kings, she points out Ermenfrois Crespin and Jacquemes Louchars, powerful bankers "of very good account" (or, perhaps, "in well with the count," sont bien du conte, v. 790). Their sons are depicted as climbing after them, ready to displace their fathers at the top, while another powerful Arrageois, Thoumas de Bouriane, is shown on his way down, victim of Fortune's fickleness. At the bottom is the once prominent local entrepreneur Leurins li

cleric with connections to the abbey of Vivier and some valuable real estate in Bruges. He died between 1294 and 1297, at which time he would have been in his seventies or early eighties. See the discussion that follows and Dufournet, Le Jeu, 215.

Cavelaus.[16] Whether this play-within-the-play should be construed as a good-humored roast or a sharp exposé of immoral behavior and its consequences—we recall the lambasting sustained by certain shrewish women of Arras earlier in the play—is unclear. Much depends on theories of the play's setting and sponsorship, to which we will return.

Having reminded the audience of Fortune's fickleness, the fairies recall that they have an appointment to meet with a group of local women at the Croix-au-Pré in the northwestern quarter of Arras. Dame Douce chimes in to remind them of their obligation: Morgue has promised to help local girls acquire the charms that will attract certain men. Douce herself has recently been slighted by the chap she fancies and is eager to bring him to heel and into bed, just as she claims to have captured Jakemon Pilepois the previous year and Gillon Lavier the previous night. (Again, the way this joke would play depends a great deal on who these men were, and what Dame Douce's age and reputation were.) So the fairies exit singing—a line of musical notation is provided in the manuscript—and Adam and his companions take center stage once more. They agree that it is high time for a drink, and repair to the tavern of Raoul le Waidier. Here, the Monk takes a nap and wakes to find that the others have run up a large tab at his expense, a predicament in which Courtois had also found himself. The Physician, Dervish, and Father reappear, confirming my hypothesis that the four actors who played these roles and that of the Knave (now playing Raoul) doubled as the fairy trio and Crokesos.

Finally, Guillos recollects that it is time for all present, which seems to include everyone in the audience, to pay their respects to the *fiertre* of Notre-Dame. Mentioned for the first time in these closing lines, this portable reliquary (from the Latin *ferertrum*, a bier) has apparently been visible to the audience throughout the entire play, like the fairies' table and the tavern. And like them, it is situated under the leafy branches of a bower:

Ains irons ancois, s'on m'en croit,		We all should go, if you'll believe,
Baisier le fiertre Nostre Dame	1077	To kiss Our Lady's relic chest
Et che chierge offrir, qu'ele flame,		And give this candle, that our best
No cose nous en venra mieus.		Affairs will prosper, by its light.

Adam and his friends accordingly go about their pious business, to which the "The Play of the Bower"—renamed in its concluding rubric—has been tending all along. In the light of this devotional candle, Adam's farewell, the fairies' banquet, and all the other incidents of the play are cast into shadow, just as the fairies' bower and the tavern's bush are retroactively disclosed as trumpery simulacra of the Virgin's sheltering canopy. The Dervish and his Father and the Monk, clutching his own silly relics, are left behind, and our attention is called to the sound of bells from the parish church of Saint-Nicolas nearby.

16. Dufournet, *Le Jeu*, 205–206, 208–210, 214.

Many years ago Ernest Langlois offered a concise summary of what we can state with certainty about the career of Adam de la Halle, and subsequent scholarship has added little to his sketch.[17] By the same token, all that can be determined about "the play" or "the speech by Adam" or "The Play of the Bower," to quote its enveloping rubrics, is that it is set in Arras, in or just after the year 1276.[18] One can also say that it was evidently designed to make use of mechanisms for communication familiar to audiences in Arras, where the wily ways of charlatans, clergy, and actors were regularly compared; where the commodification of relics and the cult of celebrity were matters of concern; where the *tromperies* of professional fools and the *bêtises* of foolish naturals were often played against each other; where the bells sounding a revel's timely end could be heard as clearly in a real tavern as in a made-up one. And we know that the play was considered by its scribe to be defined in relation to a bower. That fact bears investigation. What was the *fuellie*? What was its relationship to the *fiertre* of Notre-Dame, which draws the worshipful gaze of the play's cast? How would an Arrageois audience have responded to these objects? And what can the answers to these questions contribute toward our understanding of the play's occasion, performers, and purpose?

The Fuellie and the Fiertre

The *fuellie* and the *fiertre* were intimately connected in the minds of Adam's contemporaries in Arras by the time the play known to us as the *Jeu de la feuillée* was mounted there. The latter term referred to a certain reliquary belonging to the cathedral of Notre-Dame d'Arras, the former to a temporary structure decked with foliage which had both general and specific uses, all associated with hospitality. In nearby Cambrai, a *foeullie* was erected for feasting in the bishop's court.[19] In 1237 a *folleie* built in the meadows of Compiègne for the wedding of Count Robert I of Artois cost over 237 livres, but another made inside the king's lodgings on that same occasion cost only a little more than 30 livres, a sum that included "tables and trestles" for both structures.[20]

Variously spelled, then, bowers could be humble or grand; but they always suggested welcome, shelter, and festivity. Licensed taverns selling wine advertised this fact by putting out signs garlanded with foliage, and often had courtyards or forecourts roofed

---

17. Ernest Langlois, *Adam le Bossu, trouvère artésien du XIIIe siècle: Le Jeu de la feuillée et le Jeu de Robin et de Marion* (Paris, 1923), v–xxxi.

18. Guesnon, "Adam," 174, 186, 194–203, 213.

19. Godefroy, *Dictionnaire*, 4:171.

20. Achille Peigné Delacourt, *Compte des dépenses de la chevalerie de Robert, comte d'Artois à Compiègne, en juin 1237* (Amiens, 1853), 14 and 20: "Summa pro folleia facta in domibus regis ad Compendium et tabulis et tretellis factis pro rege et tabulis et tretellis paratis in folleia pratorum."

with greenery; the streets and marketplaces of Arras were full of these.[21] Courtois succumbed to the inviting atmosphere of one such, just as the actor who portrayed him may have lured a crowd by playing in front of another. The entertainer under a bower was a familiar sight: the Carité's funerary register boasts a crude drawing executed in red and black inks depicting a jongleur—wearing a doublet with slashed sleeves, a motley coat, and a cockscomb—performing under a leafy wood-frame structure.[22] Indeed, singing in a bower appears to have been a characteristic activity throughout the North: the image for the month of May in the *travaux des mois* of the cathedral at nearby Amiens shows a man seated under a bower, his mouth open in song. (Representations of May elsewhere rely on its association with the chivalric pursuits of falconry: evoking May for a pan-European audience, the knight and his hawk make an appearance in the first scene of Adam's *Jeu de Robin et de Marion*.)[23] Bowers were also associated with acts of devotion. "The Meaning Which One Ought to Enact within Oneself at Mass" compares the worshiper's spiritual preparations to the ministry of angels "who come to dress the place and the table where God feasts his friends," advising, "so one ought to do just the same as when a king is about to enter a city, and everyone goes out to meet him." The bower becomes, in this attractive metaphor, a frame of mind, for "in that sweet place, everyone ought to show forth all his virtues, of heart and body," in order to give a fitting reception to the Lord, who "is so courtly to his friends." Only when this bower is properly decked and its table spread is one ready to hear "the news saying that the Lord is coming speedily" and to greet "the bannerbearers, the jongleurs, the musicians, the *vielles* who come before the Lord to honor him."[24]

These were the general meanings of *fuellie*, and they would certainly have informed the way an audience responded to a play of that name, and to the decking of bowers in the course of performance. But the bower to which the rubric *Li jeus de le fuellie* alludes specifically was erected every year in the Petit Marché of Arras by 1221, and was still being

---

21. Camille, "Signs," 102. For regulations of tavern signage in fifteenth-century Arras, see Guesnon, "Publications," 74. Paoli ("Taverne," 75–76) counts over 146 taverns (selling wine) and 46 brasseries (selling beer) extant by the later fifteenth century, and a good proportion of these were probably extant in the thirteenth century, since the population at that time was larger.

22. BnF fr. 8541, fol. 42r[a]. It is reproduced by Berger in *Le nécrologe*, 2:55.

23. Reproduced by Fossier, *La terre*, 1:390; compare Émile Mâle, *L'art religieux du XIIIe siècle en France: Étude sur l'iconographie du moyen âge et sur ses sources d'inspiration* (Paris, 1948), 139–157.

24. BmA 657, fol. 126v and 127r[b]: "qui descent pour apareillier le lieu et le taule ou dieus repaist les siens amis si doit on ausi faire que qant uns rois doit entrer en une cite. tout lun a la desasient al encontre et li moustre cascuns se plus grant maladie pour mieus recouvrer . . . nouveles qui dist ke li sires venrra hasteement . . . les banieres. li iougleour les muses les vieles qui vienent devant le signour pour lui honnourer. . . . En cele douce venue tout le doivent aourer de toutes leur vertus de cuer et de cors. . . . Car Diex est si courtois a ses amis quil les garde en tous perieus." See also chapter 3.

erected annually at least through 1328. Once constructed, it remained on that site between Pentecost and the morning of the feast of the Assumption, sheltering a consecrated altar on which the *fiertre*, central to the play's closing scene, was displayed. This was a chest decorated with images of the Assumption and containing the cathedral's precious Marian relics, attested for the first time in the Carité's coutumier.[25] It was thus exposed to public view in the most public of all places for a period of two to three months: an unusually long time, considering that it was the practice in most northern cathedral towns for relics to be set out for veneration only on the Monday, Tuesday, and Wednesday after Pentecost, when annual pilgrimages to the diocesan seat were encouraged.[26] Given what we already know about strained relations between City and Town, it is clear that the practice of displaying the cathedral's relics in the heart of the abbey's patrimony must have represented a significant compromise between the canons and the monks, since the abbey could claim the ownership of all real estate in its ancient domain and was, prior to the creation of the county of Artois in 1237, the sole beneficiary of its market tax. Moreover, it had recently made significant concessions in order to accommodate the potent relic of the jongleurs' Carité, sanctioning and perhaps financing the construction of the Sainte-Chandelle's Pyramide in the Petit Marché in 1200. At the same time, we have seen that Saint-Vaast was attempting to raise the profile of its own collection of relics, which included those of its founder as well as those of Saint Acaire.

How, then, did it come about that the cathedral was allowed to display a rival reliquary in this same lucrative locale for the express purpose of raising revenue? The story begins in 1232, according to an awkwardly labeled narrative copied into a fourteenth-century cartulary kept at Saint-Vaast: "What was done about the demolished structure called the *follye* in which the chest of Blessed Mary had been kept while in the *place* of Saint-Jean-en-Ronville." Preserved side by side with the census of Guiman, it borrows something of the earlier document's tone: "First of all, it is known that in all public places, in the streets and houses within the walls of the citadel of Arras, and in the suburbs wherever there is commerce, the church of Saint-Vaast has [jurisdiction]."[27] Prior to the troubling incident that prompted the composition of this account, the abbey's apologist explains that the

---

25. Coutumier, fols. 46v^b, ll. 39—47r^a and l. 2.

26. Mansfield, *Humiliation*, 152.

27. *Factum de domo destructa ad reponendum capsam Beatæ Mariæ in Platea Joannis de Rotunda Villa quæ vocatur Follye* (hereafter cited as *Follye*), ed. Henri Loriquet, in "Le trésor de Notre-Dame d'Arras," MCdMhPC 1, no. 2 (1892): 127–208 at 198–201: "In primis sciendum est quod in omnibus plateis, in vicis et in domibus infra muros civitatis Attrebatensis, et in suburbiis ubicumque mercaturæ fiunt, habet ecclesia Sancti Vedasti." The significance of this text was originally noted by Guesnon, "Adam," 206–207 and 219–220. Ungureanu (*La bourgeoisie*, 206–207) mistook the clause "vocatur Follye" as modifying "platea," thus wrongly asserting that the *place* of Saint-Jean was called "the folly" and engendering confusion in subsequent scholarship.

cathedral canons had come to an arrangement whereby their *fiertre* was displayed "in the marketplace of Arras, where there is commerce, in order to solicit the alms of the faithful," a much more advantageous location than any in the City. "There, the dwelling would be built and the chest placed within it, and there it would remain from the time of the day of Pentecost up to the Assumption of the Blessed Virgin, and after the said Assumption the said chest would be carried back to Notre-Dame and the dwelling dismantled."[28]

How might this have benefited the abbey, so little disposed to encourage competitors or trespassers? All of these arrangements hinged on the observance of important protocols, for "such was the lordship of Saint-Vaast in Arras, that when the bishop or chapter of Arras wanted to carry the reliquary of Notre-Dame into the market of Arras . . . it was first necessary for them to beg leave."[29] In other words, the abbey's power to grant or withhold permission served as a check on the freedoms of the cathedral, whose canons were aware that any diplomatic misstep at any other time of the liturgical year might deprive them of a lucrative privilege. If Saint-Vaast's permission were not properly sought or granted, the *fiertre* was supposed to "remain inside the church of Notre-Dame, outside the walls of Arras, placed at the foot of the cloister," far from the mercantile center of the Town. Here we are gaining some insight into the prehistory of the dispute *ad phalam Attrebatensem* in 1293, by which time the canons had taken steps to foster their own commercial ventures during major Marian feasts, bringing the *fiertre* back to the City on the day of the Assumption to be the spiritual focus of their claustral market and thereby safeguarding themselves against the caprice of the abbey's lordship, which could so easily deny them access to the marketplaces of Arras.

For in 1232 a predictable crisis had occurred. The canons craftily attempted an end run around the abbey's claim of total jurisdiction by the simple expedient of erecting their bower in the tiny market square in front of the church of Saint-Jean-en-Ronville. This was one of the cathedral's parishes, and the one most strategically situated for commercial traffic. Its *place* opened onto "the Street," the broad Roman road bisecting the Town from the Porte de Ronville to the Porte de la Cité and running into the City itself, past the cathedral; and it was already in use as a regular marketplace. Hearing that such a plan was afoot, the abbey promptly declared that the place Saint-Jean was not within the cathedral's jurisdiction, being neither "holy land nor cemetery" attached to the parish church, and

---

28. *Follye*, 198; "In Foro Attrebatensi] ubi fiunt mercaturæ, ad petendum fidelium eleemosinas. . . . [Æ]dificatur ibi domus et altare et ponitur capsa, et est ibi tantum modo a die Pentecostes usque ad Assumptionem Beatæ Virginis et post dictam Assumptionem, dicta capsa ad ecclesiam Beatæ Mariæ reportatur et domus destruitur et altare."

29. *Follye*, 198–199: "Tale etiam dominium habet Sanctus Vedastus in Atrebato, quod quando Episcopus vel Capitulum Atrebatensi deportare volunt feretrum Beatæ Mariæ in Foro Attrebatensi . . . a Sancto Vedasto licentia debet peti. . . . [I]n ecclesia Beatæ Mariæ remanebat vel extra muros Atrebati ad pedem sui atrii deponebant."

therefore counting as one of the commercial spaces controlled by Saint-Vaast. On a more practical note, the monks also protested that the area was too small to support the bower and its business side by side with the local market. Furthermore—and this is the most telling argument—the abbey's delegation reminded the canons that the Petit Marché was generally regarded as the usual and appropriate venue for the exhibition of relics and the performance of liturgical rites honoring them. It was, said the monks, "more convenient and pleasing to all the people of the Town gathering there for the sake of prayers and devotions, and indeed more worthy and greatly pleasing to God and to Blessed Mary," probably because of the jongleurs' chapel dedicated to her on that site.[30] Finally, they warned the canons that unless the *follye* was erected in its usual location, the monks would tear down the shrine and carry away the pieces.

This is precisely what happened on the eve of Pentecost in 1232, when the bower was constructed outside the church of Saint-Jean: the monks came in the night, broke it down, and removed it. Yet on the following day the canons further defied the monks by putting up a tent made of local cloth to shelter the *fiertre*, which was then "carried in forcefully [i.e., illegally], accompanied by a multitude of armed men."[31] Installing the reliquary in the *place* Saint-Jean, the canons and their supporters reconstructed the bower all that night and the following day, guarding their labor "forcefully, with arms," setting up the altar, celebrating divine service, and remaining encamped around the church for the remainder of the week. According to the abbey's report, all the men from the manors belonging to the bishop and chapter were called in from the countryside to help defend the cathedral's cause, so that the number of armed guards at the "sepulchre" amounted to more than fifteen hundred.[32] Even if the numbers are exaggerated, one can readily imagine how embarrassing it was for the abbey to have a crusading army—the term "sepulchre" suggests the fervor of a religious war—laying siege to the Town from within. (This was not what Mansfield called the "delicate diplomacy" of liturgical negotiation.)[33] Yet the monks al-

---

30. Follye, 199: "magis conveniens et placens toti villæ populo ibi confluenti causa orationis et devotionis, et etiam honestior et magis placens Deo et beatæ Mariæ."

31. Follye, 199: "violenter adportarunt cum multitudine armatorum." The "cloth of Arras" mentioned in the text could not have been, in 1232, a tapestry, as Loriquet and others have supposed. The seeming reference to tapestry, however, does corroborate the narrative's own assertion that it was recopied some eighty years after the events of 1232, hence after 1312; see Jean Lestocquoy, "Origine et décadence de la tapisserie à Arras," *Revue belge d'archéologie et d'histoire de l'art* 10 (1940): 27–34. Since 1313 marks the beginning of the tapestry industry in Arras, this is an instance of retroactive "product placement," designed to advertise a new commodity.

32. Follye, 201: "Semper de die et nocte existentes armati et omnes homines villarum suarum cum armis secum venire coegerunt, et fuit numerus armatorum cum prædictis canonicis custodientibus sepulcrum plusquam mille et quingenti viri."

33. Mansfield, Humiliation, 145–146.

legedly chose to exhibit their piety rather "than to fight it out with force and arms, preferring to bear with indignation and derision from the people and clergy alike." As usual, their strategy of attrition paid off, since the canons, "fatigued by the filth of arms and the very great expense," eventually withdrew their troops at the end of the week, on Trinity Sunday, carrying their relic and its bower back to the City.[34]

Thanks to this preliminary "play of the bower," we have more information about the context in which Adam's "Play of the Bower" was received, and may even have been performed. We have learned that the summer season from Pentecost (a moveable feast which fell between May 10 and June 13) to the Nativity of the Virgin (September 8) was a busy time of ritual and commercial activity centered on the display of relics, and that the *fiertre* in its bower was a regular occupant of the marketplace through the feast of the Assumption (August 15). It was therefore the near neighbor of the jongleurs' Sainte-Chandelle. Sheltered by its bower, the cathedral's relic chest would have been prominent during the Carité's ritual distribution of holy water on the three evenings inaugurated by its grand siège in the week after Trinity. In fact, it would already have been set up by the time the confraternity held the first of its thrice-annual "drinkings" at Pentecost, and it would be in situ on the eve of the midsummer feast of Saint John the Baptist (June 24), when members of the confraternity "put a wreath of red roses on each of the thirteen apostles who are around the chapel in the Petit Marché," according to the *Ordinance* drafted at least a decade prior to the *Jeu de la feuillée*. The *follye* and the *fiertre* were still in place when the maieurs of the confraternity led the commune of Arras in procession from the Petit Marché to the abbey, where the Sainte-Chandelle was placed on the high altar next to the relics of Saint-Vaast on July 15. And the bower and its relics were there when elaborate preparations were made for the performance of the Carité's founding miracle on Assumption Eve, when a "foursquare arbor decked with greenery" (*parc quarre espardie de verde herbe*) was erected next to the chapel.[35]

The prominence of relics in the marketplace not only helps to explain the setting and props referred to in the *Jeu de la feuillée* but also complicates our received idea of the play's alleged secularism. Just as many modern readers have mistakenly assumed that Saint Acaire and his relics are bogus, they have assumed that the dramatic display of relics in the marketplace was an invention original to the play and therefore intended to appear ridiculous, even blasphemous.[36] Certainly the exposure of relics was a risky business,

34. *Follye*, 201. "Quam ipsos vi et manu armata debellare, tam in clero quam in populo scandalum ponerent et derisum. . . . [S]qualore armorum fatigati et expensis nimiis."

35. *Ordinance*, fol. 6r: "Item on doit meitre le nuit saint iehan sur les .xiij. ap[ost]les qui sont en tour le cappellete v petit markiet sur cascun .i. capel de roses vermeiles."

36. E.g., Roussel, "Notes," 284; Michel Rousse, "Le *Jeu de la feuillée* et les coutumes du cycle de mai," in *Mélanges Charles Foulon* (Rennes, 1980), 313–327 at 323. Dufournet invents a false etymology for "Acaire"; see *Le Jeu*, 13.

since they could become the targets of transgressive behavior, as the monks and canons well knew. At the nearby priory of Aubigny, which was closely associated with Saint-Vaast, parishioners were actually in the habit of seizing the relics of another Irish saint, Killian, from the church and carrying them "outside into a certain public place in Aubigny to be made a spectacle for the people assembled there, daring to profane those relics by involving them in dances among the harvesters and in other disgraceful activities." One such complaint was registered in 1277, and is therefore almost exactly contemporary with the *Jeu de la feuillée*. Moreover, the perpetrators were "not only laymen, but knights," so this was not an incident that could be laid to the charge of ignorant peasants.[37] It bespeaks, in fact, a fascination with relics and their uses which spanned all echelons of society, and helps to explain the function of the bower, which, as I have already explained, provided a type of shelter that was understood to be powerfully significant in and of itself. The canopy of leaves, like the canopied arch of the Gothic cathedral, "implied security," according to Michael Camille. The objects enshrined within it were therefore domesticated, in contrast with profane entities like gargoyles, "whose very isolation in space, jutting out into the street beyond, signals their ungodly ejection from the church." Camille further observes, "The envelope of the arch thus not only contains and protects the figure, it elevates it."[38] By the same token, the presence of the relics would have elevated their surrounding foliage, as well as the places in which they were displayed.

Most "plays of the bower" in thirteenth-century Arras—ludic or liturgical—appear to have been relatively benign. Yet the Pentecostal fracas of 1232 clearly expressed or released pent-up tensions, some of which can be discerned rising to the surface on other occasions involving relics and their rites. A decade before the *Jeu de la feuillée* was composed, the bishop's sergeant was sent to demolish a booth that the monks of Saint-Vaast had built around the time of another Marian feast, Candlemas (February 2), in 1266, on land owned by the abbey in the bishop's City. This may have been a wintertime shelter for relics; it was certainly of great symbolic importance to the monks, since they not only resisted the sergeant's intervention but also seized him, beat him up, and had him imprisoned. The case was later heard in the Parlement of Paris, which found in favor of the bishop—although both sides were told, in no uncertain terms, that instigators of future violence

37. AdPC ser. H "non coté"/Cartulaire du prieuré d'Aubigny, fols. 30v–31r: "nonnulli laici tam milites quam alii predictas reliquias ab ecclesia Albigny in qua sunt contra dictorum prioris et eius con-canonicorum voluntatem. Impisdenter extrahere easdemque in quadam platea publica apud Albigny ad spectaculum publice collocare et easdem reliquias choreis commessatoribus et aliis deformitatibus sicut alias hoc facere presumpserunt prophanare intendiunt." This incident has also been noted by Bernard Delmaire in "Religion festive en Artois au XIIIe siècle," in *Nos ancêtres les paysans: Aspects du monde rurale dans le Nord/Pas de Calais*, ed. R. Muchembled and G. Sivéry (Lille, 1981), 99, and in *Le diocèse*, 1:374. (I have corrected the manuscript foliation cited in both of these studies.)

38. Camille, *Gothic Art*, 38.

would answer to the king's bailiff at Amiens.[39] Even so, battle was joined again at Pentecost two years later, in 1269, further evidence that this was a fraught season in Arras, and one likely to expose the latent stratum of enmity that subsisted between Town and City, abbey and cathedral.[40] Indeed, we have seen that the feast of the Assumption, which marked the end of this season for "acting out," was the occasion on which Count Robert II's companions had caused a major disturbance by loosing a falcon in the cathedral during Mass and vandalizing property belonging to the bishop and chapter, infractions that led to the staging of their public humiliation in the City on the Virgin's Nativity, and thus in the presence of the *fiertre*.

Did Adam de la Halle have such incidents in mind when he composed his own play? And could his "Play of the Bower" have commented on, or contributed to, the volatile atmosphere surrounding reliquaries and their protective structures? Was it performed—as seems quite likely—in the Petit Marché, with the *fiertre* and its folly in full view, juxtaposed with the bower of the fairies and the bush of the tavern, beneath which the Monk is left behind with his relics, in the company of the Dervish and his Father?

Less than a decade after the *Jeu de la feuillée* was produced, the *fiertre* of Notre-Dame was once again a prop in a much more serious "play of the bower," a very literal "plot" (*conspiracio*), described in the official record of the Parlement in Paris as "a *taquehan*," a word that is the ancestor of the modern French noun *taquin*, "a tease," or a malicious prank.[41] This was in 1285, when Adam de la Halle was far away in southern Italy with Count Robert, whose long absences from Arras occasioned a great deal of unrest among those left behind—échevins, comital agents, abbey, and cathedral, as well as townspeople. Astonishingly, we have three separate accounts, representing three very different perspectives: that preserved in the *Olim*, that of the count's bailiff in Artois, and that of the cathedral canons. As the registrar in Paris tells it, "some of the people of the Town carried out a conspiracy or *taquehan* against the échevins and great men of the Town," the object being "a reliquary chest displayed in the marketplace of Arras, sent there out of piety by the chapter of Arras, next to the place where the candle of Blessed Mary is kept and where it is customary for God to work many miracles." According to the *Olim*, these anonymous men seized the chest "impetuously and violently and to the scandal of the whole population, and took it and carried it away from that place." Then, "violently going into the houses of the masters of the guilds," they made off with the guilds' ceremonial standards (*vexilla*) and "stirred up the community of the Town of Arras against the échevins and maieurs, even making armed threats against the échevins and others of the said Town, and running about through the Town with the aforesaid standards, crying out for death, and commit-

39. *Olim*, 1:244–45 (no. 4 within the octave of Candlemas).

40. *Olim*, 1:295 (no. 3 at Pentecost).

41. Godefroy, *Dictionnaire*, 1:781.

ting many other enormities, to the grave peril of the whole Town of Arras." Finally, the wrongdoers sought sanctuary in the abbey of Saint-Vaast, and the monks had to be ordered by the king's court to surrender them to his bailiff.[42]

Further inquiry undertaken by one of the count's agents in 1286, submitted after a public investigation into the state of affairs, clarifies some key aspects of this account, which had been prepared by someone unfamiliar with local politics—though familiar, significantly, with the importance of the *fiertre* and the miracle-working Saint-Chandelle. This second report states explicitly that Arras "is very badly managed in many ways" (*est moult mal menée en moult de cas*) by its échevins, and hints that this mismanagement was the real cause of the uprising. The perpetrators, it reveals, were five men due to be executed, who had escaped from the castellan's prison; and the castellan, himself charged by the échevins with aiding or abetting their escape, was afterward imprisoned at Bapaume. The desperate men had made their way "into the Petit Marché, to the *foillie*, the *fiertre* of Notre-Dame" (*u Petit Marchiet, a la foillie, la fiertre Nostre Dame*), which they then seized and carried into the City, "with evil intent and to the disturbance of the Town and the justice of my lord the Count." Furthermore, they took banners from the houses of the guilds' maieurs "and ran about through the Town, displaying the banners, and crying out death to the échevins and to the rich men, whom they planned to kill and assault as soon as they had seized the keys to all the gates and had closed them and cried their ban."[43] Eventually, some of the men were captured and then hanged, drawn, and beheaded, presumably at the instigation of the échevins. It would be instructive to know where such executions usually took place, but it is safe to presume that the communal gallows and pillory would have been centrally located, perhaps in the Place du Castellan, where the prison was, or possibly in the Grand Marché, where blood was also shed in tournaments, and larger crowds could be accommodated for the sake of the spectacle. After 1315, executions and other forms of punish-

---

42. *Olim*, 1:245 (no. 19 among the cases held after Pentecost): "Cum in villa Attrebatensi quidam de plebe dicte ville, contra scabinos et majores ville Attrebatensis conspiracionem seu *taquehanum* fecissent, capsam reliquiarum plenam in foro Attrebatense, causa devocionis a capitulo Attrebatensi ibi missam, juxta locum ubi candela Beate Marie et reposita et ubi consuetum est a Deo multa miracula operari, impetuose ac violenter et in scandalum tocius populi, cepissent et extra locum detulissent, domosque magistrorum guendarum violenter intrantes, vexilla ipsorum cepissent, et communitatem ville Attrebatensis, contra scabinos et majores movissent, insultum eciam in scabinos et alios dicte ville facientes cum armis, et discurrendo per villam cum vexillis predictes, ad mortem clamantes, et alia plura enormia committentes in grave periculum tocius ville predicte."

43. *Che sunt les besoingnes d'Arras*, ed. Guesnon in "Adam," 219–220: "en l'emportant en Cité en mal et en torblement de la vile et en destourbement de la vile et de la justice Msgr le conte, et prisent les banières chiés les maieurs des geudes, et coururent par le vile, banieres desploiies, et crierent a la mort contre eschevins et contre les riches hommes, et les vaurent ochirre et assalirent et prisent les clés des portes et les fremerent et crierent leur ban."

ment were carried out at the commune's "cross" in the Petit Marché, the erection of which had been sanctioned by the abbey of Saint-Vaast, and for which the townspeople paid yearly homage as part of the same ceremony in which the jongleurs of the Carité disported themselves.[44] This may represent the institutionalization of a more long-standing practice which associated public correction with other public business *a le breteske;* if this is so, the sanctifying presence of the *fiertre* would have charged the scene of judicial bloodshed with additional power.

The third testimony to this "play of the bower" is that of the cathedral canons, who recalled these events a year later. It is less informative than the other two accounts, although it too conveys the impression that the calculated plans of a few historical actors tapped into a deeper vein of popular discontent. Writing to the bishop of Châlons on the octave of the feast of Saints Peter and Paul (July 6) in 1286, the canons announce that they have had a new *fiertre* fashioned to contain the precious relics annually set out for veneration in the Petit Marché, where they "happily increase the benefits accruing to the faithful and contribute to our construction funds," and they allude to an incident caused by "much madness" (*tanta insania*) in the course of the previous summer's display.[45] From their perspective, it seems that "certain cunning men," evidently inspired by Satan, were the instigators of a riot, "which they carried out among the people with scandalous uproar, the insurgents inciting them to crazy things, wielding swords and cudgels in the performance of their aims and dealing out death and confusion among the people who came, in the course of this, into our very church," where some damage was done.[46] Unlike the count's agent, the canons seem uninterested in the causes of the rebellion or the motives of the insurgents, although they are willing to admit that the violence enacted in their cathedral, with the *fiertre* as its object, may have been partly accidental. But they spend more time describing the beauty of the new reliquary and the sanctity of its contents than they do delving into the meaning of events that must surely not have been entirely mysterious to them. Their hyperbolized, almost hysterical account serves a rhetorical purpose only, and was not intended to be coolly inquisitive, as were the appraisals of Parlement and the count's bailiff. Their purpose in writing was to curry favor with a sympathetic bishop, and to publicize upcoming opportunities for pilgrims to obtain indulgences for the veneration of their treasure; they may not have wanted, consequently, to go further into the tangled details of political unrest at home.

44. De Locre, *Chronicon,* 448. See chapter 3.

45. The letter is quoted by De Locre, ibid., 431–432: "ac eorum fidei meritum feliciter augmentandum, ad nostram quoque Fabricam fabricandam."

46. Ibid., 431–432: "illius versutiis qui Sathanas dicitur, tumultu cum scandalo & seditionis Zizaniâ exortis in plebe, eodem actore cum gladiis & fustibus, strage in plebe & nece factis, ad nostram Ecclesiam huismodi sanctuarium, malorum more, partim cassum, partim fractum, per incuriam forsan raptum, pertumultus rabiem partimque concussum inhumaniter, reportarunt."

Clearly, a great deal was going on in Arras around Pentecost of 1285, though it is hard to determine precisely *what*. On the one hand, the *Olim* refers to the central incident as a popular plot; on the other, it suggests that the actions of the key perpetrators were "impetuous" and impassioned, not planned. This was very much the impression that the canons also received, or that they wanted to convey to the outside world. Then, the casual mention in two of the reports of the monks' provision of sanctuary (and the canons' silence on this topic) are suggestive, and may help to explain the charge of conspiracy leveled in the *Olim* and that of "cunning" articulated by the canons. The bailiff's inquiry reveals that the five men in question had been imprisoned by the communal government of Arras, which was later cited for abuse of justice during the count's absence. The monks, either sympathetic to the insurgents' plight and/or seeing a way to pay back injuries they had sustained at the hands of commune and count, may have forced or bribed the castellan to release his prisoners while making it known that they would find a safe haven at the abbey: they had done this sort of thing in the past, and would again.[47] Moreover, a letter from Philip III preserved in the abbey's sixteenth-century cartulary, dated January 1284, shows that the monks had taken advantage of the count's absence in order to renew their claim to the exercise of high justice within their *castrum*, and it may have been on these grounds that they released the prisoners.[48] Perhaps they also encouraged the condemned men to steal the *fiertre* and carry it back to the cathedral, where it belonged: note that the keeper of the record in Parlement was not apprised of the fact that the insurgents' first action was to do so, while the canons regarded the reliquary chest and the church of Notre-Dame as the main targets all along. Were the monks thereby registering another protest against the cathedral? Were they also supportive of the civil unrest that followed, or did the situation get out of hand?

While it is impossible to offer a definitive interpretation of this episode or its place in the history of Arras, it is clear that the principles of equal association and mutual support which had informed the establishment of the twelfth-century commune had been severely eroded by the third quarter of the thirteenth century, as the wealth of the Town's great banking families and their political influence expanded. The office of the commune's *maieur* had become a largely hereditary honor, possibly in the gift of the count. And although the échevinage was still an elected body whose members held office for a fourteen-month term, it was reconstituted as an *eschevinage nouvel* prior to Robert II's departure for the kingdom of Sicily in August 1282: this according to the report, made in 1286, suggesting that the échevins were now accountable directly to the count.[49] There is also good

---

47. See chapters 3 and 5.

48. These disputes were renewed after Robert's return, in 1296 and in 1299. See AdPC ser. 1 H.1, fols. 184v, 188r.

49. The contemporary memorandum enumerating *Les besoingnes d'Arras* says that the count "fist

evidence to suggest that the échevinage, in the year immediately prior to this incident, was raising taxes and cracking down on "foreigners" resident in Arras—recent immigrants or poorer residents who were evading taxes by not placing themselves formally under the *bannum* of the town. A petition submitted on January 17, 1284, testifies that it had recently been "decided and ordered and commanded by the échevins of Arras" that all those "who were not or who did not want to be numbered among the townspeople of Arras should leave the Town of Arras." At the same time, the échevins were once again tightening the screws on minor clerics, whose commercial activities were being more and more closely scrutinized; they were so insistent that Philip IV intervened to back the clerics' privileges in August 1284.[50]

Furthermore, it appears that the trade guilds which had been established in the early part of the century were periodically "forbidden" after 1253—although the sole reference to this is an oblique entry in a series of "extracts from old books" made by a modern antiquary.[51] At the same time, a powerful corporation known as the Vintaine, or "the Twenty," had been put in place by 1242, established to oversee the various branches of the cloth industry.[52] Two of the three accounts of the *taquehan* in 1285 clearly indicate that guilds continued to exist—or had, perhaps, been revived—since it was in the houses of their "masters" (*magistri* in the *Olim*) or maieurs (according to the bailiff) that the guilds' standards were kept. But the events of the uprising suggest that the guilds may have been reorganized in such a way as to place more power in the hands of certain élite representatives of each craft, who were in the habit of keeping the potent symbols of corporate solidarity (the banners) in their own houses rather than in the guilds' halls; hence, these maieurs were among the "big men" (*maiori*) or "rich men" (*riches hommes*) targeted by the escaped prisoners and their supporters after Pentecost in 1285.

The fact that Pentecost was a time already reserved for the expression of tensions within this very complex society—the *Jeu de la feuillée* itself can be and has been read as a scathing commentary on social injustice—illuminates the symbolic importance attached to the *fiertre* without fully explaining all the ramifications of the events that took place around it. As Steven Justice has shown in his analysis of the English peasants' rising in 1381, that rebellion was timed for Corpus Christi precisely because it was a day for the air-

---

l'eschevinage nouvel en son praiel." See the text edited by Guesnon in "Adam," 219–220. The names of the échevins in office at the time of Robert's departure in 1282 are listed in the record of the inquest held in 1289: AdPC ser. A 1009, ed. Guesnon, in "Adam," 222–233 at 223–224.

50. *Cartulaire*, 43–44: "Comme jadiz fust atiré et ordené et commandé par les echevins d'Arraz qui en ce temps estoient que tout cil qui n'estoient ou ne voloient estre de la bourgeoisie d'Arraz widassent la ville d'Arraz."

51. These notes by Claude Doresmieux were later recopied by Adophe Guesnon: "furent les caritez deffendues en Arras." See Berger, *Littérature*, 84, n. 536.

52. Guesnon, "Adam," 183; Berger, *Littérature*, 69, 83.

ing of social, political, and economic grievances, although this was usually accomplished through the dramatization of violence, not by actual violence.[53] Whitsuntide obviously served a similar function in thirteenth-century Arras, with the Carité's grand siège, which fell ten days after Pentecost itself, later coinciding with the feast of Corpus Christi. Given that the monks appear to have been responsible for the prisoners' release, are we to understand that they were behind the conspiracy, its timing, and its targets? Or do we see in this incident a mixture of motives, monastic and popular, united in a common cause? Like the peasant rebels of Kent and Essex, who selected certain people, documents, and buildings as the objects of violence in June 1381, the escaped prisoners of Arras and those who rallied to their cause seem to have been making a series of powerful gestures which may have been carefully calibrated in advance, and which were the necessary preliminaries to any seizure of power. Yet, unlike the appropriation of the guilds' banners and the attempt to close the Town's gates, the symbolic significance of the *fiertre* in this "play of the bower" is not obvious. Did it offer a type of portable sanctuary, guaranteeing the prisoners' safety while they revenged themselves upon the communal officers and men of local industry who had imprisoned them, perhaps for seditious attempts to strengthen the guilds? Or had the display of the *fiertre* in its *follye* become associated with the oppressions of a new plutocracy? After all, it was housed in the Petit Marché as a moneymaking venture. Was it therefore an act of piety to rescue the Virgin's reliquary and return it (albeit somewhat roughly) to her cathedral, before breaking into private houses and bringing out the banners that symbolized the workers' *bannum*, the power they derived from being able to act in a corporate body, which either had been denied to them since 1253 or was being newly withheld since the departure of the count three years earlier?

The absence of the count, like the involvement of the monks, is certainly significant; on his return to Arras in 1291, Robert would be busy responding to crises that had arisen in the interim and had been mounting since his coming of age. As I have already noted, the delicate balance of powers that had been achieved in Arras following its annexation in 1191 had been somewhat disturbed by the establishment of the county of Artois in 1237, but not very much; the first Count Robert had merely pressed his claims to a share of the abbey's *tonlieu* and had performed certain ceremonial functions as the count of Artois, but he never took up permanent residence in the town and hardly ever used his comital title, preferring to style himself "fils du roi" in his charters.[54] When he died in 1250, leaving an infant heir, the county was ruled in absentia by the boy's mother, Mahaut of Brabant. But after Robert attained his majority and showed himself willing and able to take an active role in governance, the competition among representatives of the commune, the cathe-

---

53. Justice, *Writing*, 147–169.

54. Menche de Loisne, "Catalogue," 138–139 (nos. 1 and 2); Richebé, *Les monnaies*, 52, 137, 172 (no. 33), and plate 8.

dral, and the abbey flared up, perhaps because there was now a smaller share of power to be divided among these older institutions, owing not only to the young count's energetic exercise of authority (see chapter 5) but also to the agency of newer corporations, such as the guilds and confraternities. We have already seen that the Carité's extraordinary position derived, in part, from its capacity to mediate among these powers. In turn, this suggests that the *Jeu de la feuillée*, if it *was* devised for performance by the Carité, may have been intended to intervene in the ongoing process of these powers' reconciliation—aided by the intercession of the Virgin, whose presence in the Pyramide of the Petit Marché was effectively doubled between Pentecost and Assumption Day, when her *fiertre* was on display next door.

What happened in the decade that followed the composition of this play, which saw the performance of other "plays of the bower"? Did Adam, "sighing in a foreign land" (*souspirant en terre estrange*), get wind of the renewed unrest at home? The *taquehan* of 1285 had occurred when he was busily occupied under the patronage of Count Robert at the court of King Charles of Sicily, perhaps at the very time when he was devising the *Jeu de Robin et de Marion*, in which violence is contained by laughter, games, and music. The second strophe of one of his five extant motets suggests that he did know of it, or at least of the troubles that had been brewing since he had left Arras in August 1282: it is the complaint of a loyal lover constantly betrayed, who turns a song of farewell and longing into an angry commentary on the dire situation in Arras. Bidding adieu to all his unnamed amours, the singer commends them to God and tells his audience that he is mourning for the "sweet little ones" (*douchettes*), so far from "the sweet country of Artois" (*douc païs d'Artois*), which is now "so silenced and distraught" (*si mus et destrois*) because the townspeople have been deprived of their rights and laws, since the greed for money (*Gros tournois*) has blinded "counts and kings" (*contes et rois*) to their plight.[55] It is a song intended to capture the attention of those patrons whom he could not address directly on such topics, and reinforces the subtext of social injustice informing the *Jeu de Robin et de Marion*. Two of Adam's monophonic songs strike a similar chord, praying to the Virgin on behalf of those needing protection from the clergy's pride and gluttony, the monks' envy and avarice, and the robbery and rapacity of knights.[56]

These poetic petitions had an effect, or at least bore the same burden as petitions that did. A year or two later, just after Adam's death and two years prior to Robert's return to the Artois in 1289, the count's agents made a formal inquest into numerous allegations against the échevinage, which included wrongful imprisonment, harsh and unusual punishments, the sale of offices and privileges to unfit men, and the acceptance of bribes—

---

55. "Aucun se sont loé d'Amours," in AHOEc, 196–199.

56. "Qui a puchele ou dame amee" and "Glorieuse Vierge Marie," in AHOEc, 104–107 and 118–121, respectively.

including the sum total of 1,200 livres for the making of false charters. Worst of all, the échevins were accused of having made an example of the first courageous man who publicly stood up to these abuses *en plaine hale*, in the open air and in the presence of the assembled townspeople, whose collective deposition of grievance was headed by the harrowing story of his mistreatment. This was one Jehans Cabos, who had often "reprimanded and denounced the échevins and their misdeeds, as well as their accounts," and whose testimony "the commons in great plenty had marked well, and vouched for his word and all that he had shown." In consequence of this very public defiance, and its public support, Jehans had been "apprehended by night" and imprisoned "uglily and villanously" among thieves and murderers, deprived even of those criminals' right to post bail and further denied the opportunity to speak with anyone, "neither his wife nor his household nor his parents nor his friends," for twelve whole days, while he "saw neither sun nor moon." Thereafter, it was thought best to remove him from Arras altogether, so he was transferred stealthily to an even worse prison in Saint-Omer, and from thence taken in the dark hours before dawn "by false ways and by false paths" to Aubigny, to "the ugliest prison that anyone knew of in any part of the world, three floors below ground, which no one would have spent three days in for 3,000 livres." (The deposition preserves the conditions of its making: one hears many outraged voices contributing to its composition, especially in clauses like this one.)[57] Evidently, the échevins were willing to stoop to torture in order to keep the people of Arras from rallying around a common cause with the help of the Blessed Virgin, whose *fiertre* had been viewed by the insurgents of 1285 as a safeguard against the cruelty of such "big men." Their vile efforts did not, in the end, succeed. The memory of past wrongs continued to be publicly voiced, as did the verses of Adam de la Halle, and the count of Artois heeded their call.

57. AdPC ser. A 1009: "A sages homes et honestes ki en Arras estes venut de le volonté et du consentement mon signeur d'Artois pour enkuerre et pour savoir l'estat de le vile d'Arras. . . . Si vos disons que Jehans Cabos par pluseurs fois en plaine hale, devant eskievins, le consel de le vile et du kemin de le vile . . . reprendoit et [blasmoit] les eskievins de leur mesfais, si comme de leur contes . . . et dont li kemuns [a grant ple]nté si paiioient bien et awouoient bien se parole et tout chou k'il moustoit. Et eskievin l'aquellirent si en hé ke il le fisent prendre nuitantre par x sierjans le conte et metre en prison si laidement et si vilainement ke avoec larons et larnesses, ne ne pooit mi avoir biele warde par ais le sien, aussi comme li laron et li mourdreur ont, ne se feme ne se maisnie ne se parens ne amis ne peurent onkes a lui parler en xii jours, ne ne vit lune ne solel. Et . . . le prisent en cele prison, entour matines . . . et le misent en le plus laid prison de Saint-Omer. . . . Et commanda a ces meismes serjans ke on le ramenast a Aubigny, et le fisent oster de le prison ii liues devant le jour . . . et l'amenerent par fauses voies et par fauses sentiers . . et le misent a Aubigny en le plus laide prison c'on sache nule part [u] monde, iii estages desous tiere, ne ne vausist avoir esté iii jous pour iii mil lb." See Guesnon, "Adam," 221–222.

Carnival in Embryo?

Casting about for the medieval antecedents of François Rabelais's *Gargantua* and *Pantagruel*, Mikhail Bakhtin saw in the *Jeu de la feuillée* a primordial and "remarkable example of a purely carnivalesque vision" containing "in embryonic form many aspects of Rabelais' world."[58] It is easy to see why he was so impressed: nonlinear in narrative, catholic in taste, the play ridicules convention, trifles with the holy, and ultimately deconstructs its own plot. It appears to be a prototypical carnival play. Yet according to Bakhtin, "carnival" was supposed to be a distillation of folk culture and a rejection of religion and order, an embrace of the grotesque and the unruly, a season when "the authority of the official realm of Church and state [was] suspended, with all its norms and values."[59] Highly influential, this thesis galvanized a generation of cultural historians, especially those of medieval and early modern France, and continues to inform the work of literary critics and theater scholars. More recently it has informed the widely read theories of Jürgen Habermas. But as Aron Gurevich has pointed out, its formulation owed more to Bakhtin's own experiences in Stalinist Russia than it did to his reading of Rabelais or Adam de la Halle.[60] How applicable is it to the *Jeu de la feuillée* and to the theater of thirteenth-century Arras?

"The Play of the Bower" actually combines all the elements that Bakhtin regarded as polar opposites: the popular and the aristocratic, the spontaneous and the institutional, the festive and the liturgical, the profane and the sacred. Its script insists that it was staged in the presence of a powerful relic, which means that it could have been viewed as performed under the aegis of the Blessed Virgin herself. It has survived to become the object of scholarly interest because it was preserved in an expensive manuscript commissioned by an affluent patron and produced by some of the most skilled scribes in Europe. Moreover, we have seen that other "plays of the bower" which took place in Arras during the thirteenth century happened at times of the year that Bakhtin would not associate with carnival, and were the products of a very mixed milieu: urban, regional, royal, mercantile, communal, comital, episcopal, popular, and monastic. If any of these plays is carnivalesque, it is a carnival that does not readily conform to Bakhtin's conception or to the many studies based on it, such as Emmanuel LeRoy Ladurie's description of carnival in Ro-

---

58. Bakhtin, *Rabelais*, 15.

59. Ibid., 259. Ungureanu, who could not have read Bakhtin's book, nevertheless cherished a similar theory, while at the same time refusing to believe that Adam de la Halle could have been the play's author (*La bourgeoisie*, 110–111, 196, 211).

60. Aron Gurevich, "Bakhtin and His Theory of Carnival," in *A Cultural History of Humour: From Antiquity to the Present Day*, ed. Jan Bremmer and Herman Roodenburg (Oxford, 1997), 54–60 at 55–58. See also Yelena Mazour-Matusevich, "Writing Medieval History: An Interview with Aron Gurevich," *Journal of Medieval and Early Modern Studies* 35 (2005): 121–157; and Thomas J. Farrell, *Bakhtin and Medieval Voices* (Gainesville, 1995), 1–14.

mans.[61] They are not so much "embryonic" of "Rabelais' world" as expressive of indigenous tensions in their own. The *follye* of the small marketplace in Arras became the catalyst and target of spiritual, political, and social unrest because it occupied and enhanced a space both holy and public; and as such, it was put to various uses that could conceivably be said to "perpetuate certain values of the community (even guarantee its survival), and on the other hand criticize political order," as Natalie Zemon Davis has said of carnivalesque activity in early modern France.[62] Yet among the most visible participants in these activities were some conservative upholders of the status quo, the abbey of Saint-Vaast and the cathedral of Notre-Dame, in creative and often uneasy alliance with popular factions, potential criminals, and (as occasion suited) any royal, comital, or communal officers whose own powers were in need of positive reinforcement.

In other words, thirteenth-century Arras had no monolithic "Church and state," no single "political order" of a kind understandable to either contemporaries of Rabelais or followers of Bakhtin. Not only was it medieval, not modern, but also it was odd, a place where jongleurs had a "lordship" and control of a powerful cult. This world was perpetually topsy-turvy, and "the world of Carnival" depends on an everyday world of strict confinement for its periodic existence.[63] The *Jeu de la feuillée*, Bakhtin's locus classicus, therefore undermines its own paradigm. In this sense, it *is* truly—gloriously—carnivalesque; but it cannot be "purely carnivalesque" in Bakhtin's sense unless it is cleansed of contemporary associations, cut from its cultural frame, and isolated from its manuscript context.

In Arras and elsewhere, the institutional boundary lines that produced Bakhtin's carnival were still undrawn during the thirteenth century, and there were not even fixed temporal boundaries within which it could be contained. The Church had not yet arrived at a universal consensus with regard to the beginning of the Lenten fast, so the "Battle between Carnival and Lent" which was so productive of the visual and performing arts in the sixteenth century was not yet raging.[64] Once again, we see that a medieval theater is not governed by binary oppositions of this familiar, modern kind. Is Dame Douce being deliberately vague when she says that her pregnancy was conceived "a little before Lent," or is she really uncertain as to when it began? In any case, the distinction meant little in the North, where there were many times throughout the year when the impulses and practices of carnival found expression. These included Quadragesima Sunday, which marked the

61. Emmanuel LeRoy Ladurie, *Le carnaval de Romans: De la Chandeleur au mercredi des Cendres, 1579–1580* (Paris, 1979).

62. Natalie Zemon Davis, "The Reasons of Misrule," in *Society and Culture in Early Modern France* (Stanford, 1975), 97.

63. Burke, *Popular Culture*, 182.

64. Mansfield, *Humiliation*, 137–141 and 154–155. See also Jacques Heers, *Fêtes, jeux et joutes dans les sociétés d'occident à la fin du moyen-âge* (Montreal, 1971), 53–55.

forty days before Easter and was technically the first Sunday of Lent, yet was anything but Lenten in its regional observance. It was called "Brandons" in the vernacular, from the torches borne through the streets and fields (purifying them with fire), or "Béhourdis," from the wooden lances brandished by revelers in the jousting matches known as *hastiludia*.[65] Its imagery appears to have been an important influence on the actions of those who took part in the uprising of 1285, and it is also possible that the tournament described by Crokesos in the *Jeu de la feuillée* should be understood as a fight with wooden swords. Indeed, the "Lenten" carnival of Quadragesima was also called the *fête de la folie*, as were the feasts of Saint John the Baptist (June 24) and Saint Christopher (July 25), and the feast of the Assumption (August 15), when similar forms of merrymaking occurred.[66] Pentecost was a season of carnival, too, hosting tournaments and dubbings, crown-wearings, community caroling, and other rites.[67] So was the entire month of May, when townspeople, peasants, and courtiers all took pleasure in gathering flowers and branches, asserting the "right of Maying," which was a jealously guarded universal privilege—as the boys of Saint-Omer demonstrated to the new count of Flanders in the spring of 1127, according to Galbert of Bruges, and as the citizens of two villages in the Ostrevant discovered in the 1230s, when they lost their *droit de Mariole* in the court of the count of Hainaut, a result of their extravagant misbehavior at that season.[68]

Furthermore, there is no indication, in the sources from Arras or anywhere else in the North, that these activities were socially segregated. The relics of Aubigny were stolen to join the dances of villagers *and* knights. The display of relics in the marketplace of Arras inspired many different kinds of foolish behavior, as well as many pious practices, in keeping with the premise of Pentecost, which commemorated the day on which the fire of divine inspiration had descended upon the disciples of Jesus in the marketplace of Jerusalem, so that representatives "from every nation under heaven" heard the Gospel, each in his own language (Acts 2).

Any theory of carnival that hinges on the strict regulation of behavior is thus inapplicable to the reality of the way times and seasons were observed in medieval communities, at least prior to the mid-fourteenth century. This is not to say that some days were not considered holier than others; but the range of meanings attached to the very words denoting "holy day" (or "holiday"), "feast" (or "fête"), betrays this ambiguity. The appropriate manner of observing these days was open to local interpretation, in keeping with the spirit

65. Juliet R. V. Barker, *The Tournament in England, 1100–1400* (Woodbridge, U.K., 1986), 148–149; Richard Barber and Juliet Barker, *Tournaments: Jousts, Chivalry, and Pageants in the Middle Ages* (New York, 1989), 179.

66. Mansfield, *Humiliation*, 141 and 154; Heers, *Fêtes*, 53–55; Warning, *Funktion*, 18–19.

67. Mansfield, *Humiliation*, 151; Rousse, "Le Jeu de la feuillée," 316–327.

68. Galbert of Bruges, *De multro*, c. 66. See Geoffrey Koziol, "England, France, and the Problem of Sacrality in Twelfth-Century Ritual," in Bisson, *Cultures*, 124–148. See also Delmaire, *Le diocèse*, 1:373.

of a liturgical calendar which had, from its earliest inception, been designed for maximum flexibility and cultural consonance, so that practices of playing and of worship which appear contradictory to us were really coincident. As Lambert of Liège found, to his annoyance, more than two thirds of all the games played during the week were played on Sunday, the only day of leisure.[69] Rather than trying to beat the gaming spirit, he joined in. His strategy therefore differed little from that of the Church at large, which had so thoroughly digested so many pagan holidays and natural rhythms of the agricultural year that its achievement often escapes notice, as in Jacques LeGoff's influential theory of the different worldviews supposedly produced by peasants' time, merchants' time, and Church time, a theory which ignores the fact that the Church's schedule had long been arranged to accommodate the needs of the peasant, while successful mercantile ventures inevitably tied themselves, with evident success, to the Church. Many markets were occasional, and as such they depended not just on the protection of temporal lords but on the patronage of the saints, while the great fairs were annual or biennial events held during the octaves of important feasts.[70] And in many places, including Arras, the very spaces reserved for trading were the special province of a saint or his earthly executors. Everyone knew which saints were important because of the days when markets were held, and vice versa.[71] The uses of time were therefore as malleable as the uses of space.

Just as they have endowed the antitheatrical fulminations of a beleaguered Tertullian or a guilt-ridden Augustine with the power to close the theaters of Rome, so have scholars of medieval drama allowed the vitriol of later theologians to limit the possibilities of a common stage. We are told that plays were "driven out" of churches after Innocent III prohibited "theatrical plays" (ludi theatrales) in a letter to the archbishop of Gnesen, dated two days after Epiphany in 1207, when Christmas festivities would have just drawn to a close. But when this letter was eventually copied into the decretal collection of Gregory IX in 1234, an added gloss makes it clear that this ban did not include liturgical plays of the kind familiar to most medieval audiences, and that Innocent's target was secular entertainments irreverently performed in church, which was the only convenient gathering-place, either indoors or out, in most medieval communities.[72] And there is little evidence to suggest that this prohibition was enforced. In fact, there is ample evidence to suggest that it was unenforceable.

More specifically, it is not possible to argue that the "birth" of "profane" theater in Arras, or anywhere else, was engendered by restrictions placed on the use of church space, or that a "tavern-church dichotomy is inscribed on the geography and history of the town

69. Mehl, Les jeux, 237–249 and tables 20 and 23.

70. Derville, L'économie, 170; Carpentier and Le Mené, La France, 189.

71. Murray, "Time and Money," 24–25; contra Le Goff, "Au Moyen Age."

72. The relevant canons are cited in Young, Drama, 2:416–417.

just as it is on the scenography and history of the theater," as Guy Paoli asserts.[73] There was no such dichotomy for most of the Middle Ages. It can actually be proved that very few ludic pastimes took place in taverns. Most types of play required light, and thus occurred during the day, usually after the midday meal, and in well-lit locations, often out of doors. Only dice games, especially the Hasard of Jehan Bodel's thieves and Arras's Courtois, could be played at night or in the murky confines of the tavern (where the chronic darkness, either real or pretended, may be another factor adding to the confusion over scorekeeping in the Jeu de saint Nicolas). Other games, particularly those we might call mimetic, were best played in the open, which meant in marketplaces, fields, streets, cemeteries, and cloisters. Moreover, the ideological and physical space between the church and the outside world could just as well be construed as a gray area, or a continuum.[74] How else could Saint Nicholas appear to thieves in a tavern or the Prudhomme pray to the saint of market forces? How else could the parable of the Prodigal Son be played out in the setting (real or imagined) of a tavern, and a chapel be founded in the marketplace of Arras, in and around which the liturgy was overseen by jongleurs? God met Mammon regularly, both in the medieval marketplace and in the churches of Christendom. The canons of the cathedral of Arras fought picaresquely to safeguard their relic and to defend the establishment of a market in their cloister; at the same time, there was a tavern in Arras that kept the cathedral's Feast of Fools all year long, the "Bishop of Asses" (Evesque des asnes).[75] So an anonymous sermon preached around 1200 in Latin and Picard made a casual comparison between frequent confession and the wine sold in a tavern (the vernacular portions are quoted in italics): "There are some who make their confession *in bulk*, just as merchants sell bread and wine *in bulk*. But it should not be done this way; rather it should be *by the glass* or *à la carte—each sin by itself and in its circumstances. That way, it will be like the taverner who sells by the glass, because he makes more that way, than if he sold in bulk."[76]* Far from condemning the taverner's practice, the preacher holds it up as an analogy for thrifty spirituality.

A medieval tavern may have been "a place of free speech," as the Comédie-Française billed it, but it cannot have been the original performance venue of the *Jeu de la feuillée.* Me-

73. Paoli, "Taverne," 82.

74. McSheffrey, "Place," 975–983. Barbara D. Palmer has exploded the myth that plays were usually performed in taverns or innyards, even in the sixteenth century; Palmer, "Early Modern Mobility: Players, Payments, and Patrons," *Shakespeare Quarterly* 56 (2005): 259–305 at 282–284.

75. Delmaire, *Le diocèse*, 1:372.

76. BnF lat. 14925, fol. 127: "Quidam sunt qui faciunt confessionem suam *en gros*, sicut mercatores vendunt pannos vel vinum en gros; sed non est sic facienda, imo *a broche, sive a detail, chascun peché par se et la circonstance; autresi, come li taverners qui vent a broche, quar plus i gaigne que se il vendet en gros.*" Excerpted from a codex of sermons by Alain of Lille and others; see Hauréau, *Notices,* 316. On preachers' frequent use of taverns—as spaces and as metaphors for preaching—see Bériou, *La prédication,* 537–540.

dieval taverns were small and dark. Even if the bower of the play's *explicit* does refer to the "bush" advertising the sale of wine, as well as to the Virgin's bower, it still makes more sense to imagine it performed in the Petit Marché, with the tavern as tiring-house and set. (In fifteenth-century Saint-Omer, which also had two marketplaces, the Golden Eagle tavern in the smaller of these is often cited as the backdrop for plays, which were performed in front of it, on the *place*.)[77] I have already suggested as much for the *Jeu de saint Nicolas*, regardless of whether or not this play was ultimately linked to the saint's major feast on December 6, as the supplementary prologue alleges. For it does not appear to me that performance on this date "precludes an outdoor site," presumably because of the cold.[78] There can have been little difference in temperature between the interior of a limestone church and the marketplace of Arras, which still hosts a winter carnival beginning on the eve of Saint Nicholas's day. Indeed, Jean-Michel Mehl has demonstrated that three times as many games were played during the month of December as in any other month, and these included as many outdoor pursuits as indoor ones; William FitzStephen's description of winter sports in late-twelfth-century London corroborates this. If we *do* entertain conjecture of an indoor venue, the only likely one in Jehan Bodel's lifetime would have been a church, possibly the cathedral, and this alone defuses any notion of the "church-tavern dichotomy" mooted earlier, since a tavern would then be contained within a church, as it was in yearly productions of Nativity plays.

In any case, churches throughout Latin Christendom provided the space as well as the time for winter carnivals when they framed the youthful follies performed in honor of the Holy Innocents (December 28) or on the feast of the Circumcision (New Year's Day) or at Epiphany (January 6), as Innocent III's ill-humored missive testifies.[79] The election of a Boy Bishop at this season was a custom widely observed in cathedral towns, and one of the mock-prelate's first duties was to go in procession to the bishop's palace to demand a reckoning of the incumbent's conduct of affairs.[80] When this occurred in Arras, the cathedral would then be handy for the production of a play about a bishop and his questionable accounting practices. Perhaps this is how Adam de la Halle first came to know the *Jeu de saint Nicholas*, and perhaps this is why it eventually found its way into the scripted commemoration of his life in the theater, along with the *Jeu de la feuillée*. Why shouldn't the role of the saint have been played by the Boy Bishop, if not in the original production

77. Justine de Pas, "Mystères et jeux scéniques à Saint-Omer aux XVe et XVIe siècles," *MSAM* 31 (1913): 345–377 at 364–365.

78. Tydeman, *Theater*, 67.

79. Mehl, *Les jeux*, 227 and 231–232 (aable 19), and "Games in Their Seasons," trans. Thomas Pettitt in *Custom, Culture, and Community in the Later Middle Ages: A Symposium*, ed. Thomas Pettitt and Leif Søndergaard (Odense, 1994), 71–83. See also Fassler, "Feast of Fools," 69–74.

80. Fassler "Feast of Fools," 70–71. See, e.g., the Paduan *episcopellus* ceremony printed in Young, *Drama*, 2:100.

conceived by Jehan Bodel, at least in subsequent revivals at the Feast of Fools or on the eve of the saint's feast, as the play's later prologue declares? I have shown that Jehan may have modeled his usurious saint on Bishop Raoul "Hornèd Hat," and that the thrifty bishop may have taken this in good part, since he subsequently left a generous legacy for the care of independent lepers; it may have been he who supported Jehan's own independence for the eight years between his retirement and his death in 1210. If the play *was* conceived for performance by choirboys at a time of constructive misbehavior, then its often pointed political commentary—its representation of the king of France as a rapacious pagan prince, its forthright acknowledgment of the bishop's support for big business—would have been both sanctioned and softened. Placing the play in this context not only helps to explain it but also helps to explain Adam de la Halle's connection with it: as a choirboy at the cathedral, he may have performed in it many times.

Contemporary evidence for the flexible placement and timing of *theatrica* is vitally important to our understanding of the *Jeu de la feuillée* and its possible meanings, which are in part dependent on conjectures about the occasion of its performance. According to Bakhtin, the play's social agenda (similar, perhaps, to his own) made it appropriate for May 1, a significant date in Russia in 1940, when his theory of carnival was first articulated, and in 1965, when it was finally published.[81] A similar idea was attractive to the re-founding members of the confraternity of Notre Dame des Ardents, but for very different reasons. They celebrated May 1, 1876, as the sexcentenary of the play's premiere, on the basis of their association of its fairy visitation with the apparition of fairies and the reenactment of "traditional" medieval May games.[82] Other scholars who have placed the play's performance in May have attempted to associate it with the springtime feast of Saint Nicholas on May 9.[83] And apparently a Breton confraternity dedicated to Saint Nicholas did observe that day in a particularly seasonal manner by the middle of the fourteenth century, gathering to hear Mass and then riding out into the forest before returning home "with branches of leaves and flowers, and to make up stories about anything at all for entertainment before going in to dinner," stories that were evidently scripted prior to performance, since "he who makes the rhymes for the story" (*celui qui fera les rimmes de listoire*) was awarded a sum of money.[84] Many of the ingredients one might imagine as contribut-

81. Bakhtin, *Rabelais*, 59. Gurevich, "Bakhtin," 55–58.

82. Cavrois, *Cartulaire*, 35–36. See Joel-Henri Grisward, "Les fées, l'aurore et la fortune (mythologie indo-européenne et *Jeu de la feuillée*)," in *Études de langue et de littérature françaises offertes à André Lanly* (Nancy, 1980), 121–136.

83. Guesnon, "Adam," 204. See also the "theatrical calendar" of André de Mandach, "Le rôle du théâtre dans une nouvelle conception de l'évolution des genres," *Stylistique, rhétorique et poétique dans les langues romanes* 8 (1986): 27–46 at 36–37.

84. "Item devent les dits freres aler touz a cheval por chacun an a matin aupres la messe le jour de la dite feste hors de la ville, le plus coitement que ils pourront ot retourner en la ville o branches de foilles

ing to the genesis of the *Jeu de la feuillée* are here: greenery and flowers (*branches de foilles et de flours*), made-up stories, a contest for poets. Yet the local ones are missing, most notably the *fiertre*, which was not on display in Arras until the Sunday of Pentecost, which could fall no earlier in the year than May 10 and would therefore never coincide with the feast of Saint Nicholas. (That said, a local tradition associating the Carité with the cult of Saint Nicholas had certainly grown up by the sixteenth century, when the practice of displaying the *fiertre* in its *follye* had fallen into abeyance and the plays of Jehan and Adam were forgotten. In 1581 a witness noted that the story of the Sainte-Chandelle was the subject of a fifteen-panel wall painting in the parish church of Saint-Nicolas.)[85]

Misunderstanding the Latin text describing the first "play of the bower" in 1232, Ungureanu opted for a possible performance on the feast of the Assumption, having noted that the Carité's *Ordinance* calls for the building of an arbor the evening before.[86] But that was to showcase the Virgin's apparition in yet another "play of the bower," as we shall see. Roger Berger also concluded that the *Jeu de la feuillée* was intended for performance by the Carité, but at its grand siège. He accordingly calculated the date of its first performance as June 3, 1276; actually, it should be June 4.[87] Yet he located the performance not in the Petit Marché but in the Carité's hall, a room reported to have been some twenty-five meters long, a generous size for the time but hardly large enough to support a cast of twelve and all the spectators who would be gathered to celebrate the grand siège.[88] And why would the confraternity go to the trouble of re-creating the sightlines, soundscapes, settings, and associations ready-to-hand in the Petit Marché, where the ritual consecration of the Sainte-Chandelle's potion would have taken place that very day? It was there that the bushy signs of numerous taverns would have underscored the ambiguity of the play's message and rivaled the bower of Notre-Dame, where the *fiertre* was displayed. In my opinion, any evening in the Petit Marché between Pentecost and Assumption would achieve the desired effects.[89] What the presence of powerful relics might mean for the carnivalesque content of Bakhtin's locus classicus, however, is now open to question.

---

et de flours, et faire hystoires d'aucunes choussez pour esbalement avant aler disner." L'Abbé Gallard, *Les trouvères guerrandais et la fête de saint Nicolas, aux XIVe siècle: Chronique rimée inédite* (Nantes, n.d.), 2–3.

85. *Épigraphie*, 2:742–743 (no. 1830 bis); Terninck, *Notre-Dame du Joyel*, 261.

86. Ungureanu, *La bourgeoisie*, 85, 206–207.

87. Berger, *Littérature*, 114–116. The error is politely noted by Badel, AHOEc, 22.

88. *Ordinance*, fols. 2r–3v. See also Cavrois, *Cartulaire*, 37.

89. This was also the view of Edmond Faral, expressed in *Histoire de la littérature française illustrée*, ed. Joseph Bédier and Paul Hazard, 2 vols. (Paris, 1923–24), 1:82. See also Gsell, "Das 'Jeu de la feuillée,'" 93–95.

Carité and Puy

In direct opposition to all theories of the *Jeu de la feuillée*'s popular appeal, radical politics, and association with the confraternity of jongleurs is that which ascribes it to another milieu entirely: a courtly one. The conversation between the Dervish and his Father, in which a "prince of the *puy*" presides over song-making contests, and the later exchange between Crokesos and Morgue, in which that prince is said to have jousted in the marketplace, have over the past two centuries spawned an independent "literary society, elegant and worldly," which supposedly set itself up in opposition to the jongleurs' Carité.[90] Arguments in favor of its existence are essentially circular. "The Puy" was founded to encourage the "writing" of poetry and jeux-partis during the thirteenth century; jeux-partis and poetry certainly survive in manuscripts of the fourteenth and fifteenth centuries, some mentioning a *puy*; therefore "the Puy" must have been established to encourage their publication, flourishing briefly under the leadership of princely poets but soon falling into "decline" before achieving a brief renascence in 1276, when Robert Sommeillon was its "prince."[91] Even those who have continued to argue that the *Jeu de la feuillée* was devised for performance at a feast sponsored by the Carité have been attracted by the idea that there was another such organization in Arras, arguing that the play's unflattering references to a *puy* are evidence of their rivalry. Berger has accordingly imagined the "literary" landscape of Arras as divided between the "bourgeois" confraternity and "the Puy, run by a handful of educated townspeople," which "devoted itself to science and lyric poetry. Like our modern academies, it held meetings closed to all but its members and organized public exhibitions."[92]

This description might apply to the varieties of cultural exchange available in a class-conscious provincial capital of the nineteenth century, but it corresponds with little that we know about the conditions creating the messy vibrancy of performance in thirteenth-century Arras. The Arrageois entrepreneur Jehan Bretel (d. 1272) was undoubtedly a master of the gamesmanship required of jeux-partis—some ninety contributions to this genre, nearly half the extant corpus, can be attributed to him—but it is hard to imagine him wielding the gavel at the meeting of something "like our modern academies," run along austere lines and "closed to all but its members" at a time when not even the princely court of the count was "closed." This drily intellectual idea of "the Puy" owes much to Petit de Julleville's statement of 1885, "The Puys are the academies of the Middle Ages," and is even harder to reconcile with the evidence than Cavrois's charming vision of "le Puy académique" as a Pre-Raphaelite country club, a sylvan gathering of pretty youths "dans la belle saison, en plein air, sur l'herbe fleurie des champs."[93]

90. Ungureanu, *La bourgeoisie*, 205 and 13, 76–77.

91. Berger, *Littérature*, 86–87, 111–114; see also his "Les bourgeois," 433–435.

92. Berger, "Les bourgeois," 433; idem, *Littérature*, 115.

93. L. Petit de Julleville, *Les comédiens en France au moyen age* (Paris, 1885), 43; Louis Cavrois, "Le Puy

Further complicating matters, ever more disjointed and decontextualized references to "the Puy," to a confraternity of jongleurs, and to a Carité de Notre Dames des Ardents have given rise to the notion that there were two—or even three—poetic societies in Arras, that they were all formed simultaneously and expressly for the purpose of producing plays, and that there was a natural antipathy among jongleurs, "the bourgeoisie," and the "patricians" of thirteenth-century Arras.[94] This idea has had a curious staying power, undoubtedly because it helps to perpetuate the cultural distinctions that are in fact demolished by the "disconcerting juxtapositions between courtly, urban, and clerical" milieus in the poetry and music of thirteenth-century Arras, where performing artists were not committed to maintaining the integrity of modern generic constructions.[95] Ursula Peters was so frustrated by the historical malapropisms generated by this scholarly game of "Telephone" that she denied the existence of any performance tradition whatsoever in Arras.[96]

To put it bluntly, these conceptions of "the Puy" are myths, not unlike the myth of the Platonic "Academy" of Florence exposed by James Hankins as a product of the romantic tendency "to reify informal contacts into institutions."[97] "As for the puy of Arras, one knows absolutely nothing about it," said Adolphe Guesnon frankly in 1915.[98] Edmond Faral, whose century-old account of the jongleurs' confraternity has been the most perceptive to date, was not quite sure what to do with scattered references to a puy, but he certainly did not regard it as the adversary of the Carité. Quite the contrary: as far as he was concerned, it must have been a splinter group, a result of overproductivity rather than exclusivity. Moreover, he admitted that what he did know about puys he had gleaned from studying the courtly puys d'amour of the fifteenth century, whose features might not be relevant to understanding the situation in Arras two centuries before.[99] He was right. Apart from the puy mentioned in the Jeu de la feuillée, in a group of local "songs and say-

académique d'Arras ou l'art de la menestrandie au Moyen-Age," MAA, ser. 2, 19 (1888): 225–243 at 228–229.

94. E.g., Louise Barbara Richardson, "The Confrérie des jongleurs et des bourgeois and the Puy d'Arras in Twelfth- and Thirteenth-Century Literature," in Studies in Honor of Mario A. Pei, ed. John Fisher and Paul A. Gaeng (Chapel Hill, 1972), 165; Tydeman, Theater, 201; Carpentier and Le Mené, La France, 271; Dane, "Parody," 4–5; Cowell, At Play, 70–71. Even Graham Runnalls was convinced that there were several "Puys" operating in Arras and suggests that the Jeu de saint Nicolas was commissioned by yet another confraternity dedicated to that saint; see Runnalls, "Medieval Trade Guilds and the Miracles de nostre Dame par personnages," Medium Ævum 39 (1970): 257–287 at 270.

95. Ardis Butterfield, Poetry and Music in Medieval France: From Jean Renart to Guillaume de Machaut (Cambridge, 2002), 135.

96. Peters, Literatur in der Stadt, 64–67 and 76–81.

97. James Hankins, "The Myth of the Platonic Academy of Florence," Renaissance Quarterly 44 (1991): 429–475 at 433 and 441.

98. Guesnon, "Adam," 203–204.

99. Faral, Les jongleurs, 128–142.

ings" known as the *chansons et dits Artésiens*, and in the jeux-partis composed in Arras, the only roughly contemporary reference to it occurs in the fiscal accounts of Mahaut of Artois, the daughter of Adam's sometime patron, Robert II. In 1328 the countess gave the generous sum of 80 livres to finance some unspecified festivities held at Pentecost, to which the échevins of the commune contributed 10 livres, while "those who belong to the *puy*, the knights as well as the other people" (*chauls qui sont du puy, tant chevaliers que autres gens*), gave 6l. 7s. 6d.[100] Placed firmly in context, this is clearly a reference to the Carité itself, or, by synecdoche, to the special manner in which some members' devotion to the Virgin manifested itself at Pentecost, when the *fiertre* was first placed beneath its *follye*, atop its consecrated altar in the Petit Marché.

At least up to 1328, therefore, the Carité and the *puy* were one and the same, alternative terms for the confraternity founded by the jongleurs of Arras and chartered by the cathedral of Notre-Dame during the twelfth century.[101] The word *puy* derives from the Latin *podium*, and refers to the high perches, altars, or pedestals on which relics were elevated for display. (Petit de Julleville, in keeping with his academic vision of "the Puy," said that it "designated the platform whereon sat the masters of the meeting and the most qualified witnesses.")[102] *Puy* is therefore a synonym for *fiertre*, which has the same meaning. Anne Sutton has observed that "the cult of the Virgin is crucial to understanding the inspiration behind all *puys*," and Roseanna Brusegan has shown that most of the *puys* founded in the late thirteenth and fourteenth centuries throughout France formed themselves around the veneration of relics, particularly those of the Virgin, their purpose being to promote the celebration of her feasts in ways that redirected the natural and festive recreations of midsummer.[103] Furthermore, many of these *puys* were based, directly and indirectly, on the customs of the Carité de Notre Dame in Arras, knowledge of which was widely disseminated by merchants and travelers, by pilgrims attending its grand siège, and by the vernacular redaction of its foundation narrative.[104] Far away in Castile, Alfonso X el Sabio heard the story and included it in his collection of *cantigas* dedicated to the Virgin.[105] Closer to home, in Bruges, the municipal accounts record modest sums paid out

100. AdPC ser. A 481.2. See also Berger, *Littérature*, 87.

101. To my knowledge, the only person since Faral to make this connection is Nigel Wilkins, in *The Lyric Art of Medieval France*, 2nd rev. ed. (Fulbourn, 1988), 9–12.

102. Petit de Julleville, *Les comédiens*, 44.

103. Anne F. Sutton, "Merchants, Music and Social Harmony: The London Puy and Its French and London Contexts, *circa* 1300," *London Journal* 17 (1992): 1–17 at 5; Roseanna Brusegan, "Culte de la Vierge et origine des puys et confréries en France au Moyen Age," in Dufournet, *Naissances*, 31–58.

104. Wilkins, *Lyric*, 13–35; Sutton, "Merchants," 5–6; A. Breuil, "La confrérie de Notre-Dame du Puy d'Amiens," *Mémoires de la société des antiquaires de Picardie*, 2nd ser., 3 (1854): 485–680.

105. Alfonso X el Sabio, "Como santa Maria fez aviir na ssa eigreja d'Arraz dous jograres ue sse querian mal," in *Cantigas de S. Maria*, ed. Walter Mettmann (Madrid, 1986), 370–371 (no. 259).

by the échevins of that town "to actors traveling to the Candle of Arras" (in 1292) and "to Pinpernele and the other actors traveling to the Candle at Arras" (1294).[106] Since the bill was being footed by the commune, it is reasonable to suppose that "Pinpernele and other actors" were being sent to Arras as ambassadors. Their charge may have been to return with those fragments of wax that were used to dedicate altars in honor of Notre Dame des Ardents throughout the North. At the same time, Pinpernele and his companions may have studied the customs and the rites of the Carité for the purposes of imitation: hence the confraternities founded in Amiens, Tournai, and other locales which eventually drew censure from the Council of Noyon in 1344, when it was noted that "jongleurs or actors have recently held up wax tapers as though they were holy objects, and have gone so far as to carry them in processions, such that the people have worshipped these candles as holy objects and have thus been led into idolatry."[107]

To be sure, none of these newer foundations could replicate the range of interests, activities, membership, venerable traditions, or miraculous pedigree of the jongleurs' confraternity in Arras. Some appear to have copied only its charitable and devotional aspects, like the confraternity of Notre-Dame-du-Jardin in Arras. Others, most notably the wealthy London Puy, were more worldly and paid only lip service to the Virgin's cult, endowing a chapel and presenting it with a half-hundredweight candle every year, but concentrating more energy and resources on poetic competitions and merrymaking, with a sideline in weddings and funerals. Its statutes reveal an intimate knowledge of the Carité's customs while at the same time providing potentially valuable information on the protocols of after-dinner competitions at its grand siège, which either were never written down in Arras or do not survive. (The London Puy's records were also fragile, despite the fact that its own bylaws legislate the careful keeping of archives. We owe our entire knowledge of them to Andrew Horn, the city chamberlain from 1320 to 1328, who included a copy of the Puy's statutes in his *Liber custumarum*, along with William FitzStephen's "Description of London.")[108] Hence, we learn that the annual *feste roiale* of the London Puy "is held and established principally in order to crown a *chanson royale*" (*est maintenue e establie principaument pur un chaunsoun reale corouner*), and is to be celebrated in a hall hung with silk and tapestries and decked with "flowers and foliage" (*florie et foillez*) and overseen by the Prince of

106. Wyffels and De Smet, *De Rekeningen*, 1:342, l. 2 (7l. 6s. 4d.): "Item istrionibus pergentibus ad Candelam Attrebatensem"; and 454, ll. 27–28 (7l.): "Item Pinpernele et aliis ystrionibus Attrebati ad Candelam pergentibus."

107. "Item, sicut audivimus in multis civitatibus et nostræ Remensis provinciæ, joculatores seu histriones de novo candelas cereas tanquam res sacra deferunt, et nituntur processionaliter deportare; populum dictas candelas tanquam res sacras adorantem ad idolatriam inducendo." Cited by Brusegan, "Culte," 44.

108. *Liber custumarum*, in *Munimenta Gildhallae Londoniensis*, vol. 2, pt. 1, ed. Henry Thomas Riley (London, 1860), 216–228 at 220.

the Puy—selected for his wealth and inclination to hospitality, not his musical artistry— and that the winning song is to be "clearly and fairly written, without mistakes" (*apertement et droitment escrite, saunz defaute*) and hung on the wall in a place of honor, beneath the Prince's arms.[109] It is more than possible that many of these procedures were based on those of the Carité, yet there are also notable differences. Had the Carité's bevées and grand siège been closed to all but its members, none of these other *puys* could have copied its customs. Indeed, it is very interesting that nearly all the spin-off confraternities and *puys* of the ensuing centuries made significant alterations to the Carité's egalitarian admissions policy, a salutary reminder that Arras was so politically, socially, and culturally distinctive that it was inimitable in certain respects.

Sutton has suggested that well-to-do Londoners were probably moved to establish "a feast which men call Puy" (*une feste ke hom apele Pui*) in the 1270s, when merchants traveling to Arras on business would have had ample opportunity to witness the impressive range of performative artistry on display there.[110] This was the heyday of Baude Fastoul and Jehan Bretel, the years when Adam de la Halle and Robert II of Artois both came of age, and when the future king of Sicily, Charles of Anjou, and the future king of England, the Lord Edward, took part in at least one poetic contest in Arras, probably during their well-publicized visit of 1263. On this august occasion, the topic of debate was obviously chosen to honor those tourneying sportsmen, with Lambert Ferri, a canon of the cathedral, posing the following musical question to one Robert de Caisnoi: Would you rather carry off all the prizes on the tournament circuit or remain utterly unknown yet secure in the love of your lady? Robert's response, favoring an amorous obscurity, pleased the Lord Edward well, as the prince's parting envoi declared: "To love, for so it's true: That is the Queen of all virtues" (*A Amours; c'est de ça jus, | Li souveraine des vertues*).[111]

But most of the Carité's customs and practices did not translate well. In London, the relationship between feasting and fellowship was the reverse of that in Arras. In Arras, the confraternity had been born of the love fostered by the Virgin, which made a miracle; the feasts of the Carité commemorated this. In London, the *confrarie du Pui* expressed "loyal love" (*loial amour*) to the king and his barons, not to the Virgin. In fact, its statutes state explicitly that the confraternity existed for the purpose of feasting. Moreover, the London Puy was the exclusive club of well-to-do professionals and gentlemen, with no women or non-members allowed at its meetings. In Arras and elsewhere in the North, by contrast, the building of urban *hôtels* by the wealthy and the nobility actually encouraged interaction

109. Ibid., 224–225. On the cultural context of the London Puy's foundation, see Nigel Wilkins, "Music and Poetry at Court: England and France in the Late Middle Ages," in *English Court Culture in the Later Middle Ages*, ed. V. J. Scattergood and J. W. Sherborne (New York, 1983), 183–204 at 185–186.

110. Ibid., 216; Sutton, "Merchants," 8–12.

111. Arthur Långfors and L. Brandin, *Recueil général des jeux-partis français*, 2 vols. (Paris, 1926), 2:18–21 (vv. 71–72).

among a wide array of social and economic classes, as Christopher Page has shown.[112] Perhaps it was the case in Arras that real princes like Count Robert or honorary ones like Robert Sommeillon were in the habit of hosting gatherings, but it is equally possible that the Carité itself played host, at home in its own *praiiel*, where a *maisnie* very like that of a (modest) lord saw to the company's refreshment. In fact, the poetic fame of Arras, which inspired the London merchants to institute a *puy* and build a hall to house it, coincides precisely with the aggrandizement of the Carité's "court," the establishment of its house-hold, and the drafting of the *Ordinance*.

What, then, was the contribution of the Carité's wealthiest members to its endow-ment? It certainly stands to reason that it was partly funded by men like Jehan Bretel, who was not only a preeminent poet but also a very wealthy banker. To which of these talents did he owe his occasional title of "prince"? The statutes of the London Puy make it clear that the role of its prince and his companions was to win honor by conspicuous expendi-ture and consumption. In Arras, we recall that the Carité's maieur of ardents and his échevins were also supposed to foot the bill for many of its yearly feats: this is suggested in the coutumier and outlined more fully in the *Ordinance*. Was "prince," then, another name for maieur? Or was "prince" not so much an office as an honorific bestowed on those whose support of the confraternity consistently went above and beyond the de-mands of office? The latter makes sense, and with this in mind, the capacity of the Carité to support a household and a hospital, endow a chapel, and commission a lavish reliquary can be better explained. But so, admittedly, can the social, economic, and political ten-sions that did, from time to time, threaten the harmony of brotherly love, tensions that in-form the earliest narratives of the Carité's foundation (the enmity of Pierre Norman and Ithier, the revolt of the knights) and are also evident in the *Jeu de la feuillée*.

The play's ambiguous treatment of Robert Sommeillon, whose princely tenure was clearly based on wealth rather than the poetic prowess with which his predecessor Jehan Bretel was endowed, may also be exemplary of these tensions, for it can be read either as a convivial ribbing or a cruel satire. Much would depend on whether any of the things said about Robert corresponded with real aspirations and actions, and on the way these were generally perceived. We cannot know. Scion of a prominent banking family, Robert would have been a near contemporary of both Adam de la Halle and Robert of Artois, and may well have resembled the hard-nosed sycophant spoken of in the *Jeu de la feuillée*. He was certainly well acquainted with the count in later life, since in 1301 the latter's bailiff sent word that Robert Sommeillon was "gravely ill," from which we can infer that this was a matter of concern—although whether the count's concern was friendly or financial cannot be discerned. Robert Sommeillon does not appear to have been actively em-ployed as a banker, as were his father, Jehan, and his grandfather Thomas, who were

112. Page, "Court and City," 204–205 and 214.

often paired with the wealthy Crespin family in business dealings, and this could be another indication that he was giving more of his time, energy, and money to other pursuits.[113] It is even possible that his red-and-green-slashed finery made a brave showing in the lists of one of the costly tournaments held in the Grand Marché from time to time, since the enormous sums expended by the count on such occasions are well documented, and the Sommeillon family may have been among those who helped to finance them, or held promissory notes sealed by the count.[114] It is possible, too, that Sommeillon once wore the favor of a lady masquerading as the fairy Morgue in a mock mêlée similar to that described by the herald Crokesos: Count Robert was himself famous for jousting in the flamboyant costume of the Arthurian hero Yvain at tournaments where combatants and spectators came dressed and masked as characters popularized in the romances of Chrétien de Troyes (see chapter 5).

Sommeillon does not appear among either the poets or the judges in the chansonniers preserving the songs and jeux-partis of Arras, though the testimony of the Dervish and his Father suggests that he was a stickler for keeping unruly participants and auditors in line. And nothing further is known of Thomas de Clari, who is mentioned in connection with him and apostrophized by the Dervish as a "paragon" of poets: this in itself is evidence that many of the songs sung at the gatherings designated by the term puy were never preserved. Perhaps many were too obscene or incompetent to warrant repetition or transcription; the reported contribution of Master Gautier Big-Toe (identifiable as a priest from a wealthy Franco-Flemish family who would have been approaching sixty in 1276) is described as tantamount to a loud fart. Do we take these disparagements as the boorish ravings of a cretin, or as a reliable description of proceedings at certain reunions of the Carité? Berger believed that the unflattering remarks made about the activities of a puy in both the Jeu de la feuillée and the group of twenty-four "songs and sayings" composed in Arras prior to 1265 "show that these works could not have been composed by it," and must therefore have been malicious parodies circulated by the confraternity of jongleurs.[115] Yet these lyrics, which Berger describes as "literature" (he glosses their frequent mention of singing and singers as references to "writing" and "writers"), are really a series of dicing-and-drinking ditties with catchy refrains which probably circulated for decades before they found their way onto the leftover folios of the famous Chansonnier de Noailles,

---

113. AdPC ser. A 45.31. On the business dealings of the family, see Bigwood, "Les financiers" (1925), 382–410 (nos. 21, 50, 124, 152 bis, 158, 176, 201, 209). Further materials relating to three generations of the Sommeillon family, dating from as early as 1232, are preserved in AdPC ser. 3 G Carton 15 "Sailly o Bois," v–vi, and ser. A 16.14.

114. For the participation of other wealthy townspeople, see Berger, Littérature, 109. On the tournaments themselves, see chapter 5.

115. Berger, Littérature, 114–115.

copied at Arras toward the end of the thirteenth century and later bound together with a fourteenth-century gathering of Adam's motets.[116]

Given that the *puy* and the Carité were identical, it is sensible to suggest that these "songs and sayings" were exercises in self-mockery, as the *Jeu de la feuillée* so clearly was, at least in part. Nor is there reason to insist that they were "declaimed" solely at the Carité's grand siège, as Bernard Delmaire imagines.[117] In any case, "declaiming" is hardly the mode of performance best suited to sexual and scatological sing-alongs: they probably went the rounds of taverns, too, even if they were originally devised and sung by members of the Carité. For not surprisingly, it appears that the confraternity's pious thrice-yearly bevées involved—or regularly devolved into—raucous celebrations intended to enliven the memory of dead confrères with drink. Although the Carité's miracle narratives and coutumier had strenuously insisted that the confraternity "was not founded for lechery or for folly" and that excessive love of wine had caused the death of one ardent on the day of the Virgin's miracle, there is a difference between insisting on an organization's spirituality of purpose and the secondary, social activities in which it engages. The Carité's *Ordinance* clearly demonstrates that a great deal of food and wine was consumed at the grand siège, and the humor of these songs—again, like that of the *Jeu de la feuillée*—is in part dependent on the listener's knowledge of what might go on at a gathering of poet-clerks, jongleurs, and festive townspeople:

Arras: that's a school. You'll hear everything there.	*Arras est escole de tous biens entendre.*
The worst wretch you know, if he comes from elsewhere,	*Quant on veut d'Arras le plus caitif prendre*
Bring him to Arras and he'll sell at the fair.	*En autre païs se puet por boin vendre.*
The fame of Arras, see, it spreads everywhere.	*On voit les honors d'Arras si estendre*
Just yesterday, I saw the sky split and tear:	*Je vi l'autre jor le ciel lasus fendre:*
God's eye's on Arras; he can learn motets there.	*Dex voloit d'Arras le motés aprendre.*[118]

116. BnF fr. 12615, fols. 197–217v. They were originally edited by Alfred Jeanroy and Henri Guy under the title *Chansons et dits artésiens du XIIIe siècle* (Bordeaux, 1898), and analyzed by Adolphe Guesnon, "La satire à Arras au XIIIe siècle: La bataille de l'enfer et de paradis," MA 12 (1899): 156–168 and 248–268. Berger gives a brief description of the codex and its contents in his edition (*Littérature*, 7–19). On the different (and interlocking) performance genres contained in the chansonnier, see Mark Everist, *French Motets in the Thirteenth Century: Music, Poetry, and Genre* (Cambridge, 1994), 104–125.

117. Delmaire, *Le diocèse*, 2:383.

118. C&D, 120–122 (no. 1), vv. 1–6.

The song goes on to say that God, feeling melancholy, decides to visit Arras for his health. Welcomed "at the hostel of the prince" (*A l'ostel le prince*, v. 10), he finds himself in the company of earnest minds who have set themselves to investigating "the humors and astronomy" (*De compleusïon et d'astrenomiier*, v. 13), polite terms for boozing and pissing around. God is then taught something about music, and hears a certain Gilbert sing an ardent song in praise of "his waxen lady" (*se dame ciere*, v. 22), perhaps a playful reference to the Lady of the Sainte-Chandelle. But God is cured only when "Bretiaus" (the name by which Jehan Bretel was remembered in the Carité's funerary register) treats him to a performance so comic that he laughs his illness away—although he soon falls victim to a new malady after he immerses himself "in the study of gorging and farting and shitmaking" (*ki met s'estudi / En trufe et en vent et en merderie*, vv. 33–34), in which some of his new friends are deeply engaged.

If God can be humored thus, why not Jehan Bretel, Robert Sommeillon, and Adam de la Halle? Must all the recreations of a confraternity be either pious or polite? Not in Arras, it seems. Another song, composed around 1252 and therefore roughly contemporary with the drafting of the Carité's *Ordinance*, describes a confraternity dedicated to Saint Oisin (Saint Gosling), whose miraculous powers are so great that he can cure anyone who hasn't drunk enough, a terrible disease. This carité has strict entrance requirements, elects a new maieur every fourteen days, and holds its siège before Pentecost, when fat goslings are cheap and plentiful.[119] The "miracles" attributed to the patron saint of drinkers, Saint Tortuel (Saint Turtledove), inspire another song that seems appropriate for the feasts of the Carité, and appears also to have inspired Adam de la Halle, who praises Saint Tortuel in one of his motets.[120] Yet another song along the same lines describes a confraternity founded for the benefit of henpecked husbands (*aduïns*), perhaps not unlike those whose shrewish wives are mentioned by name in the *Jeu de la feuillée*. It lays down the law for its sorry confrères, who are ordered to let their spouses alone when they profess to have headaches, who should never carouse, who always speak softly, and who constantly help around the house. It ends with a warning: these rules have been ratified by a special synod held at Rome, which has decreed that anyone who beats his wife will not receive a Christian burial.[121]

These party pieces reflect the healthy sense of satire that one might expect a gathering of jongleurs to possess, and the chief poetic activity long associated with "the Puy" is actually very similar in many ways: this is the jeu-parti, also known as the *parture*, a "part-game" or "part-song" competitively performed by two poet-musicians and frequently

---

119. C&D, 184–189 (no. 10: "Signor, li sains recorde, et si est verités").

120. C&D, 141–146 (no. 5: "Il n'est miracle ki rataigne"). See also "Entre Adan et Hanikiel," in *AHOEc*, 202–205, v. 9.

121. C&D, 198–203 (no. 17: "Signor, noveles sont venues").

adjudicated by guest artists, each of whom commented briefly on the efforts of one competitor. (Some of the judges named in the later manuscript collections are fictional, but many more appear to have been real.) Deeply entrenched habits of scholarship persist in describing the jeux-partis as "literary" exercises, and although it is possible that one could engage in a musical sparring match by correspondence, as one can play a game of chess, part of the challenge implicit in the form appears to be the element of surprise and immediacy involved in countering the poetic arguments and melodic schema of one's opponent with little or no advance warning. If so, that would make the job of the respondent the bravura role, since he (or she: there were female competitors) would have to reply to the questioner's initiative, and to do so within the structure inaugurated by it. This exercise was facilitated by the predictability of the major theme and its subtopics—predominantly, love—and by the formal division of each game into six alternating stanzas and two shorter envois, or "parting shots," in which the judges offered their opinions. It is noteworthy that Adam de la Halle, famed for his skill, always took the part of respondent in the eighteen jeux-partis that he composed with (or, rather, against) his older counterpart and mentor, Jehan Bretel. Perhaps this was one of the latter's princely prerogatives, the privilege of initiating debate:

Adam, s'il estoit ensi		Adam, what if it were the case
Que joie fust otroiie		That you could only have the grace
A vous dou cors de cheli		Of your love's body, pretty face,
Que vous volés a amie		And those delights of each sweet place
.x. foys en tout vostre eage	5	Just ten times in your whole lifespan.
Sans plus, or me faites sage		Then tell me, what would be your plan?
Se vous les prendriés briement		Take all ten chances, very fast,
Ou atendriés longement?		Or spread them out, and make them last?[122]

Adam's task is to state his preference—he'd take his ration all at once—and subsequently to defend his position after Jehan has offered a rebuttal; each then has a stanza for closing remarks.

If one imagines a live and largely impromptu process, then it may have been the case that competitors were allowed a set amount of time to compose their successive replies, since the length of the stanza, its meter, and its rhyme scheme would vary significantly from game to game. In the intervals, the audience would be happily employed in drinking and discussing the merits of the verses and their tunes. And on occasion it seems that either the composers or someone in the audience would record the results of the performance for posterity. Eventually, toward the very end of the thirteenth century and throughout the fourteenth, some of these successful efforts were collected and circulated in

122. Långfors and Brandin, Recueil, 2:32–36 (no. 108); AHOEc, 126–129.

manuscript books, to be read and reduplicated by admirers increasingly incapable, in a new age of scripted composition, of imitating performive poetics.[123] Arras contributed the lion's share of these transcripts: of the 182 jeux-partis extant, 114—nearly two thirds of the corpus—originated there.[124]

The statutes of the London Puy allow us to glimpse the process whereby "winning" entries were written down, but it is again important to note how different were the competitions held there and in Arras: a contest of *chansons royales* for members only, in which just one song would be "crowned," versus an improvised debate among social unequals which usually ended in a draw, and which was open to all comers, including women and many men about whom we otherwise have no information. The language of the jeux-partis may be more circumspect than that exhibited in some of the "sayings and songs," but the subject matter is often similar, and both have much in common with the Jeu de la feuillée. In one jeu-parti, for instance, Jehan asks Adam if he would consent to live in Arras all his days if he had a *bele amie* and all the other necessities of life, even if he could never leave there or look at another woman. Adam says, essentially, yes, very much as he is eventually persuaded to do in the course of his famous speech.[125] Another makes a joking reference to Adam's scholarly reputation, when Jehan Bretel begs him to explain his theories in "layman's terms" (*Con lais hom*) because he himself "knows nothing of grammar" (*Car ne sai point de gramaire*), while Adam is so "well read" (*bien letrés*): here the literacy in question is that of love, not Latin.[126] In another exchange, Jehan himself strikes a pretentious pose by recounting an anecdote about Aristotle, whose learning did not make him immune to the folly induced by sexual attraction.[127]

Where is the Blessed Virgin in all of this? In some cases she is a silent presence, seen but not spoken of, represented in the Carité's hall by her Sainte-Chandelle or in the Petit Marché by her Pyramide and *fiertre*. In others, she may well be lauded as the Lady whose affections must be strenuously won, or masked in courtly wise by stand-ins like the fairy Morgue, who also needs a sheltering bower. Perhaps some jeux-partis no longer extant were debates in her honor and made this more explicit. A few of Adam's songs, as I have

---

123. This shift in artistic technique and sensibility is charted by Sylvia Huot in *Song to Book* and by Nagy in *Poetry and Performance*. For a thoughtful analysis of the jeu-parti as a performance genre, see Michèle Gally, "Poésie en jeu: Dès jeux-partis aux fatrasies," in Castellani and Martin, *Arras*, 71–80. See also Everist, *French Motets*, 126.

124. That is, 62.637 percent, a calculation based on the edition of Långfors and Brandin.

125. "Adan, vaurriés vous manoir," in Långfors and Brandin, *Recueil*, 2:37–40 (no. 109); AHOEc, 128–133.

126. "Adan, a moi respondés," vv. 1–4, in Långfors and Brandin, *Recueil*, 2:51–54 (no. 113); AHOEc, 140–143.

127. "Adan, mout fu Aristotes sachans," in Långfors and Brandin, *Recueil*, 2:63–66 (no. 116); AHOEc, 151–153.

indicated, invoke her name directly. Who is to say that many of the poetic products that found their way into manuscript did not begin, in some sense, as devotional exercises, tantamount to the tumblings of Our Lady's legendary acrobat, who did his customary act in honor of the Virgin, or to the minstrelsy which had originally brought Norman and Ithier to her notice? The more we contemplate the twinning of Carité and *puy* in thirteenth-century Arras, the more we are encouraged to make such connections.

The Virgin's Play of the Bower

According to the *Ordinance*, preparations for the Carité's grand siège began two weeks after Easter and a full six weeks before the Trinity triduum, when the échevins and maieurs met "to do the offices of bread and wine and beef."[128] Then, on the eve of Trinity Sunday, five days prior to the feast, the maieurs and two échevins appointed to the "office of beef" collected the freshly butchered meat (conveniently, the Pyramide in the Petit Marché adjoined the butchers' stalls) and saw to its being properly jointed and salted. At that time they also set aside special cuts for the bailiff of Arras and for the members of the Carité's household, who would be working overtime all that week. On Tuesday, two days prior to the feast, the *Ordinance* notes that "the maieurs ought to be in the hall of the house making merels," the token coins that were distributed during the festivities.[129] On Wednesday night there was to be a dinner for all minstrels at the house of the maieur of jongleurs living at large in Arras (*en hors*), at the Carité's expense.[130] On Thursday itself, the first day of the grand siège, there was the solemn procession which encompassed the Town and City of Arras and which culminated in the ritual potation of holy water in the Petit Marché, followed by a feast that could not be wholly contained within the Carité's hall, so carefully calibrated gifts of money, wine, bread, and meat were distributed to various benefactors and friends. First among them was the priest of La Madeleine, an important downtown parish controlled by the abbey of Saint-Vaast in which the Carité's court was situated, who "lets us have the same rights for the bodies of our dead at the altar of his church as we have at other churches, even though the church is outside the demesne of the bishop."[131] The Carité also sent gifts to the abbot of Saint-Vaast and the cathedral chapter, as well as to the many men who would help to protect the Saint-Chandelle during its journeys to and from the chapel in the marketplace, the court, and around the town: the bailiff of Arras, his

128. *Ordinance*, fols. 7v–8r: "pour semonre le plait as eschevins de le carite bien et sousfisaunnt . . . les osfices du pain du vin et des boes."

129. *Ordinance*, fol. 1v; see also fols. 5r–v. "Item le mardi apres disner doivent estre li maieur en salle et faire les meriaus."

130. *Ordinance*, fol. 2r.

131. *Ordinance*, fol. 3r: "Pour che que par grace il nous laist avoir a sen moustier autel drois as corps que nous avons as autres moustiers ia soit che que li moustiers soit exens de levesque."

clerks and sergeants, the sergeants of the commune who would provide an armed guard, the sergeants of the castellan of Arras, and the bailiff's lieutenants.[132]

All this we know. Yet we know nothing, directly, about the feasting, about what went on in the hall of the Carité's court, or about the entertainments on offer, either during or afterward. It was not the custom of the Carité to commit the scripts of its rituals to writing. Perorations for funerals and the reception of new members are outlined in the coutumier, but oaths and other forms of words, gestures, and speeches are not included. The minutiae of festal preparations along with the salaries and benefits of the household staff are delineated in detail, but no mention is made of the way the bevées were observed, no description of the rites to be performed for Bishop Lambert on the anniversary of his death, no script for the threefold administration of holy water on the three nights of the grand siège, no information as to why the Pyramide's apostles were to be wreathed with roses on the feast of Saint John, and no mention or description of the performance for which a flowery arbor was erected on Assumption Eve. We know about the oaths taken by the confraternity's mayor on July 15, but only because these were written out by the ever careful monks in 1315, and copied again on a leftover leaf of the Carité's register in 1531.[133] The story of the Sainte-Chandelle, so creatively composed in Latin and eventually translated and expanded in the vernacular, is the closest thing we have to a conventional play script, but only because concrete, written testimony was an evidentiary requirement when the Carité sought official recognition of its cult from local ecclesiastical authorities in the latter part of the twelfth century and again from Rome in 1241. If the texts of "songs and sayings," some jeux-partis, and the plays by Jehan Bodel and Adam de la Halle do represent the residue of live entertainments undertaken by members of the Carité, these texts were made and kept separately and sporadically, and must therefore represent only a fraction of all otherwise unrecorded happenings. When the confraternity's members got together, each played or sang or disported himself "according to his art," as the abbey's account of the annual procession to Saint-Vaast put it. Only at certain special times did the jongleurs or their brother clerics find it necessary to repeat what had already been written, such as when the official "charter" of foundation, the account of the Virgin's miracle, had to be read aloud.

It was to frame a special performance of that "charter" that an arbor was annually constructed adjacent to the Pyramide in the Petit Marché on the eve of the Virgin's Assumption on August 14, the set for yet another "play of the bower." According to the Ordinance, it was surrounded by seven candelabra, each holding three candles, and the light from their twenty-one flames disclosed the maieur of ardents standing "in the doorway of the Tower with a large group of friends to accompany him," stationed there "until the singers

---

132. Ordinance, fols. 2v–3v. See also AdPC ser. 3 G 4/Oblations III–VII (Delmaire handlist no. 55).
133. BnF fr. 8541, fol. 45v.

who sing at that time leave off singing." Meanwhile, "every member of the household of Our Lady, men, women, and minstrels," was given a candle, and all walked together from the court to the Petit Marché in a group.[134] This is all that the *Ordinance* says about the performance, save that each of the singers should be paid 4 deniers, and that everyone should be escorted to the maieur's house by candlelight afterward, where there would be spiced wine for breakfast. For the vigil of the Assumption was a fast day in the calendar of Arras, and even mild privation was put to symbolic use in this reenactment of the Carité's founding miracle, since the civilian members of the confraternity standing in the chapel doorway were meant to represent the suffering ardents, waiting patiently for the Virgin's cure. It mattered little whether the miracle was supposed to have happened on that night; in nearby Tournai, a yearly procession commemorating a cure of the *mal des ardents* had originally been celebrated on the feast of the Exaltation of the Holy Cross (September 14) but was later moved ahead a week, to coincide with the more apposite feast of the Nativity of the Blessed Virgin, to whom the cure was attributed.[135] To the people of Arras, it would make perfect sense to perform the Virgin's apparition on the anniversary of the occasion when she had been taken up into heaven to preside over the merciful judgment of sinners at the side of her Son. Observing the vigil's short fast, they would imagine themselves preparing, as their ardent ancestors had, for the Blessed Lady's marvelous appearance just before the early summer's dawn. Moreover, they would await her coming amid a blaze of burning light, for on the eve of the Assumption even the abbey church of Saint-Vaast remained lit with candles from sunset to sunrise.[136]

The "four-square arbor" next to the Pyramide in the Petit Marché therefore represented the choir of the cathedral in which the Virgin had made her appearance on the night of the Carité's foundation, and it is possible that the nearby presence of the *fiertre*—these were the last few hours when it would still be sheltered in the *follye*—was instrumental in furnishing a simulacrum of Notre-Dame in the City. The protagonists Norman, Ithier, and Lambert were portrayed by the singers mentioned in the *Ordinance*, their rendition of the story presented in the same ritually charged manner as the Passion of Christ, with one chanting in a higher or lower register (*Hault*), another in a low (*Bas*), and the third intoning his part "as though reading" (*En lisant*). Moreover, as with the singing of the Passion, a subtle dramatization was achieved through the distribution of parts, with the sung voices belonging to the jongleurs and the measured tones of the reader reserved for the prayers of the tormented ardents, the sermon of reconciliation preached by Lambert, and

---

134. *Ordinance*, fols. 6r–v: "a lentree de le tour et grant plente de ses amis pour lui conpagnier . . . si longuement que li canteres qui cante en che meismes leur laisse le canter . . . cascuns de le mainnie nostre dame hommes femmes et menestrel."

135. Dumoulin and Pycke, *La grande procession*, 13–18.

136. BmA 230, fol. 136v.

the speeches of the Virgin. This may sound staid, but there is every reason to believe that those who sang for Norman and Ithier improvised their roles, "each according to his art," and there is no denying the mimetic effect of the moment commemorating the Virgin's gift of the Sainte-Chandelle:

A vous deux qui viviez de chant	To both of you, who live by song
Et de vielle ung jeu plaisant	And pleasant play of violon,
Ceste chandelle sans tarder	This candle now without delay
Vous baille en enjoings à garder	Is trusted to your guard always
A tousiours permanablement.	Forever, to eternity.

Simultaneously, an emphatic stage direction reads: "The Holy Candle must now be shown" (Il faut monstrer le Saint Cierge). Thus the very relic that had been bestowed on the legendary trinity was re-presented to the audience, perhaps with the sudden drawing aside of greenery from the curtained opening of the arbor, cued by the reader's enunciation of the words "This Candle now without delay."

This, at least, is how the mise-en-scène is presented in the oldest surviving script, possibly dating from the late fourteenth century at the earliest. Consisting of 853 rhyming octosyllabic lines, it was eventually titled "The Coming of the Holy Candle in Old-Style Verse Which Was Chanted on the Eve of the Assumption" (Advenement de sainct Chierge en vers anciens quy se chantent la veille de l'Assomption) and preserved in the "Régistre Thieulaine," copied during the seventeenth century by Philippe Thieulaine, a local landowner and former maieur of the confraternity, and onetime owner of the manuscript codex that now contains the register and coutumier.[137] Thieulaine thought that the text dated from the thirteenth century, while Edmond Faral regarded it the oldest "semi-dramatic" expression of the Carité's miracle, "to be sung, and apparently in the church."[138] While this text does not by any means represent the oldest version of the story, and it was not sung in a church, it does confirm that a local rendition of the miracle narrative circulated independently of the extant Francien translation, eventually to become the specimen of "Old-Style Verse" that found its way into the archives of the early modern confraternity, to survive the sixteenth-century wars of religion and the wars of Habsburg occupation, the reconquests of France, the crises of the French Revolution, the disasters of Napoleonic imperialism, the disillusionment of the Franco-Prussian War, and the global chaos of the twentieth century.

The Advenement drapes a little flesh on the skeletal rubrics of the Ordinance, providing concrete evidence that the consecrated altar of the Pyramide had inspired the creation of

137. It has been edited by Cavrois, Cartulaire, 127–154. I have used my own transcription from the "Régistre Thieulaine."

138. Faral, Les jongleurs, 137. The existence of the Advenement is also noted by Verhuyck, "Et le quart," 120; Richardson, "Confrérie," 170; and Espinas, Les origines, 1:110.

an indigenous set of ceremonies, most of which were probably unscripted in the time of Adam de la Halle. Was it for one of these occasions that "The Play of the Bower" was originally conceived? Was it for the coming of the fairies that the apostles wore their rosy chaplets on Midsummer Night? Or was it in honor of the Virgin that Adam and Rikiers decked that festal board? When Guillos says that it's time to go and offer a candle at the *fiertre* of Notre-Dame, is he on his way to stand with the other ardents in the doorway of the chapel in the marketplace, to await the coming of the Sainte-Chandelle? If so, the performance of the *Jeu de la feuillée* had whiled away the short late summer night as a prologue to the Virgin's holy rites. This would have been regarded, by contemporaries, as perfectly appropriate. As I noted earlier, "The Meaning Which One Ought to Enact within Oneself at Mass" describes the act of readying oneself for worship as the preparation of a bower, for "in that sweet place, everyone ought to show forth all his virtues, of heart and body," the better to honor a God who "is so courtly to his friends" and to welcome the members of his train, "the banner-bearers, the jongleurs, the musicians, the *vielles* who come before the Lord to honor him." By 1315 the abbey's cartulary records that the annual sojourn of the *fiertre* in its *follye* had become a time when "the townspeople sponsor youthful plays [*ludisque juvenilibus*] and honor it eagerly with an array of offerings."[139]

139. "Cum igitur estivo tempore . . . feretrum et reliquias S. Marie de Civitate ob nascentia ejusdem ecclesie edificia in parvo foro [ubi] nunc Cruz lapidea juxta Monetam sita est, cives posuerant ludisque juvenilibus et offerendarum ambitione certatim honorabant." Noted in a sixteenth-century copy of Guiman's cartulary and related documents (AdPC ser. 1 H 1); cited by Guesnon, "Adam," 206 (n. 1).

It is beyond the scope of this book to attempt the reconstruction of another common stage, one engendered by the interactions of itinerant courts, the tangle of Mediterranean politics, and the complex culture of the Angevin Regno in the years after the Sicilian Vespers of 1282.[1] The goal of this chapter must be more modest: to shed light on the conditions in which Adam de la Halle worked when he was in the employ of Count Robert II of Arras, to illuminate the lives of the entertainers with whom he collaborated, and to inquire further into the mechanisms that might have led to the preservation of the *Jeu de Robin et de Marion* in an unusual authorial corpus and in company with the *Jeu de saint Nicolas* of Jehan Bodel. Who was making these connections? Who had the means to commission this expensive manuscript? And who was in possession of the necessary texts? There are a few possible candidates, among them Robert himself, a man who spent a formative part of his life in the theater of Arras, and who had mastered some of the documentary procedures necessary to the preservation of the texts on which we rely for its history. In fact, Robert probably learned more about record keeping from the communes and confraternities of his domain than from the example of his noble peers.[2] Unlike them, he was scrupulous in the reckoning of accounts, and the rich archive that survives him (and that alone escaped the otherwise total conflagration of 1915) has allowed Malcolm Vale to demonstrate that the organization of his household exercised "a formative influence upon the other courts" of medieval Europe, including that of England.[3]

Robert's recourse to writing is important for several reasons, not least because the accounts dating from the 1290s allow us to glimpse the workings of entertainers at his court, barely a decade after the death of Adam de la Halle. But it is also important because of the vital linkage among plays, public life, and public record that is a major theme of this book. The *Jeu de saint Nicolas* survives, in part, because Jehan himself was trained to make and

---

1. For a glimpse of the performance culture that prevailed prior to the Angevin monarchy, see Karla Mallette, *The Kingdom of Sicily: A Literary History* (Philadelphia, 2005), especially 110–129.

2. Dirk Heirbaut, "Le cadre juridique: Institutions et droit in Flandre vers 1302," in *1302, le désastre de Courtrai: Mythe et réalité de la bataille des éperons d'or*, ed. Raoul C. van Caenegem (Anvers, 2002), 106–139.

3. Vale, *Princely Court*, especially 8, 30, 82. See also Fossier, *La terre*, 2:623.

preserve documents. The confraternity of jongleurs rivals even the greatest lords of the era in the redaction of customary law, the keeping of accounts, and the making of a household ordinance. Adam de la Halle's advanced education taught him to compose complicated polyphonic motets whose creation, transmission, and reception presuppose high levels of literacy. And not only are we able to study the theater of Arras because of the unique documentary culture that flourished there, but also we have seen that documents themselves constantly functioned as theatrical artifacts, playing a role in performances as props, or as the records of what went on, or as the scripts to be enacted. Whoever put together the anthology of Adam de la Halle's work had an exemplar of the *Jeu de saint Nicolas* on his desk, along with copies of the *Jeu de la feuillée*, the *Jeu de Robin et de Marion*, and Adam's other compositions: the very *existence* of those texts in the latter part of the thirteenth century points to one horn of a dilemma, while the fact that they exist no longer points to the other. Whether or not Robert was directly responsible, both his archives and that deluxe manuscript can be seen as products of a milieu that instilled a deep respect for performance and its written remembrance. Perhaps most remarkably, this body of evidence opens a window onto a world in which another set of actors had access to some of the same tools of power that had lent themselves, earlier in the century, to the establishment of the jongleurs' lordship in Arras. The self-conscious theatricality of Robert's own career, and the close relationship between the count and his minstrels, thus offers a further challenge to long-standing suppositions about the incompatibility of urban and aristocratic cultures and the alleged limitations of the professional entertainer's social status and diplomatic roles.

The Play about Robin and about Marion

"Here begins the Play about Robin and about Marion, that Adam made," its opening scene the very image of May.[4] Marion is warbling a song of the kind ascribed to shepherdesses, singing that Robin loves her and plans to marry her soon. Meanwhile, Aubert, a knight, is riding home from a tournament, singing self-referentially about the adventures he will have: "As from the tournament I went toward home, / I found Marote, so fair of body, all alone" (*Je me repairoie du tournoiement, / Si trouvai Marote seulete, au cors gent*, vv. 9–

---

4. The play survives in three different formats, one lavishly illustrated (Aix-en-Provence, Bibliothèque Méjanes 166) and one lacking musical notation (BnF fr. 1569, fols. 140–144). A detailed digital facsimile of the Aix manuscript (132 miniatures on 11 folios) has been prepared by Jesse D. Hurlbut, available at http://toisondor.byu.edu/dscriptorium/aix166. All citations, abbreviated JRM, refer to the edition of Schira I. Schwam Baird and Milton G. Scheuermann Jr., *Adam de la Halle: Le Jeu de Robin et de Marion* (New York, 1994). A newer edition, based on BnF fr. 25566, has been prepared by Olivier Bettens and is available at http://virga.org/robin.

10). They meet. Aubert asks Marion to tell him about her song and then questions her about the types of birds she is used to seeing. She asks him about the strange hooded bird he carries on his fist. He explains that it's a falcon, used for hunting; she replies that Robin's pastimes are far more amusing, since "In our town, all the noise is stilled / While he is playing on his pipes" (*A no vile esmuet tout le bruit / Quant il joue de se musete*, vv. 55–56). When asked whether she wouldn't rather give her love to a knight (that is, a *rara avis*), she replies spiritedly that she loves no one better than Robin, whom she expects at any moment:

Nan, bregiere?		"No," shepherdess?
Nan, par ma foi!	85	No, on my word!
Cuideriés empirier de moi		You dare to rule over a lord,
Qui si lon jetés me proiere		Dismiss my prayers and my distress?
Chevaliers sui, et vous bregiere!		I am a knight, and you shepherdess!

Finally, Aubert backs down and rides away, while Marion trills triumphantly behind his back. He takes up the mocking tune and uses it to craft a story for performance back at court: "When by the wood this morning I was riding, / I found a gentle shepherdess, a beauty fit for kings!" (*Hui main jou chevauchoie lés l'oriere d'un bois, / Trouvai gentil bergiere, tant bele ne vit roys*, vv. 97–98).

There follows a parallel scene between Marion and Robin in which the dialogue is a sexy mixture of broad innuendo, studied naïveté, and earthy humor, featuring a ubiquitous series of jokes about cheese. This banter gives way to an even more titillating duet, with Robin asking Marion if she will give him her garland (*chapelet*), Marion asking Robin if he wants to put it on his head, and Robin replying that he will give her his belt, purse, and poker. Willingly, she says—but breaks off the song to propose some new amusement. (We gather that Marion is a tease.) They dance and sing, but this entertainment requires more society; so Robin proposes that he get some of their friends to join the fun. At this, three new characters are introduced: Gautier le Testu ("Fathead"), his sidekick Baudons, and another shepherdess, Peronnele.

All but Marion depart to make convivial preparations, clearing the field for another encounter between our heroine and the amorous Aubert, who claims to have lost his falcon. This time the knight presses his suit more emphatically. Still, Marion rejects him with passionate denials until, once again, his imperious demands require her to sing. When Robin re-enters, he brings the knight's dead falcon, which he has unwittingly killed. Furious, Aubert begins to exercise the privilege of his outraged manhood and rank, while Robin calls on God and the audience for help (*Hareu, Diex! Hareu, omne gent!* v. 315). He is ultimately saved by Marion's entreaties; she explains that the fault was not intentional, that Robin was never to the manner trained (*Il n'en set mie la maniere*, v. 329). Reluctantly, the knight agrees to spare him, but at a price: Marion must acquiesce. When she refuses, he pulls her onto his horse and rides away. Marion calls desperately for help, but Robin remains paralyzed until Baudon and Gautier appear on the scene. While the three pursue their quarry, the action shifts back to Marion and the knight, who is looking forward to the fine time he will soon have. Marion staunchly declares that he will never win her favors, and eventually manages to rescue herself. Meeting up with her would-be hero, she berates Robin for his cowardice and pays little heed to his protestations of valor.

Marion's safe return is hailed by her joyful friends, and the number of the company is soon increased to six by the entrance of another shepherd, Huars, whose delayed arrival (mentioned earlier in the play) is an indication that this role was probably doubled by the actor playing Aubert. This latter portion of the play is all playing; it does not develop a musical narrative like the first part. Huars proposes a game "at Kings and at Queens" (as Roys et Roïnes, v. 438), which Marion rejects as more appropriate for Christmas Eve. So Huars suggests "Saint Coisne," which Marion calls a "vulgar play" (vilains jeus, v. 442) and "too vile" (trop lais, v. 475). As Huars explains it, one person plays the "saint" and all the others come, in turn, to make an offering. Apparently, the goal of the suppliant is to make the sober, statuesque "saint" laugh at his antics without succumbing to laughter himself.

Marion and Perronele soon tire of this game and ask for something else, which provokes Gautier to suggest a game of farting (Faisons un pet pour nous esbatre, v. 466). When Robin rebukes him for his vulgarity, Baudons proposes that they try "playing at Kings and at Queens" after all. This is a species of "Truth or Dare": the "king" or "queen" has the right to make any request of those in the "court," thus mocking the arbitrary nature of royal power. The very fact that no one can agree on how the monarch should be chosen might be taken as a commentary on kingly election—daringly apt if the Jeu de Robin et de Marion was conceived for performance at the court of King Charles of Sicily, whose claim to the throne was constantly in dispute. The lot falls on Baudons, who is enthroned and furnished with a garland for a crown. (He is even designated "The King," Li Rois, in manuscript rubrics.) Several rounds of questions follow, in which Marion and Robin are tested in expressions of love.

Then Gautier interrupts with the news that a wolf has just stolen one of Marion's sheep, a reminder of the fate that almost befell the shepherdess herself when she was nearly raped by Aubert. Robin asks Gautier to lend him his club—a machue of the kind that Courtois had used to mind his pigs—and rushes off to scare the wolf away, bringing back the sheep and giving it to Marion rather the worse for wear: it has, Gautier suggests, been violated. At this point, as though to change the subject, the peacemaker and "King," Baudons, reminds the couple of their amorous declarations, proposing that they marry immediately and suggesting that one of the men make an offer for Peronnele. She, however, is disinclined; her brother Guiot tends to beat up her suitors. Instead, she busies herself getting ready for a feast. Robin runs home to fetch his pipe and, when he returns, brings two horn players to accompany the dancing. But Gautier forestalls him by offering to recite a *chanson de geste*. Baudons, still playing the king, agrees, and Gautier launches into a well-known ditty with the promising entré: "Audigier, remarked Raimberge, kiss my ass, I say" (*Audigier, dist Raimberge, bouse vous di*, v. 728). At least according to the script, Robin doesn't let him sing more than this before he bursts in, accusing Gautier of being a "renegade minstrel" (*ors menestreus*, v. 731—a phrase that invokes the terminology of the jongleurs' Carité). Peronnele intervenes just in time, and the dancing begins. Robin leads Marion forward, bidding the company to follow him, and ending the play with a bergomask.

Like the *Jeu de la feuillée*, the *Jeu de Robin et de Marion* plays with tropes drawn from courtly, bawdy, and liturgical models.[5] It also shares the open-endedness of its predecessors, its loosely scripted star turns indicative of the fact that most medieval plays were once the product of improvisation, devised to meet the needs of many different venues and audiences. On the one hand, the scenes featuring the trio of main characters, Marion and Aubert and Robin, could constitute a satisfying musical entertainment all by themselves; indeed, the piece might well be considered complete after Robin and Marion's initial reunion, or Marion's successful self-rescue from the clutches of Aubert. On the other hand, the version of the play described here is significantly expanded in the most authoritative of its three extant manuscript copies, the anthology of Adam's work in which the *Jeu de la feuillée* and the *Jeu de saint Nicolas* are also preserved. There, a dramatic prologue, *Li ius de pelerin*, "The Play about the Pilgrim," and two new segments of dialogue have been added, changing the tone, the ostensible occasion, and even the purpose of the play.[6]

Addressing his audience in the formal meter of historical poetics, the Pilgrim of the play introduces himself as a wanderer from exotic places, among them Arbre Sec, one of the fanciful emirates mentioned in the *Jeu de saint Nicolas*:

From far Apulia I've returned, where everyone told me	*Par Puille m'en revieng, ou on tint maint concille*
About a clever cleric, wise, noble, and worthy:	*D'un clerc net et soustieu, gracieus et nobile,*
A peerless nonpareil, and born in this city:	*Et le nomper du mont; nés fu de ceste vile.*

5. Sylvia Huot, "Intergeneric Play: The Pastourelle in Thirteenth-Century French Motets," in *Medieval Lyric: Genres in Historical Context*, ed. William D. Paden (Urbana, 2000), 297–314; Linda Speck, "The Lives and Loves of Robin and Marion: Subjects Juxtaposed in the Late Thirteenth-Century French Motet," and Matthew C. Steel, "A Reappraisal of the Role of Music in Adam de la Halle's *Jeu de Robin et de Marion*," in *Music: From the Middle Ages through the Twentieth Century. Essays in Honor of Gwynn McPeek*, ed. Carmelo P. Comberiati and M. C. Steel (New York, 1988), 4–39 and 41–60, respectively.

6. This text, some 134 verses long, and the texts of the two accompanying scenes, are edited in JRM, 129–153. It should be noted that they are seemlessly incoporated into the manuscript between verses 680–681 and 706–707, respectively (vv. 694–695 and 719–720 in Badel's edition), and are not presented as "interpolations."

Master Adam le Bochu, he's called here, or so they say,	Maitres Adans li Bochus estoit chi apelés
And abroad, Adam d'Arras. 25	Et la Adans d'Arras.

He has come to bring us shocking news:

Now Master Adam's dead, O God grant him mercy!	Or est mors maistre Adans, Diex le fache merchi!
I was there at his grave, O Jesus have mercy!	A se tomble ai esté don Jhesucrist merchi!
The count showed it to me, out of his great mercy,	Li quoins le me moustra, le soie grant merchi,
When I was there last year. 45	Quant jou i fui l'autre an.

The audience's scripted response is even more shocking: a familiar, foul-mouthed Knave (li vilains), who soon identifies himself as the same Gautier "Fathead" who features in "The Play about Robin and about Marion," heckles the Pilgrim and interrupts his solemn announcement. Accompanied by a trio of locals named Guiot (Peronnele's brother?), Warniers, and Rogaus, he offers a mock-mournful recollection of Adam's talents, after which they agree to skip the Pilgrim's eulogy in favor of a local fair. The Pilgrim struggles to capture their attention:

Now stop a moment, friends! Just wait and you will hear:	Or veilliés un petit, biaus dous amis, atendre;
They made me learn his pieces, very far from here	Car on m'a fait mout lonc de ceste vile entendre,
That in the cleric's honor, who's gone to God's own sphere	Qu'ens en l'onnour du clerc que Dieus a volut prendre,
The people in this town could learn them and take cheer—	Doit on dire ses dis chi endroit et aprendre;
That is why I made for this place. 55	Si sui pour che chi enbatus.

The Pilgrim intends to showcase Adam's most recent achievement: "Because he made this dis to show off his talents" (Que il feïst uns dis pour son sens esprouver, v. 40), "Therefore it's fair to hear and good to learn" (Car biaus est a oïr et bons a retenir, v. 43). He even quotes a celebrity testimonial: the count would not have exchanged it for 500 livres, and was himself the one who commissioned Adam to compose it. The dis he means is the Jeu de Robin et de Marion.

So this play begins, handsomely produced on the manuscript page. An illuminated miniature shows the knight cantering in on horseback, his falcon on his left fist, and Marion with her shepherd's crook raising her right hand in greeting (Figure 3). It is as if they have entered the playing place just as Warniers, Rogaus, and Guiot exit, since the Pilgrim's prologue carries no *explicit* and segues immediately into Marion's song. But what is the reader—or viewer—to make of the fact that, in this revival, the knavish Gautier appears as himself a few scenes later, to be joined toward the end of the play by the local bit players who've returned, liquored up, and are conscripted into the action at two key moments, in additional scenes of seventy and eighteen lines apiece? The first time, they waylay Robin as he goes home to fetch his pipes; in answer to their questions, the shepherd admits that he actually lives in Bailleul, a suburb of Arras. The second time, they come bursting in to join the feast, just as Gautier launches into his aborted performance of "Audigier." Robin's protestations of its vulgarity may well have been shouted down in this performance.

Once again we find ourselves confronted with a play that is participating in public life and approximating a lived reality. And this play also provides us with information of an unprecedented kind: we are told why it was composed, for whom, and (roughly) when. At the same time, however, it forces us to come to terms with Adam's death in a peculiarly theatrical way, by turning it into a joke and leaving us little alternative but to rely on the testimony of a fictional character attached to one of his own plays. For in fact the Pilgrim is our only witness that Adam ever took service with the count of Artois, that he went with the count to southern Italy, presumably in August 1282, and that he composed the *Jeu de Robin et de Marion* under the count's patronage. We, like the—actual? virtual?—audience of the Pilgrim's play, must therefore work our imaginations in order to situate Robin and Marion in an exotic milieu of which we can know little, while at the same time accepting the fact that a play composed for counts and kings came home to find a welcome in Arras. We must also accept, from him, the fact of Adam's death. In order to make sense of this, we need to explore the circumstances in which Adam took service with the count and the sorts of opportunities afforded by this new career.

The Public Person of the Count

On November 24, 1265, King Louis IX told the échevins of Arras that his sixteen-year-old nephew, the second Robert of Artois, would soon take an oath to confirm their charters and privileges, even though he was still "quite young" and did not possess "much of a seal."[7] Robert was knighted two years later. Finally, at the age of twenty, he came into full possession of his patrimony and marked the occasion on March 12, 1269, with a char-

---

7. *Cartulaire*, 35 (no. 34): "verum cum ipse sit satis juvenis . . . nec sigillum habeat multum."

ter issued from Paris, confirming the oath he had taken at age sixteen and repeating the terms of the charter issued to the men of Arras by his grandfather in 1211. Communicating through the medium of parchment, he reminded all who saw and heard that he was the son of the first Count Robert of Artois, who was the royal scion of Louis VIII, who was the son of Philip Augustus, who had proclaimed himself the heir by conquest of Count Philip of Flanders, the first true lawgiver of Arras.[8]

These were public appearances by proxy. More important was the moment when the new count made his official debut in the theater of Arras, sometime during the previous autumn of 1268, on the occasion of his first *joyeuse entrée* into the Town. Mustering his men in the field of Saint-Michel, just beyond the northeastern gate on the road from Douai, Robert rode in procession through the Porte-Saint-Michel and along the rue Sainte-Croix, into the Grand Marché of Arras. Here, in the one place big enough to accommodate the crowds that would have turned out to catch a glimpse of their young lord, the people jostled and strained to hear his voice pronouncing words later preserved in the fourteenth-century "Book of Oaths" compiled by the échevinage of Arras. Placing his hand on the Gospels, Robert swore to maintain the town and its inhabitants; to uphold the laws and ancient customs of Arras; and not to go against its charters, privileges, uses, and customs.[9] He was then escorted in procession through his new capital along a parade route designed to dramatize the relationship between the Town and its ruler.[10]

"The Meaning Which One Ought to Enact within Oneself at Mass" evokes such an entry: the messenger bringing the news of their Lord's imminent arrival (the Epistle), the jongleurs who prepare the way (the Alleluia), and the herald who reads the charter guaranteeing their rights (the Gospel). Then, with the Sanctus, the table is spread for a feast, while each participant in the ceremony prepares to receive the Lord with a contrite and joyful spirit at the moment of Communion, "just as one does when a king is about to enter a city, and everyone goes out to meet him, and each one shows him his greatest grievance so that he might better recover."[11] But in fact, Robert's first joyeuse entrée occasioned both a display of civic harmony and a semi-staged show of grievance. A joint complaint later made by the young count and the échevins of Arras in the Parlement of Paris alleged that the abbot and convent of Saint-Vaast had rounded up the horses that were grazing on their grain in the field of Saint-Michel, where the reception began. The evidence suggests

8. *Cartulaire*, 35–36 (no. 35); see also 8–14 (no. 9).

9. *Livre aux sermens*, in *Cartulaire*, 509–510 (no. 1).

10. Jesse D. Hurlbut, "Immobilier et cérémonie urbaine: Les joyeuses entrées françaises à la fin du Moyen Age," in Johnston and Hüsken, *Civic Ritual*, 125–142; James M. Murray, "The Liturgy of the Count's Advent in Bruges, from Galbert to Van Eyck," in Hanawalt and Ryerson, *City*, 137–152; Kipling, *Enter the King*.

11. BmA 657, fol. 126v[b]; quoted in chapter 3.

that the monks had deliberately chosen this moment to make a spectacle of their strength and their new lord's inexperience. In effect, the king's court was being asked to rule on a much larger issue, the nature of the relationship between the powers of count, commune, and abbey.[12] It was the beginning of a decades-long feud between the count and the abbey which escalated during Robert's lengthy absence in Italy from 1282 to 1291, and which may have been a driving force behind the monks' engineering of the prisoners' release in 1285, the defiant gesture that fueled the *taquehan* and the seizure of the Virgin's *fiertre*. Moreover, the monks' efforts to thwart the youthful count and dissipate the joy of his entrée into public life added to the troubles he was having with the bishop of Arras, who also made trial of Robert's authority at this time. And it may have been in retaliation for this latter obstruction that Robert's companions made the cathedral and its lands the target of their pranks in 1270.

In marked contrast to these ecclesiastical hostilities is the evidence of a close and amicable relationship between count and commune over the coming years. It shows itself in the count's prompt response to abuses of justice by the échevins during his decade-long absence; in the public alliance between the two parties *ad phalam Attrebatensem* in 1295; and in the townspeople's readiness to advance his career, as when they voluntarily offered him 6,000 livres to fund his expedition to Toulouse and points south at the head of the king's army in April 1272, an undertaking impossible to execute, Robert explained, "without great expense."[13] (Mindful of his obligations, he drew up a careful record of his debts in 1274.)[14] Between 1284 and 1291, when the Angevin wars in the Regno required large sums of money, neither the king of England nor the king of France was able to advance as much as the 16,000 livres raised by Robert with the help of the Arrageois.[15] In part, this was an arrangement of mutual convenience and economic interdependence, but there was more to it than that. There is every appearance of mutual respect for the maintenance of jurisdictions, and sensitivity on the count's part to potential conflicts of interests that would violate the commune's rights.[16] In 1273, for example, it was decided between them that anyone under the *bannum* of the Town's échevins who wanted to become the count's man could honorably signal this change of allegiance by leaving the banlieue and reentering it

12. *Olim*, 1:736–737 (no. 30), 787 (no. 38), 791–792 (no. 5), and 847 (no. 25); AdPC ser. 1 H 1, fols. 184r–184v.

13. *Cartulaire*, 40 (no. 40): "sine magnis expensis." See also Bigwood, "Les financiers" (1924), 796 (no. 167), (1925), 396–397 (no. 12) and 404 (no. 170); Fossier, *La terre*, 2616.

14. AdPC ser. A 22.18.

15. Andreas Kiesewetter, *Die Anfänge der Regierung König Karls II. von Anjou (1278–1295): Das Königreich Neapel, die Grafschaft Provence und der Mittelmeerraum zu Ausgang des 13. Jahrhunderts* (Husum, 1999), 496 and 597.

16. AdPC ser. A 26.10–11, 22, and 27 (accounts of 1279); A 30 and A 31 (accounts of 1280); A 27.36 and 57, A 30.17, and A 28.1. (promissory notes of 1281); A 1 (register), fols. 8v and 12r; A 28.15.

in the count's service. When Adam de la Halle joined Robert's household in 1282, he too would have performed this ritual, effectively banishing himself from the Town that had hitherto provided his livelihood. Indeed, the repatriation of such temporary "exiles" as Adam and other commune-born men in the count's service was part of the reason for the festal revocation of recent banishments whenever the count made a joyeuse entrée, described as a custom of long standing in the charter of 1273.[17]

Although most people in Arras may have had no direct experience of Robert's person, they would have had many encounters with his public persona: not only the persona that was on view during his spectacular appearances but also that enacted by the people and symbols that spoke and gestured in his name. Undoubtedly influenced by the example of his uncle, Louis IX, he took care to set up bureaucratic structures for the oversight of justice and estate management in his absence, and even had a new seal made to his own specifications for use by his agents in conjunction with his personal device.[18] Unhappily, he would later have to hold an inquest into abuses of this authority, when he was obliged to have it "cried throughout all our lands that all those who have letters carrying the aforesaid seal" must have them newly authenticated and exchanged for others by a more trustworthy bailiff.[19] In future he would keep a closer watch on all his public business, making numerous inventories of the documents in his muniment chests and regularly requesting confirmations of ancient and recent charters from the royal archives.[20]

Robert would also take greater care in the selection of his lieutenants, the men who performed the count's role in his absence, and who occasionally impersonated him in overtly dramatic ways. An example of this, a bailiff's performance of the comital persona, survives in the description of a ceremony of exfestucation that took place during April 1283, the first spring of Robert's absence in Italy, when one of his noble tenants came before "the count" to renounce his claims to the lands he held from him. According to Galbert of Bruges, writing a century and a half before, if a man wanted to break the contract of faith between himself and his lord, he would throw down the wand (*festuca*) he had re-

17. *Cartulaire*, 42 (no. 43).

18. De Germiny, *Les lieutenants*, 9–11, 15, and 32; Derville, *Saint-Omer*, 127. On the bureaucratic innovations of Louis's reign, see William Chester Jordan, *Louis IX and the Challenge of the Crusade : A Study in Rulership* (Princeton, 1979), especially 35–64, 141–142, and 171–213. See also Brigitte Bedos-Rezak, "Signes et insignes du pouvoir royal et seigneurial au Moyen Age: Le témoignage des sceaux," in *Actes du 105e Congrès national des Sociétés savantes (Caen, 1980)* (Paris, 1984), 47–62 at 53.

19. AdPC ser. A 27.48 (register containing the letter, issued from Compiègne): "Nous vous mandons et conmandons que vous facies crier conmunement par toute nostre terre que tuit cil qui letres ont du devant dit seel de quel conques condicion quil soient les envoient ou aportent devant vous et devant nostre conseil qui est en artois aus jour et aus termes que vous le ferez crier."

20. E.g., AdPC ser. A 48.13 and 14; A.118 (inventories); A 36.4, 9, and 10 bis (requests for confirmation).

FIGURE 21. The Coutumier of Artois describes the ritual of exfestucation, which should be perfomed "as this figure demonstrates" (BnF fr. 5249, fol. 19v: detail)

ceived during his investiture ceremony.[21] A similar gesture, more violent than stylized, may have been made toward the end of the *Jeu de saint Nicholas*, when the emir d'Outre Arbre Sec refuses to convert to the new religion of his King: "Here I defy you, on my oath, / Renounce your homage and your fief" ("*Garde de moi, je te deffi / Et renç ton hommage et ton fief*"). These passionate words signal an appropriate action, which had become stylized by the time it was depicted in the *Coutumier of Artois* (Figure 21) and duly performed by the bailiff acting for Robert, who played his role entirely by the book.[22]

On other occasions, those acting the part of the count could become involved in dramas that were anything but stylized. A particularly violent incident reveals that Robert's relatively good relationship with the commune of Arras was not necessarily normative. The story is told in four brief lines inscribed on a piece of parchment in outsized letters, a "screaming headline" that was literally cried in the streets of Calais:

IN THE YEAR OF GRACE 1297

THE 17th DAY OF MARCH—THE MEN OF CALAIS HAVE LOST THEIR

21. Galbert of Bruges, *De multro*, cc. 38 and 95.
22. BnF fr. 5249, fol. 19r–v; AdPC ser. A 29.9.

LAW FOR THE SAKE OF THE BAILIFF & SOLDIERS OF MY LORD
OF ARTOIS, WHOM THEY KILLED.[23]

The slaughter of the counts' representatives was not just violent but *symbolically* violent, "because it was a great and terrible thing, to kill and murder the bailiff who represented the person of my lord of Artois, and to murder and kill the soldiers who were stationed there by my lord to guard the honor of the kingdom and that of the town of Calais."[24] Therefore the punishment meted out had to be similar in magnitude and metaphor. The citizens of Boulogne had lost their bell and belfry two decades before, a heavy blow, but those of Calais lost more than the capacity for publicity; they lost the substance of their power: their officers, the seals that allowed them to participate in affairs of business and state, and their archive.[25] In retrospect, this highlights the gravity of the situation in Arras at Pentecost in 1285, a dozen years before, when insurgents "ran about the Town, crying out death to the échevins and to the rich men." It shows that the threatened violence could very well have occurred and points to the very different political situation that prevailed in Arras, where it was not the count's personae who were endangered but the townspeople's and guilds' own elected representatives. Still, Robert's role had not been well played on that occasion, and the popular deposition taken down in 1289 was frank about this: the outrageous behavior of the échevins, who had been sworn in by Robert himself, made a mockery of their oaths of office and the customs of the Town. "Certainly, it placed very great shame on my lord of Artois."[26]

When acting for himself, however, Robert of Artois was a figure out of romance—quite literally. Conceived just before his father's departure for the Holy Land in 1249, he was born several months after his father's death at the battle of Mansourah on February 12, 1250, possibly in June, when his older sister, Blanche, was a toddler of two.[27] For the first few years of his life he would have had little contact with his royal uncles, since both Alphonse and Charles were captured in the same battle, and King Louis's absence from

---

23. AdPC ser. A 43.1: "En lan de grace . mil . deuschens . quatrevins . & disesept / Le diseptime jour de march. Perdirent chil de Calais leur / loi por locoison du baillieu & des saudoiers mon seingneur / dartois que il ochisent."

24. AdPC ser. A 43.5 (accord dated April 14, 1298): "Li communs de Calais a perdu leskevinage, leur chartes, leur sceaus, leur frankisses par jugement pour le ki fu grans et horibles cum dochirre et de murdrir le bailli ki representoit le persone msgr dartois et murdrir et ochire les soudoiiers ki estoient estauli de par msgr a garder lonneur du royalme et la dite vile de Calais."

25. Bedos-Rezak, "Diplomatic," 318–319, and "Civic Liturgies," 38.

26. AdPC ser. A 1009, ed. Guesnon in "Adam," 221–233 at 222: "ciertes il fisent mout grant vergogne a mon signeur d'Artois." ·

27. Auguste Menche de Loisne, "Itinéraire de Robert II, comte d'Artois (1267–1302)," BHP (1913): 362–383.

France was prolonged. During this time his mother, Mahaut de Brabant, had charge of the Artois, assisted by her adviser and protector, Gui II de Chatillon, whom she married in 1254. Thereafter, Robert appears to have been raised largely by his mother's sister Beatrice, widow of the dashing Guillaume III de Dampierre, count of Flanders, a knight celebrated in song and story who had managed to survive the carnage of Mansourah only to die a year later at a tournament in Hainaut. The seeds of many future ironies were sown in these years. Beatrice of Brabant lived at Courtrai, so the boy Robert played at warfare in the very fields where he would later meet his death. His aunt's brother-in-law, Gui de Dampierre—who was slightly younger than Robert's own father had been, and who later accompanied him on crusade in 1270—became the count of Flanders against whom he would lead that ill-fated army in 1302. (Gui himself would die three years later, at the age of seventy-eight, in a French prison.)[28] It may have been from Gui's most famous minstrel, Adenet le Roi, that Robert first heard the tales of chivalry that would captivate him all his life, tales augmented by those told of his own father.[29] Was he already a special devotee of Chrétien's Yvain, "the Knight with the Lion," when he first visited his capital of Arras as a boy and was taken around the abbey church? There he would have seen the gilded lions of a fallen knight gleaming among the dusky tombs of Merovingian abbots, and could have spelled out the inspiring legend: "A well-formed youth, both wise and brave in arms: / This was Renaud, whose form a lion adorns." By the time he was an adolescent, certainly, he identified strongly with the chevalier au lyon. The seal of which his Uncle Louis thought so little probably bore his personal device, "the head of a full-maned lion," which he continued to use as a counterseal for official documents.[30]

When Robert actually played the lion's part in a grandiose mise-en-scène of Chrétien's romances at Le Hem on October 9, 1278—the feast of France's patron, Saint Denis—he was twenty-eight years old, veteran of numerous foreign campaigns, a trusted diplomat, and a counselor to kings. He was also newly married for the second time, to Agnès de Bourbon, a powerful widow thirteen years his senior. He had been betrothed to his first wife, Amicie de Courtenay, at the age of nine, and had married her in Paris at twelve, a full four years before he was dubbed a knight by his uncle Louis at Compiègne on June 5, 1267. Their first child, christened Mahaut for her paternal grandmother, was born in the year Robert made his joyeuse entrée into Arras; the second, bearing the dynastic name Philip,

28. Marc Boone, "Une société urbanisée sous tension: Le comté de Flandre vers 1302," in van Caenegem, 1302, 26–77 at 33–41. For the intertwined genealogies of the Capetians and the comital families of Flanders, Hainaut, and Artois, see Flament, L'Artois, table 1.

29. Albert Henry, Les œuvres d'Adenet le roi, vol. 1, Biographie d'Adenet: La tradition manuscrite (Bruges, 1951), 11–64.

30. AdPC ser. A 22.17 (June 12, 1274): "capud leonis crinosum."

in 1269. A third baby, Robert's namesake, died in 1271. Shortly thereafter, Robert had his first experience of governance in Arras and of war in Tunis. He then traveled widely in Occitania and Italy, accompanied always by the bride he had known since childhood. He lost her during the winter of 1275, in the kingdom of Sicily, where he had his first taste of viceregal power, a taste that would sour during the long years he would later spend there. Barely returned to Paris in 1276, he was dispatched by his cousin King Philip III in the command of an army bound for Navarre, which Robert's sister Blanche was ruling on behalf of her young daughter, Jeanne. Laying siege to Pamplona, he found himself on Roland's legendary battlefield of Roncevaux, where he finally put down the rebellion that threatened his sister's throne. (Blanche, who had inherited the counties of Brie and Champagne from her husband, Henri, would soon wed Prince Edmund of England.)[31]

None of this real strife seems to have dulled his appetite for the theatricality of mock warfare, which was as keen as that of his peers.[32] Robert was a favorite on the tournament circuit, a lover of its pageantry, and a lavish spender (in 1281 he would still be paying for a tournament held in 1274).[33] And he received rave reviews for his bravura impersonation of Yvain in 1278, admired as much for his own qualities as for the role in which he was cast, and even won himself a special place in a chivalric romance that imitated those he had loved from boyhood. Here is what "Dame Fortrece," attendant on "Queen Guinevere," said of him as the ladies of "King Arthur's" court watched the jousting, according to Jean Sarrazin's *Roman du Hem*:

Que mesires li quens d'Artois	Who save my lord count of Artois
Est si largues et si courtois	Is so well mannered, so *courtois*,
Et si loiaus et si entiers	So constant, generous, and right
Et tant aime les chevaliers	So well beloved of ev'ry knight,
Qu'il n'en penra en nule terre,	That wheresoe'er his thoughts are bent—
Soit pour tournoi ou soit pour guerre,	On foreign war or tournament—
Qu'il ne truist compaignie assés;	Companions are not far to seek,

31. Menche de Loisne, "Itinéraire," 362–364 and 368–369.

32. See Joachim Bumke, *Höfische Kultur: Literatur und Gesellschaft im Hohen Mittelalter*, 2 vols. (Munich, 1986), trans. Thomas Dunlap as *Courtly Culture: Literature and Society in the High Middle Ages* (Berkeley, 1991), 247–273. On the inherent theatricality of warfare and tourneying, see Barker, *Tournament*, 84–111; and Michel Stanesco, *Jeux d'errance du chevalier médiéval: Aspects ludiques de la fonction guerrière dans la littérature du moyen âge flamboyant* (Leiden, 1988). See also Ruth H. Cline, "The Influences of Romances on Tournaments of the Middle Ages," *Speculum* 20 (1945): 204–211. For a historical analysis of a fictional tournament, see John Baldwin, "Jean Renart et le tournoi de Saint-Trond," *Annales, E.S.C.* 45 (1990): 565–588.

33. AdPC ser. A 27.52 (accounts of 1281).

Car il ne fu onques lassés	For his defense is never weak
De tous biens faire ne ja n'ert.	And all good graces with him bide.
Il fait bien çou c'a lui affiert.	He prospers who stays by side.[34]

Not far away, in Arras, Adam's *Jeu de la feuillée* had recently commemorated a tournament in which the fairy king Hellekin defeated all comers in the Grand Marché. It is more than probable that Adam had mentally cast his future patron in that supernatural role. (The fairy Morgue, for whose honor that playful duel was fought, is said to have preferred Arthurian heroes).[35] Indeed, it is more than possible that the two men had already met. They were probably close in age, and they could have encountered each other as early as 1263, when Charles of Anjou and Prince Edward of England had visited the young count's domain and participated in poetic debates. If not then, Robert would have had numerous opportunities to witness Adam's artistry in the half-decade between 1277 and 1282, when he was frequently in Arras. Adam, like everyone else, would have been familiar with Robert's many public roles and seen him in action in June 1279, when the count hosted what he grandly called "our war of Arras" in the same marketplace mentioned by Crokesos the fairy.[36]

Adam's Company

Partly on the basis of evidence furnished by Robert's accounts, Malcolm Vale has argued that royal edicts banning tournaments must have begun to take effect in the course of the 1280s, since few are mentioned in them by 1290.[37] But it is just as likely that the laws were irrelevant, and that the count's interest in mock warfare waned in the years after 1282 because he and his men were in southern Italy and constantly engaged in the real thing. By the time he returned to the North, Robert was in his forties and probably had little time and less inclination for frivolous combat. At the height of the tourneying season in 1294, for instance, he was preparing to meet a former friend and sporting rival on the field in deadly earnest, levying men at Aire "to go against King Edward, lord of the English," at Calais.[38] Beginning in 1296 and up to the time of his death in 1302, he personally con-

34. Jean Sarrazin, *Le roman du Hem*, ed. Albert Henry (Paris, [1938]), vv. 3937–47. Sarrazin's poetic account is preserved in BnF fr. 1588. See also Barber and Barker, *Tournaments*, 38–40.

35. Laurence Harf-Lancer, *Les fées au Moyen Age. Morgane et Melusine: La naissance des fées* (Geneva, 1984), 268–288.

36. AdPC ser. A 26.II, 22, 27: "nostre guere darras." See also Menche de Loisne, "Itinéraire," 369–370.

37. Malcolm Vale, "Le tournoi dans la France du Nord, l'Angleterre, et les Pays-Bas (1280–1400): Étude comparative," in Aubailly et al., *Le théâtre*, 263–271.

38. AdPC ser. A 39.28: "aler a armes a Chalais en le compaignie monsgr Robiert conte dArtois contre le roi Edouart signeur des Engles."

ducted the French king's business in Gascony, Aquitaine, the Midi, and Flanders.[39] So it is little wonder that the mature Robert's private time was given over to quieter pleasures, although he never lost his taste for pageantry, and his expenditures continued to exceed his means. On average, the yearly budget for the upkeep of his household totaled 20,000 livres, twice the available revenues of the county of Artois.[40] But then, real battles cost even more than theatrical ones, and were made more expensive by the theatrical display that was integral to chivalric morale and military tactics.

In this new phase of his life, Robert looked more and more to the professional entertainers of his household to supply his wants, not only when he entertained guests or required entertainment himself, but also in diplomatic missions and in the field. Their importance is reflected in the records of expenditures and disbursements kept assiduously from the count's return to the Artois in 1291 up to—and even after—his death, when well-oiled fiscal machinery dutifully accounted for the horses and equipment lost on the battlefield where Robert himself was trampled in the mud. Issuing payment to all the intimates of his household on one occasion, Robert listed them in the following order: his surgeon, his falconers, his minstrels, and his chaplain.[41] This reflects both the entertainers' relative status and the company they kept; Robert sometimes regarded minstrelsy as a medicine more efficacious than the surgeon's, a ministry more welcome than the priest's. Recovering from a prolonged illness in the spring of 1296, Robert gave the actor Simon, otherwise known as Chevrette, a special gift of 10 livres "for his many courtesies" during the time of his master's convalescence.[42] Guillaume le trompeor, attested since 1291 as one of Robert's favorites and almost certainly in the count's service at the same time as Adam, was called not simply "the trickster" but "our beloved knave" (nostre ame valet).[43] Other minstrels were also called by names whose diminutive forms—Jehannuce, Ernaudon, Pariset—may be expressive of the count's affection.

The importance of such frequent and casual references is underscored by the fact that Robert was not really a patron of "the arts," as his predecessor Philip of Flanders had been a century before. When we step outside his household circle, we find that his patronage was modest, consisting of occasional presents, annuities, or commissions. For example, he supported the university training of his chaplain's brother in Paris during the

39. AdPC ser. A 41.12–18: charters of Philip IV empowering Robert of Artois to hear oaths of fidelity and to transact other business in his name in Gascony and Aquitaine and in all the land that the king of England had held in Toulouse, Périgueux, Cahors, Saintes, Carcassone, and Rodez.

40. Auguste Menche de Loisne, "Une cour féodale vers la fin du XIIIe siècle. L'hotel' de Robert II, comte d'Artois," BHP (1918): 84–143; Derville, Saint-Omer, 127.

41. AdPC ser. A 140.8.

42. AdPC ser. A 140.34: "pro curialitate sue facta pro nobis" (dated April 26, 1296 at Angoulême).

43. AdPC ser. A 36.6. See Auguste Menche de Loisne, "Diplomatique des actes du Robert II, comte d'Artois (1266–1302)," BHP (1916): 184–224 at 218 (no. 16).

mid-1280s, when he and his train were in Italy.[44] And in the course of redecorating the chapel at his castle of Hesdin in 1296–1300, he set aside a certain sum for the services of "Bertrand the sculptor, for statues, images, and other things made by him for our project."[45] He was also generous when moved by pity or sentiment, as when he twice bestowed a gift of 4 livres on "a poor woman called The Archbishop, to assist in her marriage," a large dowry for a woman who must surely have been an actress or a prostitute; or when he spent nearly 50 sous on a coat "for a poor man who had been taken in the war in Flanders and who escaped from the prison at Cassel."[46] But most of his revenues went toward the upkeep of his estates and houses, the funding of military expeditions, and the feeding of those employed in such day-to-day pursuits.

The entertainers of his retinue were instrumental here since unlike university scholars they possessed a number of very practical skills. The days of tourneying were over, but wars—even real ones—required minstrels. As Frank D'Accone has observed, "It is difficult for us today to imagine the important role of musicians in medieval military operations."[47] Armies marching to the field of battle needed trumpeters to sound advances and retreats, and even garrisoned castles were provided with performers for military purposes, as well as to pass the long midwinter nights. These men faced dangers at least as great as those confronting the soldiery, and were recompensed accordingly. The accounts of Philip Fortaillié, Robert's castellan at Calais, reveal that during the winter of 1296 his men-at-arms drew pay of 12 deniers per day—and so did the two trompeurs stationed at the castle from October to mid-March. (To be sure, the captains of the fortress received much more, as befitted their rank: 2s. 6d. per day, while a Master Pierre of Marseilles earned 24 livres altogether for special services, because "he has made a machine they call 'the Smash.'")[48] Comparable wages are a strong indication that in this arena, as in those of Arras, the jongleur's talents were valued more highly than we have been led to believe. Robert even took his minstrels into battle with him, and spent nearly as much on their equipment as he did on that of his fighting men and squires. The accounts drawn up after his death at Courtrai reveal that Chevrette, Ernaudon, Jehannuce le Trompeur, Pariset, Jehan le Fol, Lyon, and a certain Entroigne received 16 livres apiece, as did Robert's chaplain, his body ser-

---

44. AdPC ser. A 31.29.

45. AdPC ser. A 140.28: "Bertando eschaketturiaro pro schakis, ymaginibus et rebus aliis factis per eum ad opus nostrum" (accounts of April 10, 1296). See also A 147.5 and A 157.

46. AdPC ser. A 2 (register), fol. 32r and 151.91 (mandates dated March 25, 1298, and June 29, 1299, respectively): "a une povre fame dite lachevesque en aide de son mariage, quatre libvres" and "pour une robe doneie par nous a un povre homme qui fu pris en le guerre de Flandres et escapa de le prison de Casselle, quarante noef sols dis deniers par." See Menche de Loisne, "Une cour," 129–131 (nos. 14 and 16).

47. D'Accone, Civic Muse, 416.

48. AdPC ser. A 140.17 : "maistre Pierre de Marselles qui a fait un engien que on apiele biffe."

vants, and other retainers; this was only 6 livres less than the sum issued to his knights.[49] Moreover, Jehannuce and Pariset both lost horses in the battle, which suggests that they either saw combat or were close enough to the mêlée that they were at risk. The fact that they were so near their noble master, whose ignominious death must have haunted his loyal followers for the rest of their lives, is itself proof of the loyalty he inspired.[50]

The total wages paid for the six-months' garrison at Calais in the winter of 1296 came to a little under 233 livres; fielding an army in Italy a decade before, when Adam de la Halle was in Robert's company, had been considerably more expensive. By the time the count returned home, he owed an estimated 40,000 livres.[51] These monies had gone for the maintenance of men-at-arms and minstrels from Artois, who not only were paid, lodged, clothed, and given passage overland, but also had to be reimbursed for the loss of horses and equipment. For example, an agreement made with Bérard de Saint-Georges in March 1284 shows that in exchange for their services abroad for one year, the knight and his men could expect to receive a lump sum of 300 livres paid in two installments, clothing, overseas passage for themselves and their horses, lodging at court, and compensation for horses killed.[52] Minstrels underwent similar hardships and received similar compensation; for not only did the entertainers of Robert's household sometimes take the field, but they acted as messengers, heralds, and emissaries as well. In so doing, they were expected to bring theater, or at least a touch of theatricality, to diplomatic missions and everyday life—so long as their lives were spared. The very real dangers to which Robert's entertainers were constantly exposed indicate that Adam's sudden death in Apulia, and the Pilgrim's tale of the count's remorse, are far from improbable. The tragic loss of a brilliant performer and composer could well have prompted Robert to commission the deluxe edition of Adam's oeuvre, intended to serve as a memorial. Had he lived, Adam might have been rewarded more conventionally, as other minstrels were. Jehan le Fol's is a case in point: a contemporary of Adam's in Italy, he was owed 200 livres by November 1289, "as much for money he is known to have loaned at our request, as for horses killed in our service. And for the jests we have had from him."[53]

---

49. AdPC ser. A 179.4; Menche de Loisne, "Une cour," 133–135 (no. 18).

50. On battlefield conditions at Courtrai and the conduct of the war, see J. F. Verbruggen, *De Slag der Guldensporen: Bijdrage tot de geschiedenis van Vlaanderens Vrijheidsoorlog, 1297–1305* (Antwerp, 1952), trans. David Richard Ferguson as *The Battle of the Golden Spurs (Courtrais, 11 July 1302): A Contribution to the History of Flanders' War of Liberation*, ed. Kelly DeVries (Woodbridge, U.K., 2002), 127–243.

51. AdPC ser. A 46.6 and 7: letters of Charles II of Sicily, dated April 3, 1302.

52. AdPC ser. A 30.6. See a similar agreement described in a charter of Iter de Mignac (A 30.9).

53. AdPC ser. A 35.9. Mandate of the count to Miles de Nangis, bailiff of Artois, to pay 200 livres to Jehan le Fol, "porteur de ces lettres, tant por monoie saiche prestee a nostre conmandement quant por chevaus quil a eu mort en nostre service, et por jouiaus que nous avons eu de lui."

It is justifiable to project the information gleaned from these later accounts back into the 1280s, when such records were never made or have not survived, perhaps owing to the constant movement of Robert's *maisnie* for nearly a decade after 1282. (The disappearance of the royal archives on the field of Fréteval in 1194 shows how easily such losses were incurred.) Although the conditions of Robert's wars in the Midi and Flanders, and those of his intermittent presence in Italy throughout the 1290s, are different from those of the extended campaigns a decade earlier, many of the expenses would have been similar. In 1296, for instance, Jehannuce and Pariset were each given a gift of 34 livres "for the expenses of their journey to and from Apulia, and for leaving their wives for a whole year."[54] Here, one cannot help but think of Adam's Maroie, who, like these women, was probably left at home in Arras while her husband went abroad. Separation from wife and family was worthy of additional compensation because those wives required means of support in their husband's absence. In November 1299 Pariset collected another 24 livres from Robert's receiver at Bapaume "for his expenses and those of his wife upon his return to France from Apulia" three years earlier, as well as 4 livres "over and above the sum that Pariset and Jehannuce spent out of the money paid out to their wives when they went to Apulia." Pariset was also reimbursed 32 livres for out-of-pocket expenses, and the itemized account reveals some of the minstrel's duties, needs, and mishaps. The sum comprised 4 livres for three trips that Pariset took from Venosa to Naples "when he went to look for Lyon le Nacaire," 6 livres "for a nag that he bought to replace the one of his that died at our hôtel in Genoa," 12 livres for money that Pariset loaned to Lyon while in Apulia, and another 10 livres "for money he loaned Lyon to buy a horse to replace the one of his that died there."[55] The rather amusing picture that emerges from this account is that of a seasoned courtier entrusted with the responsibility of keeping his more hapless colleague in line.

Considering that all the evidence for Adam's very existence is derived from his own compositions, later manuscript rubrics, or literary anecdotes, it is surprising how much we can learn about Jehannuce, Pariset, Chevrette, Lyon, Guillaume, Ernaudon, and the rest of Robert's train. We can therefore discern the outlines of the kind of life Adam might

54. AdPC ser. A 140.8: "A jan/uce et a pariset nostres trompeurs por leur despens daler en puille et revenir et por lassier a leur femmes por .un. an."

55. AdPC A 153.11. Mandate of Robert to the receiver of Bapaume dated at Paris on November 10, 1299: "Cest asavoir pour loutre plus quil et januche le trompeur despendirent de la monnoie que nous leur fesmies baillier quant il en aleren en Puille: quatre libres parisis. Item pour .iij. voies quil fist de venouse a naples, et il ala querre lyon le nacaire: quatre libres. Item pour .j. ronchi quil achata pour le sien qui fu mors en lostel nostre a gennes, sis libris. Item pour les despens de lui et de sa femme en son revenir de puille en france: vint et quatre libres. Item pour devres quil presta a lyon nostre nacaire qui vint avoeques lui de puille: douze libres. Item por devrres quil presta au dit lyon pour acheter .j. cheval pour le siequil li morutt: dis libres." See also A 153.40 (receipt of Pariset).

have led the decade before. And sketchy though the record is, the traces these men themselves have left show that their position within the court fostered a sturdy self-esteem. As with the Carité of jongleurs, evidence of documentary practices and, in particular, the use of seals allow for a measurement of this. Moreover, the changing protocols, orthography, and paleography of surviving receipts suggest that those who had seals either wrote their own *quittances* or at least dictated them.[56] (An exception is Ernaudon, who does not seem to have possessed either a seal or the knack of wording a receipt; when he claimed a bequest of 20 livres from the receiver of Artois in August 1302, the bailiff of Bapaume acted on his behalf and used his own seal to authenticate the document.)[57] The devices on the minstrels' seals are themselves revealing. That of Lyon puns on his Christian name and suggests that he may have been a favorite of the count, since the matrix bears a device similar to Robert's: a lion, with a rose. The devices employed by Jehan le Fol and Jehannuce le Trompeur are more directly representative of the jongleur's art, displaying a pair of *marottes* for juggling. That of Pariset enobles other tools of the trade, the herald's horn and minstrel's trumpet, by grounding them on a finely cut escutcheon encircled by the legend PARISET T'PLORERE (Figure 22). Maffie, the wife of Pariset, may have shared his profession at one time; she certainly modeled her seal on that of her late husband when she began collecting his annuity in 1304. Her widow's device is a single horn with a legend identifying it as "the seal of Pariset's widow" (S: PA RI SI VE.). Simon Chevrette's seal is especially beautiful, worthy of its owner's dignified appellation, "actor" (*hystrion*). It bears his own portrait in delicate high relief, and shows him wearing an elaborate cockscomb and playing on a lute (Figure 23).[58]

These instruments demonstrate that the jongleurs associated with Robert enjoyed a high profile yet retained their license as fools. One of the sealed documents left behind even records a snatch of the impromptu doggerel devised for the court's amusement, preserved among a sheaf of less entertaining receipts (Figure 24):

To all those men and women who see or hear these letters, Perres Fos greets you. Know, everyone, that we have had and received from the bailiff of Hesdin our wages for the nine days when we stayed there before Christmas, feeling sick: 3 sous a day or 27 sous

56. E.g., AdPC ser. A 160.54; A 184.89 and 90; A 193.90. A comparison of A 184.89 and 90 is particularly instructive, for while the wording of Pariset's and Lyon's receipts is almost identical, and both were written on the same day in June 1302, the hands are different. Moreover, the hand and the spelling of Pariset's name here ("Parizet") differ from the spelling ("Parisos") and hand appearing two years previously in A 160.54. This receipt is written in Picard dialect, and could represent either Pariset's own hand and/or pronunciation or that of the receiver of Artois.

57. AdPC ser. A 185.41.

58. AdPC ser. A 184.89 (Lyon); A 183.28 (Jehannuce); A 160.54 and 184.90 (Pariset); A 195.60 and 209.12, 29 (Maffie, widow of Pariset); A 186.52 and 193.90 (Simon dit Chevrette).

FIGURE 22. Seal of Pariset *le trompeur* (AdPC ser. A 160.54: author's photograph)

in the coin of Paris. *In witness of these | I, unwise as you please, | My seal do I seize | Setting here a big cheese.* Given in the Year of Grace 1300 in the month of December.[59]

One may imagine Perres Fos improvising his verse before an audience gathered in the hall of Hesdin to receive their Christmas pay and assume that he received a raucous ovation. The conflation of the act of sealing with that of farting played on a well-known proverb describing the dangers of certain gastronomic overindulgences, especially in polite society: *Jamais homme sage | Ne mangea fromage.*[60] We have already noted the predominance of jokes involving cheese, and the cheese as standard issue for the professional fool: the Knave in the *Jeu de la feuillée* is equipped with one, and so are Robin and Marion. Perres probably performed the sealing with flatulent sound effects.

By parodying legal language in this legal transaction, Perres was also drawing on a ven-

---

59. AdPC ser. A 161.133: "A tous chiaus et a toutes celes qui ches lettres verront. ou orrons. Perres fos. salus. Sachet tout ke nous avons eu et receu. du bailly de hesding—pour nostres gages. de noef jours que nous demourames malade a hesding devant noel—trois sols par iour .xxvii. s' par' En quel tesmoignage . ie qui ne sui pas sage. ai scelee ceste page. de mon seel. a fourmagedonne en lan de grasse .mil et trois cens. el mois de decembre."

60. Cited by Ménard, "Les fous," 442.

FIGURE 23. Seal of Simon, called "Chevrette," *hystrion* (AdPC ser. A193.90: author's photograph)

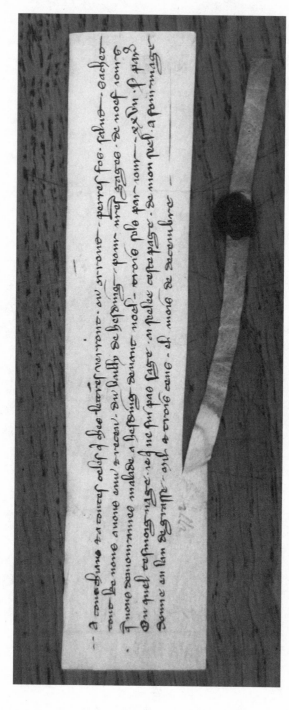

FIGURE 24. The receipt for wages composed by Perres Fos (AdPC ser. A.161.133: author's photograph)

erable genre of jokes revolving around charters and sealing which were among the staples of the jongleurs' repertoire. One such piece, *Li privilege aux bretons*, appears in the same manuscript compilation as a copy of *Courtois* and one abbreviation of the *Jeu de la feuillée*. It involves two main characters: a Breton named Yvon and an unnamed king of France (Louis IX) whose grandfather is said to have granted certain privileges to Yvon's people, notably the right to make brooms. Yvon has come to get this charter confirmed. He addresses the king and queen mother, the lords and ladies, the knights, and finally "all the little folk I've never been acquainted with," a joke that depends on an audience familiar with diplomatic protocol and Latin boilerplate.[61] Yvon makes his case, names his witnesses, and finally produces his original "charter." It turns out to be illegible because it is—or is sealed with—*un frommag | Qui est plus ian que cir*, "a cheese yellower than wax." The king laughs good-naturedly and tells him to read it aloud to the assembled company himself, "for you really seem to be a good cleric" (*Quar bien resemblez estre | Bons clers et bien proisiez*) and thus better equipped to construe the cheese than anyone else in the company. Another piece in the same collection, *La pais aux anglais*, concerns a comic plot by the English barons to win back Normandy, whose title puns on the consonance of *pes*, a fart, and *pais*, peace. It could be translated as "The Fart among the English" or "The Fart to the English." It was so popular that it spawned a sequel, *La chartre de la pais aux anglais*, a joke charter written in prose and purporting to be the actual text of an agreement made between the English barons under Henry III and Louis IX, "rich man of Paris." The audience "witnessing" it would have been struck by the absurd twists on solemn and repetitive formulae, and was also treated to a dating clause consisting of an obscene parody of the *Quem queritis?* liturgy of Easter.[62] Once again, the act of sealing becomes the excuse for a petomaniacal reference.

In the same year that Perres poked fun at the authority of written record, Count Robert issued charters to many of his household minstrels which granted them pensions for life. Pariset, who was probably the senior member of the band and almost certainly a close contemporary of Adam de la Halle, received the first installment of his in June 1300, to the tune of 20 livres per annum: the same amount Robert paid to a professor of law at Paris whom he retained as his representative in Parlement.[63] Lyon, too, was pensioned off before the battle of Courtrai, although he still rode to the wars behind his lord—and lost another horse in the process. Jehan le Fol, "knave of the late Count Robert," received his annuity on the sad occasion of his lord's demise, set like that of Pariset at 20 livres per annum. Chevrette's pension was smaller, 10 livres, but this was presumably because he

61. BnF fr. 837, fols. 190–191: "Et tut li menu gent / Que ie ne connois mi." It has been edited by Edmond Faral in *Mimes français du XIIIe siècle* (1910; reprint, Geneva, 1973), 13–28. Faral proposes the dates 1236–1252, on the basis of internal evidence (4–5).

62. Paris, BnF fr. 837, fol. 220; ed. Faral in *Mimes*, 34–51. I discuss this "charter" more fully in "A Few Odd Visits," 319–322.

63. AdPC ser. A 160.54; compare A 139.18 and 140.39.

continued to serve in the household of Robert's daughter and heir, Mahaut, now the wife of Count Othon of Burgundy.[64] Maffie, Pariset's widow, went on collecting her pension for almost three decades after her husband's death in January 1304.[65] She was so long-lived, in fact, that in 1329 the échevins of Hesdin were asked to issue a *certificate de vie* testifying to her continued survival. The countess's receiver was assured that, as of the vigil of Pentecost, Maffie was fit as a fiddle.[66] She appears to have died three years later, after collecting her Christmas installment in January 1332.[67]

Thus far did the Countess Mahaut uphold the standards of generosity dictated by her father, even though she does not appear to have shared his tastes. Hers had always been what might be termed literary. Around Christmastime in 1300, we note, she gave the duke of Brabant's minstrel 12 sous, but bestowed 40 sous on a "writer from Hainaut." And throughout her life she would employ entertainers only on an occasional basis: 10 livres to various minstrels entertaining at Candlemas in 1306; an additional 4 livres to Guillemin, the minstrel of her brother-in-law Hugh de Bourgogne; and so on.[68] Still, the aging Jehan le Fol was given a sentimental gift of 8 livres "when he parted from Madame at Amiens" in 1312 or 1313: she had probably known him since her childhood. Chevrette busied himself fulfilling various commissions, as when he "carried letters from Madame to the marriage of my lord Jehan de Chalon" on June 16, 1313, receiving 16 sous for this performance (and it probably *was* a performance).[69] Only in 1328 does Mahaut appear to have paid for a large-scale entertainment, held on or before the first of July: "To Baude de Croixilles, for many plays that were performed before my lady of Artois, for my lord the duke and the duchess of Burgundy, as well as for my lord the bishop of Arras, upon their arrival."[70] Baude was a citizen of Arras who had gotten his start in a very different theater stage-managed by Count Robert: on the eve of Courtrai he had earned 5 sous a day painting caparisons to adorn the warhorses of the knights in Robert's train.[71] A generation later he appears to have become a *metteur-en-scène*.

64. AdPC ser. A 184.89 (Lyon); A 202.3 (Jehan); A 46.25 and 186.39 (Chevrette).

65. Contrary to the statement of Jules-Marie Richard, who says that Maffie died in 1303; see Richard, *Une petite-nièce de Saint-Louis: Mahaut comtesse d'Artois et de Bourgogne (1302–1329)* (Paris, 1887), 107.

66. AdPC ser. A 496.56 and 57: note appended to Maffie's receipt, dated the morrow of Ascension Day at Arras in 1329.

67. AdPC ser. A 529.

68. On Mahaut's artistic patronage and building projects, see Richard, *Une petite-nièce*, 107–115, 256–297, and 306–360.

69. AdPC ser. A 161.123; A 217.10 and 11; A 298 (register), fols. 14v and 19r.

70. AdPC ser. A.478.1: "A Baude de Croixilles pour pluseurs ju qui furent fait tant par devant madame dartois, mons le duc et la ducesse de Bourgoigne, comme devant mons leveque darras a leur venue, ix lb. xv s. ix d."

71. AdPC ser. A 179.4. See Menche de Loisne, "Une cour," 135–143 at 142–143 (no. 19).

"Perhaps it was in Arras during the thirteenth century that jongleurs knew the best and brightest days of their history. The patronage of the townspeople weighed less heavily on their shoulders than that of the lords: it was not as brutally obvious as the price of service."[72] Edmond Faral's estimation of the jongleurs' usual lot is probably just, although his characterization of the patronage they enjoyed in Arras does not adequately reflect the fact that most of them were self-employed or held other part-time jobs. Apart from the three jongleurs on the permanent staff of the Carité's maisnie, the only one who appears to have been something other than a freelance artist was a minstrel kept by Bauduin VII, castellan of Arras in the time of the first Count Robert.[73] And when this began to change in the time of Robert II, it did not necessarily change for the worse. His court was exemplary not just for its documentary practices but because it was, like other princely courts, a perpetual theater, a moveable feast, and "a powerful force in the development of a common musical culture uniting court and city," as Christopher Page reminds us.[74]

To judge from the surviving accounts, then, Adam de la Halle would certainly have been able to rely on the talents of numerous performing artists when he devised the Jeu de Robin et de Marion, a play requiring a small cast of six, only three of whom must be able to sing well, and which was probably only very loosely scripted (if scripted at all) to leave room for the license of a motley crew described at various times as trompeurs (trumpeters, heralds, or tricksters), menestrels (minstrels), nacaires (tambourine players, musicians), and, occasionally, as "actors": Chevrette's seal had even used the Greek word. Such terminology was by no means fixed; Symon dictus Chevrette ystrion could also be called Symon Chevrete, menesterel monsegnor dartois. Lyon de Margat was Lyon le nacaire or Lyons menestrels, depending on the context. On one occasion, Jehan le Fol—probably another colleague of Adam's—appears as Jehan de Naquarre, menesterel. Pariset was a troumperes et menestreus or valles et tromperes de noble prinche monseigneur le comte.[75] Ernaudon, for his part, seems to have doubled as a falconer, a skill that would have come in handy if the play featured a real falcon. These appellations depended more on who was making the record than on the role being played, and courtly usage seems to have avoided the term jongleur, so prized by the personnel of the Carité des Ardents, at least through the middle of the thirteenth century. Yet this did not prevent the symbols of the jugglers' trade from being displayed on seals. And although none of Robert's entertainers, save Adam himself, can be shown to have had an affiliation with the confraternity, that is because we are reliant on the Carité's funerary register for information on its membership, and the Carité's own coutumier re-

72. Faral, Les jongleurs, 142.

73. Berger, Littérature, 63.

74. Christopher Page, "Court and City," 204–205. See also Vale, Princely Court, 95 and 200–246; Zumthor, La lettre, 288; Bumke, 220–228; Heers, La ville, 231–235.

75. E.g., AdPC ser. A 139.33; A 153.40; A. 160.54 and 124; A 179.4; A 184.89; A 186.39.

stricted funerals and memorial prayers to those who died within its banlieue. Given that the entertainers who sought employment with Robert were, by definition, itinerants, who often lived and died abroad (as Adam did), we cannot construe the silence of this record as an indication that separate spheres of courtly and popular entertainment were maintained. The evidence actually points the other way: the urban court was culturally porous, and not only in Arras. By 1321, all professional entertainers in Paris would be united in a corporation of jongleurs, no matter how they earned their wages. The guild's first leader was one Pariset, "ménestrel du Roy," son of that Pariset who, like Adam, had served the count of Artois.[76]

Adam Abroad

Two plays of Adam de la Halle are preserved side-by-side in the anthology that now bears the Bibliothèque nationale's shelfmark "français 25566." Despite their proximity there, and in the minds of the manuscript's compiler and audience, the *Jeu de la feuillée* and the *Jeu de Robin et de Marion* have not been viewed as companion pieces by many modern readers.[77] Marie Ungureanu went so far as to deny that they could have been written by the same person, and although hers is an extreme view, it is by no means isolated.[78] Unlike Adam's own contemporaries, scholars since the nineteenth century have reacted unfavorably to the juxtaposition of "literature," supposedly produced under the higher auspices of a court, with seemingly subversive social comedy. The Arrageois scenes associated with the *Jeu du pèlerin* have therefore been slighted as "interpolations" designed to cheapen the play and season its humor for a less refined palate.[79] Yet the manuscript tradition declares that the theater of Arras supported a pluralistic culture of performance. The count of Artois himself did not disdain to strut and fret many hours upon that stage, and he laughed at the antics of Perres Fos. It is hardly unlikely, therefore, that the townspeople shared some of his tastes, or that local jongleurs might have revived a play that was partly the product of his generous patronage. Indeed, the Pilgrim's prologue insists that Adam's *dis* was considered appropriate entertainment for the court of a king and the marketplace of a mercantile capital. The pastoral genre may be "eminently aristocratic," in Faral's phrase, but it is also particularly suited to the expression of a wistful urban ennui. Since Virgil's *Georgics*, if not before, it has been as much a product of the marketplace and

76. Richard, *Une petite-nièce*, 107.

77. Rousse and Huot are exceptional in this regard. See Jean Dufournet, "Complexité et ambiguïté du *Jeu de Robin et Marion*: L'ouverture de la pièce et le portrait des paysans," in *Études de philologie romane et d'histoire littéraire offertes à Jules Horrent*, ed. Jean Marie d'Heur and Nicoletta Cherubini (Liège, 1980), 141–159; and idem, "Du *Jeu de Robin et Marion au Jeu de la feuillée*," in *Études de langues et littérature du Moyen Age: Offertes à Felix Lecoy par ses collègues, ses élèves et ses amis* (Paris, 1973), 73–94.

78. Ungureanu, *La bourgeoisie*, 109.

79. E.g., Axton, *European Drama*, 141.

its commodification of sentimentality as of learning or pretension. This can also be seen in the medieval *pastourelles* of Macabru and Jehan Bodel.[80]

Even its Italian provenance does not place the play as far beyond the reach of the Arrageois as some have supposed. Long before Adam's journey abroad, Arras had forged strong commercial and cultural ties with many Italian cities, particularly Genoa, where Robert had a house.[81] In 1268 a party of Guelph merchants arrived from Siena, settling there under his protection.[82] By then Arras had already proved a haven for other exiled Tuscans, notably Brunetto Latini (1220–1295), the Florentine scholar and diplomat who had been ambassador to the Castilian court of Alfonso X el Sabio, the wise king who included the story of the jongleurs' miracle in his song cycle celebrating the Blessed Virgin. When Brunetto was unable to return to his native city during the Ghibellines' bid for power, he stayed in Arras, where he worked on his philosophical encyclopedia, *Li Livres dou Tresor*, originally written in the language of his new home and including material drawn from Latin translations of Aristotle's Ethics. Perhaps this project inspired the musical debate between Jehan Bretel and Adam de la Halle in which Aristotle is featured as a compliment to the Carité's Italian guest. Latini certainly made many friends and contacts while in residence, and when he returned to Italy, he did so in the train of Charles of Anjou, Robert II's uncle and another of Adam's future patrons. Meanwhile, collectors throughout Europe would continue to purchase books prepared by the atelier he had established in Arras, a scriptorium partly staffed by local clerics which turned out vernacular manuscripts written by Italian scribes and illustrated by Picard artists well into the early part of the fourteenth century.[83] One well-known codex, dated 1310 and now part of the collection of the Bibliothèque nationale, contains a copy of the *Tresor* and a collection of Adam's songs.[84]

Vibrant cultural currents also linked Arras to Provence and to the Holy Land.[85] As we

---

80. Faral, *Les jongleurs*, 258; Ada Biella, "Considerazioni sull'origine e sulla diffusione della 'pastourella,'" *Cultura Neolatina* 25 (1965): 236–267. The best reading, overall, is that of Rosanna Brusegan, "Le Jeu de Robin et Marion et l'ambiguïté du symbolisme champêtre," in *The Theater in the Middle Ages*, ed. Herman Braet et al. (Louvain, 1985), 119–129.

81. AdPC A 153.11. See Georges Jehel, "Gênes et Arras au moyen âge," in Castellani and Martin, *Arras*, 27–36.

82. AdPC ser. A 16.9, 12–13 and 16.6 bis: "cives et mercatores Senen' Guelfos."

83. Julia Bolton Holloway, *Twice-Told Tales: Brunetto Latino and Dante Alighieri* (New York, 1993), 221 and 521, and *Brunetto Latini: An Analytic Bibliography* (London, 1986), 13–25, 63–65, and 127–129. See also Brunetto Latini, *Li livres dou tresor*, ed. Francis J. Carmody (Geneva, 1998), xvii–xviii and xlvi–lvii.

84. BnF fr. 1109, fols. 311ra–325va, dated 1310 in a colophon on fol. 136[143r].

85. On the very close ties between Florence and Naples during this period, see David Abulafia, "Southern Italy and the Florentine Economy, 1265–1370," *Economic History Review* 33 (1981): 377–388; reprinted in *Italy, Sicily, and the Mediterranean, 1100–1400* (London, 1987). See also Dunbabin, *Charles I*, 83–86, 119–121, and 155–165.

have seen, the *Jeu de saint Nicolas* is predicated on its audience's sense of proximity to the crusader kingdoms of Outremer. Meanwhile, one of the manuscripts of *Courtois* and one of the abbreviated *jeux* derived from the "Play of the Bower" circulated in Italy, where French-speaking expatriates had an appetite for songs and stories in their native vernacular. Even the Boy and the Blind Man show themselves to be *au fait* with current events by singing a recruiting song of the sort authorized by Urban IV in 1265 as part of the effort to rally popular support for Charles of Anjou's claim to the throne of Sicily; others were composed by Rutebeuf (the *Chanson de Pouille* and *Le dit de Pouille*) and Jean de Meung.[86] The Angevin territories of the Mediterranean would provide another channel through which Adam's compositions would find their way into a wider European market, which partly explains the lavishly illustrated *Robin et Marion* from the Angevin capital of Aix-en-Provence (Bibliothèque Méjanes 166), a copy of the play in which lyrics and dialogue have been translated into Francien for the better understanding of audiences unfamiliar with the robust dialect of Picardy.

It is therefore reasonable to surmise that Adam took service with the count of Artois not only to satisfy the wanderlust exhibited in the *Jeu de la feuillée* but also to expand his artistic powers and extend their reach. It was a conventional career move. Over a decade before, Adenet le Roi had made the trip to Tunis in the company of his patron, Gui de Dampierre, who continued to support the Angevin cause. Moreover, King Charles of Sicily had himself been a poet and musician in his youth, and even if Adam did not meet him when he and Edward of England played at jeux-partis in 1263, everybody knew the songs attributed to him.[87] True, Charles was held to be notoriously stingy by the troubadours of his own court in Provence, but there is good evidence that he valued his household entertainers in Italy, at least one of whom was a "beloved" (*dilectus*) familiar.[88] He had also shown himself more than willing to support the endowment of the university that Frederick II had founded at Naples in 1224.[89] Adam was a scholar, too, and it is possible that

86. Nancy Freeman Regalado, *Poetic Patterns in Rutebeuf: A Study in Noncourtly Poetic Modes of the Thirteenth Century* (New Haven, 1970), 39–54. See also Alessandro Barbero, "Letterature e politica fra Provenza e Napoli," in *L'état angevin: Pouvoir, culture, et société entre XIIIe et XIVe siècle* (Rome, 1998), 159–172 at 163.

87. See Jean Maillard, *Roi-trouvère du XIIIe siècle: Charles d'Anjou* (Rome, 1967).

88. Stefano Asperti, *Carlo I d'Angiò e i trovatori: Componenti "provenzali" e angioine nella tradizione manoscritta della lirica trobadorica* (Ravenna, 1995), 9–10, 122–125, and 130–133; H. Petersen Dyggve, "Personnages historique figurant dans la poésie lyrique française des XIIe et XIIIe siècles, XXV: Charles d'Anjou," *Neuphilologische Mitteilungen* 50 (1949): 144–174; Noël Coulet, "Aix, capitale de la provence angevine," in *L'état angevin*, 217–330; Alfred Jeanroy, "La poésie provençale dans l'Italie du sud à la fin du XIIIe siècle," in *Mélanges de philologie, d'histoire et de littérature offerts à Henri Havette* (Paris, 1934), 43–48; Barbero, "Letterature," 166–167; Aurell, *La vielle*, 157; Dunbabin, *Charles I*, 199, 208–209, and 214–218.

89. Gennaro Maria Monti, "Ancora sullo studio generale di Napoli de Carlo I a Roberto," *Archivio storico per le province Napoletane* 59 (1934): 137–180; Kiesewetter, *Die Anfänge*, 521–525.

his special range of talents—his learning, his ability to compose in a wide range of styles, the polished manner honed by Paris and poetic debate—recommended him as the ideal candidate to do for Charles what Jehan Bodel had done, somewhat obliquely, for Philip Augustus: make him a *chanson de geste*. This time, however, it was not merely a song dedicated to a king; it was about a king: the *Roi de Sicile*.

Charles of Anjou was the very subject to fire the imagination of an ambitious poet. He had already captivated his nephews, not just his brother Robert's son but the two sons of Louis IX, Philip III and Pierre d'Alençon, all three of whom were his unfailing supporters until his death. Perhaps this is because he was the only surviving son of Louis VIII, who had "inherited his father's somewhat unCapetian devotion to warfare," as Jean Dunbabin remarked, thus inspiring romantic sentiments in a younger generation who had grown up without knowing the warlike count of Artois.[90] Their devotion helps to explain the somewhat odd contrast between the stern, implacable Charles of later chronicles and statute books and the resourceful, sentimental hero of Adam's unfinished epic, the *Roi de Sezile*. It may have been the way Count Robert remembered the dashing young uncle of his boyhood, so close in age and temperament to the father he had lost. Charles may have acted like a father to him, indeed; he had stood in loco parentis when Robert's young wife, Amicie, died in Italy, himself seeing to the design and installation of her tomb at Saint Peter's in Rome.[91] And there was much to be admired in him still. He was a brilliant stage manager of tournaments and dubbings, a gallant figure on horseback, a throwback to an earlier age of chivalry who, at the age of fifty-eight, had challenged a king fifteen years his junior to a duel.[92]

Charles was a self-made monarch. The youngest son of Louis VIII, he had not been included in the appanage which had endowed Robert I with the Artois; he was conceived after that arrangement had been made, and born after his father's death in 1225. He appears to have been destined for a career in the Church when, in 1246, Louis IX gifted him with the patrimony of their recently deceased brother, Jean. This included the counties of Anjou and Maine, which had been part of another Angevin empire, that of England's Henry II, confiscated by Philip Augustus in 1203. It gave Charles an entry onto the world stage. In that same year he won the hand of Beatrice, youngest daughter of the late Raymond Berengar V of Provence (1209–1245) and sole heiress to the county; her older sisters, Eleanor and Margaret, were the queens, respectively, of England and France. A few years later, ransomed and returned home from crusade, Charles also made a bid for the imperial county of Hainaut. He was obliged to give it up in 1254 but retained some influ-

90. Dunbabin, *Charles I*, 20.

91. Ibid., 210.

92. Steven Runciman, *The Sicilian Vespers: A History of the Mediterranean World in the Later Thirteenth Century* (Cambridge, 1958), 236–241; Dunbabin, *Charles I*, 197–208.

ence with the Dampierre family of Flanders. In the ensuing decade he successfully extended his Provençal domain into Piedmont and acquired, with Louis's help, the county of Forcalquier.

Then Urban IV began to seek a new king of Sicily. At odds with the Hohenstaufen dynasty and the city-states loyal to the Holy Roman emperor, he sought to replace the late Frederick II's son Manfred with a prince sympathetic to the exercise of papal power in Italy. Here was Charles's opportunity to make himself a king and Beatrice a queen equal to her older sisters. After nearly two years of fierce diplomacy, the count and countess of Provence were crowned king and queen of Sicily, on the feast of the Magi Kings at Epiphany in 1266. It was a premature gesture, but Charles proved his claim later that year when he defeated Manfred at the battle of Benevento. He proved it again when he defeated Frederick's grandson Conradin at Tagliacozzo in 1268—although he overreached himself badly when he arrested Conradin and his supporters for treason and had them executed, an affair that rubbed salt in the wounds of the imperial party in Italy (the Ghibellines) and angered the Aragonese king, Pedro, who had married Manfred's daughter. In 1270 he further aggravated Aragon when he interrupted Catalan trade with Egypt and imposed his lordship on the emir of Tunis, in the wake of the disastrous crusade in which his soon-to-be sainted brother Louis met his end. In 1278 he made a successful play for the Frankish kingdom of Greece, the principality of Morea, and he also purchased the title to the crusader kingdom of Jerusalem and its capital at Acre. This escapade made him—bizarre shades of the *Jeu de saint Nicolas*—the king of Outremer. Finally, as part of a larger effort to extend his influence farther east, he arranged the marriage of his son Charles and his daughter Isabelle to children of King Stephen of Hungary, Maria and the future King Ladislas.[93]

Dunbabin has made a good case for the relative stability of Charles's hold on the Regno, the mainland of southern Italy, showing that it was characterized by internal peace and prosperity, and buttressed by an efficient legal system, well-maintained roads, sound coinage, and strong trading networks.[94] But in Sicily, which Charles neglected, the negative consequences of the past decades' strife erupted in the full-scale rebellion known as the Sicilian Vespers. It began in Palermo, a city Charles called the capital of his realm but which he had visited only once. Its dispossessed landholders appear to have been conspiring with the king of Aragon in plans to invade the Regno as soon as Charles left to pursue an ill-advised war against the Byzantine emperor, Michael VIII Paleologus, although in the end it was the outrageous taxes levied to finance this campaign that were the immediate cause of the uprising in March 1282—taxes and a *crime passionelle*. On the evening of Easter Monday a French soldier is said to have offered unwanted attentions to the wife

---

93. Dunbabin, *Charles I*, 11–18, 37–39, 41–43, 55–58, 96–100, 184, and 193–197.
94. Ibid., 66–70.

of a citizen and was killed by her outraged husband, who raised the rallying cry "Death to the French!" The revolt spread rapidly, crossing the straits into Calabria.[95]

It was this that brought Robert down from the Artois. He was ready by August, mustering his men in Arras and marching south by way of Paris and thence to Avignon, stopping at Sisteron (Haute-Provence) in late September. He had a force of two thousand knights, according to the versified Greek *Chronicle of Morea*,[96] which follows these affairs much more closely than the local chronicle of Salimbene de Adam (who gives Robert's name as "Peter" and styles him "the brother of the king of France").[97] By early November he and his men were in Montefiescone, near Viterbo. By January 27, 1283, they were in Calabria, at the very tip of Italy's "boot," and they appear to have been stationed there, principally at Nicastro and Monteleone, for the next eighteen months.[98]

Where was Adam at this time? Nothing can be known for certain about his movements. The near-complete incineration of the departmental archives of the Pas-de-Calais during World War I is paralleled by the destruction of the Angevin registers in the archives at Naples during the German retreat of 1943. A heroic and ongoing initiative on the part of local scholars has resulted in a retrospective inventory of these registers' contents based on the publications and personal notes of local historians, but even the sixteenth-century compilations on which these nineteenth- and twentieth-century registers were based did not comprise all of the records generated by Charles I and his son Charles II.[99] If Adam had already been commissioned to compose a poetic biography of Charles, he may have been left behind in Naples, where he could consult the archives and the expertise of Saba Malaspina, the official historian of Charles's reign and one of his chief political apologists, author of "The Book of the Deeds of the Kings of Sicily" (*Liber gestarum regum Siciliae*), completed in 1285.[100] It seems likely, too, that Adam would have moved to Bari with the royal archives in November 1284, when King Charles made his last progress to Apu-

95. Ibid., 99–113. See Runciman, *Sicilian Vespers*, for a full account of these incidents and their pan-European significance.

96. *The Chronicle of Morea*, ed. John Schmitt (London, 1904), vv. 6829–35. A French translation was made toward the end of the fourteenth century: *Chronique de Morée (1204–1305): Livre de la conqueste de la princée de l'Amorée*, ed. Jean Longnon (Paris, 1911), ¶475b.

97. Salimbene de Adam, *Cronica*, ed. Giuseppe Scalia, 2 vols. (Turnhout, 1998), 2:776.

98. De Losine, "Itinéraire," 371.

99. Jole Mazzoleni, *Le fonti documentarie e bibliografiche dal sec. X al sec. XX conservate presso l'archivio di stato di Napoli* (Naples, 1974), 31–57; Andreas Kieswetter, "La cancellaria Angioina," in *L'état angevin*, 361–395; Samantha Kelly, *The New Solomon: Robert of Naples (1309–1342) and Fourteenth-Century Kingship* (Leiden, 2003), 10–11. See also Paul Durrieu, *Les archives angevines de Naples: Étude sur les registres du roi Charles Ier. (1265–1285)*, 2 vols. (Paris, 1886–1887), and "Notice sur les registres angevins en langue française conservés dans les archives de Naples," *Mélanges d'archéologie et d'histoire* 3 (1883): 3–33.

100. Claude Carozzi, "Saba Malaspina et la legitimité de Charles Ier," in *L'état angevin*, 81–97.

lia, where he later died.[101] This further suggests that it was in Bari, the pilgrimage center for the cult of Saint Nicholas, that Adam spent his last years. It also suggests that Adam was party to the propaganda campaign of Malaspina, who helped to link Charles with the legacy of Charlemagne by analogy, even referring to his ineffectual heir apparent, Charles of Salerno, as Charles Martel.[102] And we know that Adam was effective in this new role, since his poetic version of at least one key episode in Charles's life, his wooing of Beatrice, would later be picked up and embroidered by Brunetto Latini and Dante Alighieri in Italian, while at the same time finding its way into the history of Guillaume de Nangis and the *Chronicle of Morea*, translated into Greek and finally back into French.[103]

Adam would certainly have needed some outside sources of information in order to craft his heroic narrative. But his other sources of inspiration were very similar to those of Jehan Bodel, and may have included the *Chanson des Saisnes*, which had begun by warning lesser rhymesters of the challenges involved in versifying history. Adam, too, begins in that vein:

Lamentable it is, a shame to good trouvères	*On doit plaindre, et s'est hontes a tous bon troveours,*
When good material is spilled and sown with tares,	*Quant bonne matere est ordenee a rebours;*
Not placed in trust of those who with much pain care	*Car qui miex set plus doit metres paine et secours*
Can place it all in order and make the verses fair.	*A che bien ordener qui miex doit estre en cours.*[104]

Having established the difficulty of his task, he announces the topic, "The matter is of God, arms, love, and ladies fair, / And of a noble prince, of parts and virtue rare" (*Li matere est de Dieu etd'armes et d'amours / Et du plus noble prinche en proueche et en mours*, vv. 10–11), and he begins by comparing the crusading exploits of Charles and his royal brothers with those of Roland and Olivier. Then, before launching into the history of "Charles the Great," he introduces himself as the narrator who will restore all that has hitherto been missing from the poetic and historical record: "I Adam of Arras: I shall redress those wrongs" (*Mais jou, Adans d'Arras, l'ai a point radrechie*, v. 68). And lest anyone be confused as to his identity, he says, "They also call me 'hunchback,' though that I've never been" (*On*

---

101. Mazzoleni, *Le fonti*, 32; Durrieu, *Les archives*, 2:189.

102. Patrick Gilli, "L'intégration marquée des Angevins en Italie: Le témoignage des historiens," in *L'état angevin*, 11–33; Kiesewetter, *Die Anfänge*, 175.

103. *Chronicle of Morea*, vv. 5935–5954; *Chronique de Morée*, ¶¶441–457. See Holloway, *Twice-Told*, 229; and Dunbabin, *Charles I*, 199.

104. *Le Roi de Sicile*, in AHOEc, 376–394 (vv. 1–4).

m'apele Bochu, mais je ne lesui mie, v. 70). His poetic scheme is ambitious: working in twenty-line strophes, each unified by a single rhyme sound, he attempts to tell the story of Charles's life in terms that would make him the peer of heroes like Chrétien's Cligès or the medieval incarnation of Alexander the Great.

But he did not get very far: the story ends abruptly with the pope's selection of Charles as Manfred's challenger, and is clearly supposed to follow through with a description of the battles that followed. Adam was just getting to the good part when he stopped. What happened? Did the death of Charles interrupt his narrative? References to the poem's protagonist are couched in the present tense, suggesting that Charles was still alive when Adam began the work; and Dunbabin has conjectured that finished stanzas were read aloud to the king from time to time as part of his evening's entertainment. Yet if the purpose of the project was to provide a lasting memorial, why would it have been terminated at the time of Charles's death on January 7, 1285? (This was, incidentally, the day after the nineteenth anniversary of his coronation.) Did Adam begin work on a project more to his taste, the *dis* which the Pilgrim described as the superior showcase for his artistry, *li geius de Robin et de Marion*?

The historical circumstances and scenario of the *Jeu de Robin et de Marion* have led Dunbabin to posit that it was a pastiche worked up from older material, prefaced with a plot "particularly appropriate for an audience of soldiers."[105] Perhaps, but this would be somewhat risky, given that the soldiers were busily dealing with the aftermath of a crisis brought about by the molestation of a vulnerable colonial subject by an armed oppressor. But maybe that was the point: it is tempting to offer a political interpretation of the play, particularly the first scenes, but hard to make that reading fit with an Angevin agenda. It might be argued that Aubert's lost falcon symbolized the vanquished Manfred, who had been immortalized by his father, Frederick II, in his famous treatise "On the Art of Hunting with Birds" (*De arte venandi cum avibus*), which became popular in translation after a copy was brought back to Flanders by Gui de Dampierre in 1270.[106] Images of hunting birds adorn several of Frederick's castles in southern Italy as well as the basilica of San Nicola, and were as clearly associated with him as Yvain's lion with Robert of Artois.[107] So it could have been the case that members of the play's audience saw in the ignominious death of the falcon a metaphor for the ignominious defeat of the emperor's heirs.

Yet the immediate reception of Robin and Marion in the Regno would also have depended on the place and timing of the play's performance. Was it produced before or after Charles's death? In either case, how would the carnival kingship of Baudons have played to an audience concerned with a real royal succession? Was the wrangling of shep-

---

105. Dunbabin, *Charles I*, 207.

106. Mallette, *Kingdom*, 162–164; Dunbabin, *Charles I*, 209.

107. Pina Belli d'Elia, *La basilica di S. Nicola a Bari: Un monumento nel tempo* (Galatina, [1985]), 74–75.

herds over the festive crown taken as a comment on the contest among the princes of Europe for the crown of the realm? Was there anything satirical about "playing at Kings and Queens"? It is hard to imagine that the playwright of the *Jeu de la feuillée* would have been unaware of the parallels, even if he did not live to see them played out. For as it happens, the Angevin fate in the Regno hung in the balance for years after Charles's and Adam's deaths. The heir presumptive was in captivity and would remain so until 1289, and the pope did not immediately recognize his claim to the throne or the appointment of Robert of Artois as his regent. Towns in southern Apulia would also resist occupation with increased violence, emboldened by the successful rebellions in Calabria—Sicily was totally lost to the Aragonese—the death of Charles, and the absence of a viable successor. As Steven Runciman has pointed out, following Salimbene's lead, it took several more significant deaths in 1285, including that of the pope, King Pedro, and King Philip III of France, to save southern Italy for the Angevin cause.[108] But it would be another half-decade before Robert and his household could go home. And by that time, as the Pilgrim reported, Adam was left behind. Only his plays made it home to Arras.

The Death of Princes

There is nothing ambiguous about the death of Robert II. Fatefully, it was at Courtrai that Philip IV named him one of the twelve peers of the realm, in September 1297: not far from there Robert had spent his childhood, and it was there that he would meet his death.[109] A few years later, on May 10, 1302, he was appointed captain of the king's army in Flanders and, two weeks after that, empowered to levy men-at-arms in preparation for war. At the same time, Robert's agents began to make provisions for "the people of the household of my lord of Artois to equip them for the war with Flanders." Chevrette, Jehannuce, Jehan le Fol, Pariset, and Lyon each received money for the necessary equipage and a horse, according to the ex post facto expense account detailing the arrangements made by "the late count." Then, on June 28, 1302, Robert had it published throughout his host that merchants bringing supplies to the French army in Flanders were to be given safe conduct, for they brought the trappings without which the count of Artois, with his boyish love of pageantry, could not well appear: new and splendid saddles for his warhorses, one embroidered with his arms and trimmed with vermilion, another "hung all with cloth of yellow silk," pennants for the trumpeters' horns, a new banner. Costumed thus, Robert rode out at the head of his greatest army on the eleventh of July. Behind him in the throng, somewhere amid the gorgeous caparisons and fluttering standards provided for his

---

108. Runciman, *Sicilian Vespers*, 255–260.
109. AdPC ser. A 42.15.

knights, was a secondhand hack girded with "an old saddle bought for Jehan le Fol (8 sous)."[110]

Jehan came back from those wars; his noble master did not. The battle of Courtrai would come to be known among the victorious Flemings as the Battle of Golden Spurs, from the five hundred gilded pairs wrested from the boots of fallen French aristocrats, dedicated as trophies to the glory of Notre Dame in her church at Courtrai. (Robert himself had ordered twenty-two customized pairs; they head the itemized list of expenditures drawn up prior to the battle.)[111] Philip IV's ill-advised attempt at the annexation of Flanders, coming only a little more than a century after Arras had become French in the time of Jehan Bodel, had transformed the ensuing conflict into a cause célèbre, so that July 11, 1302, is still celebrated as the founding date of Flemish independence.[112]

Once again, a role played by Count Robert was immortalized. He was not Yvain this time but a poor Christ figure in the *Passio Francorum secundum Flemyngos*, a savage and theologically inconsistent parody of the Passion liturgy composed at Bruges for a monastic audience with a malicious sense of humor, and which survives because it was copied into the chronicle of the exiled English cleric Adam Usk (ca. 1360/1365–?) almost exactly a century later (when Adam can hardly have failed to note the parallels between the downfall of Robert and the deposition of Richard II, in which he had recently played a controversial role).[113] It begins with the foolish King Philip asking his "disciples," "Who do men say is the count of Flanders?" And when a sycophantic Pierre says, "Lord, you are the king of Flanders," Philip calls him the rock "on which I will build my council. And to you also I will give the keys of my kingdom in Flanders," a kingdom which, as everyone knew, was non-

---

110. AdPC ser. A 46.10, 11, and 19; A 179.4: "Item une viese sele por achetee por Jehan le Fol." On the events leading up to the battle and its aftermath, see Nicholas, *Flanders*, 191–197; and Verbruggen, *De Slag der Guldensporen*, 1–39.

111. AdPC ser. A 179; ed. Richard in *Une petite-nièce*, 387–389.

112. Raoul van Caenegem, introduction to *1302*, 10–63. See also, in the same volume, Eric Bournazel, "La royauté capétienne au XIIIe siècle," 78–105. Note Verbruggen's characterization of this battle as "Vlaanderens Vrijheidsoorlog" ("Flanders's War of Liberation") in the title of his classic study, *De Slag der Guldensporen*.

113. "When I was in Bruges," Adam says (sometime between 1402 and 1404), he consulted the chronicles of the monastery of Saint Bartholomew of Eeckhout and "found this which follows, written in mockery of the French, for that in former days they were routed by the men of Flanders." See Edward Maunde Thompson, *Chronicon Adæ de Usk, A.D. 1377–1421*, 2nd ed. (London, 1904), 107–110 and 287–288. The *Passio* is also featured in Paul Lehmann's study of *Die Parodie im Mittelalter* (Stuttgart, 1963), 85 and 202–204. I have used the edition of J.-M. de Smet, "*Passio Francorum secundum Flemyngos*: Het Brugse spotevangelie op de nederlaag van de Fransen te Kortrijk (11 juli 1302)," *De Leiegouw* 19 (1977): 289–318 (reprint, Leuven, 1978).

existent, and for which the count of Artois would take the fall.[114] When Robert's character encounters another Peter on the field of battle, the Flemish weaver Pieter de Coninck, the doomed count is made to engage him in a disconcertingly blasphemous dialogue:

> Peter struck him again, saying, "Is that how you answer the high priest?" And the count fell upon the ground and prayed, saying: "Father, if it is possible, let this cup pass from me. But let it not be according to my will, but as you wish, Peter." And a great movement was made upon the earth from the third hour up to seventh hour. And at the seventh hour, the count cried out in a loud voice, saying, "*Bayard Bayard, où es tu, pourquoi as moi refusé?*" That is, "My horse, my horse, why have you forsaken me?" And having said this, he breathed his last.[115]

There is hardly enough in this to sustain laughter (the text's first modern editor deemed it "so offensively profane that it is better left without translation")[116] and some good evidence that many of those on the winning side were more inclined to sympathize with Robert's shocking demise than to make a mockery of it. A contemporary depiction of the battle in a local redaction of the *Grandes chroniques de France* shows the gallant Flemish-reared count crushed and mangled under the weight of fallen horses, as the newly armed townsmen of Flanders, his former neighbors, close in for the kill.[117] Even the most vivid depiction of the battle sponsored by a reawakened Flemish nationalism in the nineteenth century portrays Robert sympathetically as another victim of French imperialism: in the life-sized mural commissioned for the town hall in Courtrai and executed by Nicaise de Keyser (1813–1887), he is at the center of a horrifying maelstrom, his eyes wide with terror, awaiting crucifixion.[118]

---

114. "'Quem dicunt homines esse comitem Flamdrie?' . . . . 'Domine, tu es rex Flandrie.' . . . 'Et ego dico tibi quia tu es Petrus, et super hanc petram edificabo consilium meum. Et tibi dabo claves regni mei in Flandria.'" De Smet, "*Passio Francorum,*" 311–312.

115. "Petrus iterum percussit, et ei dixit: 'Sic respondes pontificis?' Et procidit comes in terram et oravit dicens, 'Pater si possibile est, transert a me calix iste. Non tamen sicut ego volo, sicut tu vis, Petre.' Et terre motus factus est magnus ab hac hora tercia usque ad horam nonam. Et hora nona clamavit comes voce magna dicens, '*Bayard, Bayard, ou es tu? Per quey as tu me refuse?*' Hoc est, 'Equus meus, equus meus, ut quid me dereliquisti?' Et hoc dicto, expiravit." Ibid., 314–315.

116. Thompson, in *Chronicon Adæ de Usk*, 288 (n. 1).

117. Brussels, Bibliothèque royale de Belgique 5, fol. 329v. This is in stark contrast to the doctored account of the battle depicted in a later French edition: BnF fr. 2813, fol. 326 (ca. 1375).

118. An early study in oils of De Keyser's fresco (destroyed during World War I) is preserved at the Stedelijke Musea of Kortrijk, in the former abbey of Greonige. For these and other striking representations of the battle of 1302, medieval and modern, see Bert Cardon and Bart Stroobants, "L'iconographie de la bataille des Eperons d'or," in van Caenegem, 1302, 170–193; and, in the same volume, Jo Tollebeek, "Le culte de la bataille des Eperons d'or de la fin du XVIIIe au XXe siècle," 194–239.

At home in the Artois, his death marked the end of an era: 1302 is the last date in a world chronology begun by a contemporary scribe, for "in that year was fought the battle at Courtrai between the French and the Flemish in which the French were beaten. There died on that day Robert, count of Artois, and Jehan de Hainaut, knights; and many other good men."[119] In Arras the bells rang out then and thereafter on July 11, according to the cathedral obituary: "On this day there died in the year 1302 at Courtrai Robert, count of Artois, of famous memory, illustrious son of the glorious prince Robert, count of Artois, brother of Saint Louis, king of the Franks."[120]

By contrast, the time and place of Adam's death remain enigmatic, although both are reported in colorful ways. Two sources speak, unmistakably, of his demise; but both are poetic, and oddly jocular. We have already heard the testimony of the Pilgrim that Adam's tomb is to be found in Apulia. The *terminus ante quem* is based on an even more problematic witness, an entry made in the Carité's funerary register in the late spring of 1288, when a certain "Madoc. Jehans" was buried just before Pentecost.[121] A self-styled "nephew" of Adam, this Jehans was a scribe who identified himself in a colophon to his copy of Benoît de Saint-Maur's *Roman de Troyes*, later recopied by another scribe working in the fourteenth century:

Cis jehanes mados ot nom	The scribe: Jehanes Mados the name,
Con tenoit a bon conpaignon	A social guy of goodly fame.
Darras estoit bien fu connus	He's from Arras, well known to you—
Ses oncles adans li bocus	His uncle's Adam le Boçu
Que pour revel et pour conpaigni	Who for a revel, company,
Laissa arras ce fu folie	Left our Arras; that was folly,
Car il est tremus et ames	For he was much beloved at home
Quant il morut ce fu pites.	And when he died, we all made moan.[122]

Jehans's verses are wily and parasitic; they cling to the final rhyme of the preceding *roman*, making it a pedestal whereon he strikes a Goliardic pose, complaining of his poverty, enforced sobriety, and ill luck at the gaming table. In this context his avowed kinship with Adam looks a little too opportunistic, however hard it may be to refute.

119. Paris, BnF fr. 6447, fol. 8v^b: "Fu li bataille a Courtray entre les Franchois et les Flamens. Se furent desconfit li Franchois. Et i fu mors Robers quens darthoys. Jehans de Haynnau chrs' et pluseur autre bonne gent."

120. BmA 290, fol 121r: ".v.idus.iulii. Eodem die obijt Anno M CCC°. secundo apud Courtray clare memorie. Robertus comes Attrebaten. Illustris filius quondam magnificum princeps Robert comitis Attre' fratris sancti Ludovici reg' francorum."

121. Berger, *Le nécrologe*, 1:61.

122. BnF fr. 375, fol. 119v^a. See Huot, *Song to Book*, 26. On the dating of the manuscript, see Charles François, "Perrot de Neele, Jehan Madot et le MS. B.N. fr. 375," *Revue belge de philologie et d'histoire* 41 (1963): 761–779.

Yet the argument for Adam's continued health and professional well-being beyond the period 1285–1288 is vexed, to say the least. The most intriguing piece of evidence, and one far more transparent than either the *Jeu du pèlerin* or Jehans Mados, is the mention of a "Maistre Adam Le Boscu" who was paid 20 shillings for his part in the festivities at Caernarvon at Pentecost in 1306, when Edward II, then prince of Wales, was knighted amid much minstrelsy.[123] Fabienne Gégou has insisted that this Master Adam was Adam of Arras, although a salvo of criticism has denied this on the grounds that, according to the *Jeu du pèlerin*, the poet was not called Adam le Boçu outside Arras.[124] This is easily disproved, however, since Adam himself acknowledges both this name and that "of Arras" in the *Roi du Sezile*, while "le Boçu" was also the name known and supplied by a fifteenth-century scribe adding rubrics to the fourteenth-century manuscript of one of the playlets derived from the *Jeu de la feuillée*. Gégou's imaginative scenario is neat: it describes how the young Adam might have had an opportunity to meet the Lord Edward in 1263, when the future king stopped in Arras with Charles of Anjou; how Adam survived his stay in Italy to see the *Jeu de Robin et de Marion* produced in Arras, perhaps even revived for Edward I's return visit in 1290; and how the *Jeu du pèlerin* could have provided a "whimsical" prologue for these later performances.[125] When Robert II died in 1302, what would have prevented the aging Adam of Arras from seeing the world and spending some time among the English?

As attractive as the story is, it cannot be supported by further evidence. If Adam was hale and hearty throughout the 1290s, why does he not figure at all in the extensive accounts of Robert's household? Had he ceased to be employed there on a regular basis, he would at least have received a pension, like his colleagues, or occasional gifts of money, or at least a casual mention. Even Adam's old friend Rikiers Aurris turns up, as the purveyor of "wax and lights" for the count's hôtels at Saint-Omer and Tournehem in 1296—fulfilling the fairies' prophecy of bourgeois respectability after all.[126] It is far more likely that this "Maistre Adam le Boscu" of Caernarvon was an "Adam impersonator," perhaps one of many who traded (as the sycophantic Jehans had done) on his fame by working up his repertoire of songs and sketches. And this "Adam" was not even a headliner; nor is the

123. Account roll preserved as London Public Record Office MS E/101/369/6; ed. Constance Bullock-Davies as *Menestrellorum multitudo: Minstrels at a Royal Feast* (Cardiff, 1978), 1–6 at 3 (transcript) and 67 (analysis).

124. Fabienne Gégou, "Adam le Bossu était il mort en 1288?" *Romania* 86 (1965): 111–117, and "Les trouvères artésiens et la cour d'Angleterre de 1263 à 1306," in *Mélanges de langue et littérature françaises du Moyen-Age et la Renaissance offerts à M. Charles Foulon*, 2 vols. (Rennes, 1980), 1:141–146. See also Norman R. Cartier, "La mort d'Adam le Bossu," *Romania* 89 (1968): 116–124.

125. Gégou, "Les trouvères," 143–145.

126. AdPC ser. A 161.30: "nous doions a Arraz a Rikier Ourri por cire et limegnon prinse de lui por nostre hostel, vint et sept l. dis et sept s. et sis den." See Menche de Loisne, "Une cour," 130 (no. 15).

paltry sum he earned comparable to what the real Adam le Boçu would have commanded had he lived.

When jongleurs die, there are no comets seen.

Epilogue: The Translation of Saint Nicholas and the Legacy of Jehan Bodel

The manuscript anthology that contains Li gieus de Robin et de Marion qu'Adans fist and Li ius de pelerin, with its related scenes, alone preserves the full text of Li ieus de le fuellie and the sole surviving copy of Li ius de saint Nicholai. It must have been compiled by someone who had access to exemplars of these plays or who had some other, more direct and intimate knowledge of Adam's work. It was certainly paid for by someone who had an interest in preserving Adam's artistic legacy, and who knew that there would be nothing further to add. It is probable, given the manuscript's Picard provenance, its focus on Adam and Arras, and its depiction of Adam as a performer of rare attainments, that the patron was Robert II. If not, it was someone with close ties to Arras and willing to pay for a lavish collection whose purpose was to trace the trajectory of Adam's career from beginning to end, constructing a coherent (if chronologically creative) portrait of the artist and his development, emphasizing his connection with Arras, and, ultimately, alluding to some special connection with Jehan Bodel. Intriguingly, Henri Roussel once asserted that this person was Gui de Dampierre, count of Flanders, although he cited no evidence in support of this statement.[127] Gui was certainly an important patron of minstrels, as I have noted, and he clearly had dealings in Arras: by 1295 he owed the bankers there 65,000 livres. He fought for the Angevins and alongside Robert of Artois after the Sicilian Vespers, and he might well have known and valued the work of Adam de la Halle. If he did commission the manuscript, he or the compiler to whom he entrusted the task showed a remarkable sensitivity not only to Adam's artistry but to his role as a representative of Arras. So this is another possible solution to the puzzle—and a poignant one, considering that Gui would spend the final years of his life attempting to defend his county from the encroachments of King Philip IV, whose general was Gui's own protégé, Robert of Artois.[128] We might also look to one of the wealthy supporters of the Carité for a patron, or to the Carité itself. Unable, according to its own established customs, to celebrate the obsequies of members who died outside Arras, it could have chosen this memorial as a fitting tribute to a former colleague.

In this manuscript, the Jeu du pèlerin (not attributed to Adam) is positioned midway through what amounts to an artistic biography, between the lyrical pieces and the dramatic or narrative ones. Its function matches that of the play as performed in Arras: it ex-

127. Roussel, "Notes," 285.
128. Nicholas, Flanders, 145–146, 170, and 181–191.

plains the context of the *Jeu de Robin et de Marion* to an audience that has not been to the Regno. The *Jeu de la feuillée*, which follows close on the heals of *Robin et Marion*, is thus positioned to recapitulate what was already known about Adam: it returns him to Arras and "dramatizes [his] role within this community," as Sylvia Huot has put it.[129] The compilation thus erects a textual monument to match the tomb the Pilgrim says he saw in Apulia, and like the Pilgrim prepares to teach all of Adam's pieces to a new audience. To that end, the purported death of Adam, whether real or poetic, is not allowed to interfere with the liveliness of the *Jeu de la feuillée*, which opens with the reassuring rubric announcing that it is in fact Adam's own "speech," *Li dis Adan*, echoing the term used by the Pilgrim to describe *Robin et Marion*, the *dis* made for Robert of Artois. Only after enjoying Adam's plays is the manuscript's audience reminded of the artist's mortality and treated to his weightiest efforts: the unfinished epic, the *Vers d'amour*, Adam's leave-taking in the *Congé*, and the oblique eulogy of a *Vers de le mort*, based on that of the trouvère-turned-Cistercian, Hélinant of Froidmont (d. ca. 1230), which was widely imitated in the North and which also inspired Adam's older contemporary in Arras, Robert LeClerc.[130] Like the *Jeu du pèlerin*, it serves a narrative function, drawing a heavy curtain over the story of Adam's life and work. *Explicit d'Adan* ("Here ends about Adam"), writes the scribe. Yet he must finish his task with the *Jeu de saint Nicolas*, as if to remind us that Jehan Bodel's Arras is the soil out of which Adam's art grew, and where it remains rooted.

Adding another dimension to this artistic biography are the miniatures accompanying each section of the manuscript, which immortalize Adam's primary role as a performer. In the first frame (Figure 1), he is shown singing his songs with authority, legs crossed and brandishing a newly penned scroll; his audience is rapt and attentive. The image that introduces the jeux-partis shows him debating with Jehan Bretel, exhibiting the parchment page on which the winning gambit is preserved; here, the audience is absent from the frame, and the manuscript's spectators alone witness the performance.[131] Then the Pilgrim takes the stage in his own play, engaging the crowd—presumably the people of Arras (Figure 2). This scene gives way to the opening of the *Jeu de Robin et de Marion*, and once again we are the sole audience, watching a play in which, as the image suggests, Adam himself played the role of Aubert (Figure 3). This may be sheer imagination on the artist's part, but it underscores the importance of Adam as the prototypical interpreter of his own works. At the beginning of the *Jeu de la feuillée*, Adam appears again, this time costumed for his role as aspiring student (Figure 4). Finally, the *Congé* depicts him riding off in fine style, but with a longing backward glance at his friends (Figure 5). The *Jeu de saint*

---

129. Huot, *Song to Book*, 68.

130. See Arndt Wallheinke, *Die "Vers de le Mort" von Robert le Clerc aus Arras: In sprachlichem und inhaltlichem Vergleiche mit Helinands "Vers de la Mort"* (Leipzig, 1911).

131. Bnf fr. 25566, fol. 23v[b].

FIGURE 25. Adam de la Halle as evangelist: the act of musical composition reimagined in the fourteenth-century Chansonnier d'Arras (BmA, fol. 142v: author's photograph)

Nicolas, the last selection, illustrates the devotion of the Prudhomme and the blessing conferred by Saint Nicholas, patron of revelry and revenue (Figure 6).

If, as Huot has suggested, the author of the *Jeu du pèlerin* and the manuscript's overseer are one and the same, these portraits of Adam as actor of his oeuvre are likely to be evocative of contemporary performance practices, although the flourishing of scripts in the miniatures illustrating his songs and jeux-partis are a gesture in the direction of a newer type of authorial persona which would emerge in the following century.[132] The Chansonnier d'Arras, for example, copied in the mid-fourteenth-century, depicts an Adam static and studious, modeled on the Evangelists, writing at his desk (Figure 25).[133] This formal figure symbolizes the extent to which Adam and his work had become canonized within a generation or two of his death, and is thus a reminder of how much the concomitant

132. Huot, *Song to Book*, 70 and 59–63. See also John Haines, *Eight Centuries of Troubadours and Trouvères: The Changing Identity of Medieval Music* (Cambridge, 2004), 5–48 and 172.

133. BmA 657, fol. 142v.

shift from oral performance to written authorization has done to inhibit our understanding of how entertainments were conceived, devised, staged, and eventually inscribed on parchment for a posterity that was increasingly disassociated with their enactment. Such stylized portraits, presiding over texts that will henceforward be treated as immutable, are a far cry from the palpable depictions of a medieval theater which are preserved in the Arrageois anthology. These later images foster a notion of performance as past, of the text as correspondingly predominate and impermeable. We must not make that prejudice, new in the fourteenth century, our own. Instead, we must insist—as this manuscript does—on a view of Adam's life and work that neither bars him from a place among the minstrels of Robert's *maisnie* nor scorns the bustle of the Petit Marché.

But how do we explain the relevance of the *Jeu de saint Nicolas* in this context? What would this play have meant to audiences in Apulia, or Arras, nearly a century after its composition in 1191? Jehan's play responds to a very specific set of historical circumstances, as I have demonstrated. It is also a striking work of art, however, and therefore transcends those circumstances. Its remarkable preservation in this manuscript, and its positioning within that manuscript, prove that the book's maker(s) and user(s) considered it especially, perhaps newly, significant. Why? There is no single answer. It is safe to assume that the play was considered by Adam, or those who knew Adam, to provide an important clue to his artistic development. Perhaps he saw himself as Jehan's artistic apostle, composing in some of the styles and formats the former had pioneered in Arras, and offering his own innovations. Perhaps, as I have suggested, he had himself taken part in performances of "The Play of Saint Nicholas." If the manuscript's compiler were privy to these influences, and had access to an exemplar of the play, these considerations may have been persuasive enough.

Add to these conjectures what we little we can infer about Adam's experiences in Italy. Could he have brought this play with him, or had it sent to him when, after two years' hard campaigning, Robert's household established itself in Apulia? King Charles had died at Foggia on the Adriatic coast, just north of Bari, the center of Saint Nicholas's cult since 1087 and the site of the magnificent Norman basilica built to house his remains. The collection of Saint Nicholas legends preserved in the Bibliothèque municipale of Arras contains the story of the Italian sailors whose pious theft of the relics from their resting place in Myra made this one of southern Italy's few major pilgrimage sites.[134] And I have noted that it was the place where the Regno's royal archives were housed after 1284, making this a logical place for Adam to settle, since his movements were not necessarily tied to those of Robert. In any case, letters and charters in the comital archives show that Robert was

---

134. BmA 307, fols, 95v^a–117v^a. See Patrick J. Geary, *Furta Sacra: Thefts of Relics in the Central Middle Ages*, rev. ed. (Princeton, 1990), 94–103; and P. Gerardo Cioffari, *Storia della basilica di S. Nicolas di Bari*, vol. 1, *L'epoca Normanno Svevo* (Bari, 1984).

certainly based at Bari in August 1285 and February 1286, was at nearby Foggia and Bar-
letta very frequently in 1286, and again in Bari and other Adriatic towns in October 1287
and several times thereafter.[135] In fact, he was fortifying the towns against enemy attack.
An act dated May 20, 1286, shows that the papal legate, Gerardus, bishop of Sabina, and
Robert of Artois, "baillif of the kingdom of Sicily," were busily making arrangements for
the safety of religious houses outside the walls of Bari "because of the imminent wars, and
the tumult of the present times."[136] Again we are brought face-to-face with mortality, possibly Adam's own, in the year following the taking of these measures for the town's protection. Moreover, it is worth noting that Bari—because of its extraordinary preeminence
as a pilgrimage destination—continued to be the object of unusual generosity and solic-
itude on the part of Charles II, who devoted much attention to the appointments of the
church and its ceremonies, the care of pilgrims, the deportment of canons and clergy. In
all this he was known to privilege French influences on the liturgy, as well as appointing
Frenchmen to half of the vacancies in the chapter and to most of the important capitular
offices.[137]

In short, I am wondering whether Adam could have presided over a staging of the *Jeu
de saint Nicolas* in the saint's own basilica, for a diverse congregation of expatriates from
Francia, Flanders, and Picardy, as well as for local residents, pilgrims, and Apulian clerics. (Some of these last were native speakers of Greek. Coincidentally, a rare copy of
Aristophanes' comedies was housed nearby, at the monastery of San Nicola di Casole.)[138]
The prologue would have come in handy, and may even have been composed for the occasion. The play's crusading imagery was appropriate, too: papal backing of Angevin supporters in the conflict with Aragon made their cause a holy war, as did the fact that
Honorius IV had placed Sicily under interdict.[139] The pagan King of the play could therefore stand in for this new enemy, while the Arras of Jehan Bodel became the beleaguered
Christian Regno. Saint Nicholas in his shrine could play himself. And if, in after years, the
manuscript containing the play were commissioned by Gui de Dampierre, the pagan King
would once again recall the bad old days of imperial designs on Flemish territory, which
were renewed in 1298 and which eventually cost Robert his life and Gui his freedom. The
double entendre would not even require a live performance of the play: merely placing it

135. Menche de Loisne, "Itinéraire," 371–375.

136. Ferdinando Ughelli, *Italia sacra; sive, De episcopis Italiæ, et insularum adjacentium, rebusque ab iis præclare gestis, deducta serie ad nostram usque ætatem*, 2nd ed., ed. N. Coleti, vol. 7 (Venice, 1721), 631–632:
"propter imminentes guerras, & præsentis turbationem temporis."

137. Ughelli, *Italia sacra*, 7:633–639. Kiesewetter (*Die Anfänge*, 509–510) notes this uncharacteristic
behavior with surprise.

138. Robert Weiss, "The Translators from the Greek at the Angevin Court of Naples," *Rinascimento* 1
(1958): 195–266 at 201–203.

139. Runciman, *Sicilian Vespers*, 227–233 and 257–268.

in this suggestive position in the manuscript would be making a powerful point. Furthermore, it is possible that Adam, who is said to have died in Apulia, was laid to rest in Bari, perhaps in the basilica. If so, "The Play of Saint Nicholas" would be a requiem in parchment, the prophetic tribute of one dead playwright to another, with a miniature representing both in the person of a Prudhomme from Arras. The first shall be last, the last first: *Chi fine li jeus de Saint Nicholai que Jehans Bodiaus fist. Amen.*

CONCLUSION ON LOOKING INTO
A MEDIEVAL THEATER

A pagan king invades Arras and converts to Christianity; the king of France invades Arras and converts its coinage. Adam de la Halle impersonates himself in a play of his own creation; his noble patron impersonates an Arthurian hero in a romance based on an actual event. A holy icon comes to life and chastises three would-be thieves; the Blessed Virgin appears and extends her favor to two delinquent minstrels. Criers come to blows over confused rights of publicity; heralds give out confusing information in the name of conflicting authorities. A trio of fairies offers advice to the people of Arras; a confraternity of jongleurs grants them absolution from sin. The bishop Saint Nicholas miraculously increases money entrusted to him; the bishop of Arras lends money at interest. A monk displays relics and asks for donations; the cathedral canons display a reliquary and are attacked by monks. Actors impersonate preachers to win penitents; preachers imitate entertainers to please the crowd. A false charter is read aloud to elicit laughter; a real charter transcribes the telling of a joke.

This procession of paired vignettes recalls just a few of the dramas that took place in thirteenth-century Arras. Looking at them side by side, we have seen that the formal plays of medieval Europe were enacted and received by people used to a performing repertoire that included the promulgation of laws, the celebration of Mass, the punishment of wrongdoers, the ringing of bells, the recitation of epic poetry, the staged contention of lyric debates, and the real contention of politics. Together, they were mounted on a common stage.

"Those things are taken to be public that belong to all people, that is which tend toward the use of all men": so explains the treatise titled *On the Laws and Customs of England* attributed to Henry de Bracton (ca. 1210–1268), citing certain features of the natural landscape as *res publica* that can have no individual owners, such as rivers. Then, Bracton goes on to say, there is an allied class of things "said to belong to the whole community in dominion and in use," things "such as theaters, stadia and the like, and which are therefore the common property of all citizens." Like rivers, these too are defined by action, movement, flux. A *stadium*, Bracton explains, recalls the distance that Hercules was said to be able to run on a single breath. As for theaters, he says, "they are so called from *theorando*, that is 'a looking into.'" Inherent in both the verbs used by Bracton—the Greek *theoréo*, the Latin *inspicio*—is the endeavor of shared purpose, the need to find something out through involvement with others.[1]

This book constitutes an exercise in *theorando*, a "looking into" the history of a particular community and its means of communication, deliberation, and memorial preservation. The aim has been to broaden the study of a medieval theater and to rediscover the culture of performance that provided the vocabulary for its plays. And as I have demonstrated, the study of public interactions, some of which were conceived and received as fictions, adds not only to our knowledge of plays and players, audiences and performance conditions, but also to our understanding of real people with real concerns. This is because the apprehension of a truly *medieval* theater calls for the historian to "re-enact the past in his own mind," as Robin Collingwood put it.[2] Any artifact that had its origin in a public act, or was destined for public reading or display, must again be exhibited to the critical scrutiny and keen ears of an imagined audience—imagined, that is, by the historian using all the tools and knowledge of her craft. This enactment of evidence, the use of performance as analytical tool, involves excavation of the processes that have led to the production of primary sources and calls upon the historian to consider the conditions in which those artifacts were received and transmitted. It therefore has the capacity to change the way we understand the past.

In particular, this history invites us to think creatively about the manipulation and impact of premodern public media and the relationship of communication technologies to the exercise of agency. To quote Bracton's words again: "Those things are taken to be public that belong to all people, that is which tend toward the use of all men." In Arras even documentary practices fell under this rubric. All the more so did the know-how of persuasive speech, arresting behavior, demonstrative noise, eloquent gesture, commanding appearance: the ingredients of a common stage. And to those who did not have the full freedoms of their use were given the powers of interpretation; I have stressed the extent to which public opinion really mattered when it came to delineating space, wielding power, articulating custom, doing justice. Is it possible, then, to argue that the medieval marketplace of Arras prefigures the "marketplace of ideas" many times associated with modernity? A classic formulation derives from Oliver Wendell Holmes's defense of free speech, expressed as a dissenting opinion (with the support of Justice Louis D. Brandeis) and appended to the Supreme Court's judgment of the case *Abrams v. U.S.* in 1919: "If you

---

1. Henry de Bracton, *De legibus et consuetudinibus Angliæ*, ed. George E. Woodbine and trans. Samuel E. Thorne, 2 vols. (Cambridge, 1968), 2:40: "Publica autem ita accipiuntur, quæ sunt omnium populorum, id est quod spectant ad usum hominum tantum. . . . Universitas vero sunt, non singulorum, quæ sunt in civitatibus ut theatra, stadia et huiusmodi, et si qua sunt in civitatibus communia. Dicuntur vero theatra a theorando, id est inspiciendo. . . . Et dicuntur ista universitatis dominio et usu."

2. Cited in the Introduction, n. 36.

have no doubt of your premises or your power and want a certain result with all your heart you naturally express your wishes in law and sweep away all opposition. . . . But when men have realized that time has upset many fighting faiths, they may come to believe even more . . . that the ultimate good desired is better reached by free trade in ideas—that the best test of truth is the power of the thought to get itself accepted in the competition of the market."[3]

Time and time again, we have seen that the entrenched and institutionalized powers of Arras were forced to yield to the very pressures described here. Neither law nor coercion was effective in maintaining authority, delineating boundaries, keeping the peace, safeguarding revenue, and creating consensus without some appeal to the general public, which was thereby endowed with a power of its own. Nor was this merely the power of transgression; such a mitigating explanation would not account for the sustained and astonishing success of the jongleurs' Carité, or for the contest ad phalam Attrebatensem, or for the inquests held "to air" public opinion, or even for the subject matter and varied messages of the plays themselves, which have attracted the admiring gaze of readers from the eighteenth century to our own day, readers who have found them familiar, enlightened, modern.

Moreover, it is precisely those forms of communication that prove most difficult to circumscribe and regulate which have the most power to effect real change, and which merit extra efforts of detection on the part of the historian. The public sphere of modernity is said to rely on the commercial printing press, yet Edward S. Hermann and Noam Chomsky have observed that modern mass media are more easily dominated by wealthy individuals or dictatorial states.[4] A medieval public sphere, by contrast, shaped as it was by media that could not be efficiently controlled—no matter how hard kings and canonists might try—had a capacity for meaningful exchange, social innovation, and political action that the modern public sphere may lack. Ease of censorship and social constraint was, indeed, part of the insalubrious "structural transformation" of the nineteenth century to which Habermas originally referred, and it is arguable that the enclosure of theater in the late sixteenth century already made it subject to these effects. It is therefore useful to equate Öffentlichkeit, the quality of "openness" that characterizes a public sphere, with the open-air en plaine hale, and to conclude that the medieval public sphere was both larger and more buoyant than that of the Enlightenment, just as a medieval theater was more multifaceted, more immediate, and more representative (in every sense) than the playhouses of the Renaissance, to which only those with money and leisure had access.

This was apparent even to contemporaries of this later, more circumscribed theatricality. In 1598, when John Stow (1525–1605) considered the changes to the culture of Lon-

3. Abrams v. U.S. (250 U.S. 616, 1919), no 316.
4. Herman and Chomsky, Manufacturing Consent, 18–19.

don that had taken place during his long lifetime, he quoted William FitzStephen's description of its "sports" in full, with nostalgic approval, because the medieval city of 1174 was more familiar to him than the one he inhabited. And he devoted page after page to a catalogue of the Christmas revels, May games, Carnival celebrations, city festivals, athletic contests, religious processions, and staged shows which had been the focus of public life in the years before the Reformation, reminding his younger readers that "the like exercises have been continued till our time" and had only recently been banned, underscoring the rapidity with which unbounded playing places had been subsumed into buildings whose restricted, licensed confines belied their claims to universality: The Globe, The Theater. "Of late time in place of those stage plays, hath been used comedies, tragedies, and interludes, and histories, both true and fained: for the acting whereof certain public places have been erected." This was after the Court of Common Council had moved to restrict the conditions in which all of the city's "sports" were performed, an act issued—with ironic timing—on the feast of Saint Nicholas in 1574. Comparing a medieval theater with these newly closed spaces, Stow mourned the losses of the past and prophesied little good for the future: "Which open pastimes in my youth, being now suppressed, worser practises within doors are to be feared."[5]

In 1716 a large-scale wooden relief model of Arras was completed by the engineers to Louis XIV, designed to ensure accurate military intelligence of this strategic border town, whose main features had been little altered since the thirteenth century.[6] Prominent in the Petit Marché is the chapel dedicated to Notre Dame de Ardents, which was still, at that time, the center of an important cult. But this enduring landscape changed drastically in the centuries that followed. In 1791 the Pyramide was pulled down in the early stages of the French Revolution; the cathedral was targeted in 1799. (Arras was the hometown of Robespierre.) Then, between the first and second phases of the battle of Arras, persistent firebombing leveled the town and incinerated most of the sources on which a history of medieval Arras and its theater might have relied. The view of Arras therefore looks very different in a German stereotype of the town's remaining targets, issued to an artillery battalion stationed on the Vimy ridge in 1916. The only towers still standing to attract the gun-

5. Stow, SURVAY, 1:92–95. See Lawrence Manley, "Of Sites and Rites," in The Theatrical City: Culture, Theater and Politics in London, 1576–1649, ed. David L. Smith et al. (Cambridge, 1995), 35–54; and Ian Gadd and Alexandra Gillespie, eds., John Stow (1525–1605) and the Making of the English Past: Studies in Early Modern Culture and the History of the Book (London, 2004). On the licensing of playhouses and the act of 1574, see David Katham, "Citizens, Innholders, and Playhouse Builders, 1543–1622," ROMRD 44 (2005): 38–64 at 42–43, 47–48.

6. Measuring 35 square meters and made to a scale of 1/600, it was kept at Versailles before being transferred to the Invalides in Paris and ultimately purchased for the Musée des Beaux-Arts in Arras. Ironically, it was badly damaged during the bombardment of 1915, and its restoration was only completed in 1998.

ners' aim—neatly labeled for ease of reference—are those of the medieval parish church of Saint-Nicolas in the far southeastern quarter of the town, ultimately destroyed, and the church of Notre-Dame-des-Ardents.[7] This edifice, built in 1876, when the confraternity of jongleurs was formally revived, would be the only major building to survive the war intact, "attesting visibly to the protection of the Virgin over her new sanctuary."[8] Miraculous, considering that Arras was never more than a kilometer from the Western Front and was officially designated one of "the murdered towns of France" in 1918.[9]

Scarcely had the Armistice been signed than the tourist board of the Pas-de-Calais launched a public campaign to rebuild the region's decimated towns. Under the headline "Arras and the Battlefields of Artois," fundraising posters advertise scenes of devastation with lurid images of the war's "most moving ruins."[10] John Singer Sargent, billeted in Arras while working on commission for the British Ministry of Information's War Memorials Committee (Gassed would be his masterpiece), drew the surprised notice of a fellow artist when he seemed disinclined to relish the Gothic picturesque. "I never could persuade him to work in the evening," said the English painter Henry Tonks, "when the ruined town looked so enchanting."[11]

Today the visitor to Arras marvels at the brave revival of the town's venerable structures, including the late medieval belfry and hôtel-de-ville, the seventeenth-century townhouses, the arcades. One can still follow the course of the old Estrée northwestward from the train station (formerly the Porte de Ronville) and locate the place where the castellan's prison once stood (now the Place du Théâtre), the site on which the counts of Flanders and Artois had built their houses, the vicinity of the mill and wedge-shaped piece of land belonging to the bishop of Arras. But the more obvious reminders of rivalry between City and Town have been entirely erased. The cathedral now occupies the monastery church of its old nemesis, while the medieval walls and defensive ditches and even the river Crinchon have been buried beneath the surface. What looks, on maps of the medieval town, like paired, unequal cells of power is now an oblong mass. For the historian of a medieval theater, struggling to recover a sense of place, it is good to see the Grand' Place furnished with a Ferris wheel and circus tents on the feast of Saint Nicholas, and the Place des Héros (Petit Marché) crowded with stalls on market days—though not nearly so crowded as it would have been in the days when the jongleurs' chapel and the scaffolding for public proclamations took up space, and criers and preachers vied with beggars and merchants

7. AdPC ser. 4 Fi 3126; reproduced in Jean-Michelle Decelle et al., eds., 1914–1918, le Pas-de-Calais en guerre: Les gammes de l'extrême (Arras, 1998), 47.

8. F. Blondel, in Chevallot, Notre-Dame des ardents, 9–10. On the revival of the confraternity (offically dissolved on March 18, 1792), see Cavrois, Cartulaire, 3–7 and 103–104.

9. Henri Potez, Arras [Villes meurtiés de France] (Paris, 1918).

10. AdPC ser. 17 Fi b901; Arras et les Champs de Bataille de l'Artois: "les plus émouvantes ruines."

11. Quoted by Evan Charteris, John Sargent (London, 1927), 212.

for attention. It is also instructive to visit the neo-Romanesque church of Notre-Dame-des-Ardents, monument to the medieval past and to the strong hold of modern constructions upon that past. Standing before the altar, with its statue of the Virgin suspended in mid-air, we are invited to witness the drama of her apparition to a pair of wayward minstrels and the bishop of Arras. We cannot see what they saw, but it may be as close to a common stage as we will ever get.

APPENDIX

THE CURRENT "CANON" OF MEDIEVAL VERNACULAR DRAMA BEFORE 1300: PLAYS AND SCRIPTS

PLAY	DIALECT	COMPOSED	PLACE { MS PROVENANCE*	MS CODEX	DATE
"Sponsus"	Occitan/Latin	ca. 1080	Abbey of Saint-Martial, Limoges	Paris, BnF lat. 1139	before 1100
Ordo representacionis Ade ("Jeu d'Adam")	Anglo-Norman / Latin	ca. 1160?	Anglo-Norman realm { MS copied in the Midi	Tours, Bm 927	early 13th c.
Seinte Resureccion	Anglo-Norman/Latin	late 12th c.	{ Norwich Cathedral? { St. Augustine's, Canterbury	Paris, BnF fr. 902 / London, BL Add. 45103	after 1255 / ca. 1275
Auto de los reyes magos	Castilian	late 12th c.	Toledo	Madrid, BNE C. Toledo Cax-6, 8	ca. 1200
Jeu de saint Nicolas +	**Picard**	1191-1202	**Arras**	<u>Paris, BnF fr. 25566</u>	after 1288
Courtois d'Arras	Picard	before 1228	Arras { all MSS copied in northern France, either in Picardy or the Île-de-France	<u>Paris, BnF fr. 837</u> / Paris, BnF fr. 19152 / Paris, BmF fr. 1553 / Pavia, BU Aldini 219	late 13th c. / early 13th c. / before 1285 / 14th c.
Miracle de Théophile (Rutebeuf)	Francien	ca. 1261	Île-de-France { both MSS from northern France	<u>Paris, BnF fr. 837</u> / Paris, BnF fr. 1635	late 13th c. / late 13th/14th c.
Le garçon et l'aveugle	**Picard**	after 1266	**Arras** { Picardy	<u>Paris, BnF fr. 24366</u>	13th–16th c.
Jeu de la feuillée	Picard	ca. 1276	**Arras** { the two later MSS contain abbreviated versions	<u>Paris, BnF fr. 25566</u> / <u>Paris, BnF fr. 837</u>	after 1288 / late 13th c. / late 13th/14th c.
Jeu de Robin et de Marion	**Picard**	ca. 1283	Naples or Apulia { **Arras** { northern France { southern France (Francien)	<u>Paris, BnF fr. 25566</u> / Paris, BnF fr. 1569 / Aix-en-Provence, Méjanes 166	after 1288 / late 13th c. / early 14th ca.

* "Place" (Roman type) refers to the probable place of the play's origin or composition, "provenance" (in italics) to the place where a given manuscript appears to have been produced. Sometimes the two are the same (e.g., Saint-Martial, Toledo, Arras).

+ Plays associated with Arras are highlighted in boldface; the two codices containing multiple scripts are underlined.

BIBLIOGRAPHY

Primary Materials

SOURCES IN MANUSCRIPT

Aix-en-Provence: Bibliothèque Méjanes

166   Adam de la Halle's *Jeu de Robin et de Marion*, 14th c.

Arras: Bibliothèque municipale
Archives de la Confrérie de Notre Dame des Ardents d'Arras, including the *Ordinance* ("MS. 239") and
    the "Régistre Thieulaine"

230   ordinal of the abbey of Saint-Vaast, early 14th c.

269   *Liber officiorum* of Saint-Vaast, 12th c.

290   obituary of the cathedral of Notre-Dame d'Arras, 13th–15th c.

307   collection of saints' lives in the vernacular, 13th c.

309   missal from the cathedral of Notre-Dame d'Arras, 13th c.

323   *Registrum* of Gregory the Great, with 12th-c. library catalogue

334   missal and sanctoral from Saint-Vaast, 13th c.

424   necrology of the cathedral of Notre-Dame d'Arras, 13th–15th c.

437   gradual and hymnal from Saint-Vaast, 13th c.

453   *Chronicon Andreæ Marchianensis*, 12th c.

466   ritual for the diocese of Arras, 14th c.

469   pontifical of Saint-Vaast, late 13th or early 14th c.

637   prosae and Passion sequences from the cathedral of Notre-Dame, 14th c.

657   vernacular preaching materials and the "Chansonnier d'Arras," 13th–14th c.

722   *Ars temporum* from Saint-Vaast, ca. 1282

740   necrology of the cathedral of Notre-Dame d'Arras, 13th–14th c.

745   Rule of Saint Benedict with *Rituale monasticum* from Notre-Dame, 12th c.

787   Franciscan missal from the library of Saint-Vaast, 14th c.

883   *Passiones Domini cum cantu* from Notre-Dame, 14th c.

845   devotional material in French verse from the library of Saint-Vaast, 14th c.

1049   lectionary of New Testament readings from Notre-Dame, 12th c.

1051   *Codex Lamberti episcopi Attrebatensis*, 17th c.

1067   collection of sermons, late 12th or early 13th c.

1060   *Trésor* of Brunetto Latini (incomplete) from Saint-Vaast, late 13th c.

1116   register of the confraternity of Notre-Dame-de-Jardin, ca.1290–ca.1583

1266   *Cartulaire de saint-Vaast d'Arras* or "Codex Guesnon," late 11th–12th c.

Arras: Archives départementales du Pas-de-Calais
A 1–529   "Trésor des chartes d'Artois," 1237–early 14th c.

3 G 1   "Antiquum cartulare" of the diocese of Arras (collection of paper and parchment leaves),
           13th –18th c.

3 G 2   charters relating to the cathedral of Arras and its benefices

3 G 3   charters relating to dealings between the diocese and the mendicant orders

3 G 4   charters dealing with oblations to the cathedral of Arras

3 G 5   material relating to the "Grand Commun" of the cathedral canons

3 G 15   charters of the bishop and chapter of Arras, relating to outlying parishes

1 H 1   cartulary of Saint-Vaast, with the "cartulaire dit de Guimann," 16th c. copy

1 H 2   cartulary of Saint-Vaast (also known as "cartulaire dit de l'evêché" or "Livre rouge" or AdPC
           9 J/AA) 19th-c. copy

H   "non coté"cartulary of the priory of Aubigny, late 12th–early 15th c.

Atlas 29   E. Morel, "Plan de l'ensemble de la ville d'Arras en 1382"

Brussels: Bibliothèque royale de Belgique

5   copy of the Grandes chroniques de France, ca. 1320–1340

21532–35 obituary of the cathedral of Arras

London: British Library, Additional Manuscripts

45103   copy of the Seinte Resureccion from Canterbury, ca. 1275

London: Public Record Office

E/101/369/6   account roll for the knighting of the future Edward II at Caenarvon in 1306

Madrid: Biblioteca Nacional de España

Cax-6, 8   Cathedral of Toledo: Auto de los reyes magos, ca. 1200

Paris: Bibliothèque nationale de l'Arsenal

3142   chansonnier associated with Arras, 13th c.

Paris: Bibliothèque nationale de France, fonds français

155   Picard translation of the Bible by Guiart, 14th c.

160   Picard translation of the Bible by Guiart, 14th c.

375   Roman de Troie, with the colophon of Jehans Mados dated 1288

412   prose saints' lives, dated 1285

763   anonymous translation of the Bible, late 13th or early 14th c.

821   devotional material in French, written in Italy; late 13th or early 14th c.

837   anthology containing Courtois d'Arras, "uns geus," and Théophile; 13th c.

844   chansonnier of Provençal and Picard lyrics, late 13th or early 14th c.

902   collection of didactic material with a copy of Seinte Resureccion, mid-13th c.

903   sole copy of the Bible of Jehan Malkaraume, 13th c.

1109   Brunetto Latini's Trésor with Arrageois material, dated 1310

1553   anthology containing Courtois d'Arras, 13th c.

1569   Roman de la rose with the Jeu de Robin et de Marion, late 13th c.

1635   anthology containing one copy of Rutebeuf's Théophile, 13th c.

2813   copy of the Grandes Chroniques de France, ca. 1375

5249	coutumier of Artois, dated 1250
6447	Picard collection of prose hagiography with a world chronology, ca. 1279
8541	register of the Carité de Notre Dame des Ardents d'Arras, 1194–1363
9561	historiated vernacular Bible, 13th c.
12615	"Chansonnier de Noailles" with the "Chansons et dits" of Arras, late 13th c.
17229	prose saints' lives with the miracle of the Sainte-Chandelle of Arras, 13th c.
19152	anthology containing *Courtois d'Arras*, late 13th or early 14th c.
20040	saints' lives and the Passion of Jesus Christ in verse, 13th c.
24366	*Roman de Troie* with *Le garçon et l'aveugle*, mid-13th to 16th c.
25545	Flemish manuscript of fabliaux and other materials, 13th and 14th c.
25566	anthology of Adam de la Halle's works with the *Jeu de saint Nicolas*, ca. 1288

Paris: Bibliothèque nationale de France, fonds latin

1139	proser-troper from Saint-Martial, containing the so-called "Sponsus," 11th c.
1328	Psalter of the use of Arras, 13th c.
1610	synodal statutes of Arras, ca. 1350
9930	cartulary of the cathedral chaptre of Arras ("Le Livre Blanc"), 13th c.
10972	"Hostagia du chapitre d'Arras," dated 1261
12827	"Recueil historique de Jean de Thélus (1587–1589)"
17737	cartulary of the cathedral of Arras, dated 1282 (Stein no. 216)

Pavia: Bibliotheca Universitaria

Aldini 219   copy of *Courtois d'Arras*, late 14th c.

Rome: Bibliotheca Apostolica Vaticana

Reg. Lat. 1490   alternate version of the *Jeu de la feuillée*'s opening scene, late 13th/14th c.

Tours: Bibliothèque municipale

927   liturgical book containing the *Ordo representacionis Ade*, mid-13th c.

Valenciennes: Bibliothèque municipale

150   liturgical book containing the early vernacular sequence of Saint Eulalia

SOURCES IN PRINT

Acta Sanctorum. Ed. Joannes Bollandus et al. 68 vols. Reprint, Brussels: Culture and Civilization, 1965–1970.

Adam de la Halle. "Das 'Jeu de la feuillée' von Adam de la Halle: Kritischer Text mit Einführung, Übersetzung, Anmerkungen und vollständigen Glossar." Ed. and trans. Otto Gsell. Ph.D. dissertation, Würzburg, 1970.

——. *Le Jeu de Robin et de Marion*. Ed. and trans. Shira I. Schwam-Baird and Milton G. Scheuermann Jr. New York: Garland, 1994.

——. *Adam le Bossu, trouvère artésien du XIIIe siècle: Le Jeu de la feuillée et le Jeu de Robin et de Marion*. Ed. Ernest Langlois. Paris: E. de Boccard, 1923.

——. *The Lyric Works of Adam de la Hale (Chansons—Jeux Partis—Rondeaux—Motets)*. Ed. Nigel Wilkins. Corpus mensurabilis musicæ 44. [Dallas]: American Institute of Musicology, 1967.

——. *OEuvres complètes*. Ed. Pierre-Yves Badel. Paris: Livres de poche, 1995.

Alberigo, Giuseppe, et al., eds. *Conciliorum oecumenicorum decreta*. 3rd ed. Bologna: Istituto per le scienze religiose, 1973.

Alfonso X el Sabio. *Cantigas de S. Maria*. Ed. Walter Mettmann. Madrid: Sálvora, 1986.

[*Auto de los reyes magos.*] Ed. and trans. Charles E. Stebbins. "The *Auto de los Reyes Magos*: An Old Spanish Mystery Play of the Twelfth Century." *Allegorica* 2 (1977): 118–143.

Bedos[-Rezak], Brigitte. *Corpus des sceaux français du Moyen Age*. Vol. 1. *Les sceaux des villes*. Paris: Archives nationales, 1980.

Berger, Roger, and Annette Brasseur, eds. *Les séquences de Sainte Eulalie*. Geneva: Librairie Droz, 2004.

Beugnot, Arthur Auguste, ed. *Les Olim, ou Registres des arrêts rendus par la cour du roi sous les règnes de Saint Louis, de Philippe le Hardi, de Philippe le Bel, de Louis le Hutin et de Philippe le Long*. 3 vols. Paris: Imprimerie royale, 1839–1848.

Bloch, Oscar, and Walther von Wartburg. *Dictionnaire étymologique de la langue française*. 5th ed. Paris: Presses universitaires de France, 1968.

Bodel, Jehan. *La Chanson des Saisnes*. Ed. Annette Brasseur. 2 vols. Geneva: Librairie Droz, 1989.

——. *Les fabliaux de Jean Bodel*. Ed. Pierre Nardin. Dakar: Université de Dakar, 1959.

——. *Le Jeu de saint-Nicolas de Jehan Bodel*. Ed. and trans. Albert Henry. Brussels: Presses Universitaires de Bruxelles, 1962. Reprint, Geneva: Librairie Droz, 1981.

——. "Les Pastourelles de Jehan Bodel." Ed. Annette Brasseur. In Castellani and Martin, *Arras*, 257–302.

Bougard, Pierre, and Carlos Wyffels, eds. *Les finances de Calais au XIIIe siècle: Textes de 1255 à 1302*. Brussels: Pro Civitate, 1966.

Boutaric, Egard, ed. *Actes du Parlement de Paris, 1254–1328*. 2 vols. Paris: H. Plon, 1863–1867.

Bracton, Henry de. *De legibus et consuetudinibus Angliæ: On the Laws and Customs of England*. [Ed. George Edward Woodbine.] Trans. Samuel E. Thorne. 2 vols. Cambridge, Mass.: Selden Society, in association with the Belknap Press of Harvard University Press, 1968.

Brou, Louis, ed. *The Monastic Ordinal of St.-Vedast's Abbey, Arras: Arras, Bibliothèque municipale, Ms. 230 (907) of the Beginning of the 14th Century*. 2 vols. London: Henry Bradshaw Society, 1957.

Bullock-Davies, Constance. *Menestrellorum multitudo: Minstrels at a Royal Feast*. Cardiff: University of Wales Press, 1978.

Calonnes d'Avesne, Albéric. *Dictionnaire historique et archéologique du département du Pas-de-Calais: Arrondissement d'Arras*. 2 vols. Arras: Sueur-Charruey, 1873–1874.

[Carité de Notre Dame des Ardents d'Arras.] Louis Cavrois, ed. *Cartulaire de Notre-Dame-des-Ardents à Arras*. Arras: E. Bradier, 1876.

——. Chevallot, Paul, ed. *Notre-Dame des ardents d'Arras: Faits et documents*. Abbéville: F. Paillart, 1918.

——. [*De la chandele darraz*]. Ed. Berger as "Le récit du miracle" in *Le nécrologe*, 2:137–156.

——. [Register]. Ed. Berger as *Le nécrologe*, vol. 1.

——. [Coutumier]. Ed. Adolphe Guesnon as *Statuts et règlements de la Confrérie des jongleurs et des bourgeois d'Arras aux XIIe et XIVe siècles, publiés pour la première fois d'après un manuscrit de la Bibliothèque impériale*. Arras: [s.n.], 1860.

[Caron, Zéphir-François-Cicéron]. *Catalogue des manuscrits de la bibliothèque de la ville d'Arras*. Arras: A. Courtin, 1860.

"Les chansons et dits artésiens." Ed. Berger in *Littérature et société arrageoises*.

Charles of Anjou. *Roi-trouvère du XIIIe siècle: Charles d'Anjou*. Ed. Jean Maillard. Rome: American Institute of Musicology, 1967.

"Charte de l'Estrée." Ed. Guesnon in "Les origines," 256–258.

The Chronicle of Morea. Ed. John Schmitt. London: Methuen and Co., 1904.

———. *Chronique de Morée (1204–1305): Livre de la conqueste de la princée de l'Amorée*. Ed. Jean Longnon. Paris: Librairie Renouard, 1911.

Chronicon universale anonymi Laudunensis. Ed. Alexander Cartellieri and Wolf Stechele. Leipzig: Dyksche Buchhandlung, 1909.

Courtois d'Arras: Jeu du XIIIe siècle. Ed. Edmond Faral. 2nd rev. ed. Paris: H. Champion, 1922 and 1967.

———. *Li "Lais de courtois," commedia francese del secolo XIII*. Ed. Giuseppe Macrì. Lecce: Adriatica Editrice Salentina, 1977.

———. Trans. Genty de Creky as *Courtois of Arras: The Best Seller of the 13th Century, for the First Time in English*. Chicago: Sussman and Ollainville: La Tourelle, 1959.

Dante Alighieri. *De vulgari eloquentia*. Ed. Warman Welliver as *Dante in Hell*. Ravenna: Longo, 1981.

———. *De vulgari eloquentia*. Trans. Sally Purcell as *Literature in the Vernacular*. Manchester: Carcanet New Press, 1981.

De Bure, Guillaume. *Catalogue des livres de la bibliothèque de feu M. le duc de la Vallière*. 3 vols. Paris: G. De Bure, 1783.

Decelle, Jean-Michelle, et al. *1914–1918, le Pas-de-Calais en guerre: Les gammes de l'extrême*. Arras: Archives départementales du Pas-de-Calais, 1998.

Delaborde, Henri-François, ed. *OEuvres de Rigord et Guillaume le Breton*. Paris: Société de l'histoire, 1882.

——— et al. *Recueil des actes de Philippe Auguste roi de France: Chartes et diplômes relatifs à l'histoire de France publiés par les soins de l'Académie des inscriptions et belles-lettres*. 4 vols. Paris: Imprimerie nationale, 1916–1979.

Delisle, Léopold, ed. *Catalogue des actes de Philippe-Auguste*. Paris: A. Durand, 1856.

Delmaire, Bernard. "Archives du Pas-de-Calais Série 3 G, chapitre d'Arras: Analyse des actes antérieures à 1350." Inventory donated to the AdPC in Arras, 1977.

———, ed. "Le testament d'un évêque d'Arras originaire du diocèse de Vienne en Dauphine (1220)." In *Papauté, monachisme, et théories politiques: Études d'histoire médiévale offertes à Marcel Pacaut*. Vol. 2. *Les églises locales*, ed. P. Guichard et al. 453–460. Lyons: Centre Interuniversitaire, 1994.

de Locre, Ferry. *Chronicon Belgicum ab anno CCLVIII ad annum usque MDC continuo perductum*. 3 vols. Arras: Guilielmus Reverius, 1614–1616.

Demay, Germain. *Inventaire des sceaux de l'Artois et de la Picardie*. Paris: Imprimerie nationale, 1877.

Dinaux, A. *Trouvères, jongleurs, et ménéstrels du nord de la France et du midi de la Belgique*. 4 vols. Paris: Techener, 1837–1863.

Doré, Robert. *État des inventaires et répertoires des archives nationales, départementales, communales et hospitalières de la France à la date du 1er décembre 1919*. Paris: E. Champion, 1919.

Du Cange, Charles du Fresne. *Glossarium mediae et infimae latinitatis*. Rev. ed. Ed. Léopold Favre et al. 10 vols. Graz: Akademische Druck Verlagsanstadt, 1954.

Ernout, A., and A. Meillet. *Dictionnaire étymologique de la langue latine*. 2 vols. 4th ed. Paris: Librairie C. Klincksieck, 1960.

Espinas, Georges, and Henri Pirenne, eds. "Les coutumes de la gilde marchande de Saint-Omer." *MA* 14 (1901): 189–196.

État des inventaires des Archives départementales, communales et hospitalières au 1er janvier 1983. 2 vols. Paris: Archives nationales, 1984.

Factum de domo destructa ad reponendum capsam Beatæ Mariæ in Platea sancti Joannis de Rotunda Villa quæ vocatur Follye. Ed. Loriquet in "Le trésor de Notre-Dame d'Arras," 199–201.

Faral, Edmond. *Le manuscrit 19152 du fonds français de la Bibliothèque nationale*. Facsimile. Paris: Droz, 1934.

——, ed. *Mimes français du XIIIe siècle*. Paris: H. Champion, 1910. Reprint, New York: AMS Press, 1973.

FitzStephen, William. *Descriptio nobilissimae civitatis Londoniae*. In Stow, 2:218–229.

Fossier, Robert, ed. *Chartes de coutume en Picardie: XIe–XIIIe siècle*. Paris: Bibliothèque nationale, 1974.

Galbert of Bruges. *De multro, traditione, et occisione gloriosi Karoli comitis Flandriarum*. Ed. Jeff Rider. CCCm 131. Turnhout: Brepols, 1994.

Gallard, l'Abbé. *Les trouvères guerrandais et la fête de saint Nicolas, au XIVe siècle: Chronique rimée inédite*. Nantes: Société de bibliophiles bretons et de l'histoire de Bretagne, [n.d.].

Le garçon et l'aveugle. Transcribed in Symes, "The Boy and the Blind Man," 128–143.

Gautier de Coincy. *Les miracles de Nostre Dame*. Ed. V. Frederic Koenig. 3 vols. Geneva: Droz, 1961–1966.

Gentil, Charles le. *Le viel Arras, ses faubourgs, sa banlieue, ses environs: Souvenirs archéologiques & historiques*. Arras: Eugène Bradier, 1877.

Gesta abbatum monasterii Sancti Albani. Ed. Henry Thomas Riley. 2 vols. In *Chronica Monasterii S. Albani*. Rolls Series. Rerum Britannicarum Medii Ævi Scriptores. London: Longmans, Green, Reader, and Dyer, 1897.

Giry, Arthur, ed. *Documents sur les relations de la royauté avec les villes en France de 1180 à 1314*. Paris: A. Picard, 1885. Reprint, Geneva: Slatkine Megariotis Reprints, 1974.

Godefroy, Frédéric. *Dictionnaire de l'ancienne langue française et de tous ses dialectes du XIe au XVe siècles*. 10 vols. Paris: F. Vieweg, 1881–1902. Reprint, Geneva: Slatikine, 1982.

Gosse, [Antoine-Alexandre], ed. "Anciens synodes d'Arras." In *Histoire de l'abbaye et de l'ancienne congrégation des chanoines réguliers d'Arrouaise avec notes critiques, historiques, et diplomatiques*. 574–613. Lille: L. Danel, 1786. Reprint, Arras: S.A.P.I.A., 1972.

Gossen, Carl Theodor. *Grammaire de l'ancien picard*. Paris: Klincksieck, 1970.

Les Grandes Chroniques de France. Ed. Jules Marie Edouard Viard. 10 vols. Paris: Société de l'histoire de France, 1920.

Grierson, Philip. "La bibliothèque de St-Vaast d'Arras au XIIe siècle." *Revue bénédictine* 52 (1940): 117–140.

Guesnon, Adolphe. *Sigillographie de la Ville d'Arras et de la Cité*. Arras: Topino, 1865.

——, ed. "Un cartulaire de l'abbaye de Saint-Vaast d'Arras: Codex de XIIe siècle. " *BPH* (1896): 240–305.

——. "Le cartulaire de l'évêché d'Arras. Manuscrit du XIIIe siècle avec additions successives jusqu'au milieu du XVIe: Analysé chronologiquement." *MAA* (1902): 165–323.

——. [Cartulaire de la commune d'Arras: Recueil des documents tiré des archives de la mairie.] Inventaire chronologique des chartes de la ville d'Arras. [Suivi du livre aux sermens]. Arras: Topino, 1863.

——. La Chandelle d'Arras, texte inédit du XIIIe siècle. Arras, 1899.

Guibert of Nogent. De vita sua. Trans. Paul J. Archambault as A Monk's Confession: The Memoirs of Guibert of Nogent. University Park: Pennsylvania State University Press, 1996.

Guillaume de Nangis. Chronique latine de Guillaume de Nangis de 1113 à 1368. Ed. Hercule Géraud. 2 vols. Paris: J. Renouard, 1843.

Hauréau, [Jean-]Barthélemy, ed. Notices et extraits de quelques manuscrits latins de la Bibliothèque nationale. 6 vols. Paris: Klincksieck, 1889–1894.

Henry of Livonia. Chronicon Livoniæ. Ed. L. Arbusow and Albert Bauer. Würzburg: Holzner, 1959.

——. Chronicon Livoniæ. Trans. James A. Brundage. The Chronicle of Henry of Livonia. New York: Columbia University Press, 2003.

d'Héricourt, Achmet, and Alexandre Godin. Les rues d'Arras: Dictionnaire historique comprenant des notices sur leur étymologie, leur direction, et sur les établissements religieux, administratifs, militaires, etc., qui y étaient situés, précédé d'un résumé de l'histoire d'Arras. 2 vols. Arras, 1856.

Hugh of Saint-Victor. Didascalicon. Ed. Charles Henry Buttimer. 2 vols. Washington, D.C.: Catholic University Press, 1939.

Imbs, Paul, and Bernard Quemada. Trésor de la langue française: Dictionnaire de la langue du XIXe et du XXe siècle (1789–1960). 16 vols. Paris: CNRS, 1971–1994.

Inventaire-sommaire des Archives départementales antérieures à 1790. Pas-de-Calais: Archives civiles—Série A. Ed. Jules-Marie Richard. 2 vols. Arras: Imprimerie de la Société du Pas-de-Calais, 1878–1887.

——. Pas-de-Calais: Série H. Ed. H. Loriquet, J. Chavanon, and G. Tison. 3 vols. Arras: Imprimerie de la Société du Pas-de-Calais, 1902–1911.

Jarnstrom, Edward, and Arthur Långfors, eds. Recueil des chansons pieuses du XIIIe siècle. 2 vols. Helsinki: Suomalaisen tiedeakatemain toimituksia, 1910–1927.

Jeanroy, Alfred. Le Chansonnier d'Arras: Reproduction et phototypie. Paris: La Société des anciens textes français, 1875–1925.

Lambert of Liège. "L'Antigraphum Petri et les lettres concernant Lambert le Bègue, conservées dans le manuscrit de Glasgow." Ed. Arnold Fayen in Compte rendu des séances de la Commission royale d'histoire 68 (1899): 255–356.

Långfors, Arthur. Les incipit des poèmes français antérieurs au XVIe siècle: Répertoire bibliographique établi à l'aide de notes de M. Paul Meyer. Paris: E. Champion, 1917. Reprint, Geneva: Slatkine Reprints, 1977.

——, and L. Brandin, eds. Recueil général des jeux-partis français. 2 vols. Paris: Société des anciens textes français, 1926.

Leroquais, V. Les sacramentaires et les missels manuscrits des bibliothèques publiques de France. 4 vols. Paris, 1924.

Liber Custumarum. Ed. Henry Thomas Riley in Munimenta Gildhallae Londoniensis. Vol. 2, pt. 1. London: Longman, Green, Longman and Roberts, 1860.

Loriquet, Henri. "Le trésor de Notre-Dame d'Arras." MCdMhPC 1, no. 2 (1892): 127–208.

Mansi, J.-D., et al., eds. Sacrorum conciliorum nova et amplissima collectio. 53 vols. Reprint, Paris: H. Welter, 1901.

Marbach, Carolus, ed. *Carmina scriptuarum, scilicet Antiphonas et Responsoria ex Sacro Scripturæ fonte in librose liturgicos Sanctæ Ecclesiæ Romanæ*. Reprint, Hildesheim: G. Olms, 1963.

Mazzoleni, Jole. *Le fonti documentaire e bibliografiche dal sec. X al sec. XX conservate presso l'Archivio di stato di Napoli*. 2 vols. Naples: Arte tipografica, 1974.

Menche de Loisne, Auguste Charles Henri. "Catalogue des actes de Robert I, comte d'Artois (1237–1250)." *BHP* (1919): 133–206.

——. *Dictionnaire topographique du département du Pas-de-Calais*. Paris: Imprimerie nationale, 1907.

——. *Table onomastique du cartulaire de Saint-Vaast*. Arras, 1906.

——, ed. "Anciennes chartes en langue vulgaire reposant en original aux Archives du Pas-de-Calais (1221–1258)." *BHP* (1899): 65–78.

——. "Le cartulaire des chapellenies d'Arras: Manuscrit de 1282 avec additions des XIVe et XVe siècles, analysé." *MAA* (1907): 184–394.

——. *Le cartulaire du chapitre d'Arras publié ou analysé avec extraits textuels d'après le manuscrit de la Bibliothèque nationale*. Arras: Rohard-Courtin, 1897.

Menche de Loisne, Auguste Charles Henri, and Roger Rodière. *Épigraphie ancienne de la ville d'Arras et supplement*. 2 vols. (Epigraphie du département du Pas-de-Calais, ouvrage publié par la Commisssion départementales des Monuments historiques. Vol. 7.) Fontenay-le–Comte: Henri Lussand, 1925 and 1927.

"Miracles de S. Vaast." Ed. van der Straeten in *Les manuscrits hagiographiques*, 87–93.

Molinier, Auguste. *Les sources de l'histoire de France dès origines aux guerres d'Italie*. 6 vols. Paris: A. Picard et fils, 1901–1906.

Morel, Edmond. *Essai de topographie arrageoise: Plan d'Arras-Ville en 1382 reconstitué d'après les documents contemporains*. Arras: Imprimerie Rohard-Courtin, 1914.

Niermeyer, J. F., and C. von de Kieft. *Mediæ latinitatis lexicon minus*. 2 vols. Rev. ed. Leiden and Boston: Brill, 2002.

Noomen, Willem, and Nico Van den Boogard, eds. *Noveau recueil complet des fabliaux*. 10 vols. Assen: Van Gorcum, 1983–1998.

Omont, Henri, ed. *Fabliaux, dits et contes en vers français du XIIIe siècle: Facsimile du manuscrit 837 de la Bibliothèque nationale*. Paris: E. Leroux, 1932.

Ordo nuptiarum [Use of Arras]. Ed. Molin and Mutembe in *Le rituel de mariage*, 297–298.

Passio Francorum secundum Flemyngos. Ed. J.-M. Smet in *Passio Francorum secundum Flemyngos: Het Brugse spotevangelie op de nederlaag van de Fransen te Kortrijk (11 juli 1302)*. Leuven: Historia Louvaniensia, 1978. Extracted from *De Leiegouw* 19 (1977): 289–318.

——. Ed. Paul Lehmann in *Die Parodie im Mittelalter*, 202–204. Stuttgart: Anton Hiersemann, 1963.

——. Ed. Edward Maunde Thompson in *Chronicon Adæ de Usk*, 107–110.

Patrologia Latina, cursus completus. Ed. Jacques-Paul Migne et al. 217 vols. Paris: Garnieri and Migne, 1844–1891. Reprint, Ann Arbor: ProQuest Information and Learning Company, 1996 [full-text database].

Peigné-Delacourt, Achille, ed. *Compte des dépenses de la chevalerie de Robert, comte d'Artois à Compiègne, en juin 1237*. Amiens, 1853.

Pontal, Odette, and Joseph Avril, eds. *Les statuts synodaux français du XIIIe siècle*. 3 vols. (in 4). Paris: Bibliotèque nationale, 1971–1988.

Potez, Henri. *Arras*. [Villes meurtriés de France.] Paris and Brussels: G. Van Oest et cie, 1918.

Quicherat, J. *Catalogue général des manuscrits des bibliothèques publiques des départements de France.* Vol. 4. *Arras-Avranches-Boulogne.* Paris: Imprimerie nationale, 1872.

Raoul de Chapeau Cornu. [Last will and testament.] Ed. Delmaire in "Le testament d'un évêque d'Arras."

Richard, Jules-Marie, ed. *Cartulaire de l'Hôpital Saint-Jean-en-l'Estrée d'Arras.* Paris: H. Champion, 1888.

Ruelle, Pierre, ed. *Les Congés d'Arras (Jean Bodel, Baude Fastoul, Adam de la Halle).* Brussels: Presses universitaires de Bruxelles, 1965.

Rutebeuf. *Œuvres complètes.* Ed. Edmond Faral and Julia Bastin. 2 vols. Paris: Fondation Singer-Polignac, 1959 and 1960.

Salimbene de Adam. *Cronica.* Ed. Giuseppe Scalia. CCCm 125. 2 vols. Turnhout: Brepols, 1998.

Samaran, Charles, and Robert Marichal. *Catalogue des manuscrits en écriture latine portant des indications de date, de lieu ou de copiste.* 7 vols. Paris: CNRS, 1959.

Sarrazin, Jean. *Le roman du Hem.* Ed. Albert Henry. Travaux de la Faculté de philosophie et lettres de l'Université de Bruxelles 9. Paris: "Les belles lettres," 1939.

Li senefiance conment on se doit contenir a le messe. Ed. H. Sonneville in "*Li senefiance. conment on se doit contenir a le messe:* Édition et traduction d'un traité en ancien francais." *Recherches de théologie ancienne et médiévale* 44 (1977): 230–236.

Sigibert Gembloux. *Chronographia, continuatio Aquinctina.* Ed. L. C. Bethmann in MGH: *Scriptores.* Vol. 4. Hanover: Bibliopolius Hahnianus, 1841.

Stein, H. *Bibliographie générale des cartulaires français ou relatifs à l'histoire de France.* Paris: A. Picard et fils, 1907.

Stow, John. *A SURVEY OF LONDON. Conteyning the Originall, Antiquity, Increafe, Moderne eftate, and defcription of that City, written in the yeare of 1598. by Iohn Stow Citizen of London. Since by the fame Author inreafed, with divers rare notes of Antiquity, and publifhed in the yeare, 1603. [. . .] With an Appendix, contayning in Latine Libellum de fitu & nobilitate Londini: Written by William Fitzftephen, in the raigne of Henry the fecond.* Ed. Charles Lethbridge Kingsford. 2 vols. Oxford: Clarendon Press, 1908.

Taillar, M. "Recherches pour servir à l'histoire de l'abbaye de Saint-Vaast d'Arras jusqu'à la fin du XIIe siècle." *MAA* (1859): 173–501.

———. *Recueil d'actes des XIIe–XIIIe siècles en langue romane wallone du Nord de la France.* Douai: Société nationale et centrale d'agriculture, sciences et arts, du département du Nord, 1849.

Tardif, Adolph, ed. *Coutumier d'Artois: Publié d'après les manuscrits 5248 et 5249 fonds français de la Bibliothèque nationale.* Recueil des textes pour servir à l'enseignement de l'histoire du droit. Paris: A. Picard, 1883.

Teulet, A., et al. *Layettes du Trésor des chartes: Inventaire analytique suivant l'ordre chronologique (755–1270).* 4 vols. Paris: Archives nationales, inventaires et documents, 1863–1902.

Tock, Benoît-Michel, ed. *Les chartes des évêques d'Arras (1093–1203).* Section d'histoire médiévale et de philologie, 20. Paris: Bibliotèque nationale, 1991.

———."Les chartes promulgées par le chapitre cathédral d'Arras au XIIe siècle." *Revue Mabillon* (1991): 49–97.

Ughelli, Ferdinando, ed. *Italia sacra; sive, De episcopis Italiæ, et insularum adjacentium, rebusque ab iis præclare gestis, deducta serie ad nostram usque ætatem.* 2nd ed. Ed. N. Coleti. 10 vols. Venice: Sebastian Coleti, 1717–1722.

Usk, Adam. *Chronicon Adæ de Usk, A.D. 1377–1421.* Ed. Edward Maunde Thompson. 2nd ed. London: Henry Frowde, 1904.

van der Straeten, Joseph. *Les manuscrits hagiographiques d'Arras et de Boulogne-sur-Mer avec quelques textes inédits.* Subsidia Hagiographica 50. Brussels: Société des bollandistes, 1971.

van Drival, E. *Épigraphie du département du Pas-de-Calais.* Vol. 1. *Arras.* Fontenay-le–Comte: Imprimerie moderne, ca. 1883.

———, ed. *Cartulaire de l'abbaye de Saint-Vaast rédigé au XIIe siècle par Guimann.* Arras: A. Courtin, 1875.

———. *Le nécrologe de l'abbaye de Saint-Vaast d'Arras.* Arras: Académie des sciences, lettres et arts, 1878.

Viollet-Le-Duc, Eugène-Emmanuel. *Dictionnaire raisonné de l'architecture française du XIe au XVIe siècle.* 10 vols. Paris: B. Bance [etc.], 1858–68.

von Tischendorf, Constantin, ed. *Evangelia apocrypha.* Reprint, Hildesheim: G. Olms, 1987.

Wakefield, Walter L., and Austin P. Evans. *Heresies of the High Middle Ages.* New York: Columbia University Press, 1991.

Wyffels, Carlos, and J. de Smet, eds. *De Rekeningen van de Stad Brugge (1280–1319).* 2 vols. Brussels: Paleis de Academiën, 1965 and 1971.

Works Cited

Abbé, Jean-Loup. "Rayonnement urbain et seigneuries autour d'Arras et de Douai au XIIIe siècle." *RN* 65 (1983): 400–410.

Abulafia, David. "Southern Italy and the Florentine Economy, 1265–1370." *Economic History Review,* ser. 2, 33 (1981): 377–388. Reprinted in *Italy, Sicily, and the Mediterranean, 1100–1400.* London: Variorum, 1987.

Adams, Henry. *The Education of Henry Adams.* Boston: Massachusetts Historical Society, 1918. Reprint, Boston: Houghton Mifflin, 2000.

Adler, Alfred. "Le *Jeu de saint Nicolas:* Édifiant, mais dans quel sens?" *Romania* 81 (1960): 112–120.

———. *Sens et composition du "Jeu de la feuillée."* Ann Arbor: University of Michigan Press, [1956].

Altenburg, Detlef, Jörg Jarnut, and Hans-Hugo Steinhoff, eds. *Feste und Feiern im Mittelalter: Paderborner Symposion des Mediävistenverbandes.* Sigmaringen: J. Thorbecke Verlag, 1991.

Althoff, Gerd. "Demonstration und Inszenierung: Spielregeln der Kommunkiation in mittelalterlicher Öffentlichkeit." *Frühmittelalterliche Studien* 27 (1993): 27–50.

———. "Empörung, Tränen, Zerknirschung. 'Emotionen' in der öffentlichen Kommunikation des Mittelalters." *Frühmittelalterliche Studien* 30 (1996): 60–79.

———. *Verwandte, Freunde und Getreue: Zum politischen Stellenwert der Gruppenbindungen im früheren Mittelalter.* Darmstadt: Wissenschaftliche Buchgesellschaft, 1990.

Anderson, Benedict. *Imagined Communities: Reflections on the Origins and Spread of Nationalism.* Rev. ed. London: Verso, 1991.

Asperti, Stefano. *Carlo I d'Angiò e i trovatori: Componenti "provenzali" e angioine nella tradizione manoscritta della lirica trobadorica.* Ravenna: Longo, 1995.

Aubailly, Jean-Claude. "Réflections sur le *Jeu de saint Nicolas:* Pour une dramatologie." *MA* 95 (1989): 419–437.

Aubailly, Jean-Claude, et al., eds. *Et c'est la fin pour quoy sommes ensemble: Hommage à Jean Dufournet. Littérature, histoire et langue du Moyen Âge*. 3 vols. Paris: Champion, 1993.

——, eds. *Le théâtre et la cité dans l'Europe médiévale*. Stuttgart: Heinz, 1988.

Aurell, Martin. *La vielle et l'épée: Troubadours et politique en Provence au XIIIe siècle*. Paris: Aubier, 1989.

Austin, J. L. *How to Do Things with Words*. William James Lectures of 1955. Cambridge: Harvard University Press, 1962.

Axton, Richard. *European Drama of the Early Middle Ages*. London: Hutchinson, 1974. Reprint, Pittsburgh: University of Pittsburgh Press, 1975.

——, and John Stevens, trans. *Medieval French Plays*. Oxford: Basil Blackwell, 1971.

Barber, Richard, and Juliet Barker. *Tournaments: Jousts, Chivlary, and Pageants in the Middle Ages*. New York: Weidenfeld and Nicolson, 1989.

Bakhtin, Mikhail. *Rabelais and His World*. Trans. Hélène Iswolsky. Cambridge: MIT Press, 1968.

Baldwin, John W. *The Government of Philip Augustus: Foundations of French Royal Power in the Middle Ages*. Berkeley: University of California Press, 1986.

——. "The Image of the Jongleur in Northern France around 1200." *Speculum* 72 (1997): 635–663.

——. "Jean Renart et le tournois de Saint-Trond: Une conjonction de l'histoire et de la littérature." *Annales E.S.C.* 45 (1990): 565–588.

——. *The Language of Sex: Five Voices from Northern France around 1200*. Chicago: University of Chicago Press, 1994.

——. "*Persona et Gesta*: The Image and Deeds of the Thirteenth-Century Capetians. I: The Case of Philip Augustus." *Viator* 19 (1988): 193–207.

Barker, Juliet R. V. *The Tournament in England, 1100–1400*. Woodbridge, U.K.: Boydell and Brewer, 1986.

Barnish, Jonas. *The Antitheatrical Prejudice*. Berkeley: University of California Press, 1981.

Bataillon, Louis-Jacques. *La prédication au XIIIe siècle en France et Italie: Études et documents*. Aldershot: Variorum, 1993.

Battard, M. *Beffrois, halles, hôtels de ville dans le Nord de la France et la Belgique*. Arras: Brunet, 1948.

Bautier, Robert-Henri, ed. *La France de Philippe-Auguste: Le temps de mutation*. Paris: Éditions de CNRS, 1982.

Beaune, Colette. *Naissance de la nation de France*. Paris: Gallimard, 1985. Ed. and trans. Fredric L. Cheyette and Susan Ross Huston as *The Birth of an Ideology: Myths and Symbols of Nation in Late Medieval France*. Berkeley: University of California Press, 1991.

Beckwith, Sarah. "Ritual, Theater, and Social Space in the York Corpus Christi Cycle." In *Bodies and Disciplines: Intersections of Literature and History in Fifteenth-Century England*, ed. Barbara Hanawalt and David Wallace. 63–86. Minneapolis: University of Minnesota Press, 1996.

——. *Signifying God: Social Relation and Symbolic Act in the York Corpus Christi Plays*. Chicago: University of Chicago Press, 2001.

Bédier, Joseph, and Paul Hazard, eds. *Histoire de la littérature française illustrée*. 2 vols. Paris: Larousse, 1923–24.

Bedos-Rezak, Brigitte. "Diplomatic Sources and Medieval Documentary Practices." In *The Past and Future of Medieval Studies*, ed. John Van Engen. 313–343. Notre Dame: Notre Dame University Press, 1994.

——. *Form and Order in Medieval France: Studies in Social and Quantitative Sigillography*. Aldershot, U.K.: Variorum, 1993.

——. "The Social Implications of the Art of Chivalry: The Sigillographic Evidence." In *The Medieval Court in Europe*, ed. E. R. Haymes. 1–31. Munich: Wilhelm Fink, 1986.

——. "Towards an Archeology of the Medieval Charter: Textual Production and Reproduction in Northern French Chartiers." In *Charters, Cartularies, and Archives: The Preservation and Transmision of Documents in the Medieval West*, ed. Adam J. Kosto and Anders Winroth. 43–60. Toronto: Pontifical Institute of Medieval Studies, 2002.

——. "Towns and Seals: Representation and Signification in Medieval France." In *Town Life and Culture in the Middle Ages and Renaissance: Essays in Memory of J. K. Hyde*, ed. B. Pullan and S. Reynolds. *Bulletin of the John Rylands University Library* 72 (1990): 35–47.

Bell, Catherine. *Ritual: Perspectives and Dimensions*. New York: Oxford University Press, 1997.

Bellart, G., and Maison, F. *Les fortifications d'Arras du XIIe au XIXe siècle: Études et oeuvres et documents présentés à l'exposition "Arras, ville forte."* Arras: Musée d'Arras, 1979.

Belli d'Elia, Pina. *La Basilica di S. Nicola a Bari: Un monumento nel tempo*. Galatina: Congedo, [1985].

Berger, Roger. "Archidiacres, officiaux, dignitaires du chapitre d'Arras (1093–1300): Essai de chronologie." *BCdMhPC* 8 (1958–1970): 505–541.

——. *Littérature et société arrageoises au XIIIe siècle: Les chansons et dits artésiens*. Arras: CdMhPC, 1981.

——. *Le nécrologe de la Confrérie des jongleurs et des bourgeois d'Arras (1194–1361)*. 2 vols. Arras: CdMhPC, 1963 and 1970.

——. "Notes sur les évêques d'Arras antérieurs à 1300." *BCdMhPC* (1972 [1973]): 167–174.

Bériou, Nicole. *La prédication de Ranulphe de la Houblonnière: Sermons aux clercs et aux simples gens à Paris au XIIIe siècle*. Paris: Études augustiniennes, 1987.

Berkhofer, Robert F. III. *Day of Reckoning: Power and Accountability in Medieval France*. Philadelphia: University of Pennsylvania Press, 2004.

——, Alan Cooper, and Adam J. Kosto, eds. *The Experience of Power, 950–1350*. Aldershot, U.K.: Ashgate, 2005.

Bertin, Paul. *Une commune flamande-artésienne: Aire-sur-la-Lys dès origines au XVIe siècle*. Arras: Brunet, 1946.

Besnier, M. G. "Pas-de-Calais." In "Chronique des Archives départementales: Années 1926 et 1927," ed. A. Vidier and H. Courteault. 399–403. *BPH* (1926–1927): 247–464.

Bestul, Thomas. *Texts of the Passion: Latin Devotional Literature and Medieval Society*. Philadelphia: University of Pennsylvania Press, 1996.

Bevington, David, ed. *Medieval Drama*. Boston: Houghton Mifflin, 1975.

Biedermann-Pasques, Liselotte. "Quelques aspects du développement de l'écriture du français à travers des manuscrits et des incunables (IXe–XVe siècle)." In Goyens and Verbeke, *Dawn*, 215–224.

Biella, Ada. "Considerazioni sull'origine e sulla diffusione della 'pastourella.'" *Cultura Neolatina* 25 (1965): 236–267.

Bigwood, Georges. "Les financiers d'Arras: Contribution à l'étude du capitalisme moderne." *Revue belge de philologie et d'histoire* 3 (1924): 465–508 and 769–819; 4 (1925): 109–119 and 379–421.

Bisson, Thomas N. *Assemblies and Representation in Languedoc in the Thirteenth Century*. Princeton: Princeton University Press, 1964.

——. *Conservation of Coinage: Monetary Exploitation and Its Restraint in France, Catalonia, and Aragon (c. A.D. 1000–c. 1225)*. Oxford: Clarendon Press, 1979.

———, ed. *Cultures of Power: Lordship, Status, and Process in Twelfth-Century Europe*. Philadelphia: University of Pennsylvania Press, 1995.

———. "Reply" to "Debate: The 'Feudal Revolution.'" *Past and Present* 155 (1997): 208–225.

Bloch, R. Howard. *Etymologies and Genealogies: A Literary Anthropology of the French Middle Ages*. Chicago: University of Chicago Press, 1983.

Borrelli de Serres, Léon Louis. *La réunion des provinces septentrionnales à la couronne par Philippe Auguste: Amiénois, Artois, Vermandois, Valois*. Paris: A. Picard et fils, 1899.

Bossy, John. "The Mass as a Social Institution, 1200–1700." *Past and Present* 100 (1983): 29–61.

Bourdieu, Pierre. *Ce que parler veut dire: L'économie des échanges linguistiques*. Paris: Fayard, 1982.

Bourgain, Pascale. "La poésie lyrique médiévale." In *Mise en page et mise en texte du livre manuscrit*, ed. Henri-Jean Martin et Jean Vezin, 164–168. [Paris]: Éditions du Cercle de la Librairie-Promodis, 1990.

Bourgeois, Albert. *Lépreux et maladreries du Pas-de-Calais (Xe–XVIIIe siècles): Psychologie collective et institutions charitables*. Arras: CdMhPC, 1972.

Bozonnet, Marcel. "Résumé" of "Jeu d'Adam (Le Jeu de la feuillée)." In *Comédie Française: Saison 2003–2004*. 22–23. Brussels: Le Cri édition, 2003.

Braet, Herman, and Werner Verbeke, eds. *Death in the Middle Ages*. Leuven: Leuven University Press, 1983.

Brand, Paul. *Observing and Recording the Medieval Bar at Work: The Origins of Law Reporting in England*. London: Selden Society, 1999.

Breuil, A. "La confrérie de Notre-Dame du Puy d'Amiens." *Mémoires de la société des antiquaires de Picardie*, ser. 2, 3 (1854): 485–680.

Brody, Saul Nathaniel. *Disease of the Soul: Leprosy in Medieval Literature*. Ithaca: Cornell University Press, 1974.

Bruckner, Matilda Tomaryn. "What Short Tale Does Jehan Bodel's Political Pastourelle Tell?" *Romania* 120 (2002): 118–131.

Brusegan, Rosanna. "Le Jeu de Robin et Marion et l'ambiguïté du symbolisme champêtre." In *The Theater in the Middle Ages*, ed. Herman Braet, Johan Nowe, and Gilbert Tournoy. 119–129. Leuven: Leuven University Press, 1985.

Buc, Philippe. *The Dangers of Ritual: Between Early Medieval Texts and Social Scientific Theory*. Princeton: Princeton University Press, 2001.

Bumke, Joachim. *Höfische Kultur: Literatur und Gesellschaft im Hohen Mittelalter*. 2 vols. Munich: Deutscher Taschenbuch Verlag, 1986. Trans. Thomas Dunlap as *Courtly Culture: Literature and Society in the High Middle Ages*. Berkeley: University of California Press, 1991.

Burke, Peter. *Popular Culture in Early Modern Europe*. New York: Harper & Rowe, 1978.

Butterfield, Ardis. *Poetry and Music in Medieval France: From Jean Renart to Guillaume de Machaut*. Cambridge: Cambridge University Press, 2002.

Calhoun, Craig, ed. *Habermas and the Public Sphere*. Cambridge: MIT Press, 1992.

Camille, Michael. *The Gothic Idol: Ideology and Image-Making in Medieval Art*. Cambridge: Cambridge University Press, 1989.

———. "Signs of the City: Place, Power, and Public Fantasy in Medieval Paris." In *Medieval Practices of Space*, ed. Barbara Hanawalt and Michael Kobialka. 1–36. MinneapolisUniversity of Minnesota Press, 2000.

——. "Signs on Medieval Street Corners." In *Die Strasse: Zur Funktion und Perzeption öffentlichen Raums im späten Mittelalter*, ed. Gerhard Jaritz. 91–117. Vienna: Österreichischen Akademie der Wissenschaften, 2001.

Caporael, Linnda R. "Ergotism: The Satan Loosed in Salem?" *Science* 192, no. 4234 (April 1976): 21–26.

Cardevacque, Adolphe de. *Histoire de l'administration municipale de la ville d'Arras depuis l'origine de la commune jusqu'à nos jours*. Arras: Sueur-Charruey, 1879.

——, and Auguste Terninck. *L'abbaye de Saint-Vaast: Monographie historique, archéologique et littéraire*. 3 vols. Arras: Alphones Bussy, 1865–1868.

Carolus-Barré, Louis. "Les grands tournois de Compiègne et de Senlis en l'honneur de Charles, prince de Salerre (mai 1279)." *Bulletin de la Société nationale des antiquaires de France* (1978–1979): 87–100.

Carpentier, Elisabeth, and Michel Le Mené. *La France du XIe au XVe siècle: Population, société, économie*. Paris: Presses universitaires de France, 1996.

Cartier, Normand R. "La mort d'Adam le Bossu." *Romania* 89 (1968): 116–124.

Casagrande, Carla, and Silvana Vecchio. "Clercs et jongleurs dans la société médiévale (XIIe–XIIIe siècles)." *Annales E.S.C.* 34 (1979): 913–928.

Castellani, Marie-Madeleine, and Jean-Pierre Martin, eds. *Arras au moyen âge: Histoire et littérature*. Arras: Artois presses université, 1994.

Cavrois, Louis. "Le Puy académique d'Arras ou l'art de la menestrandie au Moyen-Age." *MAA*, ser. 2, 19 (1888): 225–243.

Cerquiglini, Bernard. *Éloge de la variante: Histoire critique de la philologie*. Paris: Seuil, 1989. Trans. Betsy Wing as *In Praise of the Variant: A Critical History of Philology*. Baltimore: Johns Hopkins University Press, 1999.

Chambers, E. K. *The Mediaeval Stage*. 2 vols. Oxford: Clarendon Press, 1903.

Charteris, Evan. *John Sargent*. New York: C. Scribner's and Sons, 1927.

Les chartes et le mouvement communal. Saint-Quentin: Société académique de Saint-Quentin, 1982.

Chartier, Roger. *Cultural History: Between Practices and Representations*. Ithaca: Cornell University Press, 1985.

Chaumartin, H. *Le mal des ardents et le feu Saint-Antoine: Étude historique, médicale, hagiographique et légendaire*. Vienne, 1946.

Chazan, Robert. *Medieval Jewry in Northern France: A Political and Soicial History*. Baltimore: Johns Hopkins University Press, 1973.

Cioffari, P. Gerardo. *Storia della basilica di S. Nicolas di Bari*. Vol. 1. *L'epoca Normanno Svevo*. Bari: Centro Studi Nicolaiani della basilica di S. Nicola, 1984.

Clanchy, Michael T. *From Memory to Written Record: England, 1066–1307*. 2nd ed. Oxford: Basil Blackwell, 1993.

Clark, Susan Johnson. "The Theater of Medieval Arras." Ph.D dissertation, Yale University, 1973.

Clauzel, Denis, Charles Giry-Deloison, and Christophe Leduc, eds. *Arras et la diplomatie européenne, XVe–XVIe siècles*. Arras: Artois Presses Université, 1999.

Cline, Ruth H. "The Influences of Romances on Tournaments of the Middle Ages." *Speculum* 20 (1945): 204–211.

Coleman, Joyce. *Public Reading and the Reading Public in Late Medieval England and France.* Cambridge: Cambridge University Press, 1996.

Coletti, Theresa. *Mary Magdalene and the Drama of Saints: Theater, Gender, and Religion in Late Medieval England.* Philadelphia: University of Pennsylvania Press, 2004.

Collingwood, R. G. *The Idea of History.* Oxford: Clarendon Press, 1946. Rev. ed. Ed. Jan van der Dussen. Oxford: Clarendon Press, 1993.

Comberiati, Carmelo P., and Matthew C. Steel, eds. *Music from the Middle Ages through the Twentieth Century: Essays in Honor of Gwynn McPeek.* New York: Gordon and Breach, 1988.

Coornaert, E. "Les ghildes médiévales (Ve–XIVe siècles)." *Revue historique* 199 (1948): 22–55 and 208–243.

Corbin, Alain. *Les cloches de la terre: Paysage sonore et culture sensible dans les campagnes au XIXe siécle.* Paris: Albin Michel, 1994.

Coulet, Noël. "Aix, capitale de la provence angevine." In *L'état angevin,* 217–330.

——. "Processions, espace urbain, communauté civique." In *Liturgie et musique (XIe–XIVe s.).* 381–397. Cahiers de Fanjeaux 17. Toulouse: E. Privat, 1982.

——. "Propriétaires et exploitants d'auberges dans la France du Midi au Bas Moyen Age." In *Gastfreundschaft, Taverne und Gasthaus im Mittelalter,* ed. Hans Conrad Peyer and Elisabeth Müller-Luckner. 119–136. Munich: R. Oldenbourg, 1983.

Cowell, Andrew. *At Play in the Tavern: Signs, Coins, and Bodies in the Middle Ages.* Ann Arbor: University of Michigan Press, 1999.

Crossley, Nick, and John Michael Robert, eds. *After Habermas: New Perspectives on the Public Sphere.* Oxford: Blackwell, 2004.

D'Accone, Frank A. *The Civic Muse: Music and Musicians in Siena during the Middle Ages.* Chicago: University of Chicago Press, 1997.

Dagenais, John. *The Ethics of Reading in a Manuscript Culture: Glossing the "Libro de buen amor."* Princeton: Princeton University Press, 1994.

Dane, Joseph A. "Parody and Satire in the Literature of Thirteenth-Century Arras." *Studies in Philology* 81 (1984): 1–27 and 119–144.

——. *Res/Verba: A Study in Medieval French Drama.* Leiden: E. J. Brill, 1985.

Darnton, Robert. "An Early Information Society: News and Media in Eighteenth-Century Paris." *AHR* 105 (2000): 1–35.

Davidson, Clifford, ed. *Material Culture and Medieval Drama.* Kalamazoo: Western Michigan University Press, 1999.

——, ed. *The Saint Play in Medieval Europe.* Kalamazoo: Western Michigan University Press, 1986.

Davis, Natalie Zemon. *Fiction in the Archives: Pardon Tales and Their Tellers in Sixteenth-Century France.* Stanford: Stanford University Press, 1987.

——. *Society and Culture in Early Modern France.* Stanford: Stanford University Press 1975.

de Certeau, Michel. *L'écriture de l'histoire.* Paris: Gallimard, 1975.

de Germiny, Maxim. *Les lieutenants de Robert II, comte d'Artois, gardes et maîtres de toutes ces terres (1270–1299).* Arras: Imprimerie F. Guyot, 1898.

de Linas, Charles. *La Confrérie de Notre-Dame des Ardents.* Arras, 1857.

Delmaire, Bernard. *Le diocèse d'Arras de 1093 au milieu de XIVe siècle: Recherches sur la vie religieuse dans le nord de la France au Moyen Age.* 2 vols. Arras: CdMhPC, 1994.

de Pas, Justine. "Mystères et jeux scéniques à Saint-Omer aux XVe et XVIe siècles." MSAM 31 (1913): 345–377.

Deregnaucourt, Jean-Pierre. "De l'église à la rue: Les lieux publiques de la charité privée à Douai aux dernier siècles du Moyen Age." In *Lieux publics et sociabilité.* 1–13. Fédération des sociétés savantes du Nord de la France, Actes du 22e Congrès. Bouchain, 1981.

——. "Le dernier voyage: L'ambulation funèbre à Douai au XIVe et XVe siècles." In *Actes en colloque: La sociabilité urbaine en Europe du Nord-Ouest du XIVeau XVIIIe siècles.* 81–88. Douai: Lefebvre-Lévêque, 1983.

——. "L'élection de sépulture d'après les testaments douaisiens (1295–1500). RN 65 (1983): 343–360.

Derville, Alain. *L'économie française au moyen âge.* Paris: Ophrys, 1995.

——. "Ghildes, carités, confréries dans le Saint-Omer médiéval." *Bulletin de la Société des Antiquaires de la Morinie* 19 (1959): 193–211.

——. "Les métiers de Saint-Omer." In *Les métiers au moyen âge: Aspects économiques et sociaux,* ed. Pascale Lambrechts and Jean-Pierre Sosson. 99–108. Louvain-la-Neuve: Université catholique de Louvain, Institut d'études médiévales, 1994.

——. "Le nombre d'habitants des villes de l'Artois et de la Flandre wallonne (1300–1450)." RN 65 (1983): 277–299.

——. *Saint-Omer: Des origines au début du XIVe siècle.* Villeneuve d'Ascq: Presses universitaires de Lille, 1995.

——. *Villes de Flandre et d'Artois (900–1500).* Villeneuve d'Ascq: Presses universitaires du Septentrion, 2002.

Deschamps, Jeanne. *Les confréries au Moyen Age.* Bordeaux: Imprimerie Biere, 1958.

Despy, Georges, and Pierre Ruelle, eds. *Bourgeois et littérature bourgeoise dans les anciens Pays–Bas au XIIIe siècle.* Brussels: Éditions de l'Université de Bruxelles, 1978.

Dhoehaerd, R. "Note sur l'histoire d'un ancien impôt: Le tonlieu d'Arras." MAA (1943–44): 177–201; and (1946): 27–42.

Dox, Donalee. *The Idea of the Theater in Latin Christian Thought: Augustine to the Fourteenth Century.* Ann Arbor: University of Michigan Press, 2004.

Dozier, Jane B. "Mimesis and Li jeus de la fuellie." *Tréteaux* 3 (1981): 80–89.

Duby, Georges. *Le dimanche de Bouvines: 27 juillet 1214.* Trente journées qui ont fait la France 5. Paris: Gallimard, 1973.

——. *Les trois ordres: ou, L'imaginaire du féodalisme.* Paris: Gallimard, 1978.

Dufour, Charles. "Situation financière des villes de Picardie sous saint Louis." *Mémoires de la Société des antiquaires de Picardie,* ser. 2, 5 (1858): 583–691.

Dufournet, Jean. "Complexité et ambiguïté du Jeu de Robin et Marion: L'ouverture de la pièce et le portrait des paysans." In *Études de philologie romane et d'histoire littéraire offertes à Jules Horrent,* ed. Jean Marie d'Heur and Nicoletta Cherubini. 141–159. Liège, 1980.

——. *Courtois d'Arras (L'enfant prodigue).* Paris: G. F.-Flammarion 1995.

——. "Du double unité: Les sarrasins dans le Jeu de saint-Nicolas." In *Studies in Honor of Hans-Erich Keller: Medieval and Occitan Literature and Romance Linguistics,* ed. Rupert T. Pickens. 261–274. Kalamazoo: Medieval Institute Publications, 1993.

——. *Le garçon et l'aveugle: Jeu du XIIIe siècle.* Ed. Mario Roques. Paris: H. Champion, 1989.

——. "Du Jeu de Robin et Marion au Jeu de la feuillée." In *Études de langues et littérature du Moyen Age: Offertes à Felix Lecoy par ses collègues, ses élèves et ses amis.* 73–94. Paris: H. Champion, 1973.

——. *Le Jeu de la feuillée.* Paris: Flammarion, 1989.

——, ed. *Naissances du théâtre français (XIIe–XIIIe siècles).* In *Revue des langues romanes* 95 (1991).

Du Laurens, J.-B. *Histoire de la Sainte Chandelle d'Arras.* Brussels: Henry Kristemaeckers, [1881].

Dumoulin, Jean, and Jacques Pycke, eds. *La grande procession de Tournai (1090–1992): Une réalité religieuse, urbaine, diocésaine, sociale, économique et artistique.* Tournai: Cathédrale Notre-Dame and Louvain-la-Neuve: Université catholique de Louvain, 1992.

Dunbabin, Jean. *Charles I of Anjou: Power, Kingship, and State-Making in Thirteenth-Century Europe.* London: Longman, 1998.

Dupire, Noël. "Mots picards ou wallons difficiles et rares." *Neuphilologische Mitteilungen* 50 (1949): 130–144.

Durrieu, Paul. *Les archives angevines de Naples: Étude sur les registres du roi Charles Ier (1265–1285).* 2 vols. Paris: E. Thorin, 1886–1887.

——. "Notice sur les registres angevins en langue française conservés dans les archives de Naples." *Mélanges d'archéologie et d'histoire* 3 (1883): 3–33.

Dyggve, Holger Petersen. "Personnages historiques figurant dans la poésie lyrique française des XIIe et XIIIe siècles." *Neuphilologische Mitteilungen* 50 (1949): 144–174.

Emery, Richard W. *The Friars in Medieval France: A Catalogue of French Mendicant Convents, 1200–1550.* New York: Columbia University Press, 1962.

——. "The Friars of the Sack." *Speculum* 18 (1943): 323–334.

——. "A Note on the Friars of the Sack." *Speculum* 35 (1960): 591–595.

Enders, Jody. *Death by Drama and Other Medieval Urban Legends.* Chicago: University of Chicago Press, 2002.

——. *Rhetoric and the Origins of Medieval Drama.* Ithaca: Cornell University Press, 1992.

——. "Theater Makes History: Ritual Murder by Proxy in the *Mistere de la Sainte Hostie.*" *Speculum* 79 (2004): 991–1016.

Erler, Adalbert, Ekkehard Kaufmann et al. *Handwörterbuch zur deutschen Rechtsgeschichte.* 5 vols. Berlin: E. Schmidt, 1971–1998.

Espinas, Georges. *Les origines de l'association.* Vol. 1. *Les origines du droit d'association dans les villes de l'Artois et de la Flandre française jusqu'au début du XVIe siècle.* 2 vols. Bibliothèque de la Société d'histoire du droit des pays flamands, picards, et wallons 14. Lille: E. Raoust, 1941–1942.

L'état angevin: Pouvoir, culture, et société entre XIIIe et XIVe siècle. Istituto Storico Italiano per il Medio Evo, nuovi studi storici 45. Rome: Collection de l'École française de Rome, 1998.

Fanien, P. *Histoire du chapitre d'Arras.* Arras: Rousseau-LeRoy, 1868.

Faral, Edmond. *Les jongleurs en France au Moyen Age.* Paris: H. Champion, 1910. Reprint, New York: B. Franklin, 1970; and Geneva: Slatkine, 1987.

Farrell, Thomas J., ed. *Bakhtin and Medieval Voices.* Gainsville: University Press of Florida, 1995.

Fassler, Margot. *Gothic Song: Victorine Sequences and Augustinian Reform in Twelfth-Century Paris.* Cambridge: Cambridge University Press, 1993.

Fenster, Thelma, and Daniel Lord Smail, eds. *Fama: The Politics of Talk and Reputation in Medieval Europe.* Ithaca: Cornell University Press, 2003.

Feuchère, Pierre. *Les châtelains d'Arras: De l'épée à la plume.* Arras: CdMhPC, 1948.

——. "La noblesse du nord de la France." *Annales E.S.C.* 6 (1951): 306–318.

Fixot, Michel, and Elisabeth Zadora-Rio, eds. *L'environment des églises et la topographie des campagnes médiévale: Actes du IIIe Congrès internationale d'archéologie médiévale, Aix-en-Provence, 28–30 septembre 1989.* Paris: Éditions de la Maison des sciences de l'homme, 1994.

Flament, Monique. *L'Artois à la fin du XIIIe siècle.* Poitiers: Imprimerie l'Union, 1981.

Flood, David, ed. *Poverty in the Middle Ages.* Franziskanische Forschungen 27. Werl: D. Coelde, 1975.

Fossier, Robert. *Le Moyen Age en Picardie.* Amiens: CNDP and CRDP, [1983].

——. *La terre et les hommes en Picardie jusqu'à la fin du XIIIe siècle.* 2 vols. Amiens: Université de Paris, 1968.

Foulon, Charles. *L'oeuvre de Jehan Bodel.* Paris: Presses universitaires de France, 1958.

Fournier, E. "Un cartulaire du chapitre d'Arras." *MAA* (1932): 193–203.

——. "Les chapelles et autels de l'ancienne cathédrale d'Arras." *BCdMhPC*, ser. 2, 5 (1922–1930): 286–293.

——. "Mélanges d'archéologie artésienne. II: À propos d'épigraphie. Les prémieres églises des religieux mendiants à Arras et le droit de sépulture." *BCdMhPC*, ser. 2, 5 (1922–1930): 393–402.

François, Charles. "Perrot de Neele, Jehan Madot et le MS. B.N. fr. 375." *Revue belge* 41 (1963): 761–779.

Fritz, Jean-Marie. *Le discours du fou au moyen âge, XIIe–XIIIe siècles: Étude comparée des discours littéraire, médical, juridique et théologique de la folie.* Paris: Presses universitaires de France, 1992.

Gadd, Ian, and Alexandra Gillespie, eds. *John Stow (1525–1605) and the Making of the English Past: Studies in Early Modern Culture and the History of the Book.* London: British Library, 2004.

Gallo, F. Alberto. *Musica nel castello: Trovatori, libri, oratori nelle corti italiane dal XIII al XV secolo.* Bologna: Il Mulino, 1992. Trans. Anna Herklotz and Kathryn Krug as *Music in the Castle: Troubadours, Books, and Orators in Italian Courts of the Thirteenth, Fourteenth, and Fifteenth Centuries.* Chicago: University of Chicago Press, 1995.

Ganshof, F. L. "Le roi de France en Flandre en 1127 et 1128." *Revue historique de droit français et étranger* 27 (1949): 204–228.

Garnier, François. *Le langage de l'image au Moyen Age.* 2 vols. Paris: Léopard d'or, 1982 and [1988].

Geary, Patrick J. *Furta Sacra: Thefts of Relics in the Central Middle Ages.* Rev. ed. Princeton: Princeton University Press, 1990.

——. *Living with the Dead in the Middle Ages.* Ithaca: Cornell University Press, 1994.

Gégou, Fabienne. "Adam le Bossu était il mort en 1288?" *Romania* 86 (1965): 111–117.

Genicot, Léopold. "Aristocratie et dignités ecclésiastiques en Picardie aux XIIe et XIIIe siècles." *Revue d'histoire ecclésiastique* 67 (1972): 436–442.

Ghyssens, Joseph. *Les petits deniers de Flandre des XIIe et XIIIe siècles.* Cercle d'études numismatiques: Travaux, 6. Brussels, 1971.

Gibson, Gail McMurray. *The Theater of Devotion: East Anglian Drama and Society in the Late Middle Ages.* Chicago: University of Chicago Press, 1989.

Gilson, Étienne. *Les idées et les lettres.* Paris: J. Vrin, 1932.

Goffman, Erving. *The Presentation of Self in Everday Life.* Garden City, N.Y.: Doubleday, 1959 and 1990. Reprint, Harmondsworth: Penguin, 1969.

Goldstein, Leonard. "On the Origin of Medieval Drama." *Zeitschrift für Anglistik und Amerikanistik* 19 (1981): 101–115.

Goyens, Michèle, and Werner Verbeke, eds. *The Dawn of the Written Vernacular in Western Europe*. Leuven: Leuven University Press, 2003.

Graham, William A. *Beyond the Written Word: Oral Aspects of Scripture in the History of Religion*. Cambridge: Cambridge University Press, 1987.

Grisward, Joel-Henri. "Les fées, l'aurore et la fortune (mythologie indo-européenne et *Jeu de la feuillée*)." In *Études de langue et de littérature françaises offertes à André Lanly*. 121–136. Nancy: Université de Nancy, 1980.

Grundmann, Herbert. *Religiöse Bewegungen im Mittelalter* [. . .]: *Anhang, Neue Beiträge sur Geschichte der religiösen Bewegungen im Mittelater*. 4th ed. Darmstadt: Wissenschaftliche Buchgesellschaft, 1977. Trans. Steven Rowan as *Religious Movements in the Middle Ages: The Historical Links between Heresy, the Mendicant Orders, and the Women's Religious Movement in the Twelfth and Thirteenth Century, with the Historical Foundations of German Mysticism*. Notre Dame: Notre Dame University Press, 1995.

Guesnon, Adolphe. "Adam de la Halle et le *Jeu de la feuillée*." *MA* 28 (1915): 173–233.

——. *L'atelier monétaire de la comtesse Mahaut d'Artois en 1306*. Paris: Extrait du Bulletin archéologique (1895), 1896.

——. "La collection de Sir Thomas Phillipps et les archives communales d'Arras." *MCdMhPC* 3 (1909): 1–11.

——. *Un collège inconnu des Bons enfants d'Arras à Paris du XIIIe au XVe siècle*. Paris: Extrait des *Mémoires de la Société de l'histoire de Paris et de l'Ile-de-France* 42, 1915.

——. *La Confrérie des jongleurs d'Arras et le tombeau de l'évêque Lambert*. Arras: Imprimerie Répessé [et] Cassel, 1913.

——. "Nouvelles recherches biographiques sur les trouvères artésiens." *MA* 15 (1902): 137–173.

——. "Les origines d'Arras et de ses institutions." *MAA* (1895): 183–258.

——. "Publications nouvelles sur les trouvères artésiens." *MA* 21 (1908): 57–82; and 22 (1909): 65–93.

——. "Recherches biographiques sur les trouvères artésiens." *BHP* (1894): 420–435.

——. *Le régistre de la Confrérie des jongleurs et des bourgeois d'Arras: Note sur le manuscrit fr. 8541 de la Bibliothèque nationale*. Paris, 1899.

——. "La satire à Arras au XIIe siècle: La bataille de l'enfer et de paradis." *MA* 12 (1899): 156–168 and 248–268.

Guest, Gerald B. "The Prodigal's Journey: Ideologies of Self and City in the Gothic Cathedral." *Speculum* 81 (2006): 35–75.

Gurevich, Aron Iakovlevich. "Bakhtin and His Theory of Carnival." In *A Cultural History of Humour: From Antiquity to the Present Day*, ed. Jan Bremmer and Herman Roodenburg. 54–60. Oxford: Basil Blackwell, 1997.

——. *Categories of Medieval Culture*. Trans. G. L. Campbell. London: Routledge and Kegan Paul, 1985.

——. *Medieval Popular Culture: Problems of Belief and Perception*. Trans. János M. Bak and Paul A. Hollingsworth. Cambridge: Cambridge University Press, 1988.

——. "Popular and Scholarly Medieval Cultural Traditions: Notes in the Margins of Jacques LeGoff's Book." *Journal of Medieval History* 9 (1983): 71–90.

Gurr, Andrew. *The Shakespeare Company, 1594–1642*. Cambridge: Cambridge University Press, 2004.

Gutton, Jean-Pierre. *Bruits et sons dans notre histoire: Essai sur la reconstitution du paysage sonore*. Paris: Presses Universitaires de France, 2000.

Guy, Henri. *Essai sur la vie et les oeuvres littéraires du trouvère Adan de la Hale*. Paris: Librairie Hachette, 1898. Reprint, Geneva: Slatkine, 1970.

Habermas, Jürgen. *Communication and the Evolution of Society*. Trans. Thomas McCarthy. Boston: Beacon Press, 1979.

——. *On the Pragmatics of Social Interaction: Preliminary Studies in the Theory of Communicative Action*. Trans. Barbara Fultner. Cambridge: MIT Press, 2001.

——. *Strukturwandel der Öffentlichkeit: Untersuchungen zu einer Kategorie der bürgerlichen Gesellschaft*. Darmstadt: Hermann Luchterhand, 1962. Trans. Thomas Burger and Frederick Lawrence as *The Structural Transformation of the Public Sphere: An Inquiry into a Category of Bourgeois Society*. Cambridge: MIT Press, 1989.

Haines, John. *Eight Centuries of Troubadours and Trouvères: The Changing Identity of Medieval Music*. Cambridge: Cambridge University Press, 2004.

Hanawalt, Barbara, and Kathryn L. Ryerson, eds. *City and Spectacle in Medieval Europe*. Minneapolis: University of Minnesota Press, 1994.

Hankins, James. "The Myth of the Platonic Academy of Florence." *Renaissance Quarterly* 44 (1991): 429–475.

Hardison, O. B. *Christian Rite and Christian Drama in the Middle Ages: Essays in the Origin and Early History of Modern Drama*. Baltimore: Johns Hopkins University Press, 1965.

Harf-Lancer, Laurence. *Les fées au Moyen Age. Morgane et Melusine: La naissance des fées*. Geneva: Editions Slatkine, 1984.

Havelock, Eric A. *The Literate Revolution in Greece and Its Cultural Consequences*. Princeton: Princeton University Press, 1982.

Haverkamp, Alfred, and Elisabeth Müller-Luckner, eds. *Information, Kommunikation und Selbstardellung im mittelalterlichen Gemeinden*. Munich: R. Oldenbourg Verlag, 1998.

Heers, Jacques. *Fêtes, jeux et joutes dans les sociétés d'occident à la fin du moyen-âge*. Montreal: Institut d'études médiévales, 1971.

——. *La ville au Moyen Âge en Occident: Paysages, pouvoirs et conflits*. Paris: Fayard, 1990.

Heirbaut, Dirk. "Galbert van Brugge: Een Bron voor de vlaamse feodaliteit in de XII de deuw." *Legal History Review* 60 (1992): 49–62.

Héliot, P. *Les églises du Moyen-Age dans le Pas-de-Calais*. 2 vols. Arras: CdMhPC, 1951 and 1953.

Henry, Albert. *Les oeuvres d'Adenet le roi*. Vol. 1. *Biographie d'Adenet: La tradition manuscrite*. Rijksuniversiteit te Gent Werken uitgegeven de Faculteit van de Letteren en Wijsbegeerte 109. Bruges: De Tempel, 1951.

Herington, John. *Poetry into Drama: Early Tragedy and the Greek Poetic Tradition*. Berkeley: University of California Press, 1985.

Herman, Edward S., and Noam Chomsky. *Manufacturing Consent: The Political Economy of the Mass Media*. New York: Pantheon Books, 1988.

Hermassi, Karen. *Polity and Theater in Historical Perspective*. Berkeley: University of California Press, 1977.

Hernandez, Richard L. "Sacred Sound and Sacred Substance: Church Bells and the Auditory Culture of Russian Villages during the Bolshevik *Velikii Perelom*." AHR 109 (2004): 1475–1504.

Hindley, Alan, ed. *Drama and Community: People and Plays in Medieval Europe*. Turnhout: Brepols, 1999.

———. "Preaching and Plays: The Sermon in the Late Medieval French *Moralités*." *Le moyen français* 42 (1998): 71–85.

Hobbins, Daniel. "The Schoolman as Public Intellectual: Jean Gerson and the Late Medieval Tract." AHR 108 (2003): 1308–37.

Hoexter, Miriam, Shmuel N. Eisenstadt, and Mehemia Levtzion, eds. *The Public Sphere in Muslim Societies*. Albany: State University of New York Press, 2002.

Holloway, Julia Burton. *Brunetto Latini: An Analytic Bibliography*. London: Grant and Cutler, 1986.

———. *Twice-Told Tales: Brunetto Latino and Dante Alighieri*. New York: P. Lang, 1993.

L'homme et la route en Europe occidentale au Moyen Age et aux temps modernes. Auch: Centre culturel de l'Abbaye de Flaran, 1982.

Hughes, Andrew. "Charlemagne's Chant or the Great Vocal Shift." *Speculum* 77 (2002): 1069–1106.

———. *Medieval Manuscripts for Mass and Office: A Guide to Their Organization and Terminology*. Toronto: University of Toronto Press, 1982.

Huizinga, Johan. *Herfsttij der Middeleeuwen: Studie over levens- en gedachtenvormen der veertiende en vijftiende eeuw in Frankrijk en de Nederlanden*. Haarlem: H. D. Tjeenk Willink, 1919. Trans. [F. Hopman] as *The Waning of the Middle Ages: A Study of the Forms of Life, Thought, and Art in France and the Netherlands in the Fourteenth and Fifteenth Centuries*. New York: Longmans and Green, 1924.

———. *Homo ludens: Proeve eener bepaling van het spel-element der cultur*. Haarlem: H. D. Tjeenk Willink, 1938. Trans. [R. F. C. Hull] as *Homo ludens: A Study of the Play Element in Culture*. London: Routledge and Kegan Paul, 1949. Reprint, Boston: Beacon Press, 1950.

Hunt, Tony. "The Authenticity of the Prologue of Bodel's *Jeu de saint Nicolas*." *Romania* 97 (1976): 252–267.

———. "A Note on the Ideology of Jean Bodel's *Jeu de saint Nicolas*." *Studi Francesi* 20 (1976): 67–72.

Huot, Sylvia. *From Song to Book: The Poetics of Writing in Old French Lyric and Lyrical Narrative Poetry*. Ithaca: Cornell University Press, 1987.

———. "Intergeneric Play: The Pastourelle in Thirteenth-Century French Motets." In *Medieval Lyric: Genres in Historical Context*, ed. William D. Paden. 297–314. Urbana: University of Illinois Press, 2000.

———. *Madness in Medieval French Literature: Identities Found and Lost*. Oxford: Oxford University Press, 2003.

———. "Transformations of Lyric Voice in the Songs, Motets, and Plays of Adam de la Halle." *Romanic Review* 78 (1987): 148–164.

Hüsken, Wim. "Politics and Drama: The City of Bruges as Organizer of Dramatic Festivals." In *The Stage as Mirror: Civic Theater in Late Medieval Europe*, ed. Alan E. Knight. 165–187. Cambridge: D. S. Brewer, 1997.

Huyghebaert, Nicolas. *Les documents nécrologiques*. Typologie des sources du Moyen Age occidental 4. Turnhout: Brepols, 1972.

Jauss, Hans Robert. "Littérature médiévale et théorie des genres." *Poétique* 1 (1970): 79–101.

———. *Toward an Aesthetic of Reception*. Trans. Timothy Bahti. Minneapolis: University of Minnesota Press, 1982.

Jeanroy, Alfred. "La poésie provençale dans l'Italie du sud à la fin du XIIIe siècle." In *Mélanges de philologie, d'histoire et de littérature offerts à Henri Havette*, 43–48. Paris: Presses françaises, 1934.

Jehel, Georges. "Gênes et Arras au moyen âge." In Castellani and Martin, *Arras*, 27–36.

——, and Philippe Racinet. *La ville médiévale: De l'Occident chrétien à l'Orient musulman, Ve–XVe siècle*. Paris: Armand Colin, 1996.

Johnston, Alexandra F., ed. *Editing Early English Drama: Special Problems and New Directions: Papers Given at the Nineteenth Annual Conference on Editorial Problems at the University of Toronto*. New York: AMS Press, 1987.

——. "What If No Texts Survived? External Evidence for Early English Drama." In *Contexts for Early English Drama*, ed. Marianne G. Briscoe and John C. Coldewey. 1–19. Bloomington: Indiana University Press, 1989.

——, and Wim Hüsken, eds. *Civic Ritual and Drama*. Amsterdam: Rodopi, 1997.

Jones, Charles W. *The Saint Nicholas Liturgy and Its Literary Relationships (9th–12th c.)*. Berkeley: University of California Press, 1963.

Jordan, William Chester. *The French Monarchy and the Jews: From Philip Augustus to the Last Capetians*. Philadelphia: University of Pennsylvania Press, 1989.

——. *Louis IX and the Challenge of the Crusade: A Study in Rulership*. Princeton: Princeton University Press, 1979.

Jungmann, Josef A. *Missarum sollemnia*. Vienna: Herder, 1948. Trans. Francis A. Brunner as *The Mass of the Roman Rite: Its Origins and Development*. 2 vols. New York: Benziger Brothers, 1959. Reprint, Westminster, Md.: Christian Classics, 1986.

Justice, Steven. *Writing and Rebellion: England in 1381*. Berkeley: University of California Press, 1994.

Katham, David. "Citizens, Innholders, and Playhouse Builders, 1543–1622." *ROMRD* 44 (2005): 38–64.

Kavanagh, Thomas M. *Dice, Cards, Wheels: A Different History of French Culture*. Philadelphia: University of Pennsylvania Press, 2005.

Kelly, Samantha. *The New Solomon: Robert of Naples (1309–1342) and Fourteenth-Century Kingship*. Leiden: Brill, 2003.

Kelly, Thomas Forrest, ed. *Plainsong in the Age of Polyphony*. Cambridge: Cambridge University Press, 1992.

Kiesewetter, Andreas. *Die Anfänge der Regierung König Karls II. von Anjou (1278–1295): Das Königreich Neapel, die Grafschaft Provence und der Mittelmeerraum zu Ausgang des 13. Jahrhunderts*. Husum: Matthiesen, 1999.

Kipling, Gordon. *Enter the King: Theater, Liturgy, and Ritual in the Medieval Civic Triumph*. Oxford: Clarendon Press, 1998.

Knight, Alan E. "Drama and Society in Late Medieval Flanders and Picardy." *Chaucer Review* 14 (1980): 379–389.

Kobialka, Michal. *This Is My Body: Representational Practices in the Early Middle Ages*. Ann Arbor: University of Michigan Press, 1999.

Koch, A. C. F. "Continuité ou rupture? De la justice domaniale et abbatiale à la justice urbaine et comtale à Arras." *RN* 40 (1958): 289–96.

Kolve, V. A. "Ganymede/Son of Getron: Medieval Monasticism and the Drama of Same-Sex Desire." *Speculum* 73 (1998): 1014–67.

Konigson, Elie. *L'espace théâtral médiéval.* Paris: CNRS, 1975.

Koziol, Geoffrey. *Begging Pardon and Favor: Ritual and Political Order in Early Medieval France.* Ithaca: Cornell University Press, 1992.

Kramer, Lloyd S. "Literature, Criticism, and Historical Imagination: The Literary Challenge of Hayden White and Dominick LaCapra." In *The New Cultural History,* ed. Lynn Hunt. 97–128. Berkeley: University of California Press, 1989.

Kreutzer, W. "Zum Verständnis des 'Courtois d'Arras.'" *Vox romanica* 33 (1974): 214–233.

Laharie, Muriel. *La folie au moyen âge, XIe–XIIIe siècles.* Paris: Léopard d'or, 1991.

Lancashire, Ian. *Dramatic Texts and Records of Great Britain: A Chronological Typography to 1558.* Toronto: University of Toronto Press, 1984.

Lefebvre, Henri. *La production de l'espace.* Paris: Éditions anthropos, 1974.

Le Goff, Jacques. *Pour un autre Moyen Age. Temps, travail et culture en Occident: 18 essais.* Paris: Gallimard, 1977. Trans. [Arthur Goldhammer] as *Time, Work, and Culture in the Middle Ages.* Chicago: University of Chicago Press, 1980.

Leguay, Jean-Pierre. "La propriété et le marché de l'immobilier à la fin du moyen âge dans le royaume de France et dans les grands fiefs périphériques." In *D'une ville à l'autre: Structures matérielles et organisation de l'espace dans les villes européennes (XIIIe–XVIe siècles),* ed. Jean-Claude Maire Vigueur. 135–199. Rome: École française, 1989.

Leroy, Jean-Baptiste Onésime. *Époques de l'histoire de France en rapport avec le théâtre français, dès la formation de la langue jusqu'à la Renaissance.* Paris: Hachette, 1843.

——. *Études sur les Mystères, monumens historiques et littéraires, la plupart inconnus, et sur divers manuscrits de Gerson.* Paris: Hachette, 1837.

LeRoy Ladurie, Emmanuel. *Le carnaval de Romans: De la Chandeleur au mercredi des Cendres, 1579–1580.* Paris: Gallimard, 1979. Trans. Mary Feeny as *Carnival in Romans.* New York: G. Braziller, 1979.

Lestocquoy, Jean. *L'art de l'Artois: Études sur la tapisserie, la sculpture, l'orfèvrerie, la peinture.* Arras: CdMhPC, 1973.

——. "Deux reliquaires du XIIIe siècle: La custode du Saint-Cierge et le reliquaire de la Sainte-Épine d'Arras." *MCdMhPC* 3 (1908–1935): 397–407.

——. *Le diocèse d'Arras: La vie religieuse d'une province.* Arras: CdMhPC 1949.

——. "Origine et décadence de la tapisserie à Arras." *Revue belge d'archéologie et d'histoire de l'art* 10 (1940): 27–34.

——. *Patriciens du Moyen Age: Les dynasties bourgeoises d'Arras du XIe au XVe siècles.* Arras : CdMhPC 1945.

——. "Les plus anciens documents de la Confrérie de Notre-Dame des Ardents." *BCdMhPC* 7 (1941–1949): 372–377.

——, et al. *Histoire des territoires ayant formé le département du Pas-de-Calais.* Arras, 1946.

Lever, Maurice. *Le sceptre et la marotte: Histoire des fous de cour.* Paris: Fayard, 1983.

Levine, Lawrence W. "Shakespeare and the American People: A Study in Cultural Transformation." *AHR* 89 (1984): 34–65.

Levy, Kenneth. *Gregorian Chant and the Carolingians.* Princeton: Princeton University Press, 1996.

Lippmann, Walter. *Public Opinion*. New York: Macmillan, 1922. Reprint, New York: Simon & Schuster, 1997.

Little, Lester K. *Liberty, Charity, Fraternity: Lay Religious Confraternities in Bergamo in the Age of the Commune*. Bergamo: P. Lubrina and Northampton: Smith College, 1988.

———. *Religious Poverty and the Profit Economy in Medieval Europe*. Ithaca: Cornell University Press, 1978.

Longnon, Jean. *Les compagnons de Villehardouin: Recherches sur les croisés de la quatrième Croisade*. Paris: Champion and Geneva: Droz, 1978.

Lopez, Robert. *The Commercial Revolution of the Middle Ages, 950–1350*. Cambridge: Cambridge University Press, 1976.

———. "The Culture of the Medieval Merchant." *Medieval and Renaissance Studies* 8 (1979): 52–73.

Lourdaux, W., and D. Verhelst, eds. *The Bible and Medieval Culture*. Leuven: Leuven University Press, 1979.

Lyon, Bryce Dale, and Adriaan Verhulst. *Medieval Finance: A Comparison of Financial Institutions in Northwestern Europe*. Rijksuniversiteit te Gent Werken uitgegeven de Faculteit van de Letteren en Wijsbegeerte 143. Providence: Brown University Press, 1967.

Maillard, Jean. *Roi-trouvère du XIIIe siècle: Charles d'Anjou*. Rome: American Institute of Musicology, 1967.

Mâle, Émile. *L'art religieux du XIIIe siècle en France: Étude sur l'iconographie du moyen âge et sur ses sources d'inspiration*. Rev. ed. Paris: Armand Colin, 1902 and 1958.

Mallette, Karla. *The Kingdom of Sicily: A Literary History*. Philadelphia: University of Pennsylvania Press, 2005.

Manley, Lawrence. "Of Sites and Rites." In *The Theatrical City: Culture, Theater and Politics in London, 1576–1649*, ed. David L. Smith, Richard Strier, and David Bevington. 35–54. Cambridge: Cambridge University Press, 1995.

Mansfield, Mary C. *The Humiliation of Sinners: Public Penance in Thirteenth-Century France*. Ithaca: Cornell University Press, 1995.

Le marchand au moyen-âge. Saint-Herblain: Société des historiens médiévistes de l'enseignement supérieur, 1992.

Matossian, Mary Kilbourne. *Poisons of the Past: Molds, Epidemics, and History*. New Haven: Yale University Press, 1989.

Mattelart, Armand. *L'invention de la communication*. Paris: Éditions la Douverte, 1994.

Mazouer, Charles. *Le théâtre français du Moyen Âge*. Paris: SEDES, 1998.

Mazour-Matusevich, Yelena. "Writing Medieval History: An Interview with Aron Gurevich." *Journal of Medieval and Early Modern Studies* 35 (2005): 121–157.

Mazzoleni, Jole. *Le fonti documentarie e bibliografiche dal sec. X al sec. XX conservate presso l'archivio di stato di Napoli*. Naples: Arte tipografica, 1974.

McGee, Timothy J., ed. *Improvisation in the Arts of the Middle Ages and Renaissance*. Kalamazoo: Western Michigan University Press, 2003.

James McKinnon, ed. *Antiquity and the Middle Ages: From Ancient Greece to the 15th Century*. Man and Music 1. Basingstoke: Macmillan, 1990.

McSheffrey, Shannon. "Place, Space, and Situation: Public and Private in the Making of Marriage in Late-Medieval London." *Speculum* 79 (2004): 960–990.

Meersseman, G. G., with Gian Piero Pacini. *Ordò fraternitatis: Confraternite e pietà dei laici nel medioevo*. 3 vols. Rome: Herder, 1977.

Mehl, Jean-Michel. "Games in Their Seasons." Trans. Thomas Pettitt in *Custom, Culture, and Community in the Later Middle Ages: A Symposium*, ed. Pettitt and Leif Søndergaard. 71–83. Odense: Odense University Press, 1994.

———. *Les jeux au royaume de France du XIIIe au début du XVIe siècle*. Paris: Fayard, 1990.

Mélanges d'histoire du théâtre du Moyen-Age et de la Renaissance offerts à Gustave Cohen. Paris: Librairie Nizet, 1950.

Mélanges de langue et littérature françaises du Moyen Age et de la Renaissance, offerts à Monsieur Charles Foulon par ses collèges, ses élèves, et ses amis. Rennes: Institut de français, Université de Haute-Bretagne, 1980.

Ménard, Philippe. "Les emblèmes de la folie dans la littérature et dans l'art (XIIe–XIIIe siècles)." In *Hommage à Jean-Charles Payen. Farai chansoneta novele: Essais sur la liberté créatrice du Moyen Age*, ed. Jean-Louis Becker et al. 253–265. Caen: Centre de publications de l'Université de Caen, 1989.

———. "Les fous dans la société médiévale: Le témoignage de la littérature au XIIe et au XIIIe siècle." *Romania* 98 (1977): 433–459.

Menche de Loisne, Auguste Charles Henri. "L'ancien dialect artésien d'après les chartes en langue vulgaire du chapitre d'Arras (1248–1301)." *MAA*, ser. 2, 29 (1898): 1–94.

———. "Chronologie des baillis d'Artois du XIIIe siècle." *BHP* (1899): 65–78.

———. "Une cour féodale vers la fin du XIIIe siècle: L''hotel' de Robert II, comte d'Artois." *BHP* (1918): 84–143.

———. "Diplomatique des actes du Robert II, comte d'Artois (1266–1302)." *BHP* (1916): 184–224.

———. "Itinéraire de Robert II, comte d'Artois (1267–1302)." *BHP* (1913): 362–383.

Mermier, Guy. *"The Play of Madness": A Translation of Jeu de la Feuillée by Adam d'Arras*. New York and Bern: Peter Lang, 1997.

Meyer, Paul. "Notice du MS. Bibl. Nat. fr. 6447: Traduction de divers livres de la Bible. Légendes des saints." In *Notices et extraits des manuscrits de la Bibliothèque nationale et autres bibliothèques*. Vol. 35, pt. 2. Paris: Imprimerie nationale, 1896.

Molin, Jean-Baptiste, and Protais Mutembe. *Le rituel du mariage en France du XIIe au XVe siècle*. Paris: Beauchesne, 1974.

Monier, Raymond. *L'administration et la condition juridique des habitants de la ville d'Arras au XIIe siècle*. Paris, 1929.

———. *Les institions financières de comté de Flandre du XIe siècle à 1384*. Paris: Domat-Monchrestien, 1948.

———. *Les institutions judiciaires des villes de Flandre des origines à la rédaction des coutumes*. Lille: Bresl, 1924.

Monti, Gennaro Maria. "Ancora sullo studio generale di Napoli de Carlo I a Roberto." *Archivio storico per le province Napoletane* 59 (1934): 137–180.

Mostert, Marco, ed. *New Approaches to Medieval Communication*. Turnhout: Brepols, 1999.

Muchembled, Robert, and Gérard Sivéry, eds. *Nos ancêtres les paysans: Aspects du monde rurale dans le Nord Pas de Calais, des origines à nos jours*. Lille: Centre d'histoire de la région du Nord, 1981.

Müller, Miriam. "Social Control and the Hue and Cry in Two Fourteenth-Century Villages." *Journal of Medieval History* 31 (2005): 29–53.

Murray, Alexander. *Reason and Society in the Middle Ages*. Oxford: Clarendon Press, 1978.

——. "Religion among the Poor in Thirteenth-Century France: The Testimony of Humbert of Romans." *Traditio* 30 (1974): 285–324.

——. "Time and Money." In *The Work of Jacques Le Goff and the Challenges of Medieval History*, ed. Miri Rubin. 3–25. Woodbridge, U.K.: Boydell Press, 1997.

Murray, James M. *Notarial Instruments in Flanders between 1280–1452*. Brussels: Palais des Académies, 1995.

Muscatine, Charles. *The Old French Fabliaux*. New Haven: Yale University Press, 1986.

Musso, Daniela. "Adam o dell'ambivalenza: Note sul *Jeu de la feuillée*." *L'immagine riflessa* 8 (1985): 3–26.

Nagy, Gregory. *Homeric Questions*. Austin: University of Texas Press, 1996.

——. *Poetry as Performance: Homer and Beyond*. Cambridge: Cambridge University Press, 1996.

Nicholas, David. *The Growth of the Medieval City: From Late Antiquity to the Early Fourteenth Century*. New York: Longman, 1997.

——. *Medieval Flanders*. London: Longman, 1992.

——. *The Metamorphosis of a Medieval City: Ghent in the Age of the Arteveldes, 1302–1390*. Lincoln: University of Nebraska Press, 1987.

——. *Urban Europe, 1100–1700*. New York: Palgrave Macmillan, 2003.

Nichols, Stephen G., and Siegfried Wenzel, eds. *The Whole Book: Cultural Perspectives on Medieval Miscellany*. Ann Arbor: University of Michigan Press, 1996.

Oliver, Clementine. "A Political Pamphleteer in Late Medieval England: Thomas Fovent, Geoffrey Chaucer, Thomas Usk, and the Merciless Parliament of 1388." In *New Medieval Literatures 6*, ed. David Lawton, Rita Copeland, and Wendy Scase. 167–198. Oxford: Oxford University Press, 2003.

Ourliac, Paul. "Coutume et mémoire: Les coutumes françaises au XIIIe siècle." In *Jeux de mémoire: Aspects de la mnémotechnie médiévale*, ed. Bruno Roy and Paul Zumthor. 111–122. Montreal: Presses de l'Universite' de Montréal, 1985.

Page, Christopher. *The Owl and the Nightingale: Musical Life and Ideas in France, 1100–1300*. Berkeley: University of California Press, 1990.

Palmer, Barbara D. "Early Modern Mobility: Players, Payments, and Patrons." *Shakespeare Quarterly* 56 (2005): 259–305.

Payen, Jean-Charles. *Littérature française*. Vol. 1. *Le Moyen Age*. Paris: Arthaud, 1984.

——. "Théâtre médiéval et culture urbaine." *Revue d'histoire du théâtre* 35 (1983): 233–250.

Peters, Ursula. *Literatur in der Stadt: Studien zu den sozialen Voraussetzungen und kulturellen Organisationsformen städtischer Literatur im 13. und 14. Jahrhundert*. Tübingen: Max Niemeyer, 1983.

Petit de Julleville, L. *Les comédiens en France au moyen age*. Paris: Léopold Cerf, 1885.

Pizarro, Joaquín Martínez. *A Rhetoric of the Scene: Dramatic Narratives in the Early Middle Ages*. Toronto: University of Toronto Press, 1989.

Pohl, Hans, ed. *Die Bedeutung der Kommunikation für Wirtschaft und Gesellschaft*. Stuttgart: Franz Steiner Verlag, 1989.

Pounds, N. J. G. *An Economic History of Medieval Europe*. 2nd ed. London: Longman, 1994.

Pycke, Jacques. *Le chapitre cathédral de Notre-Dame de Tournai de la fin du XIe à la fin du XIIIe siècle: Son organisation, sa vie, ses membres*. Brussels: Nauwelaerts and Louvain-la-Neuve: Collège d'Erasme, 1986.

Rabaglio, Matteo. *Drammaturgia popolare e teatro sacro: Riti e rappresentazioni del Venerdì Santo nel bergamasco*. Bergamo: Sistema bibliotecario urbano, 1989.

Raybin, David. "The Court and the Tavern: Bourgeois Discourse in *Li jeus de saint Nicolai*." *Viator* 19 (1988): 176–198.

Regalado, Nancy Freeman. *Poetic Patterns in Rutebeuf: A Study in Noncourtly Poetic Modes of the Thirteenth Century*. New Haven: Yale University Press, 1970.

Reid, T. B. W. "On the Text of the *Jeu de Saint Nicolas*." In *Studies in Medieval French Presented to Alfred Ewert in Honour of His Seventieth Birthday*, ed. E. A. Frances. 96–129. Oxford: Clarendon Press, 1961.

Rey-Flaud, Henri. *Pour une dramaturgie du moyen âge*. Paris: Presses universitaires de France, 1980.

Reynolds, Susan. *Kingdoms and Communities in Western Europe, 900–1300*. 2nd ed. Oxford: Clarendon Press, 1997.

Richard, Jules-Marie. *Une petite-nièce de Saint-Louis: Mahaut comtesse d'Artois et de Bourgogne (1302–1329): Étude sur la vie privée, les arts et l'industrie en Artois et à Paris au commencement du XVe siècle*. Paris: H. Champion, 1887.

Richardson, Louise Barbara. "The *Confrérie des jongleurs et des bourgeois* and the *Puy d'Arras* in Twelfth- and Thirteenth-Century Literature." In *Studies in Honor of Mario A. Pei*, ed. John Fisher and Paul A. Gaeng. 161–171. Chapel Hill: University of North Carolina Press, 1972.

Richebé, C. *Les monnaies féodales d'Artois*. Paris: A. & J. Picard, 1963.

Rider, Jeff. *God's Scribe: The Historiographical Art of Galbert of Bruges*. Washington, D.C.: Catholic University of America Press, 2001.

Rigaudière, Albert. *Gouverner la ville au Moyen Age*. Paris: Anthropos, 1993.

Robb, Graham. Review of *L'atelier de Baudelaire: "Les fleurs du mal,"* ed. Claude Pichois and Jacques Dupont. *Times Literary Supplement*, April 21, 2006, 5.

Robinson, David. "La tradition manuscrite de 'Courtois d'Arras.'" *Bulletin des jeunes romanistes* 6 (1962): 37–41.

Rogier, L.-J., Aubert, R., and M. D. Knowles, eds. *Nouvelle histoire de l'église*. 5 vols. Paris: Éditions de Seuil, 1963–1975.

Rollo-Koster, Joëlle. "The Politics of Body Parts: Contested Topographies in Late-Medieval Avignon." *Speculum* 78 (2003): 66–98.

Rosenwein, Barbara H., ed. *Anger's Past: The Social Uses of Emotion in the Middle Ages*. Ithaca: Cornell University Press, 1998.

———. "Worrying about Emotions in History." *AHR* 107 (2002): 821–845.

Rousse, Michel. *La scène et les tréteaux: Le théâtre de la farce au Moyen Âge*. Orléans: Paradigme, 2004.

Roussel, Henri. "Notes sur la littérature arrageoise du XIIIe siècle." *Revue des sciences humaines* 87 (1957): 249–286.

Rubin, Miri. *Corpus Christi: The Eucharist in Late Medieval Culture*. Cambridge: Cambridge University Press, 1991.

Runciman, Steven. *The Sicilian Vespers: A History of the Mediterranean World in the Later Thirteenth Century*. Cambridge: Cambridge University Press, 1958.

Runnalls, Graham A. *Études sur les mystères: Un recueil de 22 études sur les mystères français, suivi d'un répertoire du théâtre religieux français du Moyen Age et d'une bibliographie*. Champion-Varia 14. Paris, 1998.

——. "The Manuscript of the *Miracles de Nostre Dame par personnages*." *Romance Philology* 22 (1968): 15–22.

——. "Medieval Trade Guilds and the *Miracles de nostre Dame par personnages*." *Medium Ævum* 39 (1970): 257–287.

——. "The *Miracles de Nostre Dame par personages*: Erasures in the MS and the Dates of the Plays and the 'Serventois.'" *Philological Quarterly* 49 (1970): 19–29.

Saenger, Paul. *Space between Words: The Origins of Silent Reading*. Stanford: Stanford University Press, 1997.

Santucci, Monique. "Le fou dans les lettres françaises médiévales." *Les lettres romanes* 35 (1982): 195–211.

Schafer, R. Murray. *The Soundscape: Our Sonic Environment and the Tuning of the World*. Rochester, Vt.: Destiny Books, 1994. Originally published as *The Tuning of the World*. New York: Alfred A. Knopf, 1977.

Schechner, Richard. *Performance Theory*. Rev. ed. London: Routledge, 2003.

Schenk, Gerrit Jasper. *Zeremonial und Politik: Herrschereinzüge im spätmittelalterlichen Reich*. Cologne: Böhlau Verlag, 2003.

Schmitt, Jean-Claude. *La raison des gestes dans l'Occident médiévale*. Paris: Gallimard, 1990.

Simon, Eckehard. *Die Anfänge des weltlichen deutschen Schauspiels, 1370–1530: Untersuchung und Dokumentation*. Tübingen: Max Niemeyer, 2003.

——. "Organizing and Staging Carnival Plays in Late Medieval Lübeck: A New Look at the Archival Record." *Journal of English and Germanic Philology* 92 (1993): 57–72.

——, ed. *The Theater of Medieval Europe: New Research in Early Drama*. Cambridge: Cambridge University Press, 1991.

Sivéry, Gérard. *Les capetiens et l'argent au siècle de Saint Louis: Essai sur l'administration et les finances royales au XIIIe siècle*. Villeneuve d'Ascq: Presses universitaires du Septentrion, 1995.

——. *L'économie du royaume de France au siècle de Saint Louis (vers 1180–vers 1315)*. Lille: Presses universitaires de Lille, 1984.

Smail, Daniel Lord. *The Consumption of Justice: Emotions, Publicity, and Legal Culture in Marseille, 1264–1423*. Ithaca: Cornell University Press, 2003.

Smith, Bruce R. *The Acoustic World of Early Modern England: Attending to the O-Factor*. Chicago: University of Chicago Press, 1999.

Smith, Darwin. *Maistre Pierre Pathelin: Le miroir d'orgueil. Avec l'édition et la traduction de la version inédite du Recueil Bigot (XVe siècle)*. Saint-Benoît-du-Sault: Tarabuste, 2002.

——. "Les manuscrits 'de théâtre': Introduction codicologique à des manuscrits qui n'existent pas." *Gazette du livre médiéval* 33 (1998): 1–10.

Spanos, Nicholas P., and Jack Gottlieb. "Ergotism and the Salem Witch Trials." *Science* 194, no. 4272 (December 1976): 1390–94.

Spiegel, Gabrielle M. *Romancing the Past: The Rise of Vernacular Prose Historiography in Thirteenth-Century France*. Berkeley: University of California Press, 1993.

Spivak, Gayatri Chakravorty. "Can the Subaltern Speak?" In *Marxism and the Interpretation of Culture*, ed. Cary Nelson and Lawrence Grossberg. 271–313. Urbana: University of Illinois Press, 1988.

Spufford, Peter. *Handbook of Medieval Exchange*. Royal Historical Society Guides and Handbooks 13. London: Boydell and Brewer, 1986.

Stanesco, Michel. *Jeux d'errance du chevalier médiéval: Aspects ludiques de la fonction guerrière dans la littérature du moyen âge flamboyant.* Leiden: Brill, 1988.

Stern, Charlotte. *The Medieval Theater in Castile.* Binghamton: State University of New York Press, 1996.

Stock, Brian. *The Implications of Literacy: Written Language and Models of Interpretation in the Eleventh and Twelfth Centuries.* Princeton: Princeton University Press, 1983.

Strohm, Paul. "York's Paper Crown: 'Bare Life' and Shakespeare's First Tragedy." *Journal of Medieval and Early Modern Studies* 36 (2006): 75–101.

Strohm, Reinhard. *Music in Late Medieval Bruges.* Oxford: Clarendon Press, 1985.

Sutherland, D. R. "Fact and Fiction in the *Jeu de la feuillée.*" Review of *Sens et compostion du "Jeu de la feuillé"* by Alfred Adler. *Romance Philology* 13 (1960): 419–428.

Symes, Carol. "The Appearance of Early Vernacular Plays: Forms, Functions, and the Future of Medieval Theater." *Speculum* 77 (2002): 778–831.

———. "The Boy and the Blind Man: A Medieval Play Script and Its Editors." In *The Book Unbound: New Directions in Editing and Reading Medieval Books and Texts,* ed. Siân Echard and Stephen B. Partridge. 105–143. Toronto: University of Toronto Press, 2004.

———. "A Few Odd Visits: Unusual Settings of the *Visitatio sepulchri.*" In *Music and Medieval Manuscripts: Paleography and Performance,* ed. John Haines and Randall Rosenfeld. 300–322. Aldershot, U.K.: Ashgate, 2004.

———. "Manuscript Matrix, Modern Canon." In *Oxford 21st-Century Approaches to Literature: Middle English,* ed. Paul Strohm, 7–22. Oxford: Oxford University Press, 2007.

———. "A Medieval Stage: Theater and the Culture of Performance in Thirteenth-Century Arras." Ph.D dissertation, Harvard University, 1999.

———. "The Performance and Preservation of Medieval Latin Comedy." *European Medieval Drama* 7 (2003): 29–50.

———. "Theater." In *Arts and Humanities through the Eras.* Vol. 5. *Medieval Europe (814–1450),* ed. Kristen M. Figg and John Block Friedman. 377–417. Farmington Hills, Mich.: Thomson Gale, 2004.

Tatarkiewicz, W. "*Theatrica*: The Science of Entertainment from the XIIth to the XVIIth Century." *Journal of the History of Ideas* 26 (1965): 263–272.

Taylor, Andrew. *Textual Situations: Three Medieval Manuscripts and Their Readers.* Philadelphia: University of Pennsylvania Press, 2002.

Terninck, Auguste. *Essai historique et monographique sur l'ancienne cathédrale d'Arras et sur la nouvelle église Saint-Nicolas.* Arras: Victor Didron, [1839].

———. *Notre-Dame du Joyel, ou histoire légendaire et numismatique de la Chandelle d'Arras et des cierges qui en ont été tirés par les villes et villages de Lille, Desvres, Ruisseauville, Blandecques, Courtray, etc.* Arras: Alphonse Brissy, 1853.

Théâtre et spectacles hier et aujourd'hui: Moyen Age et Renaissance. Actes du 115e Congrès national des sociétés savantes: Section d'histoire médiévale et de philologie. Paris: Comité des travaux historiques et scientifiques, 1991.

Thomas, Rosalind. *Oral Tradition and Written Record in Classical Athens.* Cambridge: Cambridge University Press, 1989.

Thrupp, Sylvia. "The Creativity of Cities: A Review Article." *Comparative Studies in Society and History* 4 (1961–62): 54–64.

Tock, Benoît-Michel. "Auteur ou impétrant? Réflexions sur les chartes des évêques d'Arras au XIIe siècle." *Bibliothèque de l'École des chartes* 149 (1991): 215–248.

———. *Une chancellerie episcopale au XIIe siècle: Le cas d'Arras.* Louvain-la-Neuve: Institut d'Études médiévales de l'Université de Louvain, 1991.

———. "Les élections épiscopales à Arras de Lambert à Pierre Ier (1093–1203)." *Revue belge* (1987): 709–721.

Togeby, Knud. "*Courtois d'Arras.*" *Travaux de linguistique et de la littérature*, vol. 11. Strasbourg: Librairie C. Klincksieck, 1973.

Tracy, James D., ed. *City Walls: The Urban Enceinte in Global Perspective.* Cambridge: Cambridge University Press, 2000.

Treitler, Leo. "Oral, Written, and Literate Process in the Transmission of Medieval Music." *Speculum* 56 (1981): 471–491.

———. "Reading and Singing: On the Genesis of Occidental Music-Writing." *Early Music History* 4 (1984): 135–208.

Trexler, Richard C. *Public Life in Renaissance Florence.* New York: Academic Press, 1980.

Trotter, D. A. *Medieval French Literature and the Crusades (1100–1300).* Geneva: Librairie Droz, 1987.

Turner, Victor. *From Ritual to Theater. The Human Seriousness of Play.* New York: Performing Arts Journal Publications, 1982.

Twycross, Meg, ed. *Festive Drama: Papers from the Sixth Triennial Colloquium of the Society for the Study of Medieval Theater, Lancaster, 13–19 July 1989.* Cambridge: Cambridge University Press, 1996.

Tydeman, William. *The Theater in the Middle Ages: Western European Stage Conditions, c. 800–1576.* Cambridge: Cambridge University Press, 1978.

Ungureanu, Marie. *La bourgeoisie naissante: Société et littérature bourgeoises d'Arras aux XIIe et XIIIe siècles.* Arras: CdMhPC, 1955.

Vale, Malcolm. *The Princely Court: Medieval Courts and Culture in North-West Europe, 1270–1380.* Oxford: Oxford University Press, 2001.

Vanbossele, José. *Kortrijk anno 1302: Achtergronden en voorgeschiednis.* Kortrijk: Uitgeverij Groeninghe, 2002.

van Caenegem, Raoul C. "Coutumes et legislation en Flandre aux XIe et XIIe siècles." In *Les libertés urbaines et rurales du XIe au XIVe siècle: Actes du Colloque international, Spa 5–8 IX 1966.* 245–279. Brussels: Pro Civitate, 1968.

———, ed. *1302, le désastre de Courtrai: Mythe et réalité de la bataille des éperons d'or.* Anvers: Fonds Mercator, 2002. Published simultaneously in Dutch as *1302: Feiten en mythen van de Guldensporenslag.*

Vandeberg, Camille Kennedy. "Authorship Theory: The Case of *Courtois d'Arras.*" Ph.D dissertation, University of Illinois at Urbana-Champaign, 1984.

van Drival, E. *Le Trésor sacré de la cathédrale d'Arras. Histoire et description des reliques insignes conservées et vénérées dans la basilique Notre-Dame et Saint-Vaast d'Arras.* Arras: A. Brissy, 1860.

van Werveke, H. "La contribution de la Flandre et du Hainaut à la troisième Croisade." *MA* 78 (1972): 55–90.

Vauchez, André. *Les laïcs au Moyen Age: Pratiques et expériences religieuses.* Paris: Cerf, 1987. Trans. Margery J. Schneider as *The Laity in the Middle Ages: Religious Beliefs and Devotional Practices*, ed. Daniel E. Bornstein. Notre Dame: Notre Dame University Press, 1993.

Vincent, Catherine. *Les confréries médiévales dans le royaume de France, XIIIe–XVe siècle.* Paris: A. Michel, 1994.

———. "Lieux de piété et lieux de pouvoir à Poitiers entre le XIIIe et le XVe siècle: La confrérie du Corps de ville dite aussi du Cent." In *La religion civique à l'epoque médiévale et moderne (chrétienté et islam): Actes du colloque,* ed. André Vauchez. 429–444. Rome: École française de Rome, 1995.

Vincent, Patrick R. "Jean Bodel and the Fleury Play-Book." *Symposium* 20 (1966): 367–378.

———. *The Jeu de saint-Nicolas of Jean Bodel of Arras: A Literary Analysis.* Baltimore: Johns Hopkins University Press, 1954.

Vitz, Evelyn Birge. *Orality and Performance in Early French Romance.* Cambridge: D. S. Brewer, 1999.

Wallheinke, Arndt. *Die "Vers de le Mort" von Robert le Clerc aus Arras: In sprachlichem und inhaltlichem Vergleiche mit Helinands "Vers de la Mort."* Leipzig: Thomas & Hubert, 1911.

Warning, Rainer. *Funktion und Structur: Die Ambivalenzen des gesitlichen Spiels.* Munich: Wilhelm Fink Verlag, 1974. Trans. Steven Rendall as *The Ambivalences of Medieval Religious Drama.* Stanford: Stanford University Press, 2001.

Weiss, Robert. "The Translators from the Greek at the Angevin Court of Naples." *Rinascimento* 1 (1958): 195–266.

Wenzel, Horst. *Hören und Sehen, Schrift und Bild: Kultur und Gedächtnis im Mittelalter.* Munich: C. H. Beck, 1995.

Wenzel, Siegfried. "The Joyous Art of Preaching; or, the Preacher and the Fabliau." *Anglia* 97 (1979): 304–325.

Werner, Karl Ferdinand. "Andreas von Marchiennes und die Geschichtsschreibung von Anchin und Marchiennes in der zweiten Hälfte des 12. Jahrhunderts." *Deutsches Archiv für Erforschung des Mittelalters* 9 (1952): 402–463.

White, Hayden. *The Content of the Form: Narrative Discourse and Historical Representation.* Baltimore: Johns Hopkins University Press, 1987.

Wickham, Glynne. *The Medieval Theater.* London: Weidenfeld and Nicolson, 1974.

Wilkins, Nigel. *The Lyric Art of Medieval France.* 2nd rev. ed. Fulbourn: New Press, 1988.

———. "Music and Poetry at Court: England and France in the Late Middle Ages." In *English Court Culture in the Later Middle Ages,* ed. V. J. Scattergood and J. W. Sherborne. 183–204. New York: St. Martin's Press, 1983.

Willeford, William. *The Fool and His Sceptre: A Study in Clowns and Jesters and Their Audience.* [Evanston, Ill.]: Northwestern University Press, 1969.

Williams, Ralph G. "I Shall Be Spoken: Textual Boundaries, Authors, and Intent." In *Palimpsest: Editorial Theory in the Humanities,* ed. George Bornstein and Ralph G. Williams. 45–66. Ann Arbor: University of Michigan Press, 1993.

Wood, Charles T. *The French Appanages and the Capetian Monarchy, 1224–1328.* Cambridge: Harvard University Press, 1966.

———. "Regnum Francie: A Problem in Capetian Administrative Usage." *Traditio* 23 (1967): 117–147.

Wood, Diana. *Medieval Economic Thought.* Cambridge: Cambridge University Press, 2002.

Wright, Edith A. *The Dissemination of the Liturgical Drama in France.* Geneva: Slatkine, 1980.

Wroe, Ann. *A Fool and His Money: Life in a Partitioned Medieval Town.* London: Cape, 1995.

Wyffels, C. "Le contrôle des finances urbaines au XIIIe siècle: Un abrégé de deux comptes de la ville d'Arras (1241–1244)." *BCdMhPC* 8 (1964): 230–240.

Young, Karl. *The Drama of the Medieval Church*. 2 vols. Oxford: Clarendon Press, 1933.

Zaret, David. *The Origins of Democratic Culture: Printing, Petitions, and the Public Sphere in Early Modern England*. Princeton: Princeton University Press, 2000.

Zink, Michel. "Le Jeu de saint Nicolas de Jean Bodel, drame spirituel." *Romania* 99 (1978): 31–46.

Zumthor, Paul. *Essai de poétique médiévale*. Paris: Éditions du Seuil, 1972.

———. *La lettre et la voix de la "littérature" médiévale*. Paris: Éditions du Seuil, 1987.

INDEX